# After the Reformation

William J. Bouwsma

G. R. Elton

Elizabeth Read Foster

Robert R. Harding

Brian P. Levack

Barbara C. Malament

H. C. Erik Midelfort

Louis O. Mink

Howard Nenner

Laura Stevenson O'Connell

Linda Levy Peck

J. G. A. Pocock

Quentin Skinner

Lawrence Stone

David Underdown

# After the Reformation

essays in honor of
## J. H. Hexter

edited by
## Barbara C. Malament

*University of Pennsylvania Press   1980*

*Library of Congress Cataloging in Publication Data*
*Main entry under title:*

*After the Reformation.*

*Bibliography: p. 353*
*1. History, Modern—Addresses, essays, lectures.*
*2. Great Britain—History—Modern period, 1485–*
*—Addresses, essays, lectures. 3. Hexter, Jack H.,*
*1910–    —Addresses, essays, lectures. I. Hexter,*
*Jack H., 1910–    II. Bouwsma, William James,*
*1923–    III. Malament, Barbara C.*
*D210.A28   1980       940.2       79-5254*
*ISBN 0-8122-7774-0*

*J. H. Hexter*

Born in Memphis, Tennessee, Jack Hexter received his A.B. from the University of Cincinnati and his Ph.D. from Harvard University. From 1939 to 1957 he taught at Queens College, CUNY. He then spent seven years as a member of the faculty of Washington University, to which he returned on his retirement as Charles S. Stille Professor of History at Yale University, where he taught from 1964 to 1978. Among his numerous awards are two Guggenheim Fellowships, a Fulbright Fellowship, a fellowship from the Ford Foundation and one from the Institute for Advanced Study. In 1970–71 he served as president of the New England History Association; in 1973–75 he was president of the Conference on British Studies. His major works include *The Reign of King Pym, Reappraisals in History, More's Utopia: The Biography of an Idea, The History Primer, Doing History,* and *The Vision of Politics on the Eve of the Reformation.*

# Contents

The Problem of Ideological Adaptation

# *Preface*

## BARBARA C. MALAMENT

In presenting these essays to J. H. Hexter on his retirement from Yale University, we wish to honor a historian's historian. Justly noted for his critical reappraisals, he has served as the conscience of his fellow scholars for over thirty years. Admonishing them when the evidence adduced in support of their conclusions was inadequate or when the categories of their analysis seemed fluid, Professor Hexter has, in his own work, displayed the same emphasis on precision and rigor demanded of others.

A master of *histoire problème*, he has displayed, too, a keen sensitivity to the rhetoric and writing of history. As the lead essay in this volume points out, Professor Hexter is one of the few historians to have reflected on the discipline of history in a disciplined way. Suggesting that narrative is a cognitive form, he has tried to answer positivists, who believe that truth must be an expression of scientific laws. Suggesting that there are certain, specifiable standards for judging a narrative, he has also tried to answer relativists, who believe that one account is as good as another.

One method may or may not be as good, depending on the

subject at hand. On matters of method, Professor Hexter is a pluralist, welcoming as he does the "new history" in all of its various forms. He has reservations, to be sure. But they have to do with the retreat from politics that is everywhere current, from the *Annalistes* in France, to the Frankfurt School in Germany, and members of the faculty here in the States. To them, politics are epiphenomena, mere *événementielle*. To Professor Hexter, they are of central concern. The history that he has written is about people acting, not merely behaving: individual people making decisions and judgments and choices, however limited these last may be.

Answering cries of "Whig! Whig!" he once said, "If this be Whiggery, make the most of it." But the linear progression is missing, the imposition of modern views on contemporaries, the agony of anticipation, as it has sometimes been called. These things Professor Hexter has warned against so insistently, in fact, that to call him a Whig makes little sense. One might say that he is Aristotelian in his belief that institutions matter, that the character of a society depends on how office and authority are distributed, or humanist in his concern with the ends that they serve. If labels are needed, "humanist" would do nicely, given the themes that dominate Professor Hexter's work. The nature of political discourse, liberty and the law, good counsel and the Christian humanist dilemma, the education of the aristocracy— these themes have interested him most. And since he has pursued them with regard to England and the Continent, in the sixteenth and also the seventeenth centuries, no one volume can do justice to them all.

Certainly no volume addressed to a single theme could do justice to them. So what we did was select the contributors instead. Former students, a sampling of those who survived Professor Hexter's marine-corps version of graduate school—they are among the contributors, as are some of Professor Hexter's colleagues and friends, including two of his sparring partners, Geoffrey Elton and Lawrence Stone. That they are still on speaking terms with him is tribute in itself to all parties concerned, for it means they have distanced themselves from even the deadliest debate. A quality that allowed Professor Hexter to laugh as he said, "He has got me, I think," when it seemed (quite erroneously) as though he had been proved wrong on the Presbyterian Independents, it is also a quality that allowed him to admit mistakes, as he did in connection with his work on Sir Thomas More.

But to return to this volume, it should be explained that having made the contributors our principle of selection, we proceeded to establish certain ground rules with respect to their essays.

Though only the first was commissioned in a technical sense, the essays were to be reserved expressly for this volume. They were to appear here before being published elsewhere; and they were to be an important contribution, whether critical or interpretive in nature, or original in the sense of being based on new research. Most of the essays, it turned out, were both. And suitably enough, most were controversial, some to the point of challenging Professor Hexter's own views. That is as it should be, and as we are sure Professor Hexter would want it. "An old tilter in the lists," to him we dedicate this volume with admiration, appreciation, and affection.

Barbara C. Malament

Society for the Humanities
Cornell University

# After the Reformation

# The Theory of Practice: Hexter's Historiography

## LOUIS O. MINK

In the Age of Letters, which has ended within our own lifetimes, the scholarly disciplines had a "public" which wanted to be informed about the advancement of knowledge in all fields. Today, only history, psychology, and literary and art criticism might be said to have a public; but in the case of psychology it is rather a clientele, and in the case of criticism, communication with a public is largely through the intermediation of curators, performers, conductors, and directors. So history alone retains a true public in the traditional way, and this is both a unique advantage and a predicament—a predicament because the professionalization of the guild of historians makes it progressively more difficult for the consumers of historiography to understand the process by which a vast and disorganized mass of mute data is transformed through the mind of an individual historian into an argued illumination of the past. A colleague recently described to me the work he was doing with an archive of newly accessible government papers; "I scan eight feet of shelf space a day," he said. In two or three years I expect to read in a few hours the lucid, perspicaciously organized and well-argued book whose history of creation led foot by foot along those shelves. It seems important to recall that process when the book is finished, with its own beginning, middle, and end. Footnotes will testify that the process occurred, but, so to speak, only as tombstones testify to life that was lived.

In an epistemologically important way, historians as inquirers differ from all other professions of inquiry except anthropology. The practice of their characteristic form of inquiry requires them to build up an "apperceptive mass" of familiarity with the *otherness* of a period or culture which resembles the unconscious familiarity we have with our own circumambient and internalized culture. By contrast, if survey research can be considered a pure form of social science, no pollster feels required to live for a long time in the community from which he seeks responses to items on his questionnaire; it is even essential that the "objectivity" of his data not be tainted by conscious or unconscious interpretations which go beyond the controls of methodology. But as anthropologists traditionally have lived in the societies they were studying, not merely visited them with clipboard and a change of underwear, so historians traditionally have tried to achieve the state of virtually living in the periods they were studying. In the simplest terms, a work of historiography has a background which is not (or not entirely) part of its content; and this background is the historian's "apperceptive mass" which indispensably orders his perception and interpretation of what otherwise are raw data.

But historians go public only in written history, which tells a story or argues from evidence or makes a case, or all of these. And at this stage only a very small part of the historian's apperceptive mass can be adduced or represented. So history as inquiry proceeds to an unusual degree, and possibly uniquely, in the gap between knowing and saying. The historian all but unconsciously draws on his apperceptive mass in the very complicated process of judging the significance and relevance of evidence as he examines it; but on the other side of the gap he must find a way of giving a convincing account of his subject for an audience which lacks almost totally anything like his own apperceptive mass. Paradoxically, this gives the individual historian a certain authority, but one which he can never claim. He cannot appeal to what he knows, over and above what he says, and what he says has to be entirely open to scrutiny and criticism according to rules of argument and evidence which do not acknowledge the authority or even the existence of what is *unexpressed*. Moreover, narrative, argument, and discourse itself are linear—as we speak of the "story line" or of the "line of argument"—while an apperceptive mass functions as the simultaneous interrelationship of a great many things which cannot be sorted out one by one. As Geoffrey Elton has remarked, a historian's own knowledge "advances on a broad front." But he can say—that is, write—only one thing at a time. To the extent that the historian's public cares about truth rather than mere entertainment, therefore, it needs to understand that a history not only presents it with a narrative or an argument, in either case a series of statements each grounded in actual evidence, but also exhibits (most generally in the *ordering* of statements as against other possible orderings) something which it does not explicitly assert, and which is grounded not directly in evidence but indirectly in the range and complexity of the historian's apperceptive mass. Among other things, this partially explains why historical inquiry can profit very little by a horizontal division of labor (if division by periods or areas is "vertical"). Historical research cannot be conducted by one group of "investigators" and written up by a different group of "technical writers," as is often the practice in some other disciplines. The historian who does not know more than he says cannot know what he says.

These broad observations are made not from the point of view of a historian with actual experience of historical practice, but from the point of view of a sort of anthropological student of cognitive cultures. But historians are by no means without resources to reflect on their own discipline, and in fact any historian-watcher will observe that such reflection is very common, although it is intermittent and seldom brought to the point of formulation in writing. An indispensable function is therefore performed by the few historians who do attempt to reflect on the discipline of history in a disciplined way—which is, of course, a different discipline from that of historical practice itself. Such metahistorical reflections serve to focus, by assent or disagreement, the self-descriptions of the historical profession, but even more importantly they represent that self-understanding to an interested public. Now it is a fact to be celebrated, when one remembers the generation of Beard, Becker, and Turner, that in the second half of the twentieth century no historian in the United States has accomplished more in the way of sustained reflection on the practice of historiography than Jack Hexter. He has, in fact, while remaining a productive scholar and writer of history proper, produced an *oeuvre* in the theory of history. It would not, perhaps, be recognizable as an *oeuvre* were it not for the publication of *The History Primer* in 1971. But because that book restates and tries to relate to each other themes and illustrations which had appeared scattered in various journals, it casts a certain retrospective light on earlier contributions. Readers of *Reappraisals in History*, when it appeared in 1961, might well have thought that it was a kind of do-it-yourself *Festschrift*. It contained the classic articles in which Hexter, if he did not put to rest forever the explanation of events in Tudor and Stuart England by the "rise of the middle class," at least assumed leadership of the opposition to that mode of explanation. But it also contained articles on method in historiography which attacked such styles of explanation as being systematically misleading, and in the "Personal Retrospect and Postscript" written for the volume, it is Hexter's "irritation with relativism, economic interpretation, tunnel history and factor analysis" (*RA*, 201) which is the theme.[1]

In 1961, however, Hexter's concern to put historians and historiography right was not yet distinguished from the periodic casting up of accounts which goes on, sometimes in public, in history as in every other discipline. Its theoretical message could be summed up in a single imperative: "Do not misinterpret the life of earlier centuries by unwittingly (or wittingly) projecting into them concepts (e.g., class, revolution) which are of more recent origin and which were at that time not part of anyone's thought or perception." This is a salutary maxim. Historians will no doubt continue to divide on the methodological question whether the past can be perspicuously described by the aid of modern conceptual frameworks no less remote from the consciousness of past agents than, say, nuclear engineering—though in part the application of the maxim depends on the type of inquiry, since no one would doubt that economic history can legitimately apply such concepts as real income and marginal cost to times antedating the concepts themselves. But no one will deny that perceptions, intentions, and ideas should not be imputed to people who could not possibly have entertained them, as if our own stock of ideas and options were assumed to have no history. Yet a salutary maxim, even though argued and illustrated, is not a theory of history.

From the record, it appears that Hexter's reflections on history were transformed from *obiter dicta* to *oeuvre* sometime around 1966. Early in 1967 there appeared in the *New York Review of Books* his review of Morton White's *Foundations of Historical Knowledge* (1965) and Arthur Danto's *Analytical Philosophy of History* (1965). Although this review and the replies to it gave much pleasure to connoisseurs of literary cockfights—and even philosophers find it hard to resist artists replying to philosophers of art, scientists replying to philosophers of science, and historians replying to philosophers of history—it seemed at most another illustration of the Balkanization of the scholarly disciplines. One could say that there was less in the dispute than met the eye, to the extent that the participants systematically failed to understand each others' distinctively disciplinary presuppositions and purposes—a common fate of interdisciplinary cooperation as well as of interdisciplinary polemics. But Hexter apparently was galvanized into an effort to understand why "analytical philosophers of history" so completely missed the point about the nature of historical knowledge, while yet monopolizing the question; and within the next five years he had published (and sometimes republished) a number of articles and two books, all devoted to elaborating a theory of historiography which would at once finish off "analytical philosophy of history" and replace it with an account of knowledge and communication more adequate to the actual practice of historical inquiry and writing.

Culminating with *The History Primer* (1971), therefore, Hexter's theory of the practice of history offers a rare opportunity to peer into the historian's workshop. I do not think that its special value lies in the polemic which occasioned it. Entertaining as that controversy often is, Hexter seldom resists the temptation to caricature his philosophical adversaries, a temptation all the more seductive because those adversaries have not joined the debate and therefore appear in it only by courtesy of his imputations. But on the positive side, Hexter never caricatures the practice of history by making it appear to conform to what others might expect of it—for example, by arguing that it is *really* "scientific." On the contrary, if he has not done much to put science in its place (which is the real point of his campaign against "analytical philosophy of history"), he has done a great deal to map the territory of history's place.

Four general characteristics run through all of Hexter's discussions of the theory of historiography; they are present by implication or intent even in contexts where they are not in the focus of attention; and they all can be regarded as giving voice or at least as attempting to give voice to what the majority of working historians think and feel. In the first place, Hexter is concerned only with the practice of professional historiography as a discipline. It is only incidental that "history" sometimes means a body of knowledge and sometimes the human past into which historians inquire. The primary meaning of "history" for Hexter is the *activity* in which historians engage and for which they are trained. The mark of professionalism is craftsmanship (*HP*, 60, 65ff.; *DH*, 4; *FB*, 57), and it is as craftsman that the professional historian is to be distinguished from Everyman as historian. The craft of history, which is, of course, learned but not codifiable in explicit methodological rules, is discernible in two areas: in the use of evidence (Hexter properly emphasizes the use of evidence rather than its mere discovery), and in skill in rhetoric, that is, in every aspect of historical writing.

The emphasis on professionalism might be misperceived as merely the attempt to close the guild of historians to amateur or "popular" historians. But guilds have never needed any intellectual self-examination to exercise that power. The problem underlying Hexter's celebration of craftsmanship is not really to draw a line between ins and outs, but rather to account for the fact that historians do recognize "professionalism" as a matter of degrees on a qualitative scale. "What are the characteristics of doing history?" is not a question which greatly exercises any historian (as it might interest a philosopher). The question which does concern historians is "What are the characteristics of doing *good* history?" And the answer to this, as Hexter once observed, is that the criterion of good history is the favorable judgment of the historical profession itself, as it emerges in a kind of consensus about the quality of particular works. Such a criterion of good history is, of course, not a good criterion: it could be that the historical guild, or at least its main centers of power, might be captured by a particular ideology or fashion, and, if the criterion of "good history" were only a collective judgment, rather than the *grounds* of judgment, there would be nothing to appeal *to* from a judgment by hypothesis askew. That the likelihood of collective *folie* is not great is no reply to the theoretical question its possibility raises; and Hexter's emphasis on craftsmanship can be seen as an attempt (not a wholly successful one, as I shall argue later) to give some content to the idea of professionalism—which otherwise would merely acknowledge the collective power of a guild unable to formulate its own standards of judgment. In professional evaluation as in the courts, justice must not only be done but be seen to be done.

Unexpectedly in someone with a well-deserved reputation as an always lively and sometimes truculent polemicist, a second characteristic of Hexter's theory of historiography is its avoidance of *Methodenstreit*. Not only does his theory refuse to enter the lists of the conceptual and methodological controversies which have from time to time challenged historians to take sides, but it is in fact designed to undercut such controversies. In "Some American Observations" (reprinted as "Doing History" in *DH*), he listed a number of "polarizations" in historiography: social science-oriented history versus humanities-oriented history; quantifying versus nonquantifying history; analytical versus narrative history; *conjonctural* versus *historisant* history; "why" history versus "how" history; and advanced versus conservative history. As oppositions, he observed, all of these are "absurdly flat-footed and ham-handed," because *good* history moves back and forth across such oppositions without being constrained by them. Of course, all the "polarizations" in this list have in common (although Hexter does not point this out) that they are related reciprocally as figure and ground; that is, each side of the polarization consists of an emphasis within a field which necessarily includes the other side. As Hexter later argued in the fifth chapter of *The History Primer*, for example, "analysis" must depend at least minimally on knowledge of the collocation of persons, places, and times, and such collocation can be represented only by a story. Put differently, "factor analysis," according to Hexter, usually finds that the "factors" it identifies as involved in the causal explanation of an event were present well before the occurrence of the event; hence it becomes a question why the event did not occur earlier. Analysts therefore distinguish "underlying" or important causes from "immediate" or merely precipitating causes; but with the admission of immediate causes, there is reintroduced the particular narrative of the particular event. One can see how in the other oppositions the two sides could similarly be shown to be reciprocally dependent.

Hexter's irenic avoidance of a certain kind of *Methodenstreit*, however, clarifies by contrast the kinds of controversy his theory of historiography is designed to legitimate, and even to precipitate. One such controversy is over the *use* of evidence, that is, whether the evidence adduced to support a case actually supports it, and whether it is fairly representative of the larger body of potential evidence which is not adduced. A second kind is over the imputability to past periods of concepts which were not part of the mental equipment of that period. Hexter himself has created models of such controversy in "The Myth of the Middle Class in Tudor England" and "Storm Over the Gentry." The main line of argument of these essays is that the characteristics of the bourgeoisie as a social class simply cannot be found in the past epochs in which historians have so readily discerned the "rise of the middle class": this is a historical issue, which Hexter attacked by examining the evidence. But a strain in his argument was also that "class interest" cannot be an explanation of the actions of people who had no conception of the class to which they have been retrospectively assigned; and this is a different kind of thesis—a conceptual or methodological thesis—since it cannot be settled one way or the other merely by examining historical evidence.

There is yet a third kind of controversy on which Hexter's theory of historiography takes sides instead of embracing both sides. In the "Personal Retrospect and Postscript" which he added to the essays reprinted in *Reappraisals in History,* he expressed (in no uncertain terms) his "irritation with relativism, economic interpretation, tunnel history and factor analysis" (*RA*, 201). Now his objections to all of these except "tunnel history"—here he simply protests against artificial classification of historical materials—have a common root. His *bêtes noires* are all more or less concealed ways of reducing individual human actions to effects of general and anonymous causes. Marc Bloch suggested "history without names" as an ideal of historical understanding, but Hexter has consistently and unabashedly opposed "leaving people out." In one of his most recent exercises in straightening out other historians (*TLS*), he was essentially criticizing a methodology of history which in using evidence selectively to support a general argument makes sure that "mere people never get in the way"; thus it "depersonalizes people"—people whose variety and idiosyncrasies are so infinite that unless somehow made irrelevant they defeat every attempt to make history comprehensible in terms of generalizations. But Hexter's strictures on "lumping" are by no means merely a weapon seized upon as useful in polemics. They were expressed in the "Personal Retrospect and Postscript," in the form of reflections on the vocabulary of early modern history. Historians cannot escape the use of "words like *think, consider, weigh, ponder, judge, choose, select, pick, decide, act, do,*" he said (considered, judged, decided) there, because such words reveal what words like *trend, development, tendency, evolution,* and so forth conceal, that "very often indeed at the junction between the way things were going and the way they went were the thoughts, the decisions, and the deeds of men" (*RA*, 213–14).

Of course, this statement is qualified by the phrase "very often indeed," which sums up the acknowledgment that there are historical phenomena which were not intended (e.g., the Price Revolution), as well as human actions done out of the coercion of authority, impulse, or unconscious habit (*RA*, 213). Nevertheless, although by admitting both voluntary and nonvoluntary phenomena into the domain of history, Hexter avoids one form of the "social science-oriented" versus "humanities-oriented" *Methodenstreit,* a good deal of free play for controversy remains inevitable, since whether the "thoughts, the decisions, and the deeds of men" were *in any given case* indeed at the junction between the way things were going and the way they went can become an issue, and not one which can be clearly settled by the weight of evidence.

A third characteristic of Hexter's theory of historiography, and one which he seems to have intended as necessary prophylaxis for historians liable to be seduced by alien theories, is its sustained critique (since 1967) of "analytical philosophy of history"; it might even be said that the two sources of Hexter's theory of historiography are reflection on his own experience of doing and reading history, on the one hand, and his mortal combat against "analytical philosophy of history," on the other. The term "analytical philosophy of history" is commonly used to refer to any theory of historical inquiry and knowledge, as distinguished from "speculative philosophy of history" as the attempt to discern the meaning or the great patterns of the historical process itself. Hexter, however, means by "analytical philosophy of history" only one form of it, the application to historiography of the philosophy of science usually known as positivism or logical empiricism. In general, this is the view that all knowledge is scientific knowledge, and that the *formal* structure of knowledge and inquiry is the same for all subject matters. Although most "analytical philosophers of history" reject both of these theses, Hexter is quite right to see that logical empiricism is prescriptive for historiography of standards and practices very different from those with which historians are familiar: like those of the physical sciences, to put it briefly. Hexter identifies two main positivist models. The first is the well-known "covering-law" model of explanation. According to this model, an adequate explanation of *any* event requires showing that the description of the event is logically deducible from one or more general laws together with appropriate statements of initial conditions; a corollary of this model is that the logical structures of explanation and of prediction are identical. The second model, called by Hexter "the logic of explanation by narration," represents the cognitive content of any historical narrative as a sequence of factual statements connected by causal explanations—which latter must conform to the covering-law model; everything else in the narrative is cognitively irrelevant (*HP*, chap. 6).

There is a certain Quixotic splendor about Hexter's single-handed sallies against the philosophers, although he himself has chosen the role of Horatio at the bridge. The Quixotic element is that philosophical positivism or "logical empiricism" was already beginning to look like a windmill rather than a giant before Hexter leveled his lance. It had been largely abandoned by philosophers after a generation of unremitting philosophical criticism, some of it by logical empiricists themselves. In response to this and to the "linguistic turn" of philosophy, Hexter's adversary was already succumbing to the death of a thousand qualifications before he entered the lists. Moreover, it seems fair to observe that as a critic of analytical philosophy of history, Hexter did not adopt a strategy uniquely available to him as a historian—that is, to *understand* analytical philosophers of history by making them a subject for intellectual history. As an intellectual biographer of Thomas More, Hexter undertook to interpret More's *Utopia* by reconstructing the "nexus of ideas and feelings" below the "surface of his thought"; and in *The History Primer* he illustrates by an example from the Netherlands-Burgundy aristocracy of the fifteenth century how a historian must come to understand "what it was like to be someone [else]" (*HP*, 204). But logical empiricism appears (not unreasonably, given its own denial of historical empathy) as theses to be debated rather than as a phenomenon to be understood. There is in fact no illuminating history of the *development* of logical empiricism, although such a history would surely reveal that, as an orthodoxy which developed and changed over the timespan of a single generation, the movement is better understood by its deeper reasons for modifying its views rather than by its "official" position at any given time.

Yet, Hexter's critique is not irrelevant. For one thing, just while logical empiricism was losing force as an adequate philosophy of science, it was becoming deeply and even institutionally entrenched as a methodology of social science. In their attempt to become scientific, American social scientists tried to model themselves on the natural sciences; but what they actually modeled themselves on was the particular philosophy of science represented by logical empiricism. And this philosophy remains habitual in much social science, although it is no longer argued by philosophers or even accepted by natural scientists as an adequate account of their own practice of inquiry. Historians do find themselves, of course, constantly in the position of relating history to social science in some ways, while protecting its autonomy in other ways. So Hexter's critique has a real target, if not quite the one he had in mind. The target is not a philosophy of science, formulated, argued, and criticized by philosophers, but that philosophy as it has become lodged in the conceptual presuppositions of much social science, and expressed not directly as propositions to be argued, but indirectly as criteria of methodology: in rules for the "design" of "experiments," for example, or in concepts such as that of operational definition or of the null hypothesis.

The *lutte* against "analytical philosophy of history" remains an indispensable foil in Hexter's strategy of argument. He uses it to sharpen by contrast and opposition the expression of his own principles of historiography. Thus, it performs a rhetorical function in his writing, and this is no small office, since for Hexter rhetoric is the *speculum mentis;* that is, the rhetoric of historical writing exactly bodies forth (for better or worse) the structure of the historian's thought. This principle is in fact the fourth general characteristic of Hexter's theory of historiography, and no doubt the most pervasive one. He has discussed the rhetoric of historiography in three different versions in four different places (*HT; IESS,* reprinted in *DH;* and *HP,* esp. chaps. 2, 4, 7, and 9). But a propensity for discussing the logic of inference in terms of the features of language was evident much earlier—for example, in the "Personal Retrospect and Postscript" of *Reappraisals in History,* where the special problems of dealing with early modern history are discussed in terms of the historian's vocabulary. It was not always so. In *More's Utopia: The Biography of an Idea* (1952), Hexter regarded his task as the recovery of More's actual thought or "idea" of Utopia, beyond the very considerable gap between More's mind and the text of *Utopia.* In writing *Utopia,* Hexter observed, More "imparted an appearance" to his idea which it "did not wear in life"; so the problem of interpretation is to "separate the thinker's thought from the literary tricks of the trade" (p. 4). This seems to represent the view that the relation between thought and the expression of that thought can be rather loose. But at the beginning of his historiographical decade in 1967, Hexter asserted (at least so far as historiography is concerned) a much more intimate relation between thought and expression; no longer a matter of "literary tricks of the trade," rhetoric has become the mirror of the historian's knowledge: "a truth about the past cannot in fact be fully distinguished from the language in which a historian states it, and one is in grave danger of misapprehending the nature, quality, and character of the truth that history attains if one disregards historiography—the unique, significant, rhetorical form that historians are impelled or constrained to use in communicating it" (*DH,* 155). Very soon, he came to regard the rhetoric of historiography as essentially evocative as well as expressive, requiring of it that it not only give formal exhibition of the structure of the historian's thought, but also elicit from the reader appropriate responses which could not be evoked in any other way; in fact, "the translational and psychedelic use of affective language" becomes "an indispensable means of communicating knowledge about the past as an integral part of the proof of [historians'] statements about it" (*HP,* 107).

What begins, therefore, as the unobjectionable observation that historical writing has special features (ranging from the larger forms of organization to such typical devices as the use of footnotes and quotations) which are conditions of its intelligibility and argumentative force, ends as the very much bolder claim that rhetoric alone is the locus of the principles of historical knowledge; that is, the rules of historiographical rhetoric *are* the epistemology of history. As "Historiography: The Rhetoric of History" asserts, "In the rhetoric of history itself are embedded assumptions about the nature of knowing, understanding, meaning, and truth, and about the means of augmenting them," and these assumptions are "not congruent with the corresponding assumptions in the sciences" (*IESS*, 390). Granting that the sciences can be adequately characterized by an account of "the logic of science," Hexter's project is not merely to resist the application of any such logic to historical practice, but to elaborate a body of rules of historiographical rhetoric which would, so to speak, fill the same epistemological space for history as the logic of science does for the sciences.

Such a body of rules would have two main parts. There would be macrorhetorical rules for the construction of narrative as a complex form, that is, for the ordering and disposition of the parts of a narrative in every way which goes beyond mere chronological sequence. And there would be microrhetorical rules stating the principles of better and worse use of such historiographical devices as footnotes, quotations, and lists (as of representative figures listed in order to communicate forcefully what they are representative of), together with syntactical forms peculiarly appropriate to history, such as the hypothetical subjunctive ("He may have thought that . . . "). Hexter does in fact extract and state several such rules; and since it is at the very center of his theory of historiography that what makes history *good* is conformity to such rules (even though a merely intuitive conformity), it may be well to state them apart from their context of illustration and discussion. The "Reality" Rule (1) is: "render the best and most likely account of the human past that can be sustained by the relevant evidence" (*HP*, 229). This is admittedly a restatement of Ranke's *wie es eigentlich gewesen*, and it is obviously not a rule of rhetoric. But it is intended to justify other rules, such as the Maximum Impact Rule (2). This is: "Place in footnotes evidence and information which, if inserted in the text, diminishes the impact on the reader of what you, as an historian, aim to convey to him" (*HP*, 230). And (finally!) there is the Economy-of-Quotation Rule (3): "Quote from the record of the past only when and to the extent that confrontation with that record is the best way to help the reader to an understanding of the past *wie es eigentlich gewesen*" (*HP*, 232).

In "Historiography: The Rhetoric of History," Hexter called his discussion of such rules "a prolegomenon to a codification of principles of historiography" (*IESS*, 389). This does seem as if Hexter is chewing more than he has bitten off; one would hardly like to put these rules, or any longer list of rules resembling them, up against Karl Popper's *Logic of Scientific Discovery* or Ernest Nagel's *Structure of Science*, as if to say, "Here are the principles of historiography which for history replace your account of science." But I think that this is because two quite different kinds of "rules" have not been distinguished: rules which *state* principles and rules which are merely pragmatic *reminders* of principles. Hexter's "Rules" are of the latter sort, although he does not avoid the temptation to claim for them the former status. It might be better not to call them "rules" at all, and in fact they are revealingly described as "*maxims* generally applicable . . . leaving the identification to the *experience* of the *trained* historian" (*IESS*, 389; italics added). Now it can be seen why the examples of "rules" are so thin when they are extracted from their actual context of illuminating discussion and illustration. Their meaning lies almost entirely not in what they state but in what that total context expresses. And what that context expresses is the "experience" of a "trained historian." The "Reality Rule," for example, gives no criterion for identifying the "best and most likely account" but presumes that ability on the part of whomever it is directed to. Formally such rules are merely question-begging: they cannot be applied at all except by someone who does not need them. But this in fact means that Hexter has in discussing such rules succeeded in *expressing* his insights into what historical understanding is, although not in stating them. They are lodged not in rules or formal models but in the "experience of the trained historian." Although it was never his intention, what Hexter has succeeded in doing is to provide an elaboration and illustration of R. G. Collingwood's cryptic thesis that "the criterion of historical knowledge is the historian himself."

So far, I have only reviewed the general characteristics of Hexter's theory of historiography, with critical comments intended merely to bring to view what those characteristics actually are. It is notable that nothing in his theory of historiography enforces a particular view about the "real nature" of history or about what is more important and less important in the actual historical process to which all historical accounts point. His concern is for "good history," with no attempt to convert some antecedent view that only a certain kind of history can be good history into normative "principles of historiography" which *only* that kind of history could satisfy; with respect to historians' points of view he is a federalist. This is evident, for example, in his respectful but critical examination of Fernand Braudel as a historian (*FB*). Although judging from his own work as a historian as well as from the examples he selects and constructs to illustrate his theoretical points (e.g., the story of the collapse of the Tacoma Narrows Bridge, or the immortalization of Bobby Thomson's home run of 3 October 1951; *HP*, chaps. 5 and 7), he rejects the *Annales* school's disdain for *histoire événementielle*, he gives a very fair picture of Braudel's point of view on historical *importance*, and his criticisms of Braudel are professional rather than ideological: he finds fault with the "deployment of evidence and documentation," with the rhetorical habit of personalizing cities and geographical features, and with the absence of useful aids such as tables of equivalences for moneys and measures (*FB*, 512ff.). One might guess—although I know of no place where he has said this—that he regards no "point of view" as adequate or even relevant to every period of history, though *any* point of view may be more or less adequate to a particular period. Hexter's unremitting criticism of the once-dominant interpretation of sixteenth- and seventeenth-century English history in terms of "the rise of the middle class" and "the emergence of nationalism" is not a rejection of that mode of interpretation in general but only of its adequacy for understanding *that* period (see his "Factors in Modern History," in *RA*, 26–43). To each period its appropriate interpretive concepts; to each historian the task of arriving, through his study of the evidence, at the appropriate concepts for *his* period. What confederates historians, therefore, and unites them as professionals, cannot be any theory, conceptual approach, or method, but only the general standards for historical writing. This, of course, leaves nothing at all to be said in general about historical actuality merely as such. If one recalls the comments about the historian's "apperceptive mass" with which this essay began, one might give a reason for Hexter's position which he himself has not advanced: the limits of a "period" are roughly that span of time and space with respect to which (given the amount and kind of potential evidence which is available) a historian can hope to develop an apperceptive mass in time to put it to constructive use. But no one can hope to do this beyond the limits of a manageable period. Hence the tacit authority of a historian— his "experience" as a "trained historian"—is of no use, and may be positively misleading, when extended to other periods. So criticism across the entire range of historical studies must be limited precisely to what historians do share in greater or less degree, namely the special skills of communicating the very different kinds of things they have come to know—in a word, to rhetoric.

Hexter's theory of historiography is of especial importance for exactly those features which to many critics must make it seem of limited interest. The most obvious way in which such a theory can be interesting is the extent to which it exemplifies or serves the purposes of a philosophical or ideological *interest* by applying that more general interest either to the practice of historical inquiry or to the process of historical actuality or both. "Analytical philosophy of history" belongs to the history of empiricism and discloses something new about the strengths and limitations of that perennial philosophy. Croce and Collingwood, and many of the philosophical critics of the covering-law model of historical explanation, such as W. H. Dray, belong to the tradition of philosophical idealism but in their turn have modified that tradition by developing it in its applications to historiography. Freud's *Civilization and its Discontents* belongs to the theory of history-as-actuality and represents a whole family of metapsychological theories of history. From Plekhanov to E. H. Carr (and beyond), Marxists have tried to solve the theoretical problems of Marxism (such as the apparent conflict between determinism and the necessity for action) in the special form in which those problems arise in the theory and practice of historiography. Against all such controversial interests, Hexter opposes no philosophy but common sense and no ideology but the belief in doing justice to the past. But precisely because of this he can be understood as representative of historians, of what unites them as professionals rather than of what may divide them philosophically or ideologically.

The realm of historians' thought to which Hexter's theory of historiography provides access, I believe, is in these days increasingly affected by an epistemological problem, a kind of indecisiveness or oscillation between certain pairs of incompatible opposites; and I should like to try to indicate what this problem is by briefly examining one of the positive contributions of Hexter's theory of historiography. This is his discussion of the historian's "second record"; its import is to show that the historian must and legitimately may bring his entire personal and intellectual experience to bear on the interpretation of evidence.

The "first record" with which any historian works is simply the sum of available and relevant evidence. The traditional way of describing the historian's problem, or part of it, with this record is that he cannot simply reproduce it but must "select" from it (and this has often been thought to be the first and inescapable departure from ideal "objectivity"). On the contrary, Hexter observes, the historian's problem is most characteristically to *supplement* the record, since his aim is to construct a credible narrative, and the record, at best, establishes only certain points in the narrative. So the historian must "draw lines among the points in the record of the past" (*HP*, 78). Where do the lines come from? From the "second record": namely, *everything* that that historian brings with him from his own experience and memory, personal as well as professional. One of Hexter's own examples will make clear how much the "second record" is intended to embrace. Among other problems of interpretation in his own study of More's *Utopia* was that of accounting for More's emphasis on measures to provide security for families in cases where the breadwinner dies or is disabled. The "solution" was to see it as a reflection of More's own personal situation in 1515, struggling to provide for a large young family. There is no *direct* evidence that More was preoccupied with this problem; the sources of the solution are rather in the second record, first as knowledge of More's actual situation as a head of family, and second from Hexter's experience of his own similar problem at the very time of his study. Hexter goes on to give himself a "social science rating" of *F* (on a quality scale of *A* to *F*) for drawing on parts of his personal experience which are beyond the pale of scientific knowledge. But he staunchly insists on the legitimacy and indeed the necessity of the historian's incorporation of such portions of his own second record in the drawing of lines to connect the evidenced points. So much the worse for "social science."

It is a poor illustration but a revealing one. It is poor, I think, because it suggests, perhaps unintentionally, that one can understand only those human situations, motives, and concerns which one has directly experienced. Moreover, it might be only an illusion that in a certain situation More would feel a problem with the same anxiety which Hexter—or I—would experience. (Maybe More considered the lilies of the field, and was confident that God would provide; one cannot eliminate this possibility by consulting one's own second record.) Most of all, the example ignores one of the most sensible and generally accepted of epistemological distinctions, that between the "context of discovery" and the "context of justification." *Anything* may legitimately serve heuristically to assist the imagination in forming explanatory hypotheses; but the hypotheses suggested by heuristic aids (analogies, metaphors, etc.) must be confirmed (justified) or disconfirmed by a process different in kind from the process in which they are invented. However, my point is not that the example is imprudent, but that it stands for a whole class of "second record" examples which might seem less obviously personal and adventitious. The claim which is taken to justify them all is that the historian typically "draws lines"; that is, he may and must *construct* a complex narrative such that the *form* of the narrative account is not evidenced in the first record as its content should be.

Now Hexter's bold thesis is that historiographical form—which is governed by rules of rhetoric—is a cognitive instrument; knowledge is contained in and communicated by the rhetorical structures of narrative historiography as much as by the individual assertions ordered by those rhetorical structures. Yet what this knowledge is about is the past *wie es eigentlich gewesen,* although by hypothesis such ordering is not in the first record, that is, in the evidence, nor is it even confirmed by the first record. It could be so confirmed only if the first record were isomorphic with the narrative, in which case there would be no problem of rhetoric at all, nor any point in referring to the second record. The theoretical dilemma can be exhibited in the following series of propositions, to all of which Hexter gives assent and in so doing may be taken as representing other historians who regard narrative as a cognitive form, not merely an aesthetic or practical device.

(1) Historiography ideally represents past actuality *wie es eigentlich gewesen.*

(2) The knowledge (understanding, etc.) communicated in historiography is not only of individual matters of fact but of structures of interrelationship.

(3) The form (both "macrorhetorical" and "microrhetorical") of narrative exhibits in an essential way and is the *only* way of communicating part of the claim to historical knowledge.

(4) The form of narrative is constructed by the historian himself (although according to rules of rhetoric, and hence not entirely arbitrarily).

The dilemma is that given (2) and (3), (1) and (4) cannot both be true. Historical actuality has, we may presume, its own complex structure (or lack of it); narrative has another, and one whose sources (rhetorical rules, the historian's "second record," and the historian's effort to elicit the *reader's* second record for an appropriate comprehension of the historian's intentions) are of an entirely different order. It could be no more than a lucky accident if the structure of narrative ever successfully represented the structure of historical actuality; but even worse, no one could possibly know whether it did, since to do so would require *comparing* the two and thus would require knowing the structure of historical actuality in itself independently of *any* representation of it. But this is impossible.

The dilemma could be avoided by giving up—*really* giving up—either (1) or (4); then the remaining three propositions would be consistent, although the meaning of "knowledge" would be quite different for the two cases. If one retains (1), historical truth is essentially *correspondence* of statement to past fact; if one retains (4), historical truth is essentially *coherence* of an account with a body of evidence. The price for giving up (1) is relativism (a *bête noire* for Hexter). That the price may be worth paying is argued, for example, by Hayden White's recent *Metahistory*, which shows in its interpretation of nineteenth-century historians that the same stock of evidence can be emplotted in irreducibly different ways; but the past "as it really was" becomes an unknowable *Ding-an-sich* from the standpoint of all subsequent knowledge. On the other hand, the price of giving up (4) is a crushing dullness (also a *bête noire* for Hexter), since the only historiographical form *directly* supported by evidence is bare chronology. There has, of course, been plenty of historiography which has not ventured beyond the cautious reporting of ascertainable fact, but it is as much the antithesis of Hexter's conception of "good history" as is the cognitive chaos of incompatible accounts which relativism legitimates. His positive contribution to the theory of historiography is the attempt to elaborate criteria for the achievement and communication of historical knowledge which would be both true and illuminating. Yet if the analysis above is correct, this is achieved by holding together incompatible criteria by main strength. To sustain this precarious alliance a sort of mental oscillation is required: to forget temporarily how much imagination goes into the construction of a narrative when one is thinking about the *otherness* of historical actuality, and to forget temporarily the distance which separates one from that actuality when one is thinking about the coherence and force of the story one tells or is trying to tell. Hexter might reply that there is very little point in historians' worrying over how it is possible to do something which in fact they do all the time as a matter of course (cf. *HP*, 263). But in a *theory* of historiography one cannot evade a problem by calling it only theoretical.

At the beginning of Sartre's novel *Nausea*, his protagonist Roquentin is reflecting on his years of historical research on the courtier and adventurer Rollebon. Roquentin's strange ontological encounters with non-being are just beginning, and their first intimations are his relatively conventional doubts about his understanding of his subject:

. . . starting from 1801, I understand nothing more about his conduct. It is not the lack of documents: letters, fragments of memoirs, secret reports, police records. On the contrary, I have almost too many of them. . . . They do not contradict each other, neither do they agree with each other; they do not seem to be about the same person. And yet other historians work from the same sources of information. . . .

I am beginning to think that nothing can ever be proved. These are honest hypotheses which take the facts into account: but I sense so definitely that they come from me, and that they are simply a way of unifying my own knowledge. Not a glimmer comes from Rollebon's side. Slow, lazy, sulky, the facts adapt themselves to the rigor of the order I wish to give them; but it remains outside of them. I have the feeling of doing a work of pure imagination.

Roquentin's *crise de nerfs* throws light by contrast on Hexter's heroism. For the fictional historian and the real historian represent the practice of historiography in objectively the same way; the difference is one of courage and commitment. "Drawing lines to connect points" is described by Roquentin with despair, by Hexter with confidence and hope. The difference, one might say, is that *wie es eigentlich gewesen* remains for Hexter a constant point of reference for an assurance which cannot be certainly derived from the relation between evidence and completed narrative. Only faith in the definiteness of the past sustains the effort toward retrospective clairvoyance. Roquentin is overwhelmed by the insight—and it *is* an insight, not a pathological symptom—that of itself the past, however definite, is mute. In a way, Hexter's controlling idea is a practical imperative rather than a theoretical insight. The past *will* speak, if he has anything to say about it.

## Notes

1. For convenience, I list here the items of Hexter's bibliography mainly concerned with the theory of historiography, with abbreviations by which they will be cited in the text. Articles reprinted in books are not separately listed.

(*RA*)    *Reappraisals in History* (London and Evanston, Ill., 1961).

(*NYRB*)    Review of Morton White's *Foundations of Historical Knowledge* and Arthur C. Danto's *Analytical Philosophy of History, New York Review of Books*, 9 February 1967; reply 23 March 1967.

(*HT*)    "The Rhetoric of History," *History and Theory* 6 (1967): 3–13.

(*IESS*)    "Historiography: The Rhetoric of History," *International Encyclopedia of the Social Sciences*, 6:368–94 (1967). Reprinted in *Doing History*, pp. 15–76.

(*DH*)    *Doing History* (Bloomington, Ind., 1971).

(*HP*)    *The History Primer* (New York, 1971).

(*FB*)    "Fernand Braudel and the Monde Braudellian," *Journal of Modern History* 44 (1972): 480–539.

(*TLS*)    Review of Christopher Hill's *Change and Continuity in Seventeenth-Century England, Times Literary Supplement*, 24 October 1975; replies 7 November 1975, 28 November 1975.

# Toward a New Socio-Political Order

# Politics and the Pilgrimage of Grace

## G. R. ELTON

Few scholars these days like to be called political or constitutional historians: it is widely held that those have ceased to be useful occupations. Especially in the United States, a preoccupation with social analysis and the study of ideas and ideologies has become not only predominant but arrogant. It is, I suppose, quite just that political historians, who have for long derided the work of even earlier annalists, should now in turn suffer the contempt of the modern *Annalistes*, but neither these debates nor the prevalent attitudes are especially beneficial to the study of history. Contempt for political history arises from a sometimes justified conviction that its practitioners have in the past been too ready to rest content with surface history—with the lives and doings of kings, bishops, soldiers, politicians, and diplomats; they have ignored the great mass of the dead, allowed a few individuals much too great an influence on events, and by-passed the operation of impersonal "forces." On top of this we have the beliefs of those to whom no history is worth writing unless it fits a framework of general theory and contributes something to the search for predictable developments. The result has been to replace the political historian's simplifications with the vast simplicities of dehumanized generalization: events have given way to circumstances and men to movements. Yet, as any historian knows who has really looked at the materials of historical study, those great structures and their lesser offspring can be maintained only if the many inconvenient facts—deeds and thoughts and reactions, unpredictable outcomes and accidental stirrings—are left out. And among these inconvenient facts the constant irruption of politics, understood in its fullest sense, stands out above the rest.

Politics are the activities of men in political society, and though they may be the active concern of the few, their effects spare none. To study the history of any society without seeking to know what its government was doing is even more inadequate than to study government without reference to social structure or intellectual climate, those vague vogues that at present attract so much devoted and often misguided labor. No one means to defend inadequate forms of political history, and a concern with all that the analyzers of "function" and "structure" and indeed of ideas and ideologies can tell him is the particular duty of the political historian who wants to tell the fullest story possible about the past, a story through time and space. No more than any other human activity does political history stand still, and its critics ought not to look at long-past performances and attitudes if they really wish to know what it is doing today. The fact is that without a history of public affairs there tends to be no history at all; instead we are likely to get a rather dubious sociology of the past, unrealistically static, devoid of a sense of time passing, often devoid of humanity. I have set out the case at sufficient length elsewhere and do not mean to repeat myself.[1] But in true historical fashion, the case should be proved by example, and this is what I should like to attempt here. The example I propose to study is too large to be fully investigated in an essay, and this paper is in part designed to show the need for further research. However, I hope also to demonstrate that even in the less obvious areas of the past we cannot safely ignore the methods and concerns of political history.

There are few important things that raise our problem in more acute form than large-scale movements against the existing governmental order. They often have political programs and their behavior involves political action; yet the springs of action, the reasons for adherence, the composition of such movements (what is often called their inner reality) cannot as a rule be illuminated by political history as such. Political descriptions of such events, the word goes, stay on the surface; a real understanding depends on economic and social analysis, on the investigation of personal and familial and regional relationships, perhaps above all on theories and typologies of revolution—on all those techniques and interests of which political history remains innocent. Of course, there is some truth in this, but it is also true that when the politics of such events are forgotten the whole thing becomes unexplained and mysterious. To see whether this is so, let us once more consider the largest revolt ever mounted against the rule of the Tudor monarchy in sixteenth-century England—the northern rebellions of the autumn of 1536. Conscious as I am of the effrontery involved in attempting a reconsideration of so vast a subject in a short essay, I am quite prepared to be rapidly over-taken by the progress of research; nevertheless, the time seems ripe to take a comprehensive look.

The fullest account of these risings was provided in the magnificent two volumes which Margaret and Ruth Dodds devoted to them some sixty years ago.[2] Their narrative of events has stood unchallenged and is, indeed, in the main beyond challenge: using all the available evidence (and incidentally using the manuscripts rather than calendar versions), the Misses Dodds told the story in massive and fascinating detail. As they saw it, a spontaneous outburst of protests against Henry VIII's policies began in Lincolnshire on 1 October; within a few days, that shire was convulsed, and very soon the rising spread to the East Riding of Yorkshire, from where it traveled rapidly over all the six northern counties. Everywhere the initiative lay with "the commons," that is to say, mainly the yeomanry, husbandmen, and craftsmen; many of the gentry, compelled by threats, took the pilgrims' oath reluctantly but accepted invitations backed by force to become the leaders of the rebels. The book lays out the full story of negotiations, collapse, betrayal, and aftermath—a magnificent tale and a true drama. Though the Misses Dodds recognized some diversity in the various centers of rebellion, and though they provided some analysis of the leadership which should have cast doubt upon their conviction that the upper classes only followed the lead of the commonalty, they confined themselves essentially to an "old-fashioned" political description of events. They accepted the various sets of demands as trustworthy evidence for the desires of the rebellious body: the whole north was delineated as having risen spontaneously in defense of the old Church, for the Princess Mary's right to the throne, for the restoration of the monasteries, for much else, and in particular against the low-born heretical councillors who had perverted the king's policy and brought the realm to ruin. Above all, their exhaustive account gave lasting substance to the figure of a great and uncorrupted

leader in Robert Aske. The Doddses' volumes, so dramatic in
themselves, provided the material for an influential fictitious
treatment which for many has settled the holiness of the Pilgrimage and the saintliness of its leader.[3]

This magisterial discussion held the field quite undisputed for
some fifty years, during which little work was done on the history
of the Pilgrimage and its aftermath except for some articles by A.
G. Dickens, who gradually came to work out his conviction that
Yorkshire at least was less devotedly Catholic than had been
supposed, a conviction finally elaborated in a work on northern
heresy that undermined many of the inherited notions about the
Pilgrimage.[4] But by and large the Misses Dodds were supposed to
have done it all. In one of the curious notes which Conyers Read
occasionally appended to entries in his *Bibliography of British
History: the Tudor Period,* their work was summed up as "impartial, wealth of detail, co-ordination of materials, but little new in
conclusions. Valuable."[5] Certainly it was valuable and provided a
wealth of well-coordinated detail, but Read might have noticed
that its conclusions, though not utterly new, became orthodoxy
just because of its apparently total coverage and mastery of the
evidence. But impartial it was not: from first to last the book
breathes an animus against Henry, Cromwell, and the reformers,
something like devotion to the cause of Catherine of Aragon, and
a profound conviction that what was at stake in the Pilgrimage
was "liberty," a term never defined but frequently employed. On
one of the rare occasions on which they allowed emotion to over-
take them, they said of the pilgrims' oath that there was "a ring in
the words that, even today, sets a calm Protestant heart beating to
the tune of the Pilgrims' March."[6] The not necessarily calm heart
of a later agnostic finds that oath, well written though it is, a good
deal more resistable; but, in any case, the phrase gives the game
away. The Misses Dodds were not impartial, nor was there any
reason why they should have been. What gave their patently
biased account such authority and long life, however, was the fact
that it did seem to be entirely in accord with discoverable facts.
Even the sceptic, rereading the evidence on which they relied,
must admit that to all appearance their story of a truly popular
movement which coerced the upper sort into compliance and
promoted the restoration of the old Church against the in-
novators—a movement in which (as they said) such other motives as feudal allegiances, economic grievances, and local
distrust of interference from the center played their subsidiary
parts—truthfully reflected what had happened.

To all appearance: and it is here that the rub lies. This was a
political story handled by the conventional methods of political

history, answering the question "what happened" with the aid of the genre's established and recognized techniques. Was this the truth of events or the truth of the surface? For a long time no one troubled himself further to seek behind the carapace of the tale for the quivering live body, but by the mid-1960s interest revived in the Pilgrimage. The rebellion has never been subjected to the full treatment of structural or quantifying methods, partly because the evidence does not permit much of this and partly because the established orthodoxy suited a historiography which preferred to take its stand with the victims of Henry VIII. Nevertheless, the effects of those novel forms of enquiry were felt here and there, at some remove, and in due course more searching studies of what actually went on, who rebelled, and why they did so have begun to appear. Although no one has yet attempted a comprehensive reassessment, much recent work has made it impossible to agree any longer with any of the major interpretations offered by the Misses Dodds. This new evaluation owes much to a move away from strictly political history and thus bears out the claims of those who campaign against those old-fashioned ways: so far so good. Yet, as I hope to show, undue disregard of politics has also prevented the revisers from seeing what went on and thus from restoring the coherence of explanation that the older account possessed.

The first returns to the problem did not seriously affect the general issues. In 1940 Garrett Mattingly gave renewed currency to the idea that the Pilgrimage was associated with a "neo-feudal conspiracy" hatched around the imperial ambassador; his highly speculative account, which nevertheless grasped some important connections too readily neglected since, accepted a false sociological concept which has proved persistent.[7] In 1967 A. G. Dickens daringly suggested that the role of religion in the insurrections had been greatly exaggerated; especially he could not find that love for the monastic orders was as fervent as the conventional story alleged, and he suggested that the real grievances behind the risings—the grievances of peasants and weavers—stood rooted in economic discontent and apprehensions of further exactions. He still, however, believed that nobles and gentry assumed the leadership under duress; to him the risings were still truly popular movements.[8] A year later, C. S. L. Davies took issue with his argument: he pointed out that the economic circumstances of 1536 were markedly better than those of 1535, that the risings were in no sense a peasants' or class war against the gentry, and that the event required an ideology which it had found in religion—in the defense of the monasteries and the protection of clergy and laity against doctrinal innovation as well as fiscal exaction.[9] These papers usefully reopened the closed subject and presented some helpful insights, but they did not begin to touch the hard core of the Dodds version. At about this time, J. J. Scarisbrick was able to sum up the accepted interpretation by calling the Pilgrimage

a large-scale, spontaneous, authentic indictment of all that Henry most obviously stood for; and it passed judgment against him as surely and comprehensively as *Magna Carta* condemned John or the *Grand Remonstrance* the government of Charles I.[10]

I now mean to show that none of those three adjectives will stand the test of deeper investigation, for even as Scarisbrick wrote, the old view was being thoroughly undermined by studies on the ground—studies that owed much to the preferences and advice of the social historian and that forced upon us a new, but so far incoherent, view of the event. Let us therefore begin by considering how completely this recent work (plus some additional investigations of my own) may have demolished the opinion that the rebellions were large-scale, spontaneous, and authentic.[11]

At first sight, the risings were certainly large-scale—altogether seven counties, about one-third of England, were up in arms in the last months of 1536. This appearance, however, hides much of the reality. Despite the great hosts of "commons" (and gentry) moving about the countryside, they never roused the whole region. In Lincolnshire, the rebels made little impact south of Lincoln; in Lancashire they dominated only north of the Ribble; in the northern counties the border regions proper remained quiet; Skipton, Carlisle, and Scarborough never surrendered; in Clifford country most of the gentry remained loyal; everywhere, and especially in the West Riding, rebellious patches mingled with loyal ones, often depending on the line taken by the lords of different fiefs.[12] Moreover, by no means all the troubled areas formed parts of one single movement. There was interaction but no proper liaison between the Lincolnshire rising and the Pilgrimage of Grace. Lancashire stirred before Aske transferred some of his influence there and remained very uneasy after Aske had called off his proceedings.[13] Northumberland always stood aside from the main rising, and the Middle March (Tynedale and Redesdale) behaved in its traditional lawless fashion rather than joining in the true rebellion. Above all, the disturbances in the Craven district of the West Riding, around Kendal, and in Cumberland, a peasant protest against exploiting landlords, had little more than a chronological coincidence with the Pilgrimage. Though delegates from all parts met at Pontefract, the great host at Doncaster did not include companies from all "the north," but was really drawn only from Yorkshire and Durham. The troubles comprehended a variety of variously motivated small-scale risings, given a spurious coherence by the one great upheaval in Yorkshire and the purposeful leadership that emerged there. This is not to deny that, especially from the point of view of Henry's government, these various rebellions naturally coalesced into the semblance of one vast disaffected region; but it is important to remember that they never confronted seven counties all united on a single program and purpose.

I turn to spontaneity. What does one mean by saying that a rebellion is spontaneous? No sizable movement of this sort can occur without some degree of inducement, management, and influence: people do not suddenly, of their own minds, rise up in thousands to march in protest about the countryside or riot through the streets of towns and villages. Somebody will have persuaded them to do so. Of course, there has to be a readiness to be persuaded, though we know enough by now about the psychology of crowds and in-groups to understand something about the way in which a willingness to protest or rebel can be generated among people who had not thought of doing any such thing. In discussing spontaneity we shall therefore be content with that limited sense applicable in such cases—the sense that the outward appearance of an unprepared and unmanaged uprising represents the essential truth of the event. That was what Cromwell's investigators were told had happened in 1536. According to the examinees, the spontaneous outburst at Louth rapidly drew in sympathizers elsewhere in Lincolnshire; what at first were potentially isolated riots quickly formed a coordinated movement; the people of Yorkshire and the rest joined in of their own volition as the spark fled down the line; and the Pilgrimage was carried on by self-risen bands of the commons marching from place to place, compelling their betters to come in by threats of violence to life and property, and forcing towns to open their gates and join the rebellion. The demand for action came, so the story went, from below; it originated in the volatile dissatisfaction and distress of the generality, which the upper classes, traditionally rulers and controllers of the people, were powerless to resist.

That some such spontaneous events occurred need not be doubted. The dissolution of the smaller houses of religion provoked positive and self-generated resistance at Hexham in Northumberland and Norton in Cheshire, and at both places the monks received ready assistance from the neighborhood. However, neither Hexham nor Norton played any part in the Pilgrimage, which never even involved Cheshire at all. It looks likely that the peasant uprising at Kendal, in Craven, and around Carlisle was truly spontaneous—a continuation of earlier rioting against enclosing and rack-renting landlords, especially the earl of Cumberland. This, too, however, must be thought pretty marginal to the Pilgrimage proper: Aske experienced real difficulties in incorporating the northwest into his own movement, and the last flicker of rebellion was defeated at Carlisle early in 1537 by just those gentry-led forces that in Yorkshire and Durham constituted the pilgrims' host. Lancashire north of the Ribble also witnessed some independently spontaneous rebellion, which again had to be specifically integrated into the main rising by the despatch there of pilgrims' leaders (Sir Stephen Hamerton and Nicholas Tempest) and which continued in existence after Aske had accepted the duke of Norfolk's promises in December. There was possibly also something sufficiently spontaneous about the activities of the Lincolnshire clergy who first set light to the tinder: the vicar of Louth may possibly have preached his fatal sermon on 1 October without coordinating things with anyone else, and the reaction of threatened monks and disaffected parish clergy elsewhere in the shire may have owed little to organization. We cannot be sure (and await further investigation), but quite likely these men were truly and thoroughly worked up by the religious policy of the government—by the break with Rome, by the threat of the Dissolution, and even more by the ban on traditional devotional practices (not to mention taxation).

Or so it might seem: but there must be serious doubts about all this in the light of researches which have left in shreds the story as it was told by those involved. We may look at three aspects of these events which make the notion of spontaneity look less than convincing: the role of the gentry, the manner in which the crowds were set in motion, and the evidence of premeditation.

The gentry, nobility, and higher clergy who got involved all without exception later claimed to have been coerced: the initiative had never come from them. That, of course, is what they were bound to say if they wished to save their lives, and it is clear that the government accepted these excuses more generally than it believed them: no one wanted a holocaust which would leave six counties without settled order or leadership. But it is also evident that the tale rings very false. The gentry not only joined the rebellion in considerable numbers but invariably acted as its leaders; except among the peasant rioters of the northwest, the commons are always represented as calling for gentlemen to take charge. Such deferential unanimity is in itself not too probable in the midst of a rebellion, and very occasionally even our distorted evidence allows glimpses of a more class-structured conflict:

some of the Lincolnshire rebels expressed the desire for noble blood of which one would expect to hear in a peasant uprising and which, for instance, was prominent in the inept plotting inspired by the northern events that occurred in Norfolk in 1537.[14] The usual story is really very odd: everywhere leading gentlemen of ancient authority are shown quivering in their shoes at threats to themselves, their families, their houses and livestock, and the next moment they are seen taking a most active lead, gathering their tenantry to march to assembly points, debating the purposes and demands of the rising, imposing the terms of negotiation and treating "the commons" as cannon fodder. No doubt there were popular stirrings here and there, but that the Pilgrimage came to be entirely commanded by supposedly coerced members of the ruling classes is beyond all dispute, and Cromwell had good reason to ask why they should all have been so frightened into positive action when they could point to no single case in which a gentleman had suffered in life or limb for resisting the rebels.[15] Determined "loyalty" was indeed possible, even though it seems quite often to have been grounded in feuds between gentlemen; thus Sir Brian Hastings, an enemy of Darcy's and hostile to the Percies, never wavered even though it cost him some heads of cattle. One may believe that the crowds of riotous husbandmen and artisans scared some people, and Aske on occasion used threats to extract money and victual from reluctant monks and assistance from reluctant towns; but the overwhelming impression must be that the Pilgrimage originated among the better sort, who brought out the people, leading at first from behind and soon enough from the front. The point has been thoroughly established for Lincolnshire, while the pervasive influence of the Percy connection has been elucidated for Yorkshire, Durham, and Northumberland.[16] The government knew the truth from the first, expressing concern to find out "what personages had in deed the rule of all things whosoever bare the name thereof."[17] It is no longer possible to avoid the conclusion that in the main the northern risings were not the spontaneous work of the commons but owed far more to the activities of "alienated" members of the ruling sort, who managed and guided the outbreak from first to last—from causing it to happen to bringing it to a close. Who they were and what caused them to be so disaffected shall be discussed later.

There were real rebels among the commons, and their behavior confirms that the events of October 1536 did not come about spontaneously. Some people quite evidently accepted the gentry's leadership with a reluctance not shown by the vast majority, watched their betters' doings with deep suspicion, and felt betrayed when the gentry came to terms with the king. Hallom was only the most prominent man of this type. These differences within the commonalty need a lot more working out, but the fact remains that the "true rebels" emerged in the course of events, adopted their position as the rebellion progressed, and never succeeded in dominating it. Thus, they seem to have tried to profit from proceedings which owed their origin to the activities of others.

The fact of upper-class guidance is further confirmed by the manner in which the rebellion was spread through the north. Right from the start trouble was stirred by means of wild rumors and stories—stories of new taxes, loss of church plate, licenses for the eating of better food (white bread and capons)—and it was upon the wings of such rumors, carefully designed to disturb the common people and reinforced by subversive prophecies and ballads, that the rising spread. The idea that the commons took up arms to defend the Church or be rid of Cromwell will not stand up to the evidence: they rose because, already much unsettled by what had in fact been happening to familiar practices of daily piety, they were led to believe often extravagant tales of further doings which would touch their pockets. Money, not the faith, caused the people to stir, if the stories spread are any indication; and the government showed itself aware of this truth in its constant efforts to kill the rumors and to point out that the recent tax touched hardly anyone among the protesters.[18] Furthermore, there were specialists in this task of rumor-spreading: the job was committed to the clergy, both regular and secular, who did their work well, always to the fore in every new hearth of disturbance and for ever prophesying dire threats to people's pockets.[19] At Knaresborough the friars went so far as to post bills all over the place proclaiming the false stories of new impositions—plough money, cattle taxes, heavy charges for baptisms.[20] The clergy, and especially the monks, had assuredly most to lose and could be expected to be active; the wonder is that so many stayed aside while others really submitted to threats. But of the many who enthusiastically threw themselves into the fray and carried disaffection across the north, the important point is that they were agents, not originators. Even the apparently spontaneous action of the Lincolnshire clergy, deeply upset by episcopal pressure to conform to the 1536 Injunctions,[21] looks to have been staged. Rumors of the characteristic kind ran about the county a good month before the vicar of Louth's sermon,[22] and when the outbreak came, organized agitators who even paid to rent their crowds made their appearance.[23] In fact, the clergy most active in the business would seem to have been the clients of the disaffected gentry: Mrs. Bowker tells me that she finds convincing links between ecclesiastical patronage and involvement in rebellion in Lincolnshire, while Miss Brigden can document the use of their clergy by the Yorkshire gentry. Behind the carriers of the infection we again find the normal ruling order of the region.

The same conclusion emerges from a study of the manner in which the pilgrims' host was gathered together. Though many groups of armed rebels assembled in their parishes, and though Lancashire and the northwest relied in the main on this method (the signal being the ringing of bells), the gentry quickly took over and applied their traditional methods—the calling out of the tenantry in formal musters at assembly points.[24] When he decided to come into the open, Darcy used a convenient priest to convey his orders for the mustering of the southern West Riding, and he did so as constable of Pontefract and king's deputy for the region.[25] The essentially independent and unorganized stirrings in Lancashire did not satisfy Aske, who in late October sent orders for the systematic raising of that county.[26] Though everybody—the king as well as the rebel leaders—talked as though wild mobs were roaming the countryside with no leadership or organization (and though there were some such excesses here and there), the truth was very different. Aske from the first commanded a reasonably well founded army, to which he added further gentry-led contingents as the rebellion advanced. Anyone doubting this might care to look at the proclamation calling out Marshland and Howdenshire—which started the whole business north of the Humber—or read the account of the great captain's lordly and military bearing at Pontefract, where Lancaster herald found him holding a sort of court in a camp of war.[27]

The best argument, of course, against genuine spontaneity lies in the evidence of planning. It has already been said that the riot at Louth did not come out of the blue, and (as Mr. James has shown) the fact that what was in Tudor terms a commonplace bit of trouble should have rapidly been enlarged into a general rising demonstrates the existence of careful preparation. Rumors that by Michaelmas any common man might find it to his advantage to be in Lincolnshire were current in Norfolk by the beginning of September.[28] It is therefore important that we should know as much as possible about the preparatory activities of those who ultimately emerged as leaders, but much of this will forever remain obscure. Still, a strictly preliminary look at some of them will be useful here, if only because it at once throws a very different light upon them than that cast in the conventional account. Aske apart, about whom more in a moment, the three key figures were Lord Hussey in Lincolnshire, Lord Darcy in the West

Riding, and Sir Robert Constable in the East Riding. They are key figures not only because they so obviously commanded much of the trouble, but also because they stand well aside from the so-called feudal structure of the north, which itself requires particular consideration.[29] All three claimed to have been forced into the ranks of the rebels against their will; all three were executed for treason. Did their behavior through the rising bear out their claims: were they innocent victims? All three were old men in their seventies who had spent most of their lives in active service under the Tudor monarchy, and only Constable (the one of them who belonged to an old-established county family) had failed to profit massively from his service. According to Hussey himself, they had as early as 1534 agreed among themselves that they "would not be heretics, but die Christian men."[30]

Virtually nothing can be discovered about Constable, for whom no examination or incriminating letters survive. There are hints of disaffection: by late 1534 Cromwell received advice from Yorkshire that Constable ought to be removed from the Commission of the Peace because he was not carrying out his duties properly.[31] His attachment to the old religion is in no doubt,[32] but his tracks remain well covered in the autumn of 1536. Thus, his guilt in planning the revolt can only be inferred from his old association with the others, against whom the evidence is clearer. It may also be guessed at from the fact that he was condemned for treason when other gentlemen of the East Riding whose actions must raise suspicion (for instance Sir Ralph Ellerker the younger) remained untroubled. But those are circular arguments of little weight: let Constable's case stand unproven. Hussey's is clearer and has been sufficiently worked out by Mr. James, who concludes that he "was the central figure around whom the Lincolnshire movement both gathered momentum and eventually collapsed."[33] Hussey certainly played an equivocal part during the rising (I shall offer an explanation of his behavior later), but the man who, among much dithering, advised the rebels to take Lincoln (which they did) cannot readily be absolved from having foreknowledge of the event. His first reaction to the news of the rioting in the northern part of the county—a letter enquiring whether what had happened involved the gentry—strongly suggests the difficulties of a man who, having planned for just such an event, now needs to discover whether his plans are taking effect or he has been upstaged by an interloper.[34]

Darcy, on the other hand, leaves no doubt. He helps the historian because, in spite of his often tedious pose as the bluff and honest soldier (gruffly referring to himself in the third person—"old Tom"), he kept a careful and ordered office whose archives came to the Crown at his arrest. Thus, we know that by 1 October he had organized his military following in a long array of knights, esquires, and gentlemen (with their retinues) "promised to serve the king's grace" under his command "as he appoints upon an hour's warning." This is an outline of the West Riding's military system, wapentake by wapentake.[35] Thereafter he certainly pretended to be opposed to the rising and to be keeping an eye on it, but Henry justly complained that he was not sending the right or the full information. Having sent his second son, Arthur, on a mission to the earl of Shrewsbury, he then tried to get him back to Pontefract in an effort to avoid leaving a hostage in royalist hands, warned York of the approach of Aske's army in terms which can only be read as an encouragement to surrender, and refused to proceed against Aske or (later) to hand him over because to do so would offend his honor.[36] The speed with which he surrendered Pontefract told most urgently against him, and no wonder; but the point is that the moment the rebels entered the castle Darcy emerged as Aske's chief fellow commander, very much the second man in charge of the proceedings. So rapid a conversion makes sense only on the assumption that Darcy had been in the plot from the first. What perhaps tells most forcefully against him, as Cromwell realized who pressed him hard on the point,[37] was the famous badge of the five wounds of Christ under which the pilgrims marched. It had been Darcy's badge over twenty years before when he took his retinue to southern France in the disastrous expedition led by the marquess of Dorset in support of Ferdinand of Aragon. Its use in 1536 was lamely explained by a story that the accidental killing of a man among the rebels had suggested the need for a distinguishing badge. Well and good: but how did thousands of badges get made in one night? Or had he dug out that ancient store? The implication that Darcy had fully prepared for the rebellion is overwhelming and, as we shall see, there is in fact plenty of evidence for a conspiracy with Darcy at the center. Darcy and Hussey were in close contact in November 1536, and though the particular messenger used denied that he had ever carried messages to Constable, the very manner of his denial hints that somebody else did.[38] The chances that in early October 1536 these three men were taken totally by surprise are too slight to be seriously considered.

The most formidable case, however, lies against Aske, whose emergence as the chief leader, the great captain, is rather astounding. Unlike the others he carried no natural authority; a minor gentleman of good family and, of all things, a lawyer (the bogeyman most hated among the common people), he really makes an odd choice for the command of rebellious shires. The fact has, of course, been read as evidence of true spontaneity: driven into rebellion, the commons found an idealist deeply disturbed by the king's policy and got him to take upon himself the organizing of the protest. But that is not what really happened. Aske's own story of how he came to be involved has always been accepted without question, mainly because we have learned to believe in the axiom of his saintly uprightness.[39] Yet it hardly makes sense. As Aske told it, he was visiting the Ellerkers in the East Riding for a weekend's hunting when Sir Ralph had to go off to attend to his duties as a subsidy commissioner. This broke up the party, and Aske decided to go to London for the start of the law term. This innocent purpose was interrupted when a band of Lincolnshire rebels captured him after he crossed the Humber and made him swear the rebel's oath. Even by his own account he immediately acquired some authority among them, and he took it upon himself to ride to Caistor (even though he took care to emphasize that leaving the band put him in danger of being regarded as a treacherous turncoat) in order to find out what was going on there. In fact, as he admitted, he went over to confer with Thomas Moigne, one of the leaders of the Lincolnshire rising. He then returned to Yorkshire, allegedly to prevent any spontaneous outbreak there, but found on his rejoining the rebels south of the Humber that he was now unable to travel further toward London because, on account of his brief departure, he was threatened with assassination if he should reach Lincoln. There was nothing for it, therefore, but to cross back into Howdenshire once more; the weather delayed him, and meanwhile a forged letter pretending to run in his name raised Beverley—and so the trouble started.

It is a story full of improbabilities. The king knew of the rebellion early on 4 October;[40] yet Aske started his journey that day in alleged ignorance that anything had happened. Even when the ferryman at Barton-on-Humber told him that Caistor was up he continued his journey. His talking to Moigne (a fellow lawyer) is deeply suspicious. Having once got away from the rebels who had forced him to take the oath, he yet rejoined them. His excuse for not pursuing his professed original intention of going to London is surely unbelievably thin. Even if it was true that he had reason to fear for his life—and I do not find this credible—the alternative he chose to getting to Westminster Hall, namely the transmission of the rebellion to Yorkshire, leaves his real mind very much exposed. And even if the proclamation in his name was forged, why should Marshland and Howdenshire have risen in response to it unless they were expecting it; and why should a forger have used his name unless it was known that he was preparing the East Riding for an uprising? Aske's whole conduct in that first October week makes sense only on the assumption that he was involved in a conspiracy but was taken by surprise when Lincolnshire burst out before he was ready in Yorkshire. He then, I suggest, went to see what was going on and made some efforts to prevent premature and ill-coordinated stirrings; indeed, the speed with which the Lincolnshire rising collapsed testifies to his good sense in wanting to be convinced that the operation was being properly conducted. He managed to hold the East Riding back long enough to make sure that when he unleashed rebellion it would sweep immediately and successfully through Marshland and Howden-shire, thus at once providing the means of power which made possible the rapid march to York and the speedy link-up with Darcy and Sir Thomas Percy in the West Riding. Success here enabled Lord Latimer to mobilize the North Riding, Sir Ingram Percy to do the same in Durham, and a general rebellion to spread through the north. That Aske knew nothing of plans to rebel until he encountered those Lincolnshire men on 4 October simply cannot be believed; and the manner in which Yorkshire joined testifies impressively to the preparations that he and others had made—preparations good enough even to overcome the handicap of what must now look like a premature outbreak in Lincolnshire that came close to jeopardizing the whole enterprise.

Spontaneous, therefore, is the wrong word to apply to the northern rebellions of 1536. Nearly all of them were planned in advance and organized from above, though without any doubt at all planning and organization were effective because the materials of disaffection and protest lay thick upon the ground. These materials have usually provided the arguments for thinking the rebellion "authentic"—that the protests embodied in the pilgrims' demands represented the general and genuine grievances of those into whose mouths they were put. Is this true?

Of course, one accepts that such sets of demands—a program—cannot emerge spontaneously in any case; someone must do the drafting, and in so mixed and muddled a rising as that of 1536 the outcome is bound to include notions put forward by various sections as well as compromises between them. Such things do not deny "authenticity," but there are features about the rebels' programs that raise serious doubts. They emerged in ways that hint at total control by a small group, and they contain items that do not fit the generally projected image. The various sets of demands put up in Lincolnshire appear to have run to eight items: no taxation except for war, the restoration of the Church's ancient liberties and the abolition of first fruits and tenths, an end to the Dissolution, an end to heresy and the punishment of Cranmer, Latimer, and Longland, reliance on noble councillors and the destruction of Cromwell, Rich, Legh, and Layton, a pardon for the rebels, and the repeal of the Statute of Uses.[41] At first sight they seem both comprehensive and representative of the various elements in the insurrection—poor commons, religious houses, the ordinary clergy, conservatives in religion and politics, the land-owning and conservative gentry. However, we know that they were effectively put together by one man—George Stones or Staines—who most energetically made propaganda for them; we know that they were agreed by gentlemen only, at a meeting held while the commons were busy killing one of their victims; and we know that they had to be explained in detail to the multitude who were later alleged to have put them forward.[42] Not only were many people puzzled to know what the Statute of Uses might be, but they even had to be told who Cromwell was and why removing him should help. No doubt the houses still standing supported the call for no more suppressions, but the fact remains that no attempt was made in Lincolnshire to restore a single one of those already dissolved.[43] The list of men named as enemies of the people is surely strange. If the commons wanted heretical prelates, Cranmer, as archbishop, would readily come to mind; but was Latimer, who had never been active in the north, really known there? His fame ran in the west country and at court, a point of significance. As for Longland, whatever his position toward the reform, he was no heretic in the Latimer mold, but he happened to be the local man and had been exceptionally active in enforcing the government's orders touching the innovations. Stranger still is the roll call of offending ministers. Cromwell: well, yes; but the commons did not know him for an enemy, and he was pointed out by the gentlemen, and especially by Stones. The mention of Legh and Layton again reflects the feelings of those troubled by the Dissolution, but no one could possibly have regarded these non-councillors as leading members of the government. As for Rich, he had been active as chancellor of Augmentations since April 1536[44] and thus may have collected the hatred of the defenders of monasticism; he was certainly not a prominent man in the realm at large. However, he had sworn away Sir Thomas More's life: and George Stones had a strong connection with the late lord chancellor's family circle.[45] At one point, the master of the Rolls (Christopher Hales) joined the proscription list, a man who had never shown the slightest leaning towards heresy; on the other hand, he had been Stones's master, which might be a better reason for his pointless inclusion. Thus, there are at least strong hints here that the demands embodied not only a confusion of local grievances, many of them sold to the rebels rather than produced by them, but also a bundle of London-based court grievances which had nothing to do with Lincolnshire at all.

⌐ The demands of the Pilgrimage of Grace, better recorded and far better worked out, pose very similar problems. Aske's first proclamation, a very incendiary document claiming to speak in the name of "the barony and communalty" of "the conventual assembly or pilgrimage," listed six: the Dissolution, the Act of Uses, payment of first fruits, general taxation, the "base council about the King," the new bishops (which excludes Longland, that Lincolnshire speciality, who had held his see since 1521).[46] Elaborated and added unto, these remained the basis of the program. It was admitted that this foundation did not originate in Yorkshire but simply took over the Lincolnshire articles, which Aske brought with him when, with two Lincolnshire messengers, he transferred the rising to Yorkshire, and one of the more reluctantly involved gentlemen later stated that he had never heard any of these grievances discussed before the insurrection.[47] Thus, for instance, Aske's admission that the Statute of Uses would never have been mentioned if Stones had not with some difficulty forced it into the Lincolnshire articles must at once call in question the seriousness of that particular complaint.[48]

The final comprehensive statement of demands, worked out at Pontefract, was composed by Aske in consultation with Darcy and other leaders; though based on grievances contributed by the representatives of various parts of the north, it underwent careful recension at a very few hands; it was then agreed, article by article, with the delegation sent to Doncaster, where they were to present it to the duke of Norfolk; finally it received approval from the full assembly of leaders—that is, gentry and clergy—at Pontefract.[49] This careful procedure must not disguise the fact that Aske (with perhaps Darcy) remained personally in charge of production throughout: the Articles were very much one man's work, but they also offer some manifest clues concerning the influences behind their composition.

Following the Misses Dodds, we may discuss them under four headings: religious, constitutional, legal, and economic. The last category needs no more than a glance. The recent subsidy was widely resented, partly because all taxes annoyed but especially because this one called expressly for contributions to peacetime government;[50] on the other hand, the protest against enclosures and high "gressums" (entry fines) was, as is well known, a specialist grievance of the tenantry in Cumberland, Westmoreland and the upper Yorkshire dales. Here we seek no hidden hand. Similarly, there are some points among the religious complaints which we can readily concede as authentic, not only in the sense that certain obvious groups would sincerely (and selfishly) maintain them, but also on the grounds that many of the commons and the bulk of the gentle no doubt were genuinely attached to traditional rights, practices, and beliefs. Resentments at attacks on the clerical privileges of sanctuary and benefit of clergy were nothing new; the whole southern Convocation had demonstrated its feelings in 1515, and those of the north evidently still continued to hold much the same opinion. We may also believe without question that the clergy assembled at Pontefract wished to recover the liberties of the north (Durham, Beverley, Ripon, St. Peter of York) against the recent act which had abolished all such. After all, Archbishop Lee, owner of Ripon and Beverley, was there, though Tunstal of Durham throughout prudently hid himself from everybody. The articles attacked first fruits and tenths, as had the Lincolnshire demands, but at Pontefract they sought to protect only monasteries: again no doubt a genuine point of ordinary selfishness.

But these were not the crucial matters under the head of religion. Three issues predominated: the royal supremacy, the fate of the abbeys, and the spread of heresy. It is on the basis of those articles that the Pilgrimage has generally been regarded as primarily a movement of religious protest. Touching the first, the leaders of the rising, who throughout claimed to be loyal subjects of Henry VIII, were in a cleft stick, and the only point they dared include was one which reasserted the pope's supremacy in matters spiritual (cura animarum) and in the consecration of bishops. Even this, in the year that saw the culmination of the government's campaign against Rome, was to tread on very dangerous ground. It was also a demand, as he confirmed, that owed its inclusion mainly to Aske, who admitted that it had hardly been discussed by the leaders and was put in when he thought he heard no objections.[51] So far as the evidence goes, the Pilgrimage produced no general enthusiasm for the pope or against the royal supremacy; in the many letters describing the grievances of the people, the political revolution in the Church remains resoundingly unmentioned. The fate of the religious houses excited more interest, but again Aske's very exceptional concern emerges from his testimony. The familiar song of praise about the great good done by the monks of the north occurs solely in what he told his interrogators and is there described as his own opinion.[52] One need not take scepticism to excess: the monastic institution had undoubtedly retained more respect in the north than elsewhere. Nevertheless, the only evidence of spontaneous support for the religious comes from Lancashire; Professor Dickens has drawn attention to manifestations of a well-entrenched hostility to monasteries in parts of Yorkshire; though Aske very early in the rising ordered the restoration of dissolved houses, at most sixteen of the fifty-five affected experienced the return of the inmates, the only safely documented case once again belonging to Lancashire; the religious themselves displayed so remarkable a reluctance to grasp the helpful hand offered by rebellion that they have drawn stern censure from their foremost historian.[53] We have really been far too ready to accept the view that the whole uprising was unleashed by conservatism in religion, even if it is conceded that conservatism in religion existed and helped to create the unsettled atmosphere. Aske said that that issue alone would have caused rebellion even if there had been no other; and this has well suited a variety of historians' attitudes ranging from personal convictions about the Reformation to methodological convictions concerning the primacy of socioeconomic and ideological explanations. The evidence for Aske's statement is very meager and mostly derived from his other remarks. At most we can say that many of the clergy, especially the seculars, expressed their dislike of the innovations and indoctrinated many of their parishioners, and that Aske deliberately from the first gave to the movement that air of a spiritual protest (a pilgrimage) which correctly reflected his own convictions but which he had difficulty in keeping alive among the mass of his followers. The moderate ease with which "the north" (Lancashire excepted) settled thereafter to the Reformation should sufficiently indicate that the religious purposes of the Pilgrimage had shallow roots, except among the few who dominated its ideology, eloquence, and propaganda.[54]

But were the pilgrims not dead set against heresy, as three of the leaders (Darcy, Hussey, and Constable) had agreed they were a full two years earlier? The articles speak strongly on the subject, but in tones that are far from clear. They mention a general demand for the punishment, by burning or otherwise, of all heretics, episcopal (no names) and lay, and they charge Cromwell, Audley, and Rich with being supporters of heresy who merit condign punishment. Even the Lincolnshire rebels had been more specific about which bishops they wanted done away with, but then the pilgrims at Pontefract could not even make up their minds as to what constituted heresy.[55] They inclined to accepting the Ten Articles (which had so much troubled the parish clergy ordered to proclaim them), and the curious Rump Convocation that met at Pontefract broke up without a usable answer to the question.[56] Aske reckoned that Cranmer, Latimer, Hilsey, and Barlow were heretics, and another document added Brown of Dublin:[57] quite a reasonable list, which proves that someone in the know supplied names, though the omission of these or any names from the articles themselves argues that the general assembly had insufficient grasp to become specific. Even more mysterious is the list of heretical writings whose suppression was demanded, a list which (it is supposed without much evidence) may have derived from a memorial put up by Robert Bowyer, a citizen and lawyer of York.[58] The Continent supplied Luther, Hus, Melanchthon, Oecolampadius, Bucer, the Augsburg Confession, Melanchthon's *Apology*, "and such other heresies of Anibaptist" (did they really suppose there was a heresiarch of that name?). England added Wycliffe, Tyndale, Barnes, (William) Marshall, (John) Rastell, (Christopher) St. German. One must wonder at the inclusion of Oecolampadius and Bucer, neither of whom appeared in English translation till many years later: here one smells a degree of sophisticated, even esoteric, information. But if the rebels were so well informed about heresy, why did they include Rastell, recently dead, who had published only on the common law and common morality, and St. German, whose lay criticism of clerical abuses only Thomas More had ever thought remotely heretical? How did the men of the north even come to think of them? In fact, More supplies the missing link: he had campaigned against St. German, and Rastell was a renegade from his circle who had turned to work for Cromwell. Furthermore, these men were prominent London lawyers, a point that deserves to be remembered. This idiosyncratic list of heretics lends no support to the notion that the risings took their origin from a widespread resistance to the religious side of the Reformation. Altogether, then, the rebels' demands fail to substantiate the authenticity of the religious protest, though it is clear that there was much vague discontent concerning the reform and that some of the participants—Aske in particular—put religion first. It can be believed that without the religious shape given to the rising it would probably have lacked cohesion, drive, and endurance; whatever raised "the commons" in the first place, they found companionship and fervor under the banner with the cross and the five wounds. But the positive positions expressed in the demands were held by a group of leaders, not by "the north."

The real problems that concern us are raised by the so-called constitutional and legal articles, hardly any of which can be said to have risen from general or spontaneous demand. Perhaps the pilgrims generally abominated the 1534 Act of Treasons, and no doubt the rather blatant request that all debts incurred during the rebellion should be canceled by act of Parliament met with sober acclaim. But the Statute of Uses, so obviously offensive to the landed classes, would, as we have seen, have been forgotten ex-

cept that it was in the pronouncements transferred from Lincolnshire. Aske admitted that he disliked it because it disturbed the
settled land law, but the possible legal effects he mentioned were
marked more by perverse ingenuity than sense: he was never
more the lawyer than when he tried to persuade his interrogators
that the statute worked against the king's feudal rights.[59] Whether
such minor grievances as the act against handguns (resented by
hunting squires and poachers)[60] or complaints about escheators'
false inquisitions *post mortem* (an ancient and conventional
theme) reflected a general or a very particular opinion cannot be
settled and does not matter. The real issues under this head were
four: the restoration of the Princess Mary, the freeing of Parliament from royal influence, dislike of the Succession Act because
it empowered Henry to bequeath the crown by his last will and
testament, and the defense of the common law against recent
innovatory practices. Taken together, these four clearly reveal
who and what stood behind the real leadership of the Pilgrimage,
though I can here only summarize a provisional but compelling
conclusion.

The first and third points both arose from the consequences of
Henry's Divorce and constitute a demand that the king's first
marriage be held legitimate and its issue be recognized as the true
heir to the crown; the complaints about Parliament combine the
strangely antiquarian grumbles of Lord Darcy with an already
well established "country" (backbench) dislike of influence which
was to have a long history thereafter (after all, the first place bill
was introduced in Mary's reign), while the last constitutes
the professional protest of one faction among common lawyers
against the recent growth in the power of Chancery—against the
work of Wolsey. An Aragonese-Marian faction, "country" independents in the Commons resentful of aggressive royal policies,
conservative lawyers: these particular interests were also, as has
already been suggested, responsible for the personal attack on
Cromwell, Audley, and Rich, hated far less by "the commons"
than by disappointed courtiers and certain London lawyers. It was
Aske who hated Audley, as he said, because of the chancellor's
use of injunctions,[61] though Wolsey had been more lavish with
them and More no less convinced of their usefulness; it was St.
German who in his best known book (*Doctor and Student*) had
defended the powers of equity. Quite manifestly his so doing
offers a more convincing reason why he should have joined the
list of enemies of the commonwealth than his alleged heresy.
The significance of the More connection, and therefore of
Sir Thomas's death as one of the causes of violent hostility
especially to Cromwell, peeps through obscurely, and so does the

leading role of lawyers and their disputes. Their influence in the rising is manifest but has not yet been studied: Aske and Moigne were only the most prominent of an Inns of Court group who lent their support and leadership to the Pilgrimage and in return appear to have expected the pilgrims to endorse their professional griefs. However, until more work has been done on connections and attitudes it is not possible to do more than suggest that one of the positive origins of the risings should be tracked back to the Inns of Court and Westminster Hall.

As for Cromwell and Rich, it must be doubted whether they were so universally hated as has been alleged. Quite certainly they had their enemies, and some efficient propaganda was conducted, in songs and prophetic utterances, especially against the lord privy seal, but Aske himself said that he knew of no cause to consider him a destroyer of the commonweal.[62] The case against him was put, with much violent abuse, in a memorial submitted by (probably) Sir Thomas Tempest, who sat for Newcastle in the Reformation Parliament: here we find, most usefully, a plain expression of the state of mind of a "country" backbencher who resented conciliar management in the Commons (and it says something for the isolation of historians one from another that this typical complaint, matchable over the centuries, should regularly have been regarded as a convincing indictment of Henry's and Cromwell's relations with Parliament).[63] It was Tempest who introduced the furious complaint about influence over elections and influence in the House, because of the result: "Whatsoever Cromwell says is right, and none other." The other thing that stuck in Tempest's throat was Cromwell's severe action the year before against the grand jury of Yorkshire, who had discovered that gentle status and country independence were no protection against Star Chamber. Perhaps some really hated Cromwell as a heretic—the charge which in the end destroyed him—but quite manifestly the real complaint of the northern gentry against him in 1536 was his government of the realm and especially his competent management of the king's affairs in Parliament. Tempest, like Darcy, was objecting to political defeat—to the victory, in and out of Parliament, of religious reform and administrative centralization—and here lies the vital clue.

It is now plain that the conventional view of the northern rebellions will not stand up. All in all, the affair was not large-scale, spontaneous and authentic. It drew in many quite real grievances and dissatisfactions, and it mobilized resentments of all kinds—social, economic, religious. It was dominated, and to all appearance instigated, not by the commons who were induced to make the running, but by the gentry who, to use Mr. James's phrase, were "alienated from the court": this was as true of Yorkshire, Durham, and Northumberland as it was of Lincolnshire. Moreover, there is plain evidence of preparation, indeed of conspiracy. Who conspired, and why?

The usual answer—of those, that is, who admit the conspiracy—is the answer of the social historian: the rebellion was a feudal or (sometimes) neofeudal phenomenon, a typically northern reaction to Tudor centralization and a hangover from the fifteenth century. This view is found well embedded in the literature and requires no lengthy demonstration here. The one man who really tried to dissect the conspiracy thought that it should be called feudal.[64] The feudal north has so well settled in the historical consciousness that even those scholars whose social analysis underlies so much of the revision attempted here have not escaped from the compulsion of the tag.[65] Yet what was so feudal about the Pilgrimage (for even the convention will allow that the adjective does not fit Lincolnshire)? Of the great northern families, Clifford supported the king, and Dacre, contrary to expectations, never moved at all either way. Nevill, sadly in decline, supplied a leader of sorts in Lord Latimer, offspring of a cadet branch and a member of that antifeudal institution, the Council of the North; the earl of Westmorland kept his distance. Only the Percies behaved in a possibly feudal way, for certainly Percy influence explains many of the alignments in Yorkshire and Northumberland. But the earl of Northumberland, head of the family, took every step he could to avoid involvement; he was the only man of standing whom the pilgrims inspected as a possible conscript and left alone. His brothers, Thomas and Ingram, so prominent in the rising, were fighting not for the "Percy interest" but for their inheritance, lost to them by the earl's bequest of his possessions to the Crown; they were trying not to recreate the Percy lordship but to keep the Percy lands, in a very unfeudal and totally gentlemanlike way. When the cry of Percy was raised, as it was at York, effectively against the earl, feudalism seems a long way off. The rising did not even reveal much clannishness; families were far from standing together. Lord Darcy's two sons resolutely abstained from rebellion and never thought to avenge his death; Robert Aske's brother defended Skipton for the earl of Cumberland; Constables and Ellerkers are found on opposing sides.[66]

Thus, the two things absent from the troubles were feudalism of any convincing sort and dynasticism. The political structure of the northern shires, particularly of Yorkshire and Lincolnshire, the real heart of the rebellion, already looks much like that of the south. The relationships of various gentry groupings, involving also the members of the northern Council, themselves local gentlemen and higher clergy, dominated county politics, but the groups could be readily "polarized" by the arrival of new men within the inner circle, by the workings of Crown patronage, and by the intrusion of government, producing the sort of "court and country" situation so characteristic, for instance, of Elizabethan Norfolk.[67] This is much too large a theme to be worked out in detail here, and one must be careful of overlarge generalizations: but to my mind the situation in the north in 1536 resembled much more the structure which produced the civil wars of the seventeenth century than that which accounts for the civil wars of the fifteenth.

It was upon this situation that the actual conspiracy which did occur impinged. It itself was even less "feudal." Who were the real leaders of rebellion? Darcy and Hussey stood out among them, and they were no feudatories. Though they persuaded the often gullible Eustace Chapuys, Charles V's ambassador, that they were "great magnates on the border," a view too trustingly accepted by the historian,[68] they were nothing of the sort. Both owed their elevation to the Tudor monarchy, and both were primarily courtiers, as incidentally Constable had been before he inherited his lands and retired north. Darcy had been prominent in the court faction which overthrew Wolsey,[69] and in retrospect it must seem that one of his motives on that occasion had been his belief that Wolsey bore the responsibility for Henry's break with his first wife. For Darcy was soon an equally prominent activist in the Aragonese court faction which from 1530 or a little later attempted to arrest the Divorce and the attack on the Church's independence that went with it. Hussey, Mary's chamberlain, naturally stood always in the thick of this group. In September 1534 both men came very close to plotting violence as their only hope, though at that time they did not wish to move without assurance of at least token military support from the emperor. Hussey himself sought out Chapuys and mentioned Darcy as his closest associate and the one who would profession-ally handle the military side, but it was he who really gave the game away when he advised a manner of proceeding which would first organize an insurrection of the people and then bring in the nobility and the clergy.[70] Darcy also told Chapuys that he kept his real mind secret even from his sons: evidently their loyalty in 1536 derived from their ignorance of the conspiracy. What happened in October 1536 was plainly contemplated some two years earlier, and Hussey's remark (which has unaccountably been overlooked by the historians) clinches the case for the in-terpretation of the Pilgrimage here advanced.

The conspirators assured Chapuys that they had good hopes of several noblemen; they mentioned Derby, Rutland, Shrewsbury, and, more doubtfully, Norfolk, all by the way court peers. It is on this slender basis that the whole business has been called feudal. Perhaps the addition of Stanleys, Manners, Talbots, and Howards might have created a true feudal array against Henry, but conspirators' hopes do not equal the truth, and however much these noblemen may have disliked Cromwell or innovation in the Church, they never deserted their duty to the king and in the event were largely responsible for the failure of the rising to spread. And no wonder: with the possible exception of Shrewsbury, they were all Tudor creatures who owed their local ascendancies to the favor of the Crown, not to feudal roots. In 1534 nothing further happened, perhaps because (as has been suggested) Darcy was kept in London at the time, but also, no doubt, because Charles V never responded to the various attempts to involve him actively in the defense of his aunt. The death of that aunt in January 1536 deprived the Aragonese faction (strong in the Privy Chamber) of an impressive figurehead and turned its attentions to two political ambitions: the overthrow of the Boleyns, vulnerable since Anne had lost her hold on the king, and the restoration of the succession to the Princess Mary. The first was achieved in April, when a court line-up against the Boleyns received the accession of Cromwell, who had his own reasons for wishing to be rid of what had become highly embarrassing allies.[71] But he also had his plans for his new and highly temporary allies at court. No sooner were Anne and her associates out of the way than Cromwell used the new Succession Act (hostile to Mary) and the princess's obstinate refusal to submit unreservedly to the royal supremacy to discredit the remnant of the Aragonese faction, who in July stood in fear of execution themselves. Hussey lost his office in Mary's household, and his wife spent a spell in the Tower for allegedly encouraging the princess's obstinacy. The conservatives discovered that all they had achieved by their attack on the Boleyns was the final elevation of Cromwell to complete power under the king. Darcy, back in Yorkshire since mid-1535, played no direct part in these court battles, but it would be absurd to suppose that he did not know what was going on. The events of April–July 1536 provide ample explanation for the virulent hatred of Cromwell displayed by Darcy and other members of the faction, a hatred of which there had been no sign in the days when they concentrated their venom on Anne Boleyn.

Thus, it would appear that these events—the defeat of a court faction in one of the typical political struggles of the age—

convinced the leadership that drastic measures were needed both
to save themselves from destruction and to overthrow Cromwell,
and they therefore resolved to put the old plans for raising the
country into effect. No doubt the further disturbance caused by
the dissolution of the lesser monasteries encouraged hopes of
success and certainly provided useful agents for a rising, but the
decisive events to bring about the northern rebellions happened
at court, not in the country. On this occasion a court faction
transferred its power base to the country, a step most unusual in
the sixteenth century. It had to do so because it had lost all hope
of victory by conventional means, and it was able to do so because
the country—or at least Lincolnshire and Yorkshire—were ready
to be so politicized. Widespread consternation at Cromwell's revolution in the Church laid the foundations. In Lincolnshire the
leading gentry were deeply suspicious of the growing intrusion of
court interests (especially the Brandon Duke of Suffolk and the
Blounts, ambitious newcomers in the county);[72] in Yorkshire, the
king's forthcoming inheritance of the Percy estates reinforced
deep apprehensions about the extension of central power through
Cromwell's policy and men. Sir Thomas Tempest left explicit
record of this typically "country" reaction to the advancing tenta-
cles of the court, but that he was not the only one is clear, for
instance, from the behavior of such men as Sir Ralph Ellerker and
Sir Robert Bowes, local men in the royal service who saw in the
rebellion a means of preserving their local power against invasion
from yet newer men in the royal service. There was, therefore, a
rebellion to be unleashed, but it was actually unleashed by the
specific political ends of one of the age's political parties, namely
the restoration of Mary and the undoing of Cromwell, both intended to change the king's proceedings from revolution to reaction. That is why these "demands" figured so prominently in the
pilgrims' program; that is why the Statute of Treasons (which had
made little impact in the north before October 1536) and the
Second Succession Act made their appearance in the articles.
Among the political motives present, the desire to avenge Sir
Thomas More's death and resistance to equitable interference
with the common law may also have played their part, but these
purposes were themselves germane to the main program of the
faction and, as it were, entertained by its fringe members.

Of course, the plans of the faction soon ran into major compli-
cations. The troubles of Sir Thomas and Sir Ingram Percy offered
fertile ground for exploitation and greatly assisted the rapid
spread of rebellion, but they also reduced the singlemindedness of
the movement. The Dissolution and the cause of the Church also
provided ready material for rebellion, and fears of Reformation

and heresy stood high among the reasons for the faction's opposition to Cromwell; but the passions roused also allowed the original protest to get out of hand to a point where Henry could not concede anything without total loss of authority. The intrusion of grievances touching the law and lawyers may also have been confusing: their effect was to extend the range of the demands well beyond what the main part of the rebels cared about or even understood. Darcy's tactics were basically simple: he wished to overthrow the dominant faction at court and procure a reversal of policy by persuading the king that a change of minister would lead to loyal peace. But he came to command a movement sworn to ends which could be obtained only by total victory over the king, and that was never on the cards.[73] However, in the main the northern risings represent the effort of a defeated court faction to create a power base in the country for the purpose of achieving a political victory at court.

This fact explains many puzzling features of the troubles. It explains the constant affirmation of loyalty to the king—the sincerely meant assertion that the rising was for him, not against him. This was the necessary stance of a party intent upon ruling about the king—a stance very different, incidentally, from the truly feudal attitudes of defiance leading to the overthrow of the dynasty which had characterized the fifteenth-century civil wars. It was the leaders' perfectly honest belief that they were only continuing the power struggle of the court by novel means that enabled Darcy to believe that he was no traitor and enabled so many prominent government men to take their share in shaping the course of the rebellion. Darcy's early letters, which have been read either as demonstrating his sincere desire to prevent rebellion or as hypocrisy, in reality show him trying to get the necessary "remedies" out of Henry by the mere threat of major trouble, so as to render unnecessary "the hasty follies" planned by the hotheads.[74] The activities of a court faction explain, as I have said, the appearance of some of the demands, especially the concentration upon the succession to the throne. They explain much about the initial behavior of the leading conspirators, who evidently had not given up their old hopes of attracting important conservative court peers to their faction. Both Darcy and Hussey kept an anxious eye on the earl of Shrewsbury, for if he had come in, so assuredly would Derby have done, and the political situation would have been transformed. Both waited for the earl's decision before declaring themselves, though when he refused to move they reacted with characteristic difference. While Hussey at once threw in the towel and fled from Lincolnshire, Darcy resolved to go it without the earl and to resort to force.

The crucial significance of the court faction, of course, helps to explain the concentrated attack on Cromwell and his ministerial colleagues, enemies to the faction, not to the commons: Audley's and Rich's real offense was not their supposed favor to heresy but their role as leading members of Cromwell's own faction. Another odd little problem also becomes clearer when the realities of the situation are understood. On one occasion the pilgrims expressed great satisfaction at hearing that the king was now surrounded by councillors of noble blood and not by those despised upstarts.[75] But those allegedly noble councillors included only three peers, one of them (Sussex) of very recent making (though not quite as recent as the Lord Cromwell); the other three—Sir William Fitzwilliam, Sir William Paulet, and Sir William Kingston—were all respectable gentlemen, administrators transferred from Wolsey's stable. However, Fitzwilliam and Kingston were certainly never real friends to Cromwell and appear in the reconstruction of an anti-Cromwellian faction late in 1539;[76] they may be presumed at least to have been acceptable to the anti-Cromwellian faction of 1536. No one has ever discovered any political side-taking in Paulet (the later Lord Treasurer Winchester), but I suggest that his inclusion among this group of Cromwell's opponents does hint at something more than aloofness from faction strife.

The whole course of the rebellion—its inception, its spread, its avowed and secret purposes, its end—becomes clearer when it is recognized that it was at heart the work of a political faction which utilized the social, economic, and religious grievances to be found in the disaffected north, grievances linked not to feudal or popular uproar but to the increasing distrust felt by the regional gentry towards a thrusting and revolutionary court policy. A common interest joined the defeated court faction with the anticourt "country" and offered an opportunity for forcing Henry to change course. In this way, the Pilgrimage, so far from being the last manifestation of "medievalism," accurately foreshadowed the political mechanism of the next two centuries, though in the reign of Henry VIII the mechanism was still so novel that its use had to take the form of a treasonable conspiracy.

In Lincolnshire the conspiracy proved rather incompetent, perhaps because Hussey, old and dithery, was not up to it: he never controlled the rising which evidently started before everything was ready, and his intended allies among the gentry lost the taste for politics when they began to fear that they had set loose the elements of social rebellion. Hence the rapid termination there. Darcy and Aske were sterner metal and, mainly thanks to the younger Percy brothers, had a much better developed power base from which to operate, but they too failed to manage the northwest (where social rebellion did start, only to be put down by Darcy's hoped-for allies among the border gentry) or really even Lancashire, which went its own way. Whether the fatal revival of trouble by Bigod's outburst had links with the court, of which he had certainly once been a member, I do not know; probably not, because Bigod evidently fell victim to simple and genuine fanaticism, but the possibility might be investigated. The bad timing of the vicar of Louth very likely prevented the wider dissemination of factional action in the south, of which we hear hints here and there; this, too, could profitably be studied further.[77]

Obviously, this paper cannot discuss all the questions or settle all the details of so massive a historical event as the northern rebellions of 1536. Its purpose has been to consider the received view of that event, to assess the effect upon that view of recent analysis (mostly social and structural in kind), and to show that what happened cannot be properly comprehended from a study of the north alone and by means of currently fashionable methods. Why rebellion happened at all, and why it happened the way it did, are questions, as it turns out, that receive their answers from an understanding of the central politics of the day; baffled by the event, the social historian still needs to call upon his political brother for aid.

## Notes

1. In *Political History: Principles and Practice* (New York, 1970), the one of my books which practically nobody seems to have read. Even Professor Hexter, whose *History Primer* shows (as indeed we know) that he and I agree very widely on the true character of historical study, has never referred to it. No doubt the book justifies that neglect, but I confess to an affection for this runt of the litter, and I was delighted to find my opinion shared by the editor of this volume, who encouraged me to reinforce my assertions by a practical demonstration. I should add that the appearance of an exclusive narrow-mindedness which some have seen in the book is misleading. It was intended to be one of a series on various forms of history; my assignment to consider political history was to be matched by similar studies of economic, social, military history, and so forth. It is a mistake to produce a first volume in a series when in the end there turns out to be no series.

2. M. E. and R. Dodds, *The Pilgrimage of Grace, 1536–7; and the Exeter Conspiracy, 1538*, 2 vols. (Cambridge, 1915).

3. Hilda Prescott, *The Man on the Donkey* (London, 1952).

4. *Lollards and Protestants in the Diocese of York* (Oxford, 1958).

5. 2d ed. (Oxford, 1959), no. 489.

6. Dodds, *Pilgrimage of Grace*, 1:182.

7. G. Mattingly, *Catherine of Aragon* (London, 1940), pp. 286–90.

8. A. G. Dickens, "Secular and Religious Motivation in the Pilgrimage of Grace," in *Studies in Church History*, vol. 4, ed. G. J. Cuming (London, 1967), pp. 39ff.

9. C. S. L. Davies, "The Pilgrimage of Grace Reconsidered," *Past and Present* 41 (1968): 54ff.

10. J. J. Scarisbrick, *Henry VIII* (London, 1968), pp. 338ff.

11. For the discussion underlying the revision see the following works, which will not be cited at every point. M. E. James, "Obedience and Dissent in Henrician England: the Lincolnshire Rebellion of 1536," *Past and Present* 48 (1970): 3ff.; and also his *Change and Continuity in the Tudor North: the Rise of Thomas First Lord Wharton*, Borthwick Papers no. 27 (York, 1965), and "The First Earl of Cumberland (1493–1542) and the Decline of Northern Feudalism," *Northern History* 1 (1966): 43ff. Margaret Bowker, "Lincolnshire 1536: Heresy, Schism and Religious Discontent?" in *Schism, Heresy and Religious Protest, Studies in Church History,* vol. 9, ed. D. Baker (London, 1972), pp. 198ff. R. B. Smith, *Land and Politics in the England of Henry VIII: The West Riding of Yorkshire, 1530–46* (London, 1970), chap. 5. C. A. Haigh, *The Last Days of the Lancashire Monasteries and the Pilgrimage of Grace* (Manchester, 1969), esp. chap. 6; also his *Reform and Resistance in Tudor Lancashire* (Cambridge, 1975), chap. 9.

12. See esp. Smith, *Land and Politics.*

13. Haigh, *Lancashire Monasteries.*

14. *Letters and Papers, Foreign and Domestic, of the Reign of Henry VIII,* ed. J. S. Brewer, J. Gairdner, R. H. Brodie, 32 vols. (London, 1862–1932), 11:972; hereafter cited as *LP.* G. R. Elton, *Policy and Police: The Enforcement of the Reformation in the Age of Thomas Cromwell* (Cambridge, 1972), pp. 142–51.

15. *LP,* 12/1:900, Article 67.

16. James, "Obedience and Dissent"; Smith, *Land and Politics.*

17. *LP,* 11:944.

18. The subsidy of 1534, levied only on those worth over £20 p.a., was the lowest assessed since the beginning of the reign.

19. The role of the clergy in the rising has been well summarized in Susan Brigden's Manchester B.A. thesis (1973), "The Northern Clergy in the Pilgrimage of Grace: a Study in Resistance." I am grateful to Miss Brigden for allowing me to use that essay.

20. *LP,* 11:1047.

21. Bowker, "Lincolnshire 1536."

22. *LP,* 12/1:70 (xi).

23. James, "Obedience and Dissent," pp. 12ff., 20ff.

24. See the description of the Yorkshire assembly in *LP,* 12/1:191.

25. *LP,* 11:1402.

26. Haigh, *Lancashire Monasteries,* pp. 70–71.

27. *LP,* 11:622, 826.

28. Ibid., 543.

29. Below, p. 45.

30. *LP,* 12/1:899.

31. *LP,* 7:1669.

32. *LP,* 12/1:851.

33. James, "Obedience and Dissent," pp. 52ff.

34. *LP,* 11:532.

35. Ibid., 522.

36. Ibid., 605–6, 627, 1045.

37. *LP,* 12/1:900, Articles 73–87.

38. Ibid., 1013.

39. His narrative was printed by Mary Bateson in *English Historical Review* 5 (1890): 330ff.; summary in *LP,* 12/1:6.

40. Dodds, *Pilgrimage of Grace,* 1:107.

41. Ibid., 1:114, plus the last one, well vouched for elsewhere and strangely omitted by Dodds.

42. James, "Obedience and Dissent," pp. 24, 37. And cf. Dodds, *Pilgrimage of Grace,* 1:102–3.

43. Dodds, *Pilgrimage of Grace,* 1:112.

44. W. C. Richardson, *History of the Court of Augmentations* (Baton Rouge, 1961), p. 65. Rich was also Speaker (elected with unusual difficulty) in the 1536 Parliament, which passed the Second Act of Succession, a measure that again ignored Mary's claims; this may well have been the reason for his appearing in the rebels' grievances.

45. James, "Obedience and Dissent," p. 26.
46. *State Papers of Henry VIII* (London, 1830), 1:466–67.
47. *LP*, 11:808; 12/1:29 (2).
48. *LP*, 12/1:901 (2).
49. Dodds, *Pilgrimage of Grace*, 1:346ff. I base my discussion on the usefully classified summary of the grievances set out there, though it should be noted that the authors' comments reveal some bias and some ignorance, especially of the law.
50. See my "Taxation for War and Peace in Early-Tudor England," in *War and Economic Development*, ed. J. M. Winter (Cambridge, 1975), pp. 33ff.
51. *LP*, 12/1:909 (44).
52. Ibid., (23).
53. Dickens, "Secular and Religious Motivation"; G. O. Woodward, *The Dissolution of the Monasteries* (London, 1966), pp. 93–97; D. Knowles, *The Religious Orders in England*, vol. 3 (Cambridge, 1959), chap. 25.
54. This is a tricky business, and further research may well renovate the opinion that profound attachment to the old religion was widespread through the north. Davies, "Pilgrimage of Grace Reconsidered," makes a good case for the part played by religion as the ideology necessary to turn a series of conventional riots into a major uprising. But for the present it looks to me as though the ideology was there because Aske injected it, not because it authentically represented the views of the multitude.
55. The Dodds*es*' index says, charmingly and revealingly: "Heresy, see New Learning." It is some sort of definition, and one shared by the more obscurantist conservatives of the day, but hardly one to put before a spiritual court.
56. Dodds, *Pilgrimage of Grace*, 1:382–86.
57. *LP*, 12/1:901 (31); 11:1182 (2).
58. Dodds, *Pilgrimage of Grace*, 1:346.
59. *LP*, 12/1:407–8. No one has ever explained what his rigmarole meant, and I do not believe that he understood the statute.
60. The act was intended to improve, not to hamper, the arming of the nation; the Misses Dodds here talk liberal rubbish (*Pilgrimage of Grace*, 1:346).
61. *LP*, 12/1:6:9.
62. Ibid.
63. *LP*, 11:1244.
64. Mattingly, *Catherine of Aragon*, pp. 286–90; Scarisbrick, *Henry VIII*, p. 340, accepts his definition of the conspiracy as neofeudal.
65. In his *Faculty, Lineage and Civil Society* (Oxford, 1974), M. E. James places the transformation from a feudal to a normal, gentry-dominated, society in the generation *after* the Pilgrimage.
66. Cf. the duke of Norfolk's cry (*LP*, 11:909): "Fie, fie upon the lord Darcy, the most arrant traitor that ever was living, and yet both his sons true knights; old Sir Robert Constable as ill as he is, and all his blood true men."
67. Cf. A. Hassell Smith, *County and Court: Government and Politics in Norfolk, 1558–1603* (Oxford, 1974).
68. *LP*, 7:1206; Mattingly, *Catherine of Aragon*, p. 287.
69. Curiously enough, at the head of the charges against Darcy one of Cromwell's men added a reference to Darcy's part in Wolsey's fall (*LP*, 12/1:848). Was Cromwell thinking of avenging his old master, to whom he alone had ever shown any loyalty?
70. *LP*, 7:1206.
71. This complex story has been told twice, by E. W. Ives ("Faction at the Court of Henry VIII: the Fall of Anne Boleyn," *History*, n.s. 47 [1972]: 169ff.), and by D. R. Starkey in an unpublished paper which better analyzes the role of the Privy Chamber in the affair and brings out more clearly the second phase (July 1536) events in which Mary's faction was in turn defeated by Cromwell. I am grateful to Dr. Starkey for his kindness in letting me see his paper.
72. James, "Obedience and Dissent."
73. I have my doubts about the conventional view that the pilgrims could easily have won a decisive military victory. Once it was clear that the south, though much disturbed, would not rise, and once Lincolnshire was quiet again, a

campaign launched across the Don in mid-November or later could not seem a very promising enterprise—as Aske clearly recognized.

74. *LP*, 11:563, 566. It has sometimes been suggested that Darcy remembered Henry's surrender to the taxpayers' strike of 1526. If he did, he allowed the north to get out of hand much too quickly, for by the time Aske entered York the situation no longer permitted Henry any such tactical withdrawal.

75. *LP*, 12/1:1013.

76. *LP*, 13/2:279–81.

77. The "Exeter conspiracy" did exist, after a fashion, but failed to coordinate with the north; Exeter later blamed Darcy for mismanaging the insurrection. The hopes Darcy had of Derby in Cheshire and Rutland in Kent may not have been entirely self-delusive. Miss Susan Brigden has shown me evidence from the London archives which suggests that the mayoral elections of 1536 were affected by factionalism connected with the northern rising.

# Toward a More Perfect Union: England, Scotland, and the Constitution

## BRIAN P. LEVACK

The Union of the Crowns of England and Scotland in 1603 inspired a large number of treatises, sermons, and poems that congratulated King James VI and I on his accession to the English throne, attested to the role of divine providence in bringing about the Union, and expounded upon the superior political, religious, and metaphysical value of unity over division. Striking an optimistic as well as a celebratory note, this literature designated all the blessings that were expected to flow from dynastic union. Paramount among these was security for both nations: for England the end of the troublesome "Auld Alliance" between Scotland and France; for Scotland freedom from the danger of invasion from England. Union also promised internal stability for the entire island of Britain because James, as king of both nations, would be better equipped to tame the turbulent and hitherto ungovernable Borders. A united and secure Britain, moreover, would be able to assume a dominant position in Europe and the world. Sir William Cornwallis referred to "our increased dominions, that have made us terrible to the world without any terror to our selves," while the poet Samuel Daniel hailed the "mighty state" resulting from the Union.[1] Brightest of all were the religious prospects. Relieved at the defeat of the Catholic claim to the throne, many Englishmen, especially moderate Puritans, hoped that the two nations would strengthen the Protestant bond by which they were already united. Andrew Willet exhorted the English and Scottish churches to cast aside their suspicions of each other and, like the united tribes of Israel, "hold one worship of God, and go up to Jerusalem together."[2]

The enthusiasm of early seventeenth-century writers for the Union of the Crowns did not, however, prevent them from recognizing its limitations. Ardent unionists such as John Thornborough, Sir Francis Bacon, and John Hayward called attention to the "urgent necessity" of strengthening a union that was more nominal than real.[3] Like King James himself, who soon after his accession proposed a "perfect union" of the two countries, these men made practical suggestions for bringing the two nations closer together. In this way the authors of treatises on the union, as well as the numerous Englishmen and Scots who served as commissioners for the union in 1604 and who debated the union in the parliaments of both countries between 1604 and 1607, came to grips with one of the most complex and delicate constitutional problems in the history of both nations. As one Englishman declared, it was "the weightiest case that ever came into the parliament house," an issue that stimulated a detailed consideration of virtually every aspect of the proposed British state.[4] Of all the constitutional problems that arose during the first three decades of the seventeenth century, none forced men to deal with more fundamental questions than the union.

But as the well-known fate of King James's union scheme amply testifies, the definition of a constitutional relationship between England and Scotland proved to be an insoluble problem, at least in the early seventeenth century.[5] In addition to coping with the more extreme expressions of xenophobia, which frequently threatened to disrupt the entire process,[6] those who tried to perfect the union encountered three main difficulties: resistance to change, dissension over procedure, and uncertainty regarding objectives. First, they had to contend with the fear expressed by both Englishmen and Scots that the union would significantly alter, if not destroy, their ancient laws and constitutions, which many considered to be unchangeable. Their fear was not unfounded, since the negotiation of any meaningful and substantial union would of necessity have involved an alteration of fundamental law. But unlike some of the unionists of the early eighteenth century, who recognized and accepted this necessity,[7] the men who discussed the union in the early seventeenth century resisted change determinedly. This conservative sentiment was most vocal in Scotland, which as the smaller, poorer, and less populous nation feared that it would lose its identity through absorption into the southern kingdom. Accordingly, the Scottish Parliament strictly bound the commissioners it appointed in 1604 not to tolerate any derogation of the "fundamental laws, ancient privileges, offices, rights, dignities and liberties" of their kingdom.[8] The English Parliament did not restrain its commissioners in similar fashion, a fact that Sir Edwin Sandys and Lawrence Hyde later used to blame the failure of the negotiations on the Scots.[9] But the English fear of constitutional change proved to be every bit as strong as the Scottish. Even the simple proposal to rename the two kingdoms "Britain" evoked deep-seated constitutional fears. Many of the objections raised against this proposal were of a rather technical nature, such as the argument that the change would invalidate all foreign treaties and writs issued under the Great Seal. But one of these objections—namely that "the change of this style will be as it were the erecting of a new kingdom, and so it shall be as it were a kingdom conquered, and then may the king add laws and alter laws at his pleasure"—suggests the existence of a genuine fear that the union would jeopardize established constitutional principles.[10] Nor did this fear arise simply in response to the speeches of King James to the English Parliament of 1604. A full year before the Union of the Crowns, Sir John Harington reported that whereas in the time of Edward VI the Scots had feared that a dynastic marriage would result in a conquest by England, "some English fear the like now, foolish fears of men, that commonly draw on by fearing that which they most fear."[11]

Even if all Englishmen did not believe that the proposed name change would destroy centuries of constitutional development and remove the very foundation of the state, many did express concern that the perfect union outlined by King James would change the English constitution, despite the king's repeated assurances that he would preserve the fundamental civil and ecclesiastical laws of each nation.[12] In a parliamentary speech on the union in April 1604, Sir Edwin Sandys argued persuasively that "the king cannot preserve the fundamental laws by uniting, no more than a goldsmith, two crowns. The bare alteration of the name taketh them not away, but an union doth. . . . We shall alter all laws, customs, privileges by uniting."[13] Another English antiunionist developed this argument in greater depth:

There cannot be a complete union (whatsoever is pretended) without change of laws, customs, etc. . . . Yet could Englishmen never be drawn to alter the laws and customs of this kingdom, which if they could have needed bettering by change, some of those kings [who had conquered England] . . . would have changed them or intermixt them with others of their own, especially the Romans, who judged all the rest of the world (England excepted) by their own laws and ordinances, only preserving the English customs entire and untoucht as more agreeable to this country and commonwealth than any other . . .

The anonymous author of this statement argued further that if English laws had ever needed improvement, Sir Thomas Smith, being a Doctor of the Civil Law, would have recommended a mixture of English law with the civil law, but in *De Republica Anglorum* Smith had nothing but respect for English law. Then, after quoting Aristotle's stern warning regarding the dangers of tampering with ancient laws and thereby threatening the ruin of the entire state, he concluded with a strong recommendation against any complete or perfect union, "which must necessarily draw on at last alteration or mutual participation of laws."[14]

The conviction that union would bring about significant legal change derived in part from the writings of the unionists themselves. For when King James and his supporters, especially Bacon, Thornborough, and Hayward, referred to a union of laws as one of the main features of the projected British state, they did not intend that either English law or Scots law would remain unchanged. Rather they intended that both laws would be reformed in the process and that a genuine fusion of the two would result. Nor did they necessarily limit the scope of the proposed legal union to public law, which was their immediate concern, but looked forward to the eventual reform and union of private law as well.[15] This prospect may have appealed to reformers within the legal profession, but those who regarded the common law as both unchanging and superior to all other legal systems naturally viewed legal union as a constitutional danger. The threat these men detected in the proposed union of laws acquired an added dimension from the fact that Scots law was heavily indebted to the civil law, whose direct influence English law had managed to avoid.[16] And when John Cowell, Regius Professor of Civil Law at Cambridge, published his *Institutiones Juris Anglicani*, in which he placed the common law within the framework of the civil law in order to encourage the codification of both English and Scots law, the implications of perfect union became even more apparent.[17]

If a preoccupation with the dangers of constitutional change bedeviled the union negotiations of the early seventeenth century, the differences that arose over the method of implementing the union made the successful conclusion of those negotiations even more unlikely. The question whether the king would accomplish the various aspects of the union by himself or in conjunction with Parliament underlay the entire dispute between King James and his English Parliament over the union. A memorandum drawn up shortly after the Union of the Crowns distinguishing between what the king could do without Parliament and what required parliamentary approval reveals that the proposed union, like the king's levying of impositions, raised the delicate constitutional question of the extent of the royal prerogative.[18] But despite James's absolutist views and his belittlement of the importance of Parliament, he did not at first attempt to circumvent either the English or the Scottish Parliament. Aside from establishing a fixed rate of exchange between the currencies of his two kingdoms, which he accomplished through proclamations in both nations,[19] and aside from using his unquestioned personal power to commission a new flag for the ships of both countries,[20] the king sought parliamentary approval of all formal proposals, including the renaming of his kingdoms. Like the Tudor monarchs who preceded him, James recognized that parliamentary ratification of his program would be infinitely more desirable than the attainment of the same ends through alternative means. Yet James always managed to keep his options open and did not hesitate to have recourse to the prerogative when parliamentary cooperation was not forthcoming.[21] Soon after the English Parliament balked at James's proposal to change the names of his kingdoms in 1604, he quickly and against sound political advice proclaimed the change in the royal style, thereby antagonizing a Parliament that was already suspicious of his union project.[22] Then, during the heated parliamentary debates over the Instrument of Union agreed upon by the commissioners, the Lords warned the Commons that if they did not approve the various articles of the Instrument, the king would accomplish the same ends by himself.[23] And in fact, after the English Parliament refused to pass all but one of the four main provisions of the Instrument, James did his best to carry out this threat. He used the judiciary to obtain the naturalization of all Scots born after the death of Queen Elizabeth; he employed royal commissioners to reduce the lawlessness of the Borders after hopes for a legal and administrative union had faded; and he even tried to make trade between the two countries as free as possible through his control over the collection of the customs.[24] In the long run, however, these steps did not greatly advance the cause of stronger union. As later developments were to prove, a durable union required parliamentary support from both nations.

Even more important than fear of constitutional change and

disagreement over procedure was the uncertainty regarding the type of state that would result from the union. Much of this uncertainty stemmed from the novelty of the situation. The proposed union was one of those "rare and great matters whereof there is no precedent."[25] Lacking guidance, therefore, the authors of early Jacobean treatises on the union and the Members of Parliament who spoke on the floor of the House of Commons searched their histories and chronicles to discover the terms upon which various European states had become united. This investigation produced some remarkably detailed accounts of such unions as had taken place between Portugal and Spain, Brittany and France, and Lithuania and Poland. It also revealed that contemporary Europe contained three fundamentally different types of unified states, each of which corresponded to a plan for Anglo-Scottish union.

The gradual consolidation of the English monarchy during the Middle Ages and the Tudor period provided the best example of one of these models, that of the unitary state.[26] This state was characterized by a royal council and parliament whose authority prevailed even in the remote regions of the kingdom; a common law for all areas and people; religious uniformity maintained by a national church; freedom of commerce from shire to shire; and some measure of national consciousness, which should not be equated with the later phenomenon of nationalism. The fact that local authorities who did not receive remuneration from the central government carried on a great proportion of the administrative work of this English state did not in any way detract from its unitary character. Nor did the existence of a multiplicity of local courts or the persistence of a variety of local customs work against the legal unity of that state. As long as local authorities recognized the supremacy of the Privy Council, Parliament, and central common law courts; as long as the crown did not have to contend with semi-independent principalities and petty kingdoms insisting upon a rigid defense of their provincial liberties; and as long as all Englishmen recognized their membership in one body politic, then it is valid to classify England, even with its relatively weak central administration, as perhaps the only unitary state in early modern Europe.

There is little doubt that King James hoped eventually to blend England and Scotland into a unitary state. Political considerations forced him to abandon his pursuit of this plan and to advocate a plural state as a temporary expedient. But in 1603 he gave a clear indication of his ultimate goal when he commanded his subjects to "repute, hold, and esteem both the two realms as presently united, and as one realm and kingdom, and the subjects of both the realms as one people, brethren and members of one body."[27] The core of this projected unitary British state was, of course, to be England, and James had no difficulty, despite his Scottish birth and kingship, in adopting an Anglocentric perspective. Since London was the center from which he ruled his two kingdoms, his ultimate goal of perfect union implied the incorporation of Scotland into England rather than the formation of some sort of composite state. As he indicated to his English Parliament in 1607, he had no doubt that Scotland would "with time become but as Cumberland and Northumberland and those other remote and northern shires."[28]

The consideration which made the English unitary state especially appropriate as a model for Anglo-Scottish union was that less than a century before, Wales—which like Scotland had a large Celtic population and at one time had possessed its own law—had been successfully integrated into the English body politic. Henry VIII and Thomas Cromwell had shired Wales on the English pattern; the English Parliament had admitted a limited number of M.P.s from the Welsh counties and boroughs; and English law had completed a victory over Welsh law that had taken nearly three centuries to attain.[29] Wales did retain separate judicatures, but this in no way altered the nature of the union. Decentralization offered numerous advantages to the English government as long as the loyalty of the local officials could be ensured and the essentially English character of the law could be preserved. The judges who administered law in Wales after the Act of Union of 1543 were all trained in the common law, and they embarked upon the task of enforcing English law even in the complex and delicate area of land tenure.

Wales figured prominently in the arguments advanced by Anglo-Scottish unionists, who were eager to call attention to the obvious geographical parallels between the two countries adjacent to England. One commentator, noting that Britain was shaped like a triangle, the most perfect and indivisible of all geometric forms, observed that each of its constituent countries possessed one of the angles, and that union with Scotland was all that was needed to complete the formation of the new state, which was appropriately to be named "Trianglia."[30] Much more important than geography, however, was the permanence of the union with Wales, which derived not merely from the thoroughness of the political incorporation, but from the apparent social unity that had developed between the two peoples in less than one hundred years. Unionists agreed unanimously that any substantive union must be based on love rather than fear and that mutual naturalization, followed by intermarriage and friendly communication between the people of the two nations, would break down social barriers that years of hostility had erected. If familiarity had developed between the English and the Welsh, just as it had in the distant past between the Romans and the Sabines, there appeared to be no reason why a similar situation should not result from a perfect union of the English and the Scots.[31] This argument may have ignored the difficulty of assimilating the Celtic population of both Wales and Scotland to the Anglo-Saxon culture of England, a process that never achieved the same success as had the assimilation of the Celtic population of Cornwall.[32] But just as the English used the landed elite of Wales as the instruments of anglicization, so there was every prospect that they could use the population of Lowland Scotland, which displayed strong cultural and linguistic similarities to England, as the agents of Celtic Highland anglicization.[33]

However appropriate the precedent of Welsh union appeared to the advocates of a unitary Anglo-Scottish state, it remained in the final analysis a most unfortunate and imprecise analogy. For Wales, despite its size and importance, had more in common with smaller palatinates, duchies, and liberties that had been incorporated into the English state than it had with Scotland. The question was not so much whether Wales was a nation, which was arguable,[34] but whether it was a sovereign state, which clearly it was not. For more than three centuries it had been a principality whose subordination to the English crown, originally through an act of conquest, could hardly be denied. The unilateral legislation of the union with Wales by the English Parliament, equivalent to an act of annexation, provides the clearest indication of the constitutional status of Wales prior to 1536.

To ascribe to Scotland in the early seventeenth century the same status as Wales in the early sixteenth required a distorted if not totally perverse interpretation of both the historical record and contemporary political reality.[35] For Scotland possessed a monarchy that could trace its direct descent further back into the past than that of England, and it met all the requirements for classification as an "empire," in the sense of constituting a realm that recognized no temporal superior. Indeed, even after 1603 Scotland laid claim to its own "imperial crown," which did not become part of a more comprehensive "imperial crown of Great Britain" until 1707.[36] It also had its own parliament, national church, and legal system. Although unionists made frequent reference to the remarkably parallel development of English and Scottish institutions, they could not deny that the two nations possessed "different laws, constitutions, and customs, with different forms of proceeding in justice; . . . different prerogatives,

privileges, and jurisdictions in the two crowns; . . . [and] different estates and governments both in parliaments and privy councils, which makest several sovereign authorities."[37]

The only way that English advocates of an Anglocentric, unitary British state could call the imperial status of Scotland into
question and accord it the subordinate status of a province like
Wales was to assert that Scottish kings had in the past become
vassals of the king of England, thereby giving the present English
king title to the "sovereignty, superiority and propriety of the
realm of Scotland."[38] Such claims appear in the English chronicles of the fifteenth and sixteenth centuries; and the prospects of
Anglo-Scottish union inspired a number of seventeenth-century
treatises that developed this argument.[39] There is no doubt that
many Scottish kings of the eleventh, twelfth, and thirteenth centuries owed their position on the throne to English intervention
and did fealty to the English king. But these distinct acts of homage did not affect the status of the Scottish monarchy in the
seventeenth century, as Sir Thomas Craig illustrated in his treatise, *Scotland's Soveraignty Asserted*. As a lawyer with a profound knowledge of legal history and feudal law, Craig showed
that even if Scottish kings had performed acts of homage in the
past, the lord-vassal relationship had lapsed as soon as the vassal
failed to seek a renovation of the fee after the person of the lord or
vassal changed.[40]

Irrespective of the merits of the various arguments advanced in
the homage controversy, Englishmen had to accept the reality of
Scotland's autonomous status during the union negotiations of
1604. Since the union did not result from conquest, and since the
king wished to make his union project acceptable to the parliaments of both England and Scotland, the two nations met across
the bargaining table, each represented by roughly the same number of commissioners, just as if they were foreign powers concluding a diplomatic agreement.[41] In one respect this may have
worked against the interests of union, for English M.P.s later
rejected a number of the articles drafted by the commissioners on
the grounds that England did not receive a *quid pro quo*, much in
the same way they might have objected to an unfair diplomatic
treaty. Had they regarded Scotland as a large province that was to
be absorbed into England on unequal terms, they would not have
refused to make economic concessions that promised to benefit
Scotland more than England. Sir Edwin Sandys and Edward Alford
made this clear in 1607 when, as an alternative to the "imperfect
union" proposed by the commissioners in 1604, they advocated a
"perfect union" in which the Scots would have been completely
subject to English law. Under such an arrangement the Scots

would have acquired naturalization and all other privileges of Englishmen, including freedom of commerce.[42] Sandys and his allies might very well have suggested this perfect union simply to defeat the commissioners' recommendations, recognizing that there was no hope of either the Scots or the king accepting their plan, and shifting the blame for the failure of the union from themselves to the Scots.[43] But whatever their motives, the logic of the Anglocentric union they proposed reveals that if a truly unitary state was to emerge from the Union of the Crowns, it would of necessity involve Scotland's acknowledgment of England's superiority and acceptance of English institutions in place of its own.

Without the assistance of a cogent and relevant Welsh precedent, the advocates of a unitary Anglo-Scottish state found it difficult to adduce European examples of the type of union they envisaged. Indeed, of all the unions discussed in the context of King James's union project, only one, the union of Poland and Lithuania in 1386, provided an instance of a "perfect union" of two sovereign states that resulted from a process of free negotiation rather than conquest or forfeiture.[44] And even that precedent did not apply exactly to the Anglo-Scottish situation of 1603, since Lithuania, which became assimilated to Poland politically, socially, and religiously,[45] claimed the status of only a grand duchy and after the union accepted the precedency of the Polish kingdom.[46] Whenever the union of two kingdoms became the subject of discourse, there was "nothing more hard to prove than a perfect union."[47]

Europe did, however, offer plentiful examples of "imperfect" unions between kingdoms or other types of sovereign states that retained their individual laws, liberties, and representative assemblies after the implementation of union. These composite structures were very often nothing more than loosely assembled dynastic "empires," such as the medieval Angevin empire, the Kalmar Union of Denmark and Norway, and the sprawling Hapsburg empire of Charles V.[48] But in some cases sufficient geographical and political cohesion prevailed between the components of these empires to give them an identity as a state. The best example of this was the union of the various kingdoms of Spain. From a strictly constitutional point of view, the only link between these kingdoms was the allegiance of their respective subjects to the same ruler, since each kingdom retained its own "laws, fueros and privileges."[49] When the king visited each of these provinces, he ruled solely by his authority as king of that one area, not as king of Spain. When absent, he ruled through a viceroy in cooperation with the ancient council of that kingdom.

Nevertheless, by using the kingdom of Castile, the dominant partner in this association of kingdoms, as the linchpin of his government, the king of Spain was able to rule a state that was one of the most powerful in Europe. To many early seventeenth-century Englishmen, Spain illustrated the advantages of union in the same way that Italy manifested the evils of division.[50]

The idea of a British plural state, modeled on that of Spain, appealed to many of those Englishmen and Scots who feared the consequences of perfect union. Preservation of both England's and Scotland's laws, parliaments, liberties, and privileges promised to free both countries from the dangers of constitutional innovation and assuage national sentiment on both sides of the Tweed without preventing the two countries from seeking closer economic, religious, and social ties. Even some of the most enthusiastic unionists of the early seventeenth century, such as Sir Thomas Craig and Sir Henry Savile, expressed a preference for this type of arrangement over that of the unitary state. Since Craig did more than any other writer of his day to illustrate the compatibility of English and Scots law, his final recommendation against a union of laws or parliaments demanded careful consideration within the unionist camp.[51]

The great attraction of a British plural state was that its implementation required a minimum amount of actual state-building. The Union of the Crowns had already determined the basic structure of the new state: the king now had "two civil or politic bodies, his two kingdoms Scotland and England."[52] All that remained to be done was to tend to such matters as the repeal of hostile laws, the regulation of justice along the Borders, the determination of commercial relations, and naturalization—the problems handled by the commissioners in 1604. But despite the apparent simplicity of this process, the new arrangement suffered from serious defects, above and beyond the failure to implement all of the commissioners' recommendations. For the plural state was neither a durable nor a stable political entity. Artificial by virtue of its dynastic foundation, it tended to aggravate the tension, all too common in the early modern period, between a centralizing and consolidating dynasty and the particularism of kingdoms, duchies, and other regions that had once been independent political units. Close examination of the frequently idealized Spanish monarchy, in which kingdoms like Aragon struggled almost continuously against the Castile-based dynasty in an attempt to maintain their liberties, provided a warning to both Englishmen and Scots that a similar situation might result from an imperfect British union.[53] Sir Francis Bacon was one of the few who heeded the warning, hoping that the close union he envisaged would prevent internal dissension as had occurred in Spain.[54] Another less optimistic Englishman predicted as early as 1604 that the Union of the Crowns was likely "to breed much both private and public discontentment in both nations, which like pestilent humours in men's bodies commonly break out in the plague-sores of rebellion."[55]

Although the Scots protested vehemently against attempts to bring about a perfect union with England, they did not recognize as readily as Bacon the dangers implicit in a plural state. Only after Charles I assaulted their religion and liberties in the 1630s did they perceive the inadequacy of purely dynastic union. Their response, however, was to demand not less union but more, hoping that closer ties with England would secure their liberties in a way that dynastic union had not.[56] Sixty years later, however, under somewhat different circumstances, when neither the king nor the English Parliament appeared to be sensitive to their interests, the Scots tested the other alternative. At that time the Scots threatened completely to dissolve the regal union by selecting a separate heir to the Scottish throne unless the English Parliament agreed to "secure the honour and independency of the Crown of this kingdom, the freedom, frequency, and power of the Parliament, and the religion, liberty, and trade of the nation, from the English or any foreign influence."[57]

The quest for some sort of viable constitutional relationship between England and Scotland consisted mainly in a conflict between the advocates of an English-style unitary state on the one hand and a Spanish-style plural state on the other. Yet the political map of Europe in 1603 included numerous states that fell somewhere between those two extremes. The most prominent of these was France, which Joseph Strayer has designated as a "mosaic state," one whose government reflected the absorption of provinces that possessed their own laws, liberties, and institutions.[58] Of course, Spain might also be classified as a mosaic state, but what distinguished France from the Iberian peninsula was that the former had achieved a greater measure of constitutional and administrative cohesion between its disparate provinces and in many respects was the most highly developed state in Europe.[59] Even the relatively weak and infrequently summoned Estates-General had given France a constitutional unity that did not prevail in Spain.

The English union literature of the early seventeenth century made frequent reference to the consolidation of the French monarchy in order to illustrate the blessings of unity, but owing to the complexity of the French constitution and some confusion regarding the exact relationship between the laws of Brittany and those of France, the authors of these treatises did not use France as an explicit model for British union.[60] But two other loosely unified European states—the United Provinces of the Netherlands and the cantons of Switzerland—did serve as the model for a number of projected British constitutions. In each of these states the component provinces retained their own political institutions but also sent representatives to a common council or parliament to handle affairs that demanded united action. Sir John Doddridge proposed such an arrangement for England and Scotland in 1604,[61] and about the same time an imaginative federal plan, now preserved in the Montagu papers at Beaulieu Manor, also appeared. This plan envisaged a two-tiered structure of both temporal and ecclesiastical government, in which a "general" parliament and corresponding synod would supplement the national parliaments and synods of each country. Separate English and Scottish councils, each including four noblemen from the other kingdom, would always attend upon the king, while specific prerogatives, such as the selection of councillors, the distribution of offices, and the regulation of the coinage, would remain in the hands of the king, "as grains to make the balances equal in which both kingdoms are suspended."[62] Neither this constitutional proposal nor that of Doddridge appears to have won much support in the early years of the seventeenth century, but in the 1640s there were some attempts to establish a measure of joint control over the affairs of the two nations.[63] Even after the failure of these efforts, the idea of some sort of British federation claimed a number of adherents, both before and after the Treaty of Union of 1707.[64]

The actual union of the parliaments in 1707 appears to have constituted a victory for the advocates of a unitary rather than a plural or federal state. The appearances, however, are somewhat deceptive, since the new British state possessed neither legal, ecclesiastical, nor social unity. The hope for legal union had persisted throughout the seventeenth century, and as late as 1702 William Seton had recommended that the future parliament of Great Britain compile a single body of law out of the municipal laws of both kingdoms.[65] These hopes were dashed in 1707. To be sure, the treaty did allow a union of public law, and it specifically provided that all laws concerning the regulation of trade, the customs, and the excise be the same in Scotland as in England. But the treaty also guaranteed the independence of the private law and judicial institutions of Scotland.[66] Although the new British Parliament acquired the right to alter Scottish private law "for evident utility of the subjects within Scotland," it rarely exercised that power. By the early eighteenth century, Scots law, owing mainly to the work of Lord Stair, had developed into a coherent and vital system, capable of resisting English influence. And English law, which had already demonstrated its easy exportability through conquest and colonization, revealed, as it did later in Canada and South Africa, that it did not interact comfortably with a rival legal system.[67] Unable to accommodate each other, English and Scots law chose to stand apart, and no real influence of one upon the other occurred until the late eighteenth and early nineteenth centuries.

The treaty of 1707 also failed to create the religious and ecclesiastical unity that the advocates of a unitary British state had desired. In many ways this failure represented the greatest disappointment of early seventeenth-century hopes, for at that time it appeared that a common Protestantism would form the most durable bond between the two peoples. Yet during the seventeenth century English Protestantism strayed from its Calvinist foundations while that of Scotland did not, and Scotland succeeded, not without difficulty, in preserving its presbyterian form of church government. By the middle of the seventeenth century one religious commentator noted that difference in church government had been "the main of all the differences betwixt the two kingdoms since the reformation of religion";[68] by 1707 the only feasible solution of the problem was the acceptance of a religious and ecclesiastical pluralism.

Finally, the social unity desired by all seventeenth-century unionists, the union of love that they expected naturalization and intermarriage would bring about, never really materialized.[69] Not only were the Celtic people of the Highlands never fully assimilated to the new "nation," but even the anglicized Lowlanders, whom the English government relied upon as the agents of assimilation, often felt estranged from eighteenth-century English society.[70] From its very inception Great Britain has been, as it remains today, a multinational state, resembling in many respects the Austro-Hungarian empire that collapsed in 1918.[71]

The Treaty of Union did not, contrary to the opinion of some historians, bring about a realization of King James VI and I's union plans.[72] In fact, the treaty reflected more the policies of Oliver Cromwell than those of King James.[73] At different times James had advocated the formation of both a unitary and a plural state, but he had never envisioned the compromise between those two models that emerged from the negotiations of the early eighteenth century. On the one hand, the Treaty of Union dashed two of James's greatest hopes, the union of laws and the union of churches; on the other, it achieved an objective he had abandoned early in his reign, the union of parliaments. Shortly after the

Union of the Crowns, James had proposed a parliamentary union, but either the difficulties he encountered with his first English Parliament or the strength of both English and Scottish opposition to this plan forced him to change his mind.[74] So consistently did the king advocate the continuation of separate parliaments after 1604 that the antiunionists of the late seventeenth and early eighteenth centuries staked a better claim to be working within the Jacobean tradition than the unionists.[75]

The union policies of King James do not, however, deserve to be evaluated by the standard of the eighteenth-century treaty. In trying to determine a new relationship between England and Scotland, James was dealing with an unprecedented constitutional problem. His efforts, and those of others, failed not simply because of his political tactics, the economic jealousy of English merchants, or the xenophobia of both Scots and Englishmen, but because no one at that time was able to formulate a plan that could satisfy all the groups whose vested interests were at stake. Rather than view James as an impractical idealist, we should regard him as a pragmatist who was willing to experiment with different proposals, but who never managed to devise a plan that commanded widespread support in both nations.

If it is erroneous to consider the treaty of 1707 as the final realization of James's dreams, it is folly to see it as the working out of a preordained plan, whether that be the providence that early writers witnessed in 1603 or the "benignant fate" that a twentieth-century historian has detected in the process.[76] In the seventeenth century the exact nature of the British state, like that of many European states, was very much in doubt.[77] No cosmic historical force guided England and Scotland from the Union of the Crowns to the Union of the Kingdoms. The history of Anglo-Scottish relations, like the history of the modern state, was an open-ended process, full of uncertainty, experimentation, and compromise. The union negotiations of the early seventeenth century attest to the extent of that uncertainty, the variety of experimentation, and the failure of compromise.

## Notes

1. [Sir William Cornwallis], *The Miraculous and Happie Union of England and Scotland* (London, 1604), sig. B4v; A. B. Grosart, ed., *The Complete Works in Verse and Prose of Samuel Daniel* (London, 1885), 1:143. The author wishes to thank the John Simon Guggenheim Memorial Foundation for a fellowship that made possible the research for this essay.

2. Andrew Willet, *Ecclesia Triumphans* (Cambridge, 1603), preface.

3. John Thornborough, *A Discourse Plainely Proving the evident utilitie and urgent necessitie of the desired happie Union* (London, 1604), p. 17; J. Spedding, ed., *The Letters and Life of Francis Bacon* (London, 1861–74), 3:90–99; John

Hayward, *A Treatise of Union of the two Realmes of England and Scotland* (London, 1604), pp. 7–40.

4. British Library (hereafter B.L.), Harleian MS. 1314, fol. 44. See also the speech of Sir Edwin Sandys, *Journals of the House of Commons* (London, 1803–; hereafter *CJ*), 1:950.

5. See D. H. Willson, "King James I and Anglo-Scottish Unity," in *Conflict in Stuart England* (London, 1960), pp. 43–55; and W. Notestein, *The House of Commons, 1604–1610* (New Haven, 1971), pp. 78–85, 211–54.

6. *Somers Tracts*, vol. 2 (London, 1809), p. 125 n.; *CJ*, 1:333.

7. Daniel Defoe, *The History of the Union between England and Scotland* (London, 1786), p. 361; [D. Symson], *Sir George M'Kenzie's Arguments against an incorporating Union* (Edinburgh, 1706), pp. 4–5.

8. *Acts of the Parliaments of Scotland* (Edinburgh, 1814–75), 4:264.

9. D. H. Willson, ed., *The Parliamentary Diary of Robert Bowyer, 1606–1607* (Minneapolis, 1931), pp. 219, 238, 244.

10. B.L., Harleian MS. 292, fol. 133. See also Notestein, *House of Commons*, p. 79.

11. C. R. Markham, ed., *A Tract on the Succession to the Crown (A.D. 1602) by Sir John Harington* (London, 1880), p. 19.

12. Public Record Office (hereafter P.R.O.), SP 14/9A/35; 14/7/84.

13. *CJ*, 1:187.

14. B.L., Harleian MS. 1314, fols. 14v–16v. See also Lansdowne MS. 486, fol. 43v.

15. C. H. McIlwain, ed., *The Political Works of James I* (Cambridge, Mass., 1918), pp. 292–93, 301–2; *Letters and Life of Bacon*, 3:335–36; Thornborough, *Discourse*, pp. 2–15; Hayward, *Treatise*, pp. 14–15.

16. B. Levack, "The Proposed Union of English Law and Scots Law in the Seventeenth Century," *Juridical Review*, n.s. 20 (1975): 99–100; P. Stein, "Roman Law in Scotland," *Jus Romanum Medii Aevi* 5, 13b (1968): 3–51.

17. John Cowell, *Institutiones Juris Anglicani* (Cambridge, 1605).

18. B.L., Harleian MS. 292, fol. 137.

19. J. F. Larkin and P. L. Hughes, eds., *Stuart Royal Proclamations*, vol. 1 (Oxford, 1973), pp. 7, 99–103; R. W. Cochran-Patrick, *Records of the Coinage of Scotland*, vol. 1 (Edinburgh, 1876), pp. 210–15.

20. *Stuart Royal Proclamations*, 1:135–36. See also National Library of Scotland, MS. 2517, fols. 67v–68.

21. James used similar tactics in dealing with the General Assembly in Scotland. See M. Lee, Jr., "James VI and the Revival of Episcopacy in Scotland: 1596–1600," *Church History* 33 (1974): 50–66.

22. S. T. Bindoff, "The Stuarts and Their Style," *English Historical Review* 60 (1945): 192–97; *Stuart Royal Proclamations*, 1:94–98; P.R.O., SP 14/9A/82.

23. *Diary of Bowyer*, pp. 209 n., 245.

24. S. J. Watts, *From Border to Middle Shire: Northumberland 1586–1625* (Leicester, 1975), pp. 152–57; T. Keith, *Commercial Relations of England and Scotland, 1603–1707* (Cambridge, 1910), pp. 16–18.

25. Hampshire Record Office, Jervoise MS. 44M69, no. 79.

26. See J. Strayer, *On the Medieval Origins of the Modern State* (Princeton, 1970), pp. 36–48.

27. *Stuart Royal Proclamations*, 1:19.

28. *Political Works of James I*, p. 294.

29. R. R. Davies, "The Twilight of Welsh Law, 1284–1536," *History* 51 (1966): 143–64.

30. Beaulieu Palace House, Papers on Scotch Affairs, 3, item 1.

31. B.L., Lansdowne MS. 486, fol. 42; Hayward, *Treatise*, p. 3; *Rapta Tatio* (London, 1604), sig. F2v; Thornborough, *Discourse*, pp. 9–10, and *The Ioiefull and Blessed Reuniting the two mighty & famous kingdoms* (Oxford, n.d.), pp. 5, 29.

32. M. Hechter, *Internal Colonialism* (London, 1977), pp. 64–65.

33. Ibid., pp. 57, 78, 112; G. Donaldson, "Foundations of Anglo-Scottish Union," in *Elizabethan Government and Society* (London, 1961), pp. 282–314.

34. See B.L., Lansdowne MS. 486, fol. 42v.

35. B.L., Harleian MS. 1314, fol. 105 recognizes the irrelevance of the Welsh precedent.

36. [A. Mudie], *Scotiae Indiculum* (London, 1682), Epistle Dedicatory; W. Ferguson, "Imperial Crowns: a Neglected Facet of the Background to the Treaty of Union of 1707," *Scottish Historical Review* 53 (1974): 22–44.

37. B.L., Harleian MS. 6850, fol. 63.

38. Bodleian Library, Clarendon MS. 133, fol. 9.

39. Ibid.; P.R.O., SP 14/7/80x (uncalendared). See Ferguson, "Imperial Crowns," pp. 31–44, and Lincoln's Inn, Maynard MS. 83, item 3, fols. 3–4 for a discussion of these claims.

40. Sir Thomas Craig, *Scotland's Soveraignty Asserted* (London, 1695), p. 421. See also B.L., Additional MS. 32094, fols. 247–58.

41. See Lincoln's Inn, Maynard MS. 83, item 1, for the proceedings of the commissioners.

42. *Diary of Bowyer*, pp. 255–61, 267.

43. See Notestein, *House of Commons*, pp. 233–34, 249, for a discussion and rejection of this interpretation. See also the opinion of Hyde in *Diary of Bowyer*, p. 280.

44. P.R.O., SP 14/7/65, p. 25, and Lincoln's Inn, Maynard MS. 83, item 3, fol. 22 recognize this exception.

45. For the terms of this union see P.R.O., SP 14/7/68; Lincoln's Inn, Maynard MS. 83, item 3, fols. 16–17; *The Cambridge History of Poland: From the Origins to Sobieski* (Cambridge, 1950), pp. 196–209. Despite a union of public law, full legal union did not come about. P.R.O., SP 14/7/61; Sir Thomas Craig, *De Unione Regnorum Britanniae Tractatus* (Scottish History Society, 1909), pp. 300–301.

46. P.R.O., SP 14/7/80x. There was no doubt, however, that Lithuania was a sovereign state. Lincoln's Inn, Maynard MS. 83, item 3, fol. 2v.

47. P.R.O., SP 14/7/65, p. 1. See also SP 14/7/64, fol. 157; SP 14/9A/37 I, fol. 123v.

48. For the use of "empire" in this sense, see C. H. Firth, "The British Empire," *Scottish Historical Review* 15(1918): 185.

49. J. H. Elliott, "The King and the Catalans, 1621–1640," *Cambridge Historical Journal* 11 (1955): 258.

50. Cornwallis, *Miraculous and Happie Union*, sig. D4v; Thornborough *Ioiefull and Blessed Reuniting*, p. 21.

51. Craig, *De Unione*, pp. 464–67; Lincoln's Inn, Maynard MS. 83, item 3, fol. 22. Savile's authorship of the latter is established by Bodleian Library, MS. e. Museo. 55.

52. B.L., Harleian MS. 6850, fol. 63.

53. Sir Charles Cornwallis, "Discourse of the State of Spaine," in *Somers Tracts*, vol. 3 (London, 1810), pp. 311–12.

54. *Letters and Life of Bacon*, 96.

55. B.L., Harleian MS. 292, fol. 128.

56. C. L. Hamilton, "The Anglo-Scottish Negotiations of 1640–1," *Scottish Historical Review* 41 (1962): 84–86; D. Stevenson, *The Scottish Revolution 1637–44* (Newton Abbot, 1973), pp. 314–15.

57. Sir David Hume, *A Diary of the Proceedings in the Parliament and Privy Council of Scotland* (Edinburgh, 1828), p. 117.

58. Strayer, *Modern State*, p. 53.

59. C. Tilly, ed., *The Formation of National States in Western Europe* (Princeton, 1975), p. 35. Tilly's relatively low rating of England's degree of "stateness" does not in any way minimize its unitary character.

60. Cornwallis, *Miraculous and Happie Union*, sig. D4v; Thornborough, *Ioiefull and Blessed Reuniting*, p. 21, and *Discourse*, p. 2; *Diary of Bowyer*, p. 279; P.R.O., SP 14/7/80, pp. 7–8; Lincoln's Inn, Maynard MS. 83, item 3, fol. 22.

61. B.L., Lansdowne MS. 486, fol. 43v. See also *Vulpone* (n.p., 1707), p. 14.

62. Beaulieu Palace House, Papers on Scotch Affairs, 3, item 1.

63. Hamilton, "Anglo-Scottish Negotiations," p. 84; W. Notestein, "The Establishment of the Committee of Both Kingdoms," *American Historical Review* 17 (1912): 481–82.

64. H. J. Hanham, *Scottish Nationalism* (London, 1969), p. 66; N. MacCormick, ed., *The Scottish Debate* (London, 1970), pp. 54–55.

65. [W. Seton], *The Interest of Scotland in Three Essays*, 2d ed. (London, 1702), p. 47.

66. G. S. Pryde, ed., *The Treaty of Union of Scotland and England 1707* (London, 1950), pp. 95–98.

67. L. Scarman, *English Law—The New Dimension* (London, 1974), pp. 9–10.

68. B.L., Stowe MS. 187, fol. 43.

69. See [Daniel Defoe], *Union and No Union* (London, 1713), p. 4.

70. Hechter, *Internal Colonialism*, pp. 112–23; F. A. Pottle, ed., *Boswell's London Journal* (New York, 1956), pp. 38–41, 83, 284.

71. R. Rose, *The United Kingdom as a Multi-national State* (Glasgow Survey Research Centre, Occasional Paper, Number 6, 1970); MacCormick, *The Scottish Debate*, pp. 6, 28; H. Rothfels, "The Crisis of the Nation-State," in *The Development of the Modern State*, ed. H. Lubasz (New York, 1964), p. 121.

72. Willson, "Anglo-Scottish Unity," p. 54.

73. H.R. Trevor-Roper, *Religion, the Reformation and Social Change* (London, 1957), p. 466.

74. It is noteworthy that Sir Henry Savile, whose advice James had solicited, recommended against a union of parliaments. Lincoln's Inn, Maynard MS. 83, item 3, fol. 22v.

75. National Library of Scotland, Advocates MS. 31.7.7., pp. 136–45; Wodrow Qu. 97, fol. 195.

76. John Gordon, *A Panegyrique of Congratulation for the Concord of the Realmes of Great Britaine* (London, 1603), p. 5; R. S. Rait, *An Outline of the Relations between England and Scotland (500–1707)* (London, 1901), p. 146.

77. Tilly, *Formation of National States*, pp. 15–16, 25–31.

# Corruption at the Court of James I: The Undermining of Legitimacy

## LINDA LEVY PECK

In 1621 the House of Commons revived the procedure of impeachment, rusty with disuse over the previous one hundred fifty years, to remove Francis Bacon from office, and to assert the principle that royal officials were responsible to the nation as represented in Parliament.[1] The committee voting out the charge put it simply: "the person is no less than the Lord Chancellor . . . the matter alleged is corruption." And later, during the impeachment debate, one member made the point most vividly by railing against "those blood suckers of the kingdom. . . . The more examples we make of great men the more good we do the country."[2]

Corruption was the charge most often urged against the Jacobean court, both by contemporaries and by later historians. It became the cutting edge of parliamentary efforts to limit royal authority before the Civil War. Yet the problem of Jacobean corruption cannot be understood simply as the automatic response of an outraged Parliament to a quantitative increase in administrative abuse. Joel Hurstfield has demonstrated that many of the practices complained of, whether bribery, misappropriation, or nepotism, were characteristic of all early modern governments.[3] And the complaint of corruption was a traditional part of Tudor rhetoric. The question then is how and why corruption acquired the power to undermine the legitimacy of the Stuart court?

Some answers may be suggested by making use of social science theory. In recent years the phenomenon of corruption has been studied in contexts ranging from urban America to developing societies in Africa. Drawing on these studies, the definition of corruption adopted here is "behavior which deviates from the formal duties of a public role because of private-regarding (personal, close family, private clique), pecuniary or status gains."[4] This definition raises problems, of course, when applied to the early modern state: bureaucratic norms of behavior had not been fully worked out, and practices labeled corrupt in the nineteenth century were standard in the seventeenth. To adopt a definition peculiar to Jacobean England, however, would prevent comparative analysis; the modern Western definition describes behavior which then can be compared in different times and places. In addition to the matter of definition, there are two types of analysis developed by social scientists that are particularly suggestive for the investigation of corruption in Jacobean politics: the analysis of the structure and functions of the political system, and that of the process by which social groups label the behavior of others as deviant.[5] These models can be used to look at the relation of corrupt practices to Jacobean governmental structure and to examine the response of the political elite to court behavior. It will be argued here that, together, the dysfunctions of Jacobean administration and the development within the elite of competing concepts of office and responsibility changed corruption from a chronic complaint to an issue which discredited the monarchy.

Structural-functional analysts, following the insights of Robert Merton's well-known analysis of the political machine in American cities, have refused to treat corruption as aberrant and haphazard behavior.[6] Rather they have tried to relate corruption to the social, political, and economic structure of the society in which it exists, and to look at its manifest and latent functions. If we make a similar analysis of early modern English government, it is clear that corruption was built into its structure. The Henrician revolution had extended the size and scope of the bureaucracy as the state took over the functions of church and guild, but there existed neither a professional, salaried civil service nor established norms of conduct pertaining to abstract achievement goals. Reflecting its feudal origin, office was often treated as private property, and a lively market existed in the buying and selling of offices. Because the crown did not enjoy a system of national taxation by which to pay its servants, they were paid by those who needed to use government services; these gratuities escalated to perhaps 40 percent of the government's yearly revenue under the Stuarts.[7] Office was, in short, a profit-making proposition. The key to control of this unwieldy apparatus was the patronage system. Access to office and to other elements of royal bounty was based on patronage dispensed by the king and his ministers or favorites on the basis of kinship and purchase more often than merit.[8] These were the structural realities of early modern bureaucracy with which every monarch of the period had to cope. Its defects included the inability to solve government problems, the loss of limited royal revenues, and the dissatisfaction of those who lost out in the scramble for reward.

On the other hand, political scientists examining the developing nations today have pointed out some beneficial functions that corruption can provide in gaining support for the government.[9] They have argued that the enlargement of the public sector, though it may result in the growth of corrupt practices, provides government with greater opportunities to reward and integrate its followers. In fact, the nationalization of patronage centralizes and augments government power and minimizes centripetal pressures. Moreover, corruption allows the integration into political life of those groups, such as wealth elites, which may be outside direct political power. Similar benefits from corruption were not lacking in early modern England. The expansion of government increased the crown's ability to reward; Henry VIII secured a strong base for his Reformation policies by providing office, favor, and land to the political elite. When skillfully used by the Tudors, patronage provided the means to conciliate the powerful, and helped to turn the attention of the politically eminent from bastard feudalism to the spoils system. Under the Stuarts, the customs farmers who through bribery gained access to valuable economic resources and political influence provided continuing support to the crown.[10] Whether corrupt practices prove functional or dysfunctional, then, depends on two points: (1) how they are controlled from within the administration, and (2) how they are tolerated by important groups outside the administration. The interaction of these two points explains the extraordinary power of the issue of corruption under James.

Jacobean administration suffered from several problems which tended to waste whatever political benefits corrupt practices might have bestowed. First and foremost was the problem of supply and demand: the numbers of those competing for favor had greatly increased,[11] causing the number of disappointed place-seekers to increase too since the crown's ability to reward did have limits. Secondly, unlike Queen Elizabeth, who had distributed patronage with an eye to service rendered,[12] James was not able to ensure that the distribution of office and privilege at court fulfilled the functions of integrating the politically important, or of recruiting able civil servants. His patronage, in fact, had the opposite effect. Through the monopolization of favor after 1615 by Buckingham, the competition of factions for court favor abruptly ended, resulting in the loss of support of those not included in Buckingham's machine. Finally, the rising standard of conspicuous consumption in the period meant that the king's highest officials had to radically increase the amount of kickbacks and bribes demanded from courtiers, merchants, and foreign diplomats. Lawrence Stone has suggested that the extravagant building of Hatfield House imposed an unprecedented standard of corruption on Robert Cecil, earl of Salisbury, and that the construction of Audley End by Thomas Howard, earl of Suffolk, ultimately led to his trial for corruption on charges that he had used the Treasury almost as if it were his private bank account.[13]

But the court was not without its reformers who tried to eliminate or at least limit abuses. The efforts of Robert Cecil and Lionel Cranfield are well known. With his most ambitious project, the Great Contract, Cecil sought to exchange the king's feudal privileges for a parliamentary grant. Lionel Cranfield headed commissions on the Navy and Treasury that had some success in curbing corrupt practices; their very success may have led to his subsequent downfall. To these two should be added Henry Howard, earl of Northampton. Although his attempts at reform have been dismissed by many historians as masking attacks on his political rivals or as cloaking his greed for personal gain, these views are anachronistic. As Joel Hurstfield has pointed out in "The Morality of Early Stuart Statesman," concern for the public welfare and for personal gain were characteristic of public officials throughout the Tudor-Stuart period and even later.[14] Northampton, who vigorously pursued the task of rationalizing royal government, recognized the dysfunctional aspects of Jacobean administration.[15] In his report on the Navy, for instance, Northampton noted that the root of the kickbacks and misappropriation of funds characteristic of the middle and lower levels of Stuart bureaucracy could be found in the sale of office. Having paid dearly for their position, officials felt obliged to recoup their investment by victimizing others, including the king himself.[16] When he analyzed the college of heralds, Northampton pointed out the relationship between the heralds' low incomes and their corrupt giving of arms. Unable to maintain themselves or their families by legal means, they resorted to selling arms "for crowns, right for reward, honor for bribes."[17] Northampton was also sensitive to the importance of restraining corruption within limits which would not alienate important segments of the ruling elite. He condemned a project for concealed lands proposed by the king's favorite, Robert Carr, and Robert Treswell, Surveyor of the King's Woods, just at the time Parliament was to meet.

It is cried down by full consent as a canker to the commonwealth and thought likely to gall ten thousand people. . . . These ways of sucking satisfaction by private persons out of subjects' fortunes hath been ever so dangerously scandalous in this state. . . . For it is one thing what Treswell the king's minister is warranted to do *in terrorem* for the gathering up of the king's debt . . . but when the king's power strengthens and enables one subject to cramp and fleece another in the king's right . . . all goes to ruin and mischief follows . . . and at this time, least of all, a parliament being resolved . . . For before the undertaking of that task in a captious and tickle time . . . the subjects minds ought rather to be prepared than distempered.[18]

In short, the system of patronage and reward as it was practiced at the Jacobean court fostered the separation of favor from administrative control, encouraged the growth of abuses and corrupt practices, and hindered their reform. Such functional weaknesses help to explain why corruption became an important political issue in James's reign. But the explanation is incomplete. During the reign of Edward VI a similar breakdown in administrative control led to similar kinds of corrupt practices, and to the cashiering of officials for abuse of office. But these officials, associates of Protector Somerset, were ousted by his successor, the earl of Northumberland, not impeached by Parliament. Moreover, with the accession of Mary and then Elizabeth, administrative control was reasserted and abuses were reformed.[19] The issue receded, and had no appreciable impact on politics until the 1590s. But the situation was different under James. Attitudes toward corruption, what it was and how it should be reformed, were beginning to change. James and his ministers did not always recognize as corrupt those practices which most outraged his critics. Reform, when it came, was not enough.

Of great importance to the potency of corruption as a political issue is the degree to which politically important subgroups are tolerant of corrupt practices.[20] In fact, sociologists have developed a new theory of deviance as a process of interaction, emphasizing social response to behavior as much as the behavior itself. Howard Becker suggests that "deviance is not a quality of the act the person commits but rather a consequence of the application by others of rules and sanctions to an offender."[21] He points out that this labeling process is erratic: it can vary over time; it can vary according to who commits the act, who is harmed by it, and what are its consequences. This theory has important application to the problem of corruption. Once it has been observed that corrupt practices were an intrinsic part of the early modern state, the question of why it became a crucial political issue in undermining the crown's authority must be extended from an analysis of the dysfunctions of the Jacobean administration to an examination of the response of the political elite.

Within the court of James I, efforts to control administrative abuses and to label behavior as corrupt foundered on the king's refusal to apply sanctions to the guilty and to enforce certain standards of conduct. But at the same time that norms of behavior became blurred at court, new standards were emerging within the governing class, which labeled as corrupt practices which the court took for granted. Jacobean England was characterized by a split in the political elite on the question of what constituted corruption, a growing intolerance of previously accepted practices, and a new notion of official responsibility, all of which combined to undermine the crown's legitimacy.

Perez Zagorin has argued that the breakdown in the governing class which precipitated the Civil War defined itself in the opposing concepts of "court" and "country." The concept of the "country," which began to emerge fully only in the 1620s, was shaped by Puritanism and a newly self-conscious and active Parliament. It came to designate "persons of public spirit, unmoved by private interest, untainted by court influence and corruption."[22] Although the court in fact was not monolithic and included reformers as well as sycophants, the "country" saw only irresponsibility and immorality. In opposition to the "court" with its moral and financial dangers and its overweening favorites and extravagance, the gentlemen of the "country" emphasized responsibility to the nation. Most important, the "country" favored the continental Protestant cause and strongly attacked the court's tolerance of Catholicism and its alliance with Spain. This tension within the political elite and the development of competing norms of office and responsibility provided the environment in which corruption became a political issue.[23] On several questions, including sale of honors and offices, bribes and Spanish pensions, the court and its opponents held different views of what constituted corruption. These differences, sharpened between 1603 and 1621 by their connection to problems of status anxiety, fiscal grievance, and foreign policy, helped to shape the successful "country" attack on the royal prerogative.

The changing response of the political elite to James's distribution of honors and offices illustrates the importance of divergent attitudes in making corruption a potent political issue. The bestowing of honors was one of the most important means by which the monarch recognized the distribution of power within his kingdom. Elizabeth had been notoriously miserly in granting honors, with the result that there existed in 1603 an unsatisfied demand for status which it was hoped that James would meet. But from his accession James's distribution of titles threatened the status of members of the governing class. Where in the last ten years of Elizabeth's reign 290 had been made knights, James knighted 906 in the first four months of his reign—432 on one occasion.[24] The king allowed his courtiers to sell knighthoods indiscriminately, and the titles were wholesaled in such lots as that between Arthur Ingram and Lionel Cranfield at the rate of six knights for £373 1s.8d.[25] The reaction to such dealings was outrage at the dishonor attaching to the king and the disgrace of other knights. Phillip Gawdy wrote to his brother in August 1603:

There were a number of worthy and very choice knights made upon that great day, but with them (like cockle among good corn) a scum of such as it would make a man sick to think of them. . . . there were sheepreeves, yeomen's sons knighted . . . divers peddlers' sons of London have received the same order, amongst the rest Thimblethorpe the attorney that was called nimble chaps full of the pox was knighted for seven pound ten shillings.[26]

Gawdy wrote that his uncle Henry Gawdy disdained the manner of making knights and would not have the dignity for £500. But Gawdy was not attacking the sale of honors as inherently corrupt. Instead, he went on to make a crucial distinction. His uncle, he noted, could be one of the Knights of the Bath, "and I think he would be content to pay somewhat roundly for it, wherein I commend him and his judgement and in my opinion do the much better than to be knighted after so many mean persons as lately have been."[27] To Gawdy the method and caliber of the new knights were what made them disreputable. But the sale of honors was not in and of itself corrupt. An honor such as the Knighthood of the Bath retained its status because of the restriction of numbers and quality.

It is important to emphasize that the shift in patronage practices away from reward for service and toward cash payments, termed "market corruption" by political scientists, was not necessarily dysfunctional. Arnold Heidenheimer has made the point that in the Jacobean era "what distinguished transactions labelled corrupt . . . were not so much characteristics linked to the duties . . . [of] public offices generally, . . . as the price at which offices and honors were sold, or the level of fees and gifts which officials demanded. The thresholds between legitimate gift acceptance and corrupt extortion . . . suggest an analogy to the limits which separate accepted interest rate levels from the higher levels that were labelled [as] usury."[28] It must be emphasized however, that in the Jacobean period it was equally a question of who got what. Even a reasonable price might not prevent outcry if those rewarded were perceived as upstarts, as the fall in the price of knighthood indicates. The sale of honors might be tolerated provided that the crown was the beneficiary and that the newly jumped up did not threaten the status of the already arrived.

For the crown the sale of titles was an important source of revenue. In 1611 the king instituted the new title of baronet with the price tag of £1,095. Under Salisbury's and Northampton's direction, the quality of the nominees was monitored, the number of baronets kept under 200, and the title avidly sought. It was the emergence of Buckingham as the king's favorite that brought about the monopolization of patronage and the sale of titles not for the crown but for his clients. Within a few years the numbers of baronets had swollen and the price had fallen to £220.[29] Recent research, however, suggests that the pressure of numbers drove the price down, not the quality of the recipients: most were country gentlemen, as were the first creations. In 1615 the crown instituted the new policy of selling peerages priced at £10,000 each. By 1628, perhaps forty individuals had purchased peerages in both England and Ireland, bringing in more than £200,000 profit to Buckingham and his patronage network.[30]

As control over sales of honors slackened, the reaction sharpened. In 1609 Robert Cotton, Northampton's aide, had brought forward the precedent of the sale by Richard I of the earldom of Northumberland, adding, "I doubt not but many of these times would set their ambitions at as high a price."[31] But by 1615 Cotton had changed his mind about the suitability of selling titles. Understanding that Sir Robert Dormer was to be made a baron and that the £10,000 he had paid was to be allocated to pay Lord Sheffield's debts, he wrote that no barons should be made except from among the brothers of noblemen and that other means should be found of supplying Sheffield's needs.[32] In 1621 members of the House of Lords petitioned the king to be excused from paying the new Irish peers respect, since they were Englishmen given foreign names "only to our injury."[33] And in 1626 one of the major charges brought against Buckingham was the selling of peerages, which was described as "an offence unnatural against the Law of Nature, it extremely deflowers the flowers of the crown . . . a prodigious scandal to this nation."[34] The change from administrative control to factional free-for-all in the distribution of honors in the years after 1615 was reflected in the changing values of the court's critics. In 1603 Phillip Gawdy had tolerated the sale of Knighthoods of the Bath if standards were upheld. In 1615 John Chamberlain remarked that there was "much speech of new barons to be made for money, which were the less to be misliked if it come to the king's coffers."[35] By 1626 the selling of titles was a major accusation in the impeachment proceedings against the duke of Buckingham.

Attitudes toward the sale of offices underwent a similar change. Endemic to administration in early modern Europe, such sales existed throughout the Tudor period. Although complaints about corruption under Edward VI had produced a statute in 1552 against such sales, it included many exceptions. The practice, somewhat reduced, continued under Mary and Elizabeth, and sales were widespread under James, particularly during the ascendency of Buckingham.[36] But the gentry's view of these sales underwent the same sort of change as had its view of the king's distribution of honors. When James acceded to the throne in 1603 many offices came on the market, and gentlemen discussed their value and price matter-of-factly. One gentlemen wrote to a country friend of several positions on which he had first refusal, including that of a groom of the king's privy chamber, which would cost £600 but offered a fee of £50 per annum plus diet.[37] His friend replied by asking what the place was worth in addition to the fee.

If it be worth £100 per annum with the fee, I am then contented upon reasonable conditions and days of payment to perform the demand, although it be at a very hard rate to give above three years value for any office . . . I will, rather than fail for a good place and of credit, give four years value, but if it may be under so much the better.[38]

In 1603, it would appear, the sale of offices carried little stigma among prospective buyers. But Buckingham's monopoly and sale of both honors and offices distorted the patronage system between 1615 and 1628 and produced disaffection among those the system was meant to conciliate. The result was to solidify opposition by changing attitudes and provoking political action. In the

1620s the sale of offices was attacked along with the sale of honors and made up a prominent part of the case against Buckingham that was pressed in the Parliament of 1626. Zagorin suggests that "to the favorite's ascendence must be ascribed in no small measure the decline of the crown's moral authority—an authority indispensable to government which once lost can hardly ever be recovered."[39] Attitudinal change was thus crucial to the process by which the court was labeled corrupt by its critics, and the most fundamental difference in attitude concerned competing norms of office and responsibility.

The crucial question of private interest versus public interest was reflected in the way the court and its critics thought of gratuities and bribes. At court, duty lay in personal service to the monarch, responsibility to the public taking a decidedly second place to the king's relations with his courtiers. The king himself shared this view. Concerning a grant to one of them, James instructed Salisbury that "it may be put to an end to the gentleman's contentment, if it may possibly be: if not, as is best for the public."[40] While the favorite, Robert Carr, proclaimed, "I am the courtier whose hand never took bribes,"[41] he was wangling 2,000 marks from Lionel Cranfield in return for his favor in negotiations for one of the farms of the customs on wine.[42] But while courtiers seemed to have defined almost all official profits as gratuities, their critics, both Puritan and parliamentary, did not. They labeled such profits corrupt. Although it is difficult to distinguish traditional themes from immediate political concerns, many contemporary sermons appear to have focused on the bribery of officials.[43] So did parliamentary action. The attack on purveyors in the sessions of 1604, 1606, and 1610 included accusations of bribery. In 1610 Parliament imprisoned Sir Stephen Proctor for the wrongful use of his commission to investigate concealed debts, and the taking of bribes. The extortion of bribes through threats of legal prosecution came under particular attack. Significantly, the Parliament of 1610 also requested that the king allow his servants to be arrested and freely sued, a request never made by any Tudor Parliament.[44]

In its efforts to compel official responsibility to the public, Parliament proceeded ever more vigorously against the king's officials, using the accusation of bribery as its principal instrument. In 1621 Walter Yonge, the Puritan diarist, recorded the Commons impeachment of Sir John Bennett, Judge of the Prerogative Court of Canterbury and the Court of High Commission, for bribery and corruption. "There was found in his custody two hundred thousand pounds in coin. He was as corrupt a judge as any in England, for he would not only take bribes of both parties, plaintiff and defendant, but many times shamefully begged them."[45] But the confusion in standards at court was such that Judge Bennett, in response to these charges, had to ask Sir Robert Cotton (whose private library was a treasure house of public records) what constituted an impeachable offense. He asked for precedents from the parliament rolls for what had been done against ordinary or ecclesiastical officers, what offenses they had been charged with, what statutes had been made against their oppressions. He ended his inquiry by asking Cotton to tell him how to search the archives in the Tower.[46] But Parliament did not recognize the studied distinctions of the courtiers. Private interests were condemned in the name of public responsibility, on no issue more dramatically than that of the Spanish pensions.

That issue called into question the responsibility of the king's highest ministers and the relation of the crown to the nation perceived by most Englishmen to be England's greatest enemy. To the king's ministers on the Spanish payroll, the taking of a pension provoked no crisis of conscience because the practice was widespread, it was tolerated by the king, and it did not require them to damage what they considered the king's interests. The practice of giving gratuities and pensions was common in Renaissance diplomacy, and Cardinal Wolsey and other members of Henry VIII's Privy Council enjoyed Spanish pensions in the 1520s. Re-establishment of relations with Spain after years of war brought about a new flow of gold to English courtiers during James's reign.

The payments originated during the peace negotiations with Spain in 1604. Given in the form of presents and gratuities "for their assistance in the concluding of peace and after for their good offices in continuing amity and good correspondence betwixt their Majesties,"[47] these payments to courtiers soon became settled pensions amounting to £9,125 a year.[48] The existence of these pensions is, however, evidence neither of a few greedy grafters nor of a Spanish fifth column, but rather of the usual mode by which foreign powers operated at the Jacobean court. "Money," said one ambassador, "is the only means of succeeding in England."[49] English clients of the archduke of the Spanish Netherlands were discontented that he did not pay as much as the Dutch. The French were not laggards either in paying off English courtiers. Northampton thought Salisbury took a pension from the French as well as from the Spanish and that the duke of Lennox was "more of a Frenchman than the members of the Council of Paris for he informed the French ambassador of everything that passed in the council."[50] The Spanish ambassador claimed that France spent 80,000 ducats a year in pensions.[51] He suggested that the best thing the pope could do was to distribute several thousand ducats himself at the English court.[52] English courtiers seem to have taken the attitude that if foreign powers were willing to pay, they themselves were willing to be paid and termed such payments "ordinary courtesies."[53] The reaction of others—John Digby, the English ambassador in Spain, King James, and the court's critics—illustrate the divergence in views even within the court toward this form of official profit.

Digby discovered in 1613 the existence and identity of the Spanish pensioners by decoding the Spanish ambassador's dispatches. In great indignation he sent to the king the details of who and how much, pointing out that the Spanish ambassador had written, "they are to be bought and sold withal, as he would do with shop-keepers . . . that as nothing is to be had of them without money, so for money he thinketh they would sell their souls to hell."[54] Digby recounted Salisbury's relations with the Spanish, his demands for greater sums, and weighed the possible explanations for Salisbury's actions—that the promotion of peace and the Spanish marriage fit in with English interests, and that as England and Spain diverged Salisbury withdrew his inclination but continued his income. Nonetheless, Digby declared, "no circumstance can make his proceedings excusable or free from the name of falsehood and treachery unless he freely acquainted your Majesty with all that passed, and that your Majesty were contented not to be displeased that the Spaniards should be cozened."[55] Whether Salisbury or any other of the king's ministers had informed the king of their pensions is uncertain. But the king's reaction to the news that his highest officials were on the take was to be neither surprised nor outraged. He did precisely nothing. If this was deviant behavior, James did not label it as such. On several occasions King James received lists of Spanish pensioners; for several years he had the opportunity to read all of the Spanish ambassador's secret correspondence; at no time did he express displeasure.[56]

His subjects did. Anti-Spanish feeling, already high in England, exploded into print as James considered a Spanish bride for Prince Charles and as war broke out in the Palatinate. In a series of popular tracts James's unpopular foreign policy, which seemed to bring into question his commitment to Protestantism, was blamed on corrupt courtiers.[57] In 1620 a tract called "Vox Populi" attacked "diverse courtiers who were hungry and gaped wide for Spanish gold."[58] Another tract asserted that "these days the King of Spain's gold and his ambassador Count Gondomar act wonders in England."[59] At St. Paul's Cross, the most important pulpit in London, which was often used by the government to project its point of view, there were preachers who spoke out against the marriage of Prince Charles and the Spanish Infanta.[60] The most damaging attack on the court was featured in a publication of 1622, "Tom Tell-Troath." In it no pretense was made of distinguishing between the king and his evil counsellors: the issue of bribery was brought home to the king himself; the monarchy itself was tainted with corruption. Gondomar, it was said:

hath at his command, and is master of your cabinet without a key, and knows your secrets before the greatest part and most faithful of your council; and which is worse, they say your Majesty knows it, and therefore suspect that yourself is bribed against yourself. Otherwise they think not the devil himself could so abuse the times we live, as to make things pass in that fashion as they do, contrary to all sense and conscience and reason of state.[61]

In the case of the Spanish pensions, corruption was connected to the all-important issues of foreign policy and religion. The king appeared to have washed his hands of the Protestant cause and allied himself with England's traditional enemy. The king was accused of preferring his personal interest to that of his people. The charge that the king had corruptly sacrificed his country's interest to that of Spain was an attack on the authority of the monarchy itself.

This divergence in views about corrupt practices was not in itself capable of fostering the active political challenge which engaged the court in the 1620s. Rather, I would suggest that corruption is only capable of undermining governmental legitimacy when it becomes linked to other critical issues of policy. Thus, between 1603 and 1621 corruption became closely linked to several issues which were crucial to the parliamentary and Puritan critics of the court. The sale of honors affected the social structure and threatened the status of the politically pre-eminent. The domination of the duke of Buckingham made the patronage system a focus for disaffection. The attack on bribe taking reflected the connection between fiscal grievances and Parliament's demand that royal officials be responsible to the public. And the issue of the Spanish pensions raised the question of official responsibility, foreign policy, and religion with a vengeance. The connection of the issue of corruption to religious attitudes points up the importance of linkage in determining the political impact of corruption. It might be asked how crucial the problem of pensions would have been had the nation involved been the Dutch. Too, it is important to note that at the same session in which members of the Commons accused Sir Stephen Proctor of extortion, they also accused Henry Spiller, a clerk of the Exchequer, of neglecting to prosecute recusants. In addition, the *absence* of an overriding issue that had previously obscured domestic abuses can be important. Thus, the end of the long war with Spain in 1604, for which the crown had been able to rally widespread support, allowed a newly intense focus on the court's domestic activities. The issue of corruption became the spearhead of Parliament's attack on all these important questions.

Corruption becomes a significant issue in politics as a result of startling "critical events" which shift the level of popular thought from the pragmatic to the symbolic plane, or so suggests one recent analyst.[62] It may be argued that what helped make corruption a potent political issue in 1621 were two events which solidified the critics' view of the court's irresponsibility. The backdrop to the convening of Parliament in 1621 was a trade depression, which exacerbated criticism of the court's extravagance and waste of the state's resources,[63] and war in the Palatinate, which crystallized opposition to the king's foreign policy. Forced to go hat in hand to the Parliament he had tried so long to avoid, the king once more had to find ways to conciliate his critics. Lord Chancellor Bacon suggested that the most obnoxious delegations of royal rights, most of them patents procured by Buckingham's means, be rescinded. This advice was not heeded. The king did admit in his opening speech that his trust had been abused by corrupt servants but insisted that a thorough reform of the Household had been undertaken. The court had learned, he said ingratiatingly, that "everyday was not to be a Christmas."[64]

But members of the Commons were not deterred by excuses. They plunged into the investigation of corruption in the law courts and the abuses of monopolists such as Sir Giles Mompesson. Mompesson had patents for licensing inns, concealed lands, and a place on the commission for the manufacture of gold and silver thread. In all three cases he had practiced intimidation and extortion. Having sought precedents "to show how far and for what offences the power of this House doth extend to punish delinquents against the state as well as those who offend against this House,"[65] the Commons indicted Mompesson, and the Lords examined and condemned him. Then the Commons found bigger game. Not only had Bacon approved these patents and others, but he had taken bribes while he sat as a judge in Chancery. Bacon claimed that he was only a man of his times, that those bribes were in fact gifts, and had not, in any case, affected his judgment. The different standards of proper governmental practices that had grown up in the years before 1621 proved Bacon's undoing. He fell from office while making distinctions between bribes and gifts which many of his contemporaries no longer recognized.[66]

Corruption had become the issue by which Parliament asserted the responsibility of the king's servants to the nation. It was also the means by which Parliament extended its own power. Throughout the 1620s charges of corruption continued to be the central weapon by which Parliament attacked unpopular figures: in 1624, the Lord Treasurer Cranfield; in 1626, the duke of Buckingham. Bacon's impeachment meant the destruction of the immunity previously enjoyed by royal ministers.[67] It is ironic that in impeaching Lionel Cranfield Parliament was impeaching the court's most vigorous and successful reformer. For some parliamentarians, rooting out corruption was not as important as setting limits to the royal prerogative. James Whitelocke, for instance, attacked abuses in the Parliaments of 1610 and 1614 and took a prominent part in the impeachment proceedings in 1621. Yet, in 1613 Whitelocke challenged both the Earl Marshall's court and Northampton's naval commission as lacking the legal authority to investigate abuses and try offenders.[68] In short, the efforts of the court to answer critics by reforming abuses led to attack by the same critics on the royal prerogative.

There is a remarkable similarity between Northampton's indictment of the "desperate leeches that suck the life blood out of the king's fortune. . . . Without some care to pull up those suckers that draw this very moisture radical from the root, it is no more possible for this poor exhausted monarchy to exist,"[69] and one parliamentarian's tirade against "those blood suckers of the kingdom. . . . The more examples we make of great men the more good we do the country."[70] Both attacked the abuses fostered by a distribution of reward uncontrolled by reference to administrative needs. But the difference between them is vitally significant. To Northampton, reform could be effected by the king's ministers' investigating and extirpating administrative abuses. But because the patronage system hindered all efforts to reform it and abuses multiplied, and because the court and Parliament no longer shared a common conception of what corruption was, reform was by the 1620s no longer enough. Corruption continued to function as an important political issue even after the death of Buckingham put an end to the worst abuses of the patronage system because the divergence in systems of value had made the court itself appear to be the source of corruption. To the Commons, corruption could be uprooted only by compelling royal officials to be responsible to the nation as represented in Parliament.

The issue of political corruption undermined the legitimacy of the early Stuarts because the court was unable to capitalize on the benefits that corruption, endemic to the early modern state, had the potential to provide. In fact, court practices, particularly after 1615, tended to alienate those the crown most needed to conciliate. Perhaps of even greater significance, corrupt practices were linked to critical issues of religion, foreign policy, and status that divided the political elite. As a result, the court and the king himself were labeled corrupt. And such a label was crucial, for the crown's loss of legitimacy was a necessary prelude to the English Revolution.

## Notes

This essay grew out of a paper read at the American Historical Association meeting held in Chicago in December 1974. Quotations have been modernized throughout.

1. Robert Zaller, *The Parliament of 1621* (Berkeley, 1971), p. 76; Clayton Roberts, *The Growth of Responsible Government in Stuart England* (Cambridge, 1966), pp. 26–29. Colin Tite, *Impeachment and Parliamentary Judicature in Early Stuart England* (London, 1974), argues that impeachment was not fully revived until later in the 1620s and refers instead to the revival of "parliamentary judicature."

2. Quoted in Zaller, *The Parliament of 1621*, pp. 64–65.

3. Joel Hurstfield, "Political Corruption in Modern England: The Historian's Problem," *History* 52 (1967): 16–34.

4. J. S. Nye, "Corruption and Political Development: A Cost-Benefit Analysis," in *Political Corruption*, ed. Arnold J. Heidenheimer (New York, 1970), pp. 566–67. Nye goes on to say: "This includes such behavior as bribery (use of a reward to pervert the judgment of a person in a position of trust); nepotism (bestowal of patronage by reason of ascriptive relationship rather than merit); and misappropriation (illegal appropriation of public resources for private-regarding uses)." Nye, in developing his definition of corruption, prefers to see the question of the public interest and the question whether non-Western societies regard the behavior as corrupt as separate variables. This definition is also adopted by James C. Scott, *Comparative Political Corruption* (Englewood Cliffs, N.J., 1972), p. 4, who points out that this definition allows the comparison of practices corrupt only by modern standards, and the study of their causes and effects in different periods and places. He suggests the use of the term "proto-corruption" to describe practices of the pre–nineteenth century period which were labeled corruption only in the nineteenth century. See Heidenheimer's discussion of the problems posed in defining corruption, *Political Corruption*, pp. 4–9. He notes of definitions such as Nye's: "this 'imposition' on the rest of the world of Western standards in evaluating behavior may well be, at this stage of research and theory building, a prerequisite to meaningful comparative analysis of political corruption phenomena." Heidenheimer has also suggested the value of using market-centered definitions of corruption to delineate the borderlines of corrupt behavior in a period such as the Jacobean where the allocation and price of offices and honors were of central importance.

5. For a brief but suggestive discussion of the application of social science theory to the historical problem of corruption, see Phillip Abrams, "Sociology and History," *Past and Present* 52 (August 1971): 119–20.

6. R. K. Merton, *Social Theory and Social Structure* (New York, 1967), pp. 72–82.

7. G. E. Aylmer, *The King's Servants: The Civil Service of Charles I* (New York, 1961), p. 248.

8. For a discussion of the Tudor-Stuart patronage system, see Wallace MacCaffrey, "Place and Patronage in Elizabethan Politics," in *Elizabethan Gov-*

*ernment and Society*, ed. S. T. Bindoff, J. Hurstfield, and C. H. Williams (London, 1961), pp. 95–126; J. E. Neale, "The Elizabethan Political Scene," in *Essays in Elizabethan History* (London, 1958), pp. 59–84; Aylmer, *The King's Servants*.

9. See Samuel P. Huntington, "Modernization and Corruption," pp. 492–500; David H. Bayley, "The Effects of Corruption in a Developing Nation," pp. 521–33; J. S. Nye, "Corruption and Political Development," pp. 564–78; all in Heidenheimer, *Political Corruption*.

10. James C. Scott, "Proto-Corruption in Early Stuart England," in *Comparative Political Corruption*, pp. 36–57. This paper had gone through several revisions before I came upon Scott's treatment of the subject. Focusing on corruption as influence, Scott emphasizes the role of commercial elites who used their wealth to influence state policies informally by buying offices because their newly won economic power was not yet reflected in political power. While Scott's analysis of the customs farmers may be correct, it neglects the fact that most of the people buying offices were gentry; see Aylmer, *The King's Servants*. Moreover, much of the scramble for reward at the Stuart court was undertaken by those with impeccable aristocratic credentials. Describing the sale of office in the seventeenth century as "making room for ambitious members of the new bourgeoisie," Scott sees the attempt to prohibit such sales, although it called itself reform, as the reaction of a traditional status-based elite to the influx of wealth elites into office (p. 47). Yet Northampton, who certainly prided himself on the antiquity and high position of the Howards, Dukes of Norfolk, of whom he was a descendant, was both a reformer who wished to abolish sale of offices *and* the patron of such merchants and middling men as Lionel Cranfield and John Daccombe, whom he advanced to office for their abilities in rationalizing administration.

11. I am grateful to Wallace MacCaffrey for emphasizing this point. See Lawrence Stone, *The Crisis of the Aristocracy* (Oxford, 1965), pp. 65–128, 647, 754–58. For an extended discussion of the structural problems brought about by the imbalance in the supply of and demand for governmental patronage, see Linda Levy Peck, "Court Patronage and Government Policy: the Jacobean Dilemma," in *Patronage in the Age of the Renaissance*, ed. S. Orgel and G. Lytle (Princeton 1981).

12. See Wallace MacCaffrey, "Place and Patronage in Elizabethan Politics," p. 97.

13. Lawrence Stone, *Family and Fortune: Studies in Aristocratic Finance in the Sixteenth and Seventeenth Centuries* (Oxford, 1973), pp. 28, 283.

14. *History* 56 (1971): 235–43.

15. Linda Levy Peck, "Problems in Jacobean Administration: Was Henry Howard, Earl of Northampton, A Reformer?" *Historical Journal* 19 (1976): 831–58.

16. Public Record Office (hereafter P.R.O.), SP 14/61, 1, fol. 18.

17. B.M. Cotton MSS. Titus C I, "Certain rules to be prescribed for the reformation of all abuses and corruption that have crept into the office of arms and for prevention of all means which may bring in the like hereafter," fol. 432v. This tract is written entirely in Northampton's own hand.

18. B.M. Cotton MSS. Titus C VI, fols. 122–122v. Northampton to Robert Carr, Viscount Rochester (1613–14).

19. Joel Hurstfield, "Corruption and Reform under Edward VI and Mary: The Case of Wardship," *English Historical Review* 68 (1953): 22–36.

20. See Nye, "Corruption and Political Development: A Cost-Benefit Analysis," in Heidenheimer, *Political Corruption*, p. 575; also pp. 26–28.

21. Howard S. Becker, "Deviance and the Response of Others," in *Delinquency, Crime and Social Process*, ed. Donald Cressy and David Ward (New York, 1969), pp. 585–89.

22. Perez Zagorin, *The Court and the Country* (New York, 1970), p. 37. Stone, *Family and Fortune*, comments on corruption: "it was a powerful factor in turning the country gentry against the administration, and in the development of a group who called themselves 'the Country,' or 'the Patriots,' a new phenomenon of open political opposition to the Court and all it stood for. This suspicion of corruption goes far to explain the obstinate refusal of Parliament to contribute to the burdens of government, a refusal which in turn made even more outrageous resort to corruption almost inevitable" (pp. 56–57). Since this essay was written,

the model of "court" and "country" and the notion of a parliamentary opposition during the early Stuart period have come under attack. See especially Conrad Russell, "Parliamentary History in Perspective, 1604–1629," *History* 61 (1976): 1–27; Derek Hirst, "Court, Country and the Problem of Early Stuart Rule," in *Faction and Parliament*, ed. K. Sharpe (Oxford, 1978), and the response by J. H. Hexter, "Power Struggle, Parliament, and Liberty in Early Stuart England," *Journal of Modern History* 50 (March 1978): 1–50. This continuing controversy does not alter the analysis presented here of why corruption was so potent a political issue in the early Stuart period: the definition of corruption was changing because of its link to other crucial issues of status, finance, religion, and foreign policy, about which there was strong disagreement within the political elite.

23. See also Michael Walzer, *The Revolution of the Saints* (Cambridge, 1965), pp. 240–45; William Haller, *The Rise of Puritanism* (New York, 1957); Aylmer, *The King's Servants*, in addition to Zagorin.

24. Stone, *The Crisis of the Aristocracy*, pp. 72–76. In 1604, the year after James' accession, an anonymous pamphleteer wrote the following: "Your Majesty's followers . . . do proclaim open sale of the most noble and ancient order of knighthood, whereby some, contrary to your Highness' intent, of unworthy condition have, for bribery, been unworthily made knights, to the dishonour of your royal Majesty and the disgrace of other virtuous knights." "Advertisements of a Loyal Subject to his Gracious Sovereign drawn from the Observation of the People's Speeches," *Somers Tracts*, vol. 2 (London, 1809), pp. 144–48.

25. Stone, *The Crisis of the Aristocracy*, p. 76.

26. I. H. Jeayes, ed., *Letters of Phillip Gawdy, 1579–1616* (London, 1906), pp. 135–36; Stone, *The Crisis of the Aristocracy*, p. 76.

27. Jeayes, *Gawdy*, p. 134.

28. Comments presented at panel: "Corruption and Reform in Seventeenth- and Eighteenth-Century England," American Historical Association meeting, December 1974, at which this paper was presented. "Market corruption" is defined by Scott as "the selling of government goods and services to the highest bidder, whether he has 'connections' or not." *Comparative Political Corruption*, p. 12.

29. Stone, *The Crisis of the Aristocracy*, pp. 85, 92–93.

30. Peck, "Court Patronage and Government Policy"; Mayes, "The Sale of Peerages in Stuart England," *Journal of Modern History* 29 (May 1957): 35.

31. Quoted in Stone, *The Crisis of the Aristocracy*, p. 104.

32. B.M. Harleian MS. 7002, fol. 381v. Cotton to Robert Carr, earl of Somerset (1615).

33. Zaller, *The Parliament of 1621*, p. 60.

34. Quoted in Mayes, "The Sale of Peerages in Stuart England," p. 36.

35. Quoted in ibid., p. 36.

36. Aylmer, *The King's Servants*, p. 228.

37. Sir W. C. Trevelyan and Sir C. E. Trevelyan, eds., *Trevelyan Papers*, vol. 3, Camden Society, o.s. 105 (London, 1872), p. 55. George Montgomery to John Willoughby, 2 Dec. 1603.

38. Ibid., 3:57–58.

39. Zagorin, *The Court and the Country*, p. 59. For a discussion of the specific political context in which the parliamentary attack on Buckingham was made, see Conrad Russell, *Parliaments and English Politics, 1621–9* (Oxford, 1979).

40. Historical Manuscript Commission, Calendar of The Manuscripts of the most honourable, The Marquess of Salisbury . . . part 18 (London, 1938), pp. 247–48, Lake to Salisbury, 24 Aug. 1606.

41. P.R.O., SP 14/71, 6, 8 Oct. 1612, Carr to Northampton.

42. Cam. Univ. Lib. MS. Dd.3.63, fols. 54–56v (1613), Northampton to Rochester: "If ever I played any part artificially to give your Lord satisfaction . . . it is in Cranfield's matter. . . . I told him as a true friend . . . that an offer of 2000 marks should have been made to your Lord lately for the matter of the wines which he had valued to you at one. . . . I wished him to consider of how great value your favor was likely to be him."

43. Millar Maclure, *The Paul's Cross Sermons* (Toronto, 1958), pp. 141, 248, and 228.

44. Clayton Roberts, *The Growth of Responsible Government in Stuart England*, pp. 1–2. I am grateful to Conrad Russell for stressing the importance of extortion in the parliamentary attack on corrupt practices.

45. George Roberts, ed., *The Diary of Walter Yonge*, Camden Society, o.s. 41 (London, 1848), p. 37.

46. B.M. Cotton MSS. Jul. C. III, fol. 23, 24 June 1621.

47. P.R.O., SP 94/21, fol. 198v, Sir John Digby to King James, 16 Dec. 1615.

48. For a discussion of the Spanish pensioners, see S. R. Gardiner, *The History of England from the Accession of James I to the Outbreak of the Civil War* (London, 1883–84), 2:216–17; Charles Carter, "Intelligence from England, Spanish Hapsburg Policy-Making and Its Informational Base, 1598–1625" (Ph.D. diss., Columbia University, 1962), pp. 172–75; Charles Carter, *The Secret Diplomacy of the Hapsburgs, 1598–1625* (New York, 1964). A. J. Loomie, *Spain and the Jacobean Catholics*, vol. 1: *1603–1612*, Catholic Record Society, 64 (London, 1973); P.R.O., SP 94/21, fol. 119v; P.R.O. 31 12/35, 17 Oct. 1614, Sarmiento to King Phillip III.

48. Henry Lonchay and Joseph Cuvelier, *Correspondance de la Cour d'Espagne sur les affaires des Pays-Bas au XVII siecle*, 6 vols. (Brussels, 1923–37), 1: no. 330, p. 152.

50. Ibid., D'Arenberg au Archiduc Albert, 2 July 1603; cf. P.R.O. 31 12/36, 22 Jan. 1615, Sarmiento to the duke of Lerma; B.M. Cotton MS. Titus B VII, fol. 489; P.R.O. 31 12/35, 9 May 1614, Sarmiento to Phillip III.

51. P.R.O. 31 12/34, 6 Sept. 1613; P.R.O. 31 12/35, 9 May 1614; 9 Mar. 1614.

52. P.R.O. 31 12/34, 15 Oct. 1613, Sarmiento to Phillip III.

53. Thomas Studder, English agent in Brussels, complained to Northampton that the Spanish were behind in their payments. He had tried, he wrote, "to procure me payment of such money as the King of Spain is behind with me which are ordinary courtesies amongst them to those they affect. If I knew how to have my suit preferred again unto him so as it might take effect, I should be the more able and would employ it in the service of my sovereign and your lordship." B. M. Cotton MS. Galba E I, fol. 262, 25 Oct. 1612. Charles Cornwallis, onetime English ambassador to Spain, offered to tell Sarmiento, the Spanish ambassador, the name of an English spy at Madrid for 6,000 ducats. Sarmiento decided the story was a ruse to extort money and brushed him off. P.R.O. 31 12/35, 25 Jan. 1614, Sarmiento to duke of Lerma.

54. P.R.O., SP 94/21, fol. 200, 16 Dec. 1615. The cipher for this letter is P.R.O., SP 106/4, fols. 22v–23.

55. P.R.O., SP 94/20, fol. 59v, 9 Sept. 1615. For cipher, see P.R.O., SP 106/4, fol. 26.

56. Garrett Mattingly, *Renaissance Diplomacy* (Baltimore, 1964), pp. 225–26.

57. L. B. Wright, "Propaganda against James I's Appeasement of Spain," *Huntington Library Quarterly* 6 (1942–43): 52.

58. Thomas Scott, "Vox Populi," *Somers Tracts*, 2:513–17.

59. "Vox Coeli," *Somers Tracts*, 2:584.

60. MacLure, *The Paul's Cross Sermons*, pp. 102, 242, 244.

61. "Tom Tell-Troath," *Somers Tracts*, 2:473.

62. John Gardiner, *The Politics of Corruption* (New York, 1970), p. 59.

63. Stone, *Family and Fortune*, p. 56.

64. Zaller, *The Parliament of 1621*, pp. 22, 35.

65. Ibid., p. 59.

66. Roberts, *The Growth of Responsible Government*, pp. 27–29; Zaller, *The Parliament of 1621*, p. 90.

67. D. L. Keir, *The Constitutional History of Modern Britain, 1485–1951* (London, 1953), p. 193.

68. G. D. Squibb, *The High Court of Chivalry* (Oxford, 1959), pp. 43–45.

69. B.M. Cotton MS. Titus C VI, fol. 123, Northampton to Rochester.

70. Zaller, *The Parliament of 1621*, p. 65.

# Aristocrats and Lawyers in French Provincial Government, 1559–1648: From Governors to Commissars

## ROBERT R. HARDING

*So hidden at the bottom of a lawyer's soul one finds some of the tastes and habits of an aristocracy. They share its instinctive preference for order and its natural love of formalities; like it they conceive a great distaste for the behavior of the multitude and secretly scorn the government of the people. . . . Every time that the nobles have wished the lawyers to share some of their privileges, these two classes have found many things that make it easy for them to combine and, so to say, they find that they belong to the same family.*

Alexis de Tocqueville[1]

Why did the French aristocracy wish to "share" its dominant position in provincial government with lawyers, who, as the new commissars, gradually developed by the 1630s into the permanent and nationwide institution of the intendancy? The question is rarely posed, because the intendancy has rarely been thought of as an institution promoted by the nobility of the sword, which throughout the *ancien régime* monopolized nearly all the hundreds of charges of governor, lieutenant general, and lieutenant in the provinces.[2] On the contrary, the prevailing theory is still that of the nineteenth century. The central government installed intendants to "supplant the governors,"[3] "finish off the governors,"[4] "control the local aristocracy."[5] "The new and redoubtable power [of the intendants] was immediately opposed by the authorities who had everything to fear by their establishment. The struggle between governors and intendants long preceded the time of Richelieu."[6] "In re-establishing royal authority Henry IV was faced with the crucial task of curtailing the governors' powers. . . . He appointed *intendants* to act as a further check. . . ."[7] "Richelieu opposed the authority of the intendants of justice, *police* and finances to that of the military governors."[8] "The feudal tradition of independence and the danger of separatism in the provinces were combined in the Provincial Governors. . . . [They] did not have to be abolished, but they could be passed by so that they declined into decorative obsolescence."[9] "The governor, chosen from the greatest families of the realm, represented more the political pretensions of the high nobility than the royal will. . . . The commissar, generally a jurist from the royal *Conseil*, was, on the other hand, charged with being the incarnation of the centralizing and absolutist policies of the monarchy."[10]

This theory has the appeal of linking administrative development to a recognizable social conflict, that between robe and sword. Few historians of early modern France make any Tocquevillian assumptions about the affinity of lawyers and aristocrats. The robe-sword polarity is the mainspring of conceptual efforts to explain such phenomena as the rise of absolutism, the decline of feudalism, and the rise of middle-class influence in government. Commissars are associated with all of these developments. Governors are often pictured as innate *frondeurs*, associated with feudalism, particularism, and disorder.

It is, of course, true that *robins* and military nobles felt group solidarity and professional pride, and they were both keenly aware that the values implied by their respective callings were disparate. "I have sometimes gone to the Parlements of Toulouse and Bordeaux," Blaise de Monluc wrote after his retirement as lieutenant general in Guyenne, ". . . and have wondered a hundred times how it was possible for so many young men to eternally amuse themselves in a court, considering that the blood of young men ordinarily boils. I believe it is a fad, and the king could do no better than to drive those people out of the courts and train them in arms."[11] *Robins* could display equally bigoted disillusionment with the *noblesse d'épée*, but sometimes also resentment or jealousy: "Those who have arms never use quills except as feathers for their hats," the *maître des requêtes* Henri de Mesmes said, "and those of the long robe have no means of glorifying themselves by memorable feats.'"[12] The historian's problem is to determine what the significance of these hostilities, resentments, and jealousies was in the context of a particular problem. Social tensions that were fundamental or structural in some situations were superficial or superstructural in others. The robe-sword polarity may well be crucial to explaining, for example, the conflicts at the Estates General of 1614. However, in the case of provincial government the jealousies were diffuse, transient, superficial, and easily overcome by common interests and mutual needs.

In general, the process of State building in the early modern period no longer appears so antiaristocratic as it once did,[13] and along with this reappraisal some components of the traditional theory of the rise of the commissars have been criticized. According to Ranum, Richelieu had no conscious intention of undermining the governors, and Mousnier provides several examples of governors and intendants who collaborated under Séguier's chancellorship (1633–72).[14] Whether these arguments should lead us to revise or scrap the traditional theories could be clarified by detailed local studies, wherever possible, of individual commissars' administrations. However, the most specialized local studies already done have not produced much unambiguous evidence on the problem, although some version of the traditional theory often appears in these works.[15] This essay will examine three other aspects of the problem, beginning with the social and business relations of the governor and commissar classes, relations that centered in Paris and around the royal court. Second, the general administrative problems confronted by governors will be analyzed in the belief that these will shed light on the rise of the commissars. Third, we will see that the changing career-orientations of governors in the seventeenth century are also pertinent to a correct understanding of the transformation in local government.

The intendancy resulted from successive modifications of two institutions, both older than the mid-sixteenth century but neither very important until after the 1550s: the judicial missions (*chevauchées*) of the *maîtres des requêtes* and the practice of dispatching royal *commissaires* on varied temporary missions. The importance of the former institution was limited by the fact that there were only two or four *maîtres des requêtes* until increases in 1553–55 brought their number to twenty.[16] These officers were recruited mainly from the sovereign courts of Paris, especially the Parlement.[17] Many were dispatched in 1556 to inspect the *recettes générales* in the face of a monetary crisis and impending state bankruptcy.[18] The *"commissaires départis"* began to appear in large numbers in the wake of first War of Religion in 1562–63. Some were provincial *robins,* but most were recruited from the elite of the Paris robe as the *maîtres des requêtes* were, and some were *maîtres des requêtes.*[19] With titles of *"intendant," "surintendant,"* and *"commissaire,"* which contemporaries used interchangeably, these dynastic bureaucrats became increasingly familiar figures in local society. After 1637 they were permanently installed in every generality, and the habit of recruiting them mainly from the *maîtres des requêtes* was fixed, as the number of these officers was raised to fifty-six by 1623, to seventy in 1642, and reduced to sixty-two by 1648.[20]

The social milieu in which these agents originated was, therefore, mainly the elite of the Paris robe families. It was a world much less isolated from the provincial governors than one might suppose. Article 181 of the 1629 Code Michaud is one of those laws of the *ancien régime* that is less surprising for prohibiting certain practices than for implying the prior existence of those practices:

No one can serve in the charges of intendant of justice or finances in our armies or provinces who is a servant, councillor, employee, or close relative of the commanders of the said armies or governors of the said provinces. Our chancellors and *gardes des sceaux* are strictly forbidden to dispatch any commission to such persons.[21]

Had there actually been intendants who were in the private employ of or closely related to the governors of the regions they administered? How common was this?

No definitive answer is possible, but from research into the backgrounds of many commissar families certain facts are clear. The first is that there were some commissars very closely tied to the regional governors. Simon Marion, once a *commissaire* and once an *intendant des finances* in Languedoc in the 1580s and 1590s, was a client (*"fidèle"*) of Damville, the *gouverneur* of Languedoc, and had been his *secrétaire* in the 1570s.[22] In 1600 Marion received the *seigneurie* of Andilly from Damville as a gift "in consideration of the great and notable services done for us by M. Simon Marion."[23] We know that Antoine de Séguier was a protégé of Epernon when he accompanied him to his governorship of Provence in 1586 as a royal commissar,[24] and his nephew, Pierre V de Séguier, was simultaneously a client of Epernon's and an *intendant* in his governorship of Limousin, Angoumois, Saintonge, and Aunis in 1621–24.[25] In 1630, when this same duke of Epernon was *gouverneur* of Guyenne, he "entreated His Majesty to appoint him an *intendant* of justice," as Epernon's secretary tells us. Louis XIII "gave the duke liberty to choose whom he should think fit out of his Council." The choice was François de Verthamon, one of the more obscure *maîtres des requêtes*, who had the advantage of "great *amitié*" with Pierre V de Séguier, "with whose conduct in the same commission the duke had been so well pleased that he desired nothing more than one who would imitate his virtue to succeed him." Between Epernon and Verthamon "there was never the least difference or conflict."[26] Verthamon served in the province until 1638 and became a *fidèle* of Epernon's son, Bernard, who followed him as governor in 1643.[27] In 1630 the *gouverneur* of Provence, Charles de Guise, "requested [Dreux] d'Aubray to be *intendant* of justice; he had no resistance to the spirit of M. de Guise, but the *garde des sceaux* commissioned him anyway."[28]

There were probably other cases of commissars who were in the employ of governors or whose independence was otherwise compromised by the fact that they were handpicked by a governor for his province.[29] Nevertheless, these cases were exceptional rather than normal. The spirit of article 181 of the Code Michaud was followed generally both before 1629 and after. It was not exceptional for commissars to be household officers or clients of aristocratic governors: this was common, perhaps usual; but they were rarely commissioned as commissars in regions those aristocrats governed. We can be sure of this because it is possible to reconstruct the relations of dozens of robe commissar families with aristocrats, and in the great majority of cases a royal intendancy represented a vacation from the *"service des grands"* rather than a continuation of it.

Let us select a single aristocratic family for which abundant notarial sources survive in Paris in order to examine more closely the commissars in their private service. The dukes of Nevers governed Champagne and Brie (1545–64, 1589–1631), Picardie (1588–89), Piedmont (1565–74), and Nivernais (almost continuously until 1645). A whole slew of royal commissars were in their household service, especially on the legal and administrative *"conseil"* they maintained in Paris. The *"chef"* of that *conseil* in the 1560s was Charles I de Lamoignon, *maître des requêtes* since 1564 and twice a commissar before his death in 1572. Since at least 1551, he had served the Nevers in various capacities.[30] He was an executor of the wills of François I de Cleves, duc de Nevers, and his son Jacques, jobs that gave him mammoth responsibility for the family's financial well-being.[31] Apart from his salary, he and his sons were rewarded with lands and money gifts from the Nevers.[32] One of his colleagues on the Nevers' *conseil* was Jean Chandon, who interrupted his service to be a commissar in Lyonnais; he was a vassal of Nevers and owed his office of *maître des requêtes* to Nevers influence over royal patronage.[33]

Also in the Nevers' service from the 1560s to the 1640s were various members of the Montholon family, including Jérome de Montholon, who was simultaneously an *intendant* in Orléanais and secretary of the duke of Nevers in the early seventeenth century.[34] Jérome's elder brother, François II, had been a lawyer on the Nevers *conseil* since Lamoignon's time in the 1560s.[35] Jérome's nephew, François, was *"intendant des affaires"* of Nevers, a major creditor of theirs, and owed both his office of *conseiller* in the Parlement and that of *secrétaire du roi* to Nevers' intercession with Henri III and Henri IV respectively.[36] Finally, Jérome's nephew, Jacques, and Jacques' nephew, François III de Montholon, continued household service to the Nevers into the 1640s.[37]

The Montholons came to the Nevers' service after experience in other aristocratic houses.[38] Likewise the de Mesmes served the house of Navarre for many decades before the 1630s and 1640s, when the brothers Jean-Antoine and Claude de Mesmes appear in Nevers' service, the former as *"chef"* of their Paris *conseil* and the latter as a member of that *conseil* and executor of the estate of Charles I de Gonzague-Nevers.[39] Both were *maîtres des requêtes* and royal commissars.[40] On the other hand, the Séguiers were in the service of the Nevers until the 1570s, when their names disappear from the family papers, and Antoine de Séguier moved into Epernon's clientele.[41] There was, of course, mobility in the *service des grands;* continuous service over many generations was exceptional, and some families—the de Thous, for example— moved more often than the families tied to the Nevers.[42]

It was typical that none of these robe agents and clients of the Nevers was ever sent as a royal commissar to a province the Nevers governed, nor were any members of their immediate families. It is nevertheless apparent that the tradition of the *service des grands* resulted in a pattern of private relations between the commissar class and the elite of the sword that in no way resembles textbook generalizations about the struggle between robe and sword. The new dynastic bureaucrats sought their social identity in close interaction with the very group of patrimonial elites that had previously dominated local government alone. Instead of rivalry, their social relations were characterized by an elaborate and complex symbiosis based on mutual needs and services.

Nearly all important *noblesse d'épée* families needed a legal and administrative council in Paris to defend their interests in the numerous, often very long, lawsuits that haunted their family fortunes, and they naturally sought the most famous lawyers in town. The robe agents administered all kinds of family business; they negotiated marriage alliances, leased lands, and found creditors for the aristocrats. They also loaned enormous sums themselves to their employers. In 1588 the Nevers owed 30,531 1. of *rente* to fifty-four robe creditors in Paris or their heirs, representing a capital value of 366,000 1.[43]

The *robins* had equally compelling reasons for seeking aristocratic connections, especially the elite of the robe, who as royal councilors and *maîtres des requêtes* moved in the circles of the royal court, where, as Matignon said, "the poisoned spirits of courtiers" regularly ruined careers and "imperiled the lives and honor of all good men."[44] While serving as commissars they often complained in letters of "enemies" and "libels." Like everyone else at court they needed the protection of a faction and patron. Jean Chandon was arrested for financial swindling in 1588 but released without a trial, "some said because of the favor of the duke of Nevers, whom he served and by whom he was greatly loved."[45] More than this, however, the *service des grands* was crucial in the social mobility of many commissar families. When Christophe de Thou resigned as *"conseiller"* in the household of Henri, duc d'Orléans, he was able to secure the post for his son-in-law, Philippe Hurault, which, as Dupuy put it, "gave him access to the great dignities of the realm."[46] Through aristocratic service, *robins* gained help in preferment to royal offices and titles; they found it a fairly quick way to acquire prime *seigneuries;* and they gained the incalculable prestige benefits of sheer association with the high and mighty. Imagine the pride of a Charles de Lamoignon, who counted two duchesses of Nevers among the godparents of his children.[47]

Godparenthood was well within aristocratic traditions of social condescension. As for intermarriage, one has only to read over the genealogies of the commissar families to see that marital alliances with governors were common, but always with lower-ranking subordinate governors of towns and forts or with provincial lieutenants. Some commissars also had sons or brothers who pursued military careers and became minor governors.

In their writings some legalists like Loyseau, Pasquier, and Leschassier expressed real hostility toward governors or fear of their local power.[48] However, the tradition of aristocratic service helped to mute the class and professional conflicts that might have arisen between the two groups, and commissars normally expressed very different attitudes toward the *noblesse d'épée* in general and governors in particular. The banality that recurs in their writings is that force and justice were twin virtues, the

former wielded by the military aristocracy, the latter adminis-
tered by the robe, and neither was effective without the other.
Jean Truchon, a *commissaire* assigned to Damville's service in
Languedoc, illustrated the point with pompous analogies to
Nestor and Agamemnon, Cineas and Pyrrhus, Achates and
Aeneas, and others.[49] The duty of the nobility, as François II de
Montholon put it, was *"de tenir la main forte à la justice"* and
"to see to it that the obedience due to the king and his justice is
not transgressed."[50] These simple ideas were the ideological basis
of the collaboration of governors and commissars. Phrases similar
to Montholon's appeared in the majority of the royal commissions of intendants as a directive to the governors of the region.[51]
*Intendants* presented their commissions to the governors upon
arrival in the province. Royal letters to governors instruct-
ing them to aid these new agents employed the same ideas and
phrases.[52]

Turning to the actualities of local administration, however, we
are plainly only part of the way toward an understanding of the
relations of the two groups, if we are to believe that governors
accepted commissars into their regimes and collaborated with
them. For if commissars were not always strangers to the governors of the regions they were sent to, they usually were, and
neither their relations with other aristocratic families in Paris nor
platitudes about the alliance of force and justice would have
meant very much if a real conflict of administrative purposes
existed between the two groups. Was there such a conflict?

It is a mistake to assume that the monarchy harbored a permanent goal of centralizing administration before the 1630s, and
even thereafter this goal was subordinated to the preservation of
public order on the local level. Out of the whole volume of activity commissars engaged in, most is to be understood as aimed at
this latter goal, and only a slight amount can be construed as implementation of centralized control. In the 1630s and 1640s they
did help centralize control over the fiscal system. On the other
hand, they were, for example, involved after 1563 in enforcing
the compromise pacifications that ended each war of religion, and
these treaties, including the Edict of Nantes, were eminently de-
centralizing, since they established·a maze of Protestant states-
within-the-State.

The tendency to identify governors with particularism or "feudalism" is equally misleading. From the point of view of the
central government, the governors were the only alternative to
particularism. They had vast local power partly because they represented the royal will, partly because they were drawn from
families that traditionally commanded loyalty in their regions,

and partly because a considerable sector of the local elite was grouped around them as personal clients, household servants, and *gens d'armes* in their military companies. Governors were the crucial means of social and political co-optation for the State. When they were weak or absent, factions and parties simply formed outside all royal influence. This was why Catholic monarchs appointed Calvinist governors, and sometimes obstreperous ones, for some regions. In their roles as the keystones of local order, governors had a solid communality of interests with the commissars. Specifically, three types of chronic administrative problems developed in governors' regimes after the mid-sixteenth century for which the commissars proved palliative.

The first was the partisanship of the judicial establishment in the provinces, which became acute after the conspiracy of Amboise in 1560 when the central government began showing a more tolerant attitude toward Calvinism and instructed governors accordingly. Most of the sovereign courts and lesser jurisdictions remained dogmatically intolerant; they refused to punish Catholics who persecuted Protestants, failed to enforce edicts of toleration, and, in the case of the Parlements, resisted registering such edicts. In some regions, on the other hand, Calvinists infiltrated and took over the courts, especially low-level jurisdictions like the courts of *baillis* and *sénéchaux*; they enforced an interpretation of the law equally detrimental to Catholics. The resulting cleavage in the structure of local government, between the judges and the governors, persisted to the end of the century and even beyond in some southern provinces. It was not necessarily closed even for governors whose religious stance resembled the courts', because, as we shall see, religious differences were not the only ones. The problem of inconsistent religious policy was worsened by the vacillation in royal religious policy, the intentional ambiguity of the edicts, and the fact that private instructions to governors sometimes varied from public policy.

As early as 1561 in Languedoc, the lieutenant general, Joyeuse, wrote to the central government: "The magistrates are very negligent in imposing punishment, excusing themselves by the diversity of edicts, as a result of which no clear law tells them how to proceed. These magistrates are composed of diverse humors, and each interprets the law according to his own desires."[53] Later he complained that the Parlement of Toulouse was sending couriers and "ambassadors" around the province, "to persuade the people that what I order is out of my own head and not the intention of the king."[54] In Provence, the *gouverneur*, Tende, could not get the Parlement at Aix to act against Catholic vigilantes: "Most of the *robins* are well-satisfied because these attacks only represent their own vengeances."[55] In Guyenne the lieutenant general, Burie, secretly told the Protestants they would not be disturbed if they assembled in private while the Parlement at Bordeaux was enforcing an *arrêt* prohibiting all Protestant assemblies.[56] Etampes, the *gouverneur* of Brittany, warned that "if force pulls in one direction and the agents of justice in another, there will be a great convulsion."[57] Etampes also made a request:

Your judges cannot definitively judge because of their partialities . . . and your edicts [on religion] await verification in the Parlement, where judgments are long and expensive. . . . At Laon your *maître des requêtes*, de Cuce, administers justice. . . . Could you command him to come to me [in Nantes] to do the same?[58]

Precisely this solution was resorted to after the First War of Religion as an antidote both to the cleavages in local government and to the ambiguity of religious policy. On 18 June 1563 commissars were created for every province to enforce the pacification terms.[59] They were to supervise and "instruct" the local judges on administration of justice and adjudicate some kinds of disputes themselves. A follow-up edict elaborating on the functions of these agents justified them on the grounds that "our provincial governors have informed us of the many difficulties that come up in the interpretation of some articles of our edict [on religion]."[60]

Many later commissars were created by general edicts—in 1579, 1582, and 1598—and dispatched to enforce the provisions of pacification edicts, a function that was mainly judicial.[61] Many of the *"commissaires"* and *"intendants"* sent individually into provinces also spent much of their time implementing provisions of pacifications. Always the new agents were told in formulaic fashion to "communicate and confer" with the governors, to "maintain a perfect *intelligence*" with them, or to advise the governors "on what they judge requisite for the service of His Majesty and the good of His subjects which the said *gouverneurs* and lieutenants general can undertake to enforce as the persons who have greater knowledge of the affairs of their regions than anyone else." There is no evidence to support the proposition that these clauses were mere "courteous gestures," as if the crown were trying to hoodwink the governors with flattery.[62] Commissars dispatched individually were frequently told, in addition, to establish themselves *"près de la personne"* of a specific governor. The purpose was to repair the schism between executive and judicial authority, not create a new one.

In practice, few commissars had any choice but to collaborate closely with a governor, especially where the commissars were most needed—where the institutions of local government, the courts and town councils, were most fanatically partisan. Without the armed protection of a powerful governor, the commissars' efforts would have been futile. The most explosive decision of all—where the Protestants were to worship—was very often left to the governors alone to make and to enforce.[63] We find the commissars moving around from town to town in governors' entourages or sitting on their provincial councils, adjudicating cases of persecution and property confiscations, releasing prisoners, supervising elections to municipal offices, and so forth. It was precisely this necessity of close collaboration that appears to account for most of the instances of conflict between governors and commissars. For the governors in most regions were themselves divided by factional and family hostility, as well as by all shades of religious sympathy. They protested against the activities of commissars tied to other governors and other parties. The State was too weak simply to erect a new, impartial administrative structure on top of the old, thoroughly partisan and factionalized one; many of the commissars acquired reputations for partisanship and tended to be identified with a particular governor's faction.

To take an early example, the *gouverneur* of Languedoc, Damville, installed Catholic town councils in dozens of Calvinist towns between the First and Second Wars of Religion.[64] The Huguenots, under the leadership of the royal lieutenant Crussol and his brother, d'Acier, protested,[65] and the central government sent two commissars from Paris to enforce the election provision of the 1563 edict of pacification in eastern Languedoc.[66] This produced a long conflict between Damville and the central government.[67] Was it a classic confrontation of a governor attempting to protect his autonomy against monarchical centralization? Evidently not. It was a purely partisan conflict, for Damville already had two commissars attached to his service for enforcement of the pacification: Jean-Jacques de Mesmes and Jacques de Beauquemare.[68] Not long thereafter, the avidly anti-Calvinist lieutenant general, Joyeuse, was moving around western Languedoc repressing *"émotions"* with commissars in his entourage,[69] and there were other commissars operating around this time in the province, each cooperating with a different governor.[70] In the early 1570s, when Damville was displaying a more tolerant attitude toward the Protestants, Molé and Belot were dispatched to Languedoc and two other provinces in the south where Damville was lieutenant general. "Protestant historians greatly praised their equity and moderation.".[71]

On the other hand, the commissars in Lyonnais in the late

1560s and early 1570s aided the governors, Biraque and Mandelot, in repressive policies that nearly obliterated the Protestant community in Lyon.[72] In Maine the Calvinists detested the commissar Miron, who followed in the entourage of the rigidly Catholic governor, Montpensier.[73] The lieutenant general in Guyenne vehemently protested against the activities of two commissars who, he claimed, "strongly favored the party of the new religion," but he toured the countryside with other commissars who were apparently more to his liking.[74] In the east, commissars were twice sent between 1564 and 1568 to Auxerre, once to investigate complaints against the Protestants "at the request of the mayor, governors," and others, and once at Coligny's request to investigate his protests against the terrorism of the local *confrérie* of the Holy Ghost.[75] Naturally, each party resented the investigation aimed at it, but Condé's only complaint against the latter commissar was that he did not do enough.[76] In sum, by strengthening a particular governor, commissars embarrassed his opponents and incurred opposition from other governors, but this opposition was partisan and had no greater significance than conflicts between governors.

In one of the most commonly cited cases where a conflict with a commissar is interpreted as aristocratic resistance to centralization, that interpretation turns out to rest on another kind of misunderstanding. This is the struggle between the marshal Ornano and the *intendant* Bellièvre in Lyonnais in 1594.[77] Ornano bitterly resented Henri IV's assignment of all judicial, fiscal, and civil functions to Bellièvre.[78] However, Ornano was not the *gouverneur* of Lyonnais; that charge was vacant until the next year, nor was Ornano the holder of any subordinate governorship in the province.[79] He was only *"chef et commandant"* of the army that won the province from the League, a charge with no tradition of nonmilitary functions. The historian Pallasse has analyzed the activities of the governors and commissars in Lyonnais during the Civil Wars with great thoroughness, and he characterizes their relations as "a continual collaboration between military force and justice, between the commander of the forces of order and the chief executor of justice; such was the form of royal government during this crisis."[80]

Cleavages between governors and the provincial judicial establishments still occurred well into the seventeenth century, sometimes for purely secular reasons. In 1640, for example, the *gouverneur* of Bourbonnais repeatedly asked Séguier to send commissars to the province to try rebels because the local magistrates would not act against them out of sympathy and fear.[81] *Intendants* never ceased to be judges. Nevertheless, new and more critical problems appeared in governors' regimes, and the functions of the commissars expanded.

By the late sixteenth century, one of the most serious threats to the governors' domination was the indiscipline of their own troops. The outbreak of the civil wars meant that for the first time since the Hundred Years War, royal troops were stationed inside France in large numbers, intruding deeply into civilian society, garrisoned in every town, and encamped in the countryside. Periodically they poured out of their billets, citadels, and camps to pillage, loot, and pursue vendettas. The problem worsened and became the most serious threat to governors' regional dominance, for by the 1570s the culpable units included the very core of governors' power, their *compagnies d'ordonnance.* These units created in the fifteenth century were the monarchy's compromise with the indigenous patron-client networks in the provinces. Virtually every major governor was captain of a *compagnie d'ordonnance,* and that meant that several hundred noblemen, mainly from his government, entered his personal service as military clients.[82] Out of their *compagnies* the major governors recruited their provincial lieutenants and the subordinate governors of towns, forts, *bailliages,* and so forth.[83]

This "principal force of the realm of François I" was by the 1580s, according to La Noue, "only old torn clothes" that left France "naked to her enemies."[84] A royal ordinance of 1574 spoke openly of "the corruption of the institution . . . ; the men of our *ordonnances* should be noblemen who love their honor, but instead they have, to our great regret, pillaged our subjects as much as or more than the foreigners or vagabonds have."[85] Royal ordinances reiterated the ancient rules of discipline,[86] and the *cahiers* of the Third Estate in 1576 and of all three Estates in 1588 vilified the noble *gendarmes* who "pillage and ravage the poor people" as they ride through the countryside "followed by an infinite number of *filles de joie,*" leaving "deserted houses and ruined lands" in their wake.[87] There was no clearer sign of the weakness of the governors' regimes than their inability to control or elicit obedience from their natural clients, the armed lesser nobles from their home regions. The number of *compagnies* was sharply reduced; there were sixty-one in the spring of 1562 with 5,730 noblemen, then twenty-one *compagnies* in 1571 and twelve early in 1585.[88] Despite a revival in the 1630s, the institution disappeared after the Fronde. For governors it meant that their military base consisted more exclusively than before of mercenary levies. The problem of indiscipline steadily worsened in the sixteenth century, and in the years of the League the distinction between martial order and the tyranny of bandit thugs was blurred almost everywhere. Complaints about their inability to control their troops, dispersed in many garrisons and forts, formed one of the most persistent subjects of governors' correspondence with the central government. For want of space, it is impossible to go very deeply into the causes of the erosion of bonds of personal clientage between governors and lesser nobles that lay behind the collapse of the system of *compagnies d'ordonnance*. However, the impression is strong that one of the main reasons why governors and other military commanders promoted the introduction of commissars into enforcement of discipline was the need to compensate for the weakness of military clientage.

It is also impossible to say exactly when commissars started becoming military judges. Because no clear distinction was drawn between civilian and military affairs, many commissars of pacifications and *"intendants de justice"* released prisoners of war, investigated complaints against troops, and informed either the governors or the *prévôts des maréchaux,* who were responsible for adjudicating the crimes of disbanded troops.[89] Under Henri IV, large numbers of *"intendants d'armée"* appeared, and the institution of commissars generally was militarized.[90] Even after the civil wars, control of the troops remained a major problem along the eastern and northern frontiers. Robert Miron's 1601–2 mission to "establish order" in the garrisons of the three bishoprics, for example, resulted from "the great complaints and protests of the sieur d'Ossonville, our lieutenant general in the *gouvernement* of Verdun."[91] Sometimes subordinate governors of towns and forts were guilty of complicity or participation in ravages and ran afoul of a commissar; this was possible only because military commissars had the backing of the major governors or army general in the region, on whom they were even more dependent for protection than their colleagues involved in civilian justice. Normally *intendants d'armée* were tied by their commissions to the service of a specific governor or general.[92] In gaining these martial law judges, governors and generals were not in theory supplementing their authority, for traditionally they had supreme judicial authority over troops in their command. In practice, however, the commissars toured the camps and garrisons, hearing complaints and imposing justice, far more regularly and effectively than the aristocrats had ever done. As far as the lesser nobles were concerned, obedience, which had hitherto been purely a matter of personal *fidélité* to the governors, now become a matter of obedience to public law in fact as well as in theory.

Another cause of military disobedience was, of course, the difficulty of mobilizing supplies and revenues for the maintenance of troops. This was the third chronic problem governors confronted. The well-known inflexibility of the royal fiscal system regularly presented acute dilemmas for governors. Because the costs of troops were budgeted a year in advance, the outbreak of disorders or other unforeseen causes for expenditure obliged the central government to commission or instruct the governors to impose "extraordinary" subsidies or forced "loans" and to requisition foodstuffs and munitions. In practice there were two general ways of going about this, each with disadvantages.

The first was to use sheer armed force to extract funds and supplies, a tactic that was satisfactory for commanders of mobile armies but one no governor would resort to except in desperation. In the long run, governors knew that their authority depended upon the support of the urban elites, and to avoid alienating them, governors often opted to dissociate themselves from extortionary fiscal devices. This attitude helped to open a fiscal role for the early commissars. Out of numerous examples, I will cite two. As early as 1562, the *gouverneur* of Brittany resisted royal orders to seize funds from municipal treasuries and churches to pay his men. He claimed to "lack the means" to oblige his own supporters to do this and suggested that the crown "could create commissars who would be more appropriate to execute the tax collection than I."[93] Much later, in 1637, his difficulty in extracting a forced loan in Limoges prompted the *gouverneur* of Limousin to suggest to Séguier "that you send M. de Tonnellier, or whichever of your *maîtres des requêtes* you advise, to this province; he should make it known that he is here for an *intendance de la justice* so that the people are not alarmed at his arrival, for it is certain that those of the countryside are only too inclined to liberty and revolt."[94]

Commissars were also helpful in the very common situation where governors did actively supervise extraordinary taxation. The key was still maintaining good relations with the urban elites. Governors relied heavily on the town councils and, where they existed, provincial estates, because these institutions imposed the extraordinary subsidies through their own tax-gathering apparatus or else borrowed the sums on their own credit, hoping for eventual reimbursement from the crown. Governors commonly had a few clients within estates and major town councils, and, more importantly, a pattern of mutual service and cooperation had grown up between them during the Renaissance because governors' influence with the central government and control over troops made them valuable allies to the local elites.[95] This orderly situation was shattered all over France in the civil wars, partly because of ideological differences and partly because the demands governors made became so massive that they were regularly resisted even by religiously sympathetic corporations except in cases of immediate danger of attack or revolt. Parlements entered these conflicts with various *arrêts* usually intended to protect towns from the fiscal exploitation of their governors.

The situation was eventually stabilized in many regions through the little-known institution of provincial councils— *"conseils d'Etat," "conseils du gouverneur," "conseils du guerre,"* and, between 1589 and 1598, *"conseils de la Sainte-Union."* Dozens of these councils appeared in the 1570s and 1580s, and some survived into the reign of Louis XIV. Invariably they were headed by a major governor and included representatives of the corporations he depended upon financially. They epitomized the decentralization of the fiscal system, for their main purpose was to coordinate taxation and the supply of troops largely autonomously from the royal fisc. Yet commissars assumed active roles in these councils and in all the administrative procedures they coordinated. Some of these councils were, of course, declared by the monarchy to be in rebellion, but elsewhere commissars backed up governors' demands and helped implement them against the reluctance of corporations, taxpayers, and the merchants who resisted sequestration of supplies. Governors were regularly accused by opponents of acting without royal approval in extraordinary taxation, but the presence of commissars operating as their right-hand men, armed with royal letters and fresh from court, removed all credibility from such accusations. In Languedoc, for example, Damville's movement away from the extreme Catholic party in the early 1570s was marked by repeated clashes with the Parlement and *capitouls* of Toulouse over supply and fiscal issues. In 1573 the monarchy dispatched Jean Truchon "to assist" Damville "in his council."[96] One can trace in detail his activities, riding around the province with Damville's client-lawyer, Jean Colias, visiting the grain and wine merchants, and paying prices fixed by the governor.[97] Like other commissars, he found his role much expanded by simple instructions from the governor. In Montpellier he participated in naming the town councilors and in negotiating a treaty with the Huguenot party.[98] Raymond de Vicose had a similar relationship with Matignon, a lieutenant general of Guyenne in the 1590s,[99] and the same is true of several commissars who operated with Ventadour when he served as the lieutenant general of Languedoc late in the reign of Henri IV.[100]

For commissars on fiscal business, however, the most common situation was probably to have no significant relationship with governors at all. For it was, above all, in technical roles as auditors and fiscal reformers that commissars had the greatest opportunity for independence from governors. Except in volatile situations, they needed neither protection nor armed enforcement of their policies, and most aspects of public finance were peripheral concerns to governors.

In the seventeenth century commissars did not cease to be judges, and in this capacity they continued to cooperate closely with governors. Religious conflicts faded very gradually, and after the civil wars, Henri IV still instructed governors to "join with" the commissars of pacification, to travel and work with them.[101] Together they still appeared to subjects as a monolithic elite. Certainly this was the perspective of the nobility at the Estates General of 1614 when they protested that judicial encroachments by both governors and commissars had deprived the *baillis* and *sénéchaux* of their ancient "authorities and pre-eminences."[102] It was also the assumption made by provincial *parlementaires* at the 1626 Assembly of Notables when they protested that *"gouverneurs* and lieutenants general should not be permitted, whether by means of the *intendants* of justice or any other device, to take control over civil, criminal, and police matters or the execution of ordinances of justice."[103] Nevertheless, the roles of both commissars and governors were transformed after 1598 in ways that made their activities increasingly irrelevant to one another.

Part of the reason for this bifurcation is fairly well known: the range of commissars' concerns was increasingly confined to fiscal administration. Under Sully, they were used to reform public finances, which meant that they installed themselves in the *bureaux des finances* auditing accounts and in *hôtels de ville* arranging for the liquidation of municipal debts.[104] In the 1630s, this activity ceased to be a reform effort and became a permanent *tutelle* over the fiscal administration. As the State deepened its involvement in the Thirty Years War, it sought to mobilize more revenue by displacing the *trésoriers de France* and *élus*, who were too respectful of the fiscal privileges of *coqs de la paroisse* and of peasants whose seigneurs worked to protect them from the fisc out of a self-interested desire to insure their own incomes.[105] The town councils also felt the weight of the new administrative style. At Poitiers in 1623 the *échevins* pointed out the difference from the governors' style to Denis Amelot when he insisted on attending every town council meeting:

They tried to make him understand that it would be a novelty contrary to all practices and would compromise their liberty; they said that when the marshals of France or governors had business to treat with the *corps de ville* they were content to make their proposals and leave while the council deliberated. Then deputies were sent to communicate the decision to them.[106]

An almost identical exchange took place at Chalons-sur-Marne in 1641 when the *intendant* Orgeval insisted on attending every council meeting and prohibited the opening of letters except in his presence.[107]

While the commissars were sealing their *tutelle* over the towns and *bureaux des finances,* the role of governors in regional administration shrank as they found their best career chances either at the royal court and in the royal councils or as commanders in the armies that were increasingly committed to struggles outside France. External war, and the Thirty Years War in particular, thus had a dual effect on local government: it impelled the *tutelle* of the commissars and the conversion of governors from regional political bosses into army commanders. Both developments were to be permanent. After 1635 only a fraction of governors resided in their provinces; in 1692 an edict that created 102 offices of provincial lieutenant noted that "most of the provincial governors and lieutenants general of our provinces are serving in our armies, and we need persons to perform their functions in their absence."[108]

The influence of Paris and the court on the power elite can be seen in table 1, which gives the proportion of the 142 *gouverneurs* of the eleven major *gouvernements*[109] who were born in Paris, died in Paris, and were buried in Paris.[110] They are grouped by year of appointment in six 22.5-year cohorts beginning at the start of Francis I's reign on 1 January 1515 and ending on 1 January 1650.

*Table 1.* Percentage of governors who were born, died, or were buried in Paris

|  | I<br>*Number of governors appointed* | II<br>*Percentage born in Paris* | III<br>*Percentage who died in Paris* | IV<br>*Percentage buried in Paris* |
|---|---|---|---|---|
| 1515–1537 | 30 | 4 | 8 | 10 |
| 1537–1560 | 22 | 11 | 24 | 13 |
| 1560–1582 | 26 | 5 | 12 | 6 |
| 1582–1605 | 25 | 7 | 30 | 23 |
| 1605–1627 | 16 | 33 | 25 | 25 |
| 1627–1650 | 23 | 64 | 68 | 26 |

The reasons for the capital's appeal to governors included the same inducements that attracted other nobles: the role of Paris as a marriage market, and a center for credit sources and civil litigation, the cultural attractions of the royal court, and the competition for the *bienfaits* of the royal gift. The new career orientations of the seventeenth century gave governors a different kind of influence in their regions. Most of the powerful courtiers and ministers of Louis XIII and Louis XIV were governors. Much more exclusively than in the sixteenth century, the local power of the governors of the seventeenth resulted from their influence over policies of the central government and over royal patronage.

Sully, for example, rarely visited his governorship of Poitou; yet he exercised enormous influence over the many Protestants there and did so in a way that was highly functional to the monarchy. For, as Henri IV told him, "through your mediation will pass all the gratifications [the Huguenots of Poitou] will get from me, and you will make them understand my good intentions . . . never failing to maintain equality of affections, favors, and *bienfaits*, but distributing them according to worth and services."[111] Similarly the famous generals and courtiers Henri II de Condé and Louis II de Condé rarely visited their governorship of Burgundy; yet as a Dijon *parlementaire* wrote in 1650:

No one had acquired any office in the Parlement or any other jurisdiction except through [Louis II de] Condé's mediation or that of his father. No one had ever been provided with a benefice but by their nomination. All the officers of the towns, whether mayors, *échevins*, captains, lieutenants, or *enseignes*, had acquired these honors only through the influence of the Condés. In short, Messieurs les Princes, père et fils, had governed Burgundy with total authority for more than twenty years. And there was more. For the people, Condé obtained the cancellation of the doubling of the *taillon* and for the Parlement the cancellation of the two *écus* per *minot* [increase on salt]. And he got letters of nobility for the *conseillers* of the Parlement, thus exempting them from the usual requirement of three generations of office-holding for the nobility.[112]

If not "total authority," the governors of the absolutist State exercised great authority, their general absenteeism notwithstanding. Certainly it was a different kind of authority from that enjoyed by their fifteenth- and sixteenth-century predecessors. It resulted from the solidarity of the State and the aristocracy. As brokers between local elites and corporations on the one hand and the court and monarchy on the other, governors were bulwarks of the absolutist State. Very rarely did they try to mobilize their provincial followings against the central government, which in any case was difficult to do.

Were Sully, the Condés, and Richelieu less powerful in their governorships than their predecessors, for example, during the Holy League: Malicorne, Mayenne, and Mercoeur respectively? There may well be no sensible way of answering such a question.

Authority comes in many forms that are difficult to compare. Two things are certain. First, assertions that governors represented "the feudal tradition of independence," "reactionary particularism," or "the political pretensions of the high nobility" are reductionist, and they also prejudge the problem of the social foundations of the absolutist State. Unlike modern administrative posts, governorships imposed no definite functions or role on their holders, who were free to assume the various careers open to any sword nobleman—courtier, royal councilor, army officer, ecclesiastic, seigneur, religious party leader, regional political boss, and so forth. Their regimes and subjects' experience of them varied dramatically depending upon which of these roles or which combination of them a governor opted for, and that decision was largely (not entirely) voluntary. The historian can trace the general transformation of roles over time and analyze the forces that brought it about, but as soon as it appears that governors' power has declined in some way, new sources and new forms of power appear.

The second certainty is that as governors absented themselves from the local scene, their actual day-to-day involvement in administration waned. A variety of arguments are widespread in historical literature which point to a "policy" of the absolutist State to weaken the governors as the commissars assumed ever-larger administrative roles. It is rarely argued that the State prohibited governors from certain activities, for it is well known that governors' letters of commission were intentionally ambiguous and contained elastic clauses that conferred a generalized delegation of royal authority: "We charge you to do all that is necessary for our service," or "all that we would do ourselves and would have done if we were present there in person." Most arguments claim that the State weakened governors through "policies" of recruitment and promotion to the charges.

It is often claimed, for example, that Richelieu and Louis XIII replaced governors often, keeping their tenures short.[113] It is believed that the absolutist State prevented pluralism of governorships and prevented major governors from filling subordinate governorships or from enjoying close relatives in such charges.[114] Also widespread is the idea that the absolutist State broke up hereditary succession to governorships.[115] These ideas appeared in classic works on administrative history in the later nineteenth century and have been repeated ever since. Some more recent theories are more complex. To A. D. Lublinskaya, the early seventeenth century saw the coming of a new nobility of recent bourgeois extraction that was becoming the *"groupe moteur"* of the nobility. While the provincial *gouverneurs* remained *noblesse d'épée* and a "reactionary force" opposed to absolutism and capitalism, the composition of the lieutenants general was changing: "Henri IV always tried to make sure that there was no unanimity between the two chief men in any given region, and in his policy toward the grandees he relied on his own henchmen the lieutenants-general, who were not usually drawn from the *noblesse d'épée*."[116] There is also the influential theory of Gaston Zeller, who depicts the decline of aristocratic governors as the result of a slow, coordinated effort, largely completed in the sixteenth century, by the crown, town councils, and especially the parlements, which used their *arrêts* to usurp administrative functions from governors.[117]

Some of these propositions can, in theory, be tested quantitatively but never have been, partly because accurate lists of governors exist for very few provinces and are difficult to draw up. In table 2, information is presented on average tenure, hereditary succession,[118] and the proportion of governors allowed to hold their charges until death.

*Table 2.* Tenure and succession of governors

|  | I Number of governors appointed | II Average tenure (years) | III Percentage of governors who were heirs of their predecessors | IV Percentage of governors who died in office |
|---|---|---|---|---|
| 1515–1537 | 30 | 9.7 | 23 | 70 |
| 1537–1560 | 22 | 10.6 | 27 | 64 |
| 1560–1582 | 26 | 11.0 | 42 | 50 |
| 1582–1605 | 25 | 11.7 | 40 | 48 |
| 1605–1627 | 16 | 13.9 | 13 | 63 |
| 1627–1650 | 23 | 10.0 | 22 | 39 |
|  | 142 |  |  |  |

The first two periods, from 1515 to 1560, correspond to what may be called the Renaissance State of Francis I and Henri II; the next two periods were the time of troubles, the Wars of Religion and their immediate aftermath; the last two periods witnessed the foundation of the absolutist State. No dramatic changes are revealed in these figures. As column II shows, the average length of tenure in office was actually slightly longer for governors appointed between 1605 and 1650, and the proportion who were allowed to hold their charges until death was slightly higher than in the period from 1560 to 1605 (column IV). Hereditary succession was, in fact, significantly less common under the absolutist

State than during the civil wars (column III). However, the significance of this should not be exaggerated. There is good reason to believe that the appropriation of the charges, the tendency of their holders to think of them as family property, was much greater under absolutism than during the Renaissance. A governor who thought of his charge as his property might try to trade it or sell it, especially if he had no male heir. Only three-quarters of these 142 *gouverneurs* had a son when their tenures ended, and only one-fifth had an adult son (over the age of seventeen). In the Renaissance State, both trading and selling were unheard of. After 1559 the crown began to permit hereditary succession more frequently, both *"par resignation"* and *"en survivance,"* because it did not wish to further weaken local government by breaking up the loyalties and clienteles that formed around governors' houses.

Shortly thereafter, the central government began permitting certain trades. The first known instance involving a major *gouvernement* occurred in 1573 when Gaspard de Saulx-Tavannes traded his *gouvernement* of Provence to Albert de Gondi for that of Metz.[119] Hurault blamed the development of venality on Henri III, "the first king with whom the governors bartered and asked money to leave their charges . . . even those who had always remained loyal."[120] Although it was not until well into Louis XIV's reign that the monarchy started selling governorships to raise revenue,[121] selling by private transaction between two aristocrats was common under Henri IV and Louis XIII. The evidence is difficult to assemble because no public records were kept, but we know that between 1585 and 1648 charges as important as the *gouvernements* of Ile-de-France, Poitou, Berry, Anjou, the *château* of Angers, Amiens, and the citadels of Amiens and Lyons were sold.[122] Many other cases involving lesser posts could be cited. The phenomenon was much decried by various contemporaries,[123] but trading and selling remained commonplace through the end of the *ancien régime,* and so did hereditary succession. If it were not for trading and selling, the figures on hereditary succession would have been higher under absolutism and so would the average tenures and the proportion of governors who held their charges until death.

Pluralism and nepotism were also increasingly common. Absolute statistical precision on these matters is not possible. One cannot be sure, for example, that one knows about every governorship a given governor held. However, reasonable estimates are possible. Of the thirty-seven major *gouverneurs* appointed from 1605 to 1650, at least 70 percent held another governorship simultaneously and at least 30 percent held a governorship within their major government, such as the governorship of an important town. The corresponding figures could not have been as high in the earlier periods; in the Renaissance State (1515–60), the corresponding figures probably did not exceed 40 percent and 20 percent respectively.[124] The impression is also strong that it was increasingly common for members of the same family to monopolize several governorships in the same province or region. This had been rare in the Renaissance, and Richelieu, far from trying to abolish it, worked to provide his own relatives with a dozen subordinate governorships in his own *gouvernement* of Brittany.[125]

One of the preconditions for both of these developments was the sheer multiplication of the number of governorships. Catherine de Medici tried to cope with the revolts of the 1560s by covering the map of France with layers of governors: "that great fruit of the first War of Religion," Pasquier thought, "that has led to so much exploitation and oppression of the people."[126] Not only did every province receive a *gouverneur,* but they gained by the seventeenth century up to six lieutenants general and up to six lieutenants as well, and in 1560–62, these major figures were empowered to install clients as governors in any town or region where they thought it necessary. "There is hardly any little town," Loyseau wrote, "that does not now have its own governor dependent upon the provincial governor. . . . There are almost as many degrees of governors as of justices."[127] Some minor governors lost their charges with the demolition of forts and citadels in interior provinces in the seventeenth century, but there remained hundreds of others, many times as many as the Renaissance State had known. One of the reasons for abandoning the stereotype that governors were innate *frondeurs* is that the few who actually undertook unambiguous rebellions against the central government represented a very tiny fraction of a large power elite.

Nor is there any evidence to support the contention that Henri IV, or any later monarch, tried to alter the social complexion of this power elite. Only two of the lieutenants general appointed by Henri IV in the eleven major provinces were *noblesse de robe.*[128] It is possible to point to a few *robins* in important governorships at all times, but it was always true that the sword had a near monopoly of the charges.

The origins of the commissars cannot be traced to any effort by the State to undermine the aristocratic structure of society or supplant the governors or the patrimonial regimes they upheld in the provinces, nor did governors simply acquiesce out of loyalty to the monarch. When the process is viewed from the perspective of the governors, a very different picture emerges. Their regimes were inherently unstable in a variety of ways; they and the central government together sought an antidote to these weaknesses in the enforcement of public law by the commissars: *"selon les ordonnances"* as their commissions said. For the weaknesses were in areas that were not hitherto regulated by legislation, or were very imperfectly regulated; they were areas where governors had always elicited obedience through a combination of personal loyalty from local elites and traditional loyalty from corporations. In the crisis of the Reformation and its aftermath, these networks of extralegal loyalties were completely inadequate to meet the threat of well-organized revolts and the resistance of elites.

Groping for ways to secure public order, the State tried to strengthen governors by various means, including multiplying their numbers and permitting hereditary succession, especially if an adult male heir existed. The commissars were another means. Some of them were temporary troubleshooters who had little to do with governors; but many others were intended as antidotes to their most critical administrative weaknesses. They re-established uniformity between the execution of the law and the adjudication of violations of the law; they implemented legal sanctions to supplement personal loyalty as the guarantor of military discipline; and they supplemented the governors' authority in winning cooperation from local corporations in the collection of taxes and requisitioning of supplies for troops.

Conflicts in the process were only sporadic, partly because governors monitored and controlled the early development of the commissars. Partly it was because the social tensions that sometimes arose between robe and sword were muted by the fact that, to a surprising extent, the commissars were absorbed into the aristocratic system of private household service, and the two groups had close social and financial relations that centered in Paris and at court. Partly it was because commissars shared with governors a commitment to public order and preservation of the status quo, the "instinctive preference for order" that Tocqueville pointed to. Partly, too, the harmony of the transition was due to the new career orientations of governors in the seventeenth century. Provincial administration was an unpromising way for a nobleman to spend his life compared to foreign wars and the royal court. Yet they and their local connections remained fundamental bulwarks of the absolutist State. It was far better to establish a solid alliance with them than to undermine them.

The protests against the tyranny of governors that were so common in *cahiers* and the writings of legalists like Du Tillet, Pasquier, Leschassier, and Loyseau in the sixteenth and early seventeenth centuries were rarely heard after 1635, when France openly entered the Thirty Years War. The *intendants*, on the other hand, and the highly effective fiscal exploitation they implemented became major grievances of the Fronde of the Parlements. In an effort to defuse the revolt, Mazarin abolished the *intendants* on 18 July 1648 except in six frontier provinces, where they were to be limited to much older roles: "They will not participate in the collection of revenue or other contentious matters; they will only remain near the governors to assist in the execution of their powers."[129] Mazarin was eventually pressed to eliminate even these *intendants*, but the hiatus was short and the restoration was quick. The institution was strong because its creation and development were molded by long-term social and political changes that were permanent and could not be reversed.[130]

## Notes

1. *Democracy in America*, trans. G. Lawrence; ed. J. P. Meyer (Garden City, N.Y., 1969), pp. 264–65.

Since this essay was written in 1974, the arguments have appeared in my book *Anatomy of a Power Elite: The Provincial Governors of Early Modern France* (New Haven and London, 1978). This article contains some information not in the book and serves as a synopsis of the argument in its closing chapters.

2. For the sake of brevity I will use the English word "governor" as an umbrella term for all the agents of the politico-military hierarchy including *gouverneurs*, lieutenants general, and lieutenants of provinces and their subordinates, the *gouverneurs* of towns and regions. Similarly, the English word "commissar" will apply to all the royal agents dispatched to the provinces with titles of *commissaire* or *intendant* of justice, finance, the army, etc. The French terms will be used when precision is desirable.

3. J. Néraud, *Les intendants de la généralité de Berry* (Paris, 1922), p. 15.

4. G. Zeller, "L'Administration monarchique avant les intendants. Parlements et gouverneurs," *Révue historique* 197 (1947): 214.

5. G. Lefebvre, *The Coming of the French Revolution*, trans. R. R. Palmer (Princeton, 1973), p. 17 n. 5.

6. G. Hanotaux, *Origines des intendants des provinces* (Paris, 1884), pp. 56–57.

7. J. Shennan, *Government and Society in France 1461–1661* (London, 1969), pp. 61–62.

8. C. Crozet, *Histoire de Champagne* (Paris, 1933), p. 204.

9. G. R. R. Treasure, *Cardinal Richelieu and the Development of Absolutism* (New York, 1972), p. 170.

10. P. Deyon, "Forces et faiblesses de l'Ancien Régime," in *Histoire de Picardie*, ed. R. Fossier (Toulouse, 1974), p. 313.

11. B. de Monluc, *Commentaires et lettres de Blaise de Monluc*, ed. A. de Ruble, 5 vols. (Paris, 1864–72), 2:119 (unless otherwise noted, all translations mine).

12. H. de Mesmes, *Mémoires*, ed. E. Frémy (Paris, n.d.), p. 127.

13. See B. Porchnev, *Les soulèvements populaires en France de 1623 à 1648* (Paris, 1963), pp. 11–15, 29–44, 538–82; D. Parker, "The Social Foundations of French Absolutism 1610–1630," *Past and Present* (1972): 67–89; and P. Anderson, *Lineages of the Absolutist State* (London, 1974), which includes in chap. 1 a survey of Marxist scholarship on the class basis of absolutism.

14. O. Ranum, "Richelieu and the Great Nobility: Some Attributes of Early Modern Political Motives," *French Historical Studies* 3 (1968): 184–204; see pp. 202–3. R. Mousnier, "Les rapports entre les gouverneurs de province et les

intendants dans la première moitié du XVIIe siècle," in *La plume, la faucille et le marteau* (Paris, 1970), pp. 201–13 (reprinted from *Révue historique* 228 [1962]).

15. In addition to J. Néraud, *Intendants de la généralité de Berry*, see F. Garrisson, *Essai sur les commissions d'application de l'édit de Nantes* (Montpellier, 1964), pp. 43, 47; A. Barbier, "Les intendants de province et les commissaires royaux en Poitou de Henri III à Louis XIV," *Mémoires de la Société des antiquaires de l'Ouest*, 2d ser., 26 (1902): 319; F. Astre, "Les intendants de Languedoc," *Mémoires de l'Académie des sciences et belles lettres de Toulouse*, 5th ser., 3 (1859): 11.

16. B. N. *Imprimés*, F23610 (189), edict of Aug. 1553; E. Esmonin, *Études sur la France des XVIIe et XVIIe siècles* (Paris, 1964), p. 14; R. Doucet, *Les institutions de la France au XVIe siecle*, 2 vols. (Paris, 1948), 1:425–26.

17. B.N. FF [fonds francais] 32785–32786, anon., "Histoire des maîtres des requêtes depuis 1575," passim. On this key genealogical and biographical source, see R. Mousnier's introduction to *Lettres et mémoires adressés au chancelier Séquier (1633–1649)*, 2 vols. (Paris, 1964), 1:51–52; this latter source will henceforth be abbreviated *L.M.S.*

18. See F. Spooner, *L'économie mondiale et les frappes monétaires en France 1493–1680* (Paris, 1956), pp. 146–52.

19. Esmonin, *Études*, p. 25.

20. *L.M.S.*, 1:45.

21. François-André Isambert, et al., eds., *Recueil général des anciennes lois françaises*, 29 vols. (Paris, 1821–33), 16:250.

22. On his genealogy see B.N. FF 32785, pp. 230–33; and L. Moreri, *Le grand dictionnaire historique*, 10 vols. (Paris, 1759), 7:257–58. On his service to Damville see the letters and instructions to Marion in B.N. FF 3324, fols. 45, 46; FF 3420, fol. 18, and C. Devic and J. Vaisette, *Histoire de Languedoc*, (henceforth *H.L.*), vol. 12 (documents) (Toulouse, 1889), cols. 1170–71 (1576). On his service as *intendant* see *H.L.*, 11:859, 870, 875, 891, and F. Astre, "Intendants de Languedoc," pp. 14–15. Simon was also called "Miles," but the "Miles Marion" who twice served as commissar to Languedoc under Henri IV was probably his son, whose missions are described in D. Buisseret, "A Stage in the Development of the French Intendants: the Reign of Henri IV," *Historical Journal* 9 (1966): 34–35.

23. A.N. Y 139, fol. 339, donation of 20 Dec. 1600.

24. On Antoine's service under Epernon in 1586, see his speeches to the Parlement of Aix and the provincial estates in B.N. Dupuy 246, fols. 63ff. and Dupuy 313, fols. 19ff. His activities as a financial agent for Epernon turn up in the death inventory of Epernon's son, Bernard: Minutier centrale (M.C.) XXXV 246 (18 July 1642). See also R. Kerviler, *Le Chancelier Pierre Séguier* (Paris, 1874), p. 8.

25. See Mousnier's introduction to *L.M.S.*, 1:32, and Séguier's commission as "*intendant* of justice, police and finances in the army," printed in Hanotaux, *Origines*, pp. 248–50.

26. G. Girard, *Histoire de la vie du duc d'Espernon* (Paris, 1655), pp. 449–50, cited by N. Fessenden, "Epernon and Guyenne: Provincial Politics under Louis XIII," (Ph.D. diss.; Columbia University, 1968).

27. See, for example, Verthamon to Bernard de La Valette, 6 Dec. 1637, "I will seek any occasion to prove that I am *fidèlement*, Monseigneur, your very obedient and obliged servant" *Archives historiques de la Gironde*, 58 vols. (Bordeaux, 1859–1932), 24:386. See also M.C. XXXV 246 (18 July 1642), Bernard's death inventory, where Verthamon appears as a family lawyer.

28. Quoted from an undescribed manuscript by G. d'Avenel, *Richelieu et la monarchie absolue*, 4 vols. (Paris, 1884), 4:210. D'Aubray's commission is printed in Hanotaux, *Origines*, pp. 295–302.

29. Possible candidates are Edouard Molé, who is known to have been a household officer of Damville after service as an *intendant* in Languedoc, and Jacques II de Vignier and his son, Nicolas, who served respectively as *intendants* in Guyenne (n. 1608) and Lorraine (n. 1640). Both provinces were governed by princes de Condé, and Jacques is known to have been Condé's "*surintendant de la maison*" from 1617 to 1631. On Molé see Damville's will, B.N. FF 4507, fols. 191–96. On Vignier's service to Condé see M.C. VIII 594 (16 Sept. 1617); XXIX 170

(26 Feb. 1619); XXVI R51 (3 Jan. 1626 and 11 Mar. 1626); XXVI R53 (25 May 1628).

30. M.C. VIII, 78 (2 June 1551) and Abbé de Marolles, *Inventaire des titres de Nevers*, ed. J. Soultrait (Nevers, 1873), col. 410 (1551). (Henceforth cited as *Inventaire Nevers*.)

31. B.N. FF 5121, fols. 121–26, 26 Oct. 1561, will of François de Cleves; B.N. FF 4682, fol. 79, *arrêt* of the *conseil privé*, 16 May 1564. On his mission as executor for Jacques de Cleves, see also Catherine de Médicis to C. de Lamoignon and Pierre de Séguier, 26 June, 1564, where she speaks of their "good and worthy services" to the Nevers as "old servants," in H. de La Ferrière, ed., *Lettres de Catherine de Médicis*, 10 vols. (Paris, 1880–1909), 2:198. (Henceforth cited as *L.C.M.*)

32. M.C. VIII 78 (2 June 1551), gift of seigneurie of Launoy-Courson from François de Cleves; M.C. VIII 92 (17 Jan. 1564), gift of 6,000 l. from Henriette de Cleves to Lamoignon's adolescent son, Charles; M.C. VIII 88 (30 July 1561), gift of 100 l. *rente* from Cleves to Charles's son, Pierre.

33. On Chandon's service see *Inventaire Nevers*, col. 382 (1574) and col. 479 (1584); and J. Chandon, *Discours des droits appartenans à la maison de Nevers es duché de Brabant, Limbourg et ville d'Anvers* (Paris, 1581). His commission as commissar to Lyonnais is printed in M. Pallasse, *La sénéchaussée et siège présidial de Lyon pendant les guerres de religion* (Lyon, 1943), pp. 440–44 (9 Sept. 1579). See also his oath of hommage to Nevers in *Inventaire Nevers*, col. 189; Nevers' acquisition of the office of *maître des requêtes* for Chandon is mentioned in B.N. FF 3411, fols. 194–95.

34. A.N. 115 AP1 doc. 263, 14 Feb. 1602. Jérome had also been in the service of the previous duke of Nevers; see his letters to Louis de Gonzague in B.N. FF 3614, fols. 113, 135, 137; FF 4715, fol. 44, and FF 4716, fol. 35 (all 1589).

35. On François II's early service to the Nevers, see B.N. FF 4684, fols. 45ff. and FF 4682, fols. 93ff., and *Inventaire Nevers*, col. 347 (21 June 1565).

36. On François' service as *"intendant"* of Nevers' household, see A.N. 115 AP1 docs. 239, 240. On his loans to Nevers, totaling over 23,000 l. by constitution of *rentes*, see his *partage* inventory in A.N. 115 AP1 245. On his indebtedness to Nevers for the two offices, see the *placets* in B.N. FF 3386, fol. 2 (2 Nov. 1578) and FF 3617, fol. 27 (28 Feb. 1592).

37. On Jacques' service as *"intendant"* of Nevers' household and later as *"conseiller* and *bailli"* of Mantua, see A.N. 115 AP1 257, 277 (1600–1606). He was also a creditor of Charles I de Gonzague-Nevers; see the inventory of his papers in A.N. 115 AP2 363 (29 Aug. 1622). On François III's service as "chief lawyer and council" to Marie de Gonzague, after the failure of the Gonzague male line, see e.g. M.C. LXXIII 356 (12 Mar. 1640) and 358 (21 July 1640).

38. Moreri, *Dictionnaire historique*, 7:728. Moreover, François de Montholon, *"intendant des affaires"* of Nevers in the 1590s, had by the early seventeenth century assumed an identical charge for the duke of Montpensier (A.N. 115 AP1 docs. 294, 295). Jérome's son, Guillaume, who was twice an intendant from 1607 to 1619, was probably in the service of Philippe du Plessis de Mornay, to whom he declared his "perfect *amitié*." See P. du Plessis de Mornay, *Mémoires*, 4 vols. (Amsterdam, 1652), 3:1177–78 and 4:116, 149, 153, 155, 174, for their correspondence. On his intendancy in Lyonnais see the *arrêts* of 1607–9 in N. Valois, ed. *Inventaire des arrêts du conseil d'Etat (règne de Henri IV)*, 2 vols. (Paris, 1886, 1893), 2, nos. 11746, 12385, 14258. This source will henceforth be cited as Valois, *Inventaire*.

39. On their service to house of Navarre see H. de Mesmes, *Mémoires*, pp. 131–32, 182–84, 209, and the introduction; and M.C. VIII 370 (7 Feb. 1567); and L. Moreri, *Dictionnaire historique*, 7:494. On their service to Nevers see especially B.N. Dupuy 570, fols. 184ff., the will of Charles de Gonzague (1634).

40. B.N. FF 32785, "Histoire des maîtres des requêtes," pp. 373–76, 418.

41. Pierre I de Séguier was "principal lawyer and *conseil*" of the duchess of Nevers in the 1540s (mentioned in M.C. VIII 90, 7 Feb. 1563). He loaned her 12,000 l. in 1542 and received the *seigneurie* of Sorel and other lands in reimbursement for this and seven years' arrears in *rente* payments in 1549 (M.C. VIII 76, 29 Aug. 1549). He often cooperated with Lamoignon in Nevers family business in the

1560s; in 1567 he received Saint Brisson and other lands in Guyenne from Henriette de Cleves, partly in foreclosure of a 15,000 l. 1561 loan and partly as a gift in recompense for services to three generations of Nevers (M.C. VIII 94, 8 April 1567). He was still in the Nevers' service in 1573 (*Inventaire Nevers*, col. 557), and the death inventories of his sons Pierre II and François show gifts from the Nevers in recompense for services and loans to them (M.C. VIII 117, Apr. 1572 and LXXVII 164, 2 May 1602).

42. Christophe de Thou owed his *seigneurie* of Stains to his service to Anne de Montmorency, and Jacques-Auguste was able to acquire his presidency of the Parlement by resignation from his uncle through the intercession of Anne de Joyeuse (A.N. Y 91, fol. 27, gift of 23 July 1545 and B.N. FF 18617, P. Dupuy, "Les commentaires ou mémoires de la vie du . . . Jacques Auguste de Thou," fols. 188–90). On other ties of this family, see fols. 59, 170, 178, 200, 257 of Dupuy's "Commentaires."

43. B.N. FF 3411, fols. 194–95, a list of Nevers' creditors (1588).

44. Reported in J.-A. de Thou, *Mémoires*, ed. Joseph Michaud and J.J.F. Poujoulat (Paris, 1857), p. 303.

45. P. de L'Estoile, *Mémoires-journaux de Pierre de L'Estoile*, 12 vols. (Paris, 1875–96), 3:190–91. For a similar example see ibid., 2:15–16.

46. B.N. FF 18617, P. Dupuy, "Commentaires," fol. 178.

47. L. Moreri, *Dictionnaire historique*, 6:114–15. There are dozens of other examples of aristocrats who served as godparents for the children of their lawyers and agents in B.N. Clairambault 987, extracts from the parish registers of St. André des Arts.

48. C. Loyseau, *Les Oeuvres* . . . , ed. C. Joly (Paris, 1616), pp. 345–48; E. Pasquier, *Oeuvres*, 2 vols. (Paris, 1723), 2: cols. 448 and 1131; J. Leschassier, *La maladie de la France* (Paris, 1606).

49. B.N. FF 15903, fol. 115, Truchon to Bellièvre, Beaucaire, 15 July 1574.

50. F. de Montholon, "Remonstrance faicte . . . en l'assemblée des États" (Paris, 1588), p. 16. B.N. Le¹4.

51. There are many published commissions in Hanotaux, *Origines*, appendix; *L.M.S.*, 2, appendix II; M. Pallasse, *Sénéchaussée et siège présidial*, pp. 419ff.; and H. d'Arbois de Jubainville, *L'administration des intendants d'après les archives de l'Aube* (Paris, 1880), pp. 194ff.

52. For several examples of these letters, see *Recueil des lettres missives de Henri IV*, ed. Berger de Xivrey and J. Gaudet, 9 vols. (Paris, 1872–83), 4:122, 618, 864; 9:240, 243. (Henceforth cited as *Lettres Henri IV*.)

53. Joyeuse to Catherine of Medici, 10 June 1561, *H.L.*, 12:582–83.

54. Joyeuse to Montmorency, 17 Sept. 1561, *H.L.*, 12:583.

55. Tende to Catherine of Medici, 2 May 1562, printed in A. Lublinskaya, ed. *Dokumenty po istorii grazhdanskikh voin vo Frantsii* (Moscow, 1962). The Russian title is translated into French on the frontispiece as *Documents pour servir à l'histoire des guerres civiles en France* and will henceforth be abbreviated *D.G.C.* Tende's letter appears as document no. 15.

56. E. Gaullieur, *Histoire de la reformation à Bordeaux et dans le ressort du parlement de Guyenne*, 2 vols. (Paris, 1884), 1:327–30.

57. Instruction of Etampes to d'Avenel, 21 July 1562, *D.G.C.*, no. 38.

58. Etampes to Charles IX, 23 May 1562, *D.G.C.*, no. 22.

59. Edict of 18 June 1563, in A. de Fontanon, ed., *Les édicts et ordonnances des rois de France*, 4 vols. (Paris, 1611), 4:274–76.

60. Edict of 14 Dec. 1563 in Fontanon, *Édicts*, 4:277. For a published account of activities of these agents, see that in M. Pallasse, *Sénéchaussée et siège présidial*, pp. 286–90 on Michel Quelin and Gabriel Myron [Miron] in Lyonnais in 1563–64.

61. The general commission creating commissars in 1579 is in B.N. FF 4014, fol. 253; that of 1582 is in G. Hanotaux, *Origines*, pp. 199–218, along with the standardized letter of commission for each agent, pp. 187–98. The commissars of the edict of Nantes have been thoroughly studied by Garrisson, *Sur les commissions*.

62. Garrisson, *Sur les commissions*, pp. 46, 52. Garrisson makes the seem-

ingly contradictory judgment that the provision of commissars with authority to decide where Protestants could worship "lost its efficacy" because of the stipulations that the commissars cooperate with governors (pp. 43–44).

63. See the instructions to Tavannes, Nevers, Montpensier, Etampes, Damville, and Gordes in N. Valois, ed., "Extraits des registres du Conseil de Charles IX relatifs à l'histoire des troubles de religion," in *Le Conseil du roi aux XIVe, XVe et XVIe siècles*. (Paris, 1884), pp. 334, 335, 339, 342, 340, 350–51, 353. This source will henceforth be cited as Valois, "Extraits." For Tavannes' enforcement in Burgundy see also B.N. FF 4048, fols. 2–191, "Recueil de pièces relatives principalement aux protestants . . . durant le gouvernement de . . . Tavannes" (1561–70).

64. L. Ménard, *Histoire civile, ecclésiastique et littéraire de la ville de Nimes avec texte et notes. . .* , 7 vols. (Paris, 1873–75), 4:370–71, 374–75; 5:7–8.

65. *H.L.*, 12: cols. 738–42 and B.N. Languedoc 92, fol. 77ff., remonstrances of the Protestants of Languedoc (1563).

66. These were the *maîtres des requêtes*, Saint-Père and Reynaud de Beaune, canon of N. D. de Paris. See the *arrêts* in Valois, "Extraits," pp. 353–56.

67. Catherine to Damville, Mar. 1564, and Damville to Anne de Montmorency, Mar. 1564, in *L.C.M.*, 2:160–61 and n. 1; Damville to Charles IX, 30 Mar. 1564 in *H.L.*, 12: cols. 746–47.

68. Catherine to Damville, 22 Oct. 1563 in *L.C.M.*, 2:107.

69. Joyeuse to Catherine, 6 Aug. 1566 in G. de Joyeuse, *Correspondance inédite*, ed. E. de Barthélemy (Paris, 1876), p. 55: "I turn over prisoners to the commissars that Your Majesties have ordered for making punishment."

70. For the commission and various other documents pertaining to the mission of Villeneuve in Toulouse, see *H.L.*, 12: cols. 758–78 (1563–64). On the activities of two later commissars in Toulouse (1565) and the commissars at Pamiers and elsewhere, see Valois, "Extraits," pp. 354, 357, 370–72.

71. *H.L.*, 11:541.

72. Pallasse, *Sénéchaussée et siège présidial*, pp. 295–303.

73. See "Advertissement des crimes horribles commis par les séditieux Catholiques Romains au pays et comté du Maine" (May 1565) in *Mémoires de Condé*, ed. D. Secause, 6 vols. (London, 1743–45), 5: "Miron is the reason why the authority of His Majesty and the justice of His commissions are held in contempt in this province" (pp. 310–11; see also pp. 302–4, 325).

74. Monluc to Charles IX, 18 Mar. 1562, in Monluc, *Commentaires et lettres*, 4:128, and see 2:369.

75. Valois, "Extraits," p. 346; and see Coligny to Catherine, 29 July 1568, and Catherine to Coligny, Aug. 1568, *L.C.M.*, 3:163–64.

76. *L.C.M.*, 3:164n. "We have seen *maîtres des requêtes* at Auxerre. What do they do? Nothing!"

77. Hanotaux, *Origines*, pp. 55–60; R. Doucet, *Institutions de la France*, 1:432–33.

78. See Henri IV to Ornano, July 1594, *Lettres Henri IV*, 9:398–99.

79. See Henri IV to the *consuls* etc. of Lyon, 11 May 1594 in *Lettres Henri IV*, 4:148–50, where the king informs the town that Ornano will stay, and the governorship will be left vacant. It was vacant because the previous *gouverneur*, Charles de Savoie-Nemours, was a *ligueur* and imprisoned in a revolt in September 1593.

80. Pallasse, *Sénéchaussée et siège présidial*, p. 295.

81. Saint Garan to Séguier, 21 July 1640 in Porchnev, *Soulèvements populaires*, appendix, pp. 606–7. See also pp. 195n. and 197, where mention is made of similar requests by Saint Garan on 4 July and 28 July 1640. See also Saint Garan to Séguier, 11 Aug. 1640, *L.M.S.*, 1:457–58.

82. For background on the *compagnies* the only treatments are Doucet, *Institutions de la France*, 2:620–28 and the preface by T. Courtaux to F. Vindry, *Dictionnaire de l'Etat majeur*, 2 vols. (Paris, 1901), pp. x–xxiii. That most of the noblemen in the companies came from within the governors' governorships was determined by research in the muster rolls (*montres*), which, after 1568, list the residence of each soldier. For example, between 75 percent and 100 percent of the

troops under Gaspard de Saulx-Tavannes in Burgundy, Honorat de Tende in Provence, Henri de Guise in Champagne, and Mayenne in Burgundy, came from within their governments (see B.N. FF 21532, fols. 2034, 2055, 2054, and FF 21528, fol. 1890 for the four *montres*, all 1568–71).

83. For example, men rose through Gaspard de Saulx-Tavannes' company to become governors of Dijon, Macon, Chalon, Verdun, Toul, Auxonne, Beaune, and other towns. Two became lieutenants general of Burgundy. See both volumes of F. Vindry, *Dictionnaire*, under "Saulx-Tavannes."

84. F. de La Noue, *Discours politiques et militaires*, ed. F. Sutcliffe (Geneva, 1961), p. 257.

85. Ordinance of 1 Feb. 1574 in Fontanon, *Édicts*, 3:111–22; see preamble.

86. See ibid., pp. 105–44, edicts of 1566, 1567, 1568, 1570, 1574, 1579, 1580, Jan. 1584, Feb. 1584, and 1585.

87. *Recueil des cahiers généraux des trois ordres aux états généraux*, ed. Lalourcé and Duval, 4 vols. (Paris, 1789), 2 (1576): 286–94 (arts. 267–88); quotations are from pp. 286, 287, 294. For 1588, see ibid., 3:55–57, 150–53, 226–28.

88. A. de Communay, ed., "Abrégé de l'estat militaire de la France en l'année 1562," *Revue de l'Agenais*, 21 (1894): 384–91; A.M. Agen EE7, royal ordinance of 22 Sept. 1571; Fontanon, *Edicts*, 3:139–40, ordinance of 9 Mar. 1585. La Noue's figures (*Discours*, pp. 298–301 and notes) also show the decline of the *gendarmerie* but are evidently impressionistic and not consistent with the royal ordinances.

89. As early as 1563 the commissars of pacification were charged with these functions; see the edict of 18 June 1563. For examples of their actual involvement in military discipline matters see Valois, "Extraits," pp. 333, 336, 349, 362.

90. Hanotaux, *Origines*, pp. 37–50.

91. A phrase from Miron's commission (23 Aug. 1601), which is copied at the start of his *procès verbal* on the mission in B.N. FF 10470, fols. 1–110. This account depicts Miron's continual cooperation with the governors of Metz and Verdun. See also Miron's correspondence on this mission in B.N. FF 15899, fols. 425–39 (1602).

92. See, for examples, the standardized commission "pour l'intendance de la justice en une armée" from the reign of Henri IV and seven individual commissions of military commissars printed in Hanotaux, *Origines*, pp. 227–28, 248–50, 256–58, 279–81, 292–94, 303–6, 313–15, 322–26; and Gobelin's commission (10 Aug. 1636) in *L.M.S.*, 2:1047–49.

93. Etampes to Catherine and to Antoine de Bourbon, Nantes, 29 July 1562, *D.G.C.*, nos. 43 and 44.

94. Ventadour to Séguier, Limoges, 24 July 1637, *L.M.S.*, 1:410–11.

95. For example, in justifying a lavish *entrée* for their governor, the town council of Aix decided in 1544 "to make a great show recognizing all that he can do for the town" (A.M. Aix BB 44, fol. 34). For the same purpose the town council of Lyon pointed out in 1550 that their governor "has great access and power with the king and the lords of his council and can do much for the town: in obtaining exemption from the *solde* of troops that the king is now requesting from the town, in the matter of the *aide* on the wine and the subsidy on merchandise entering the town and in securing prompt repayment of the great sums [the king] owes this town" (A.M. Lyon BB 71, fols. 180–81).

96. Catherine to Damville, 13 May·1572, B.N. FF 3245, fol. 64. Truchon was a president of the Parlement of Grenoble. In the 1550s, he had been Guise's chief agent in his governorship of Dauphiné, but in the 1570s, he was, like his relative, Bellièvre, a protégé of the powerful courtier, Jean Morvillier.

97. A.D. Herault B22,214, unpaginated accounts of supplies (*vivres*) from the *Cour des comptes, aides et finances* at Montpellier (1573).

98. A.M. Montpellier AA9, fol. 557 and *H.L.*, 12:1088–97.

99. On Vicose's service under Matignon see Valois, *Inventaire*, 2: no. 9214, *arrêt* of 29 Mar. 1605, and Buisseret, "Development of the French Intendants," pp. 28–30.

100. Valois, *Inventaire*, 2: nos. 12583, 12623, *arrêts* of 30 Sept. 1608.

101. B.N. Brienne 7180, fol. 139, "Commission aux gouverneurs des provinces pour se joindre avec les commissaires envoyés aux dites provinces . . ." May 1599.

102. *Recueil des cahiers généraux,* 4:200–201.

103. Various sections of this remonstrance are cited by several historians; the first was apparently A. Cheruel, *Histoire de l'administration monarchique en France,* 2 vols. (Paris, 1855), 1:292–93.

104. The standardized commission for the commissars of *règlement des tailles* (B.N. FF 17311, fols. 27–32, 27 Aug. 1598) makes no mention of the governors. On the nature of Sully's reforms see Sully, *Mémoires,* ed. Joseph Michaud and J. J. F. Poujoulat (Paris, 1857), pp. 228–56, 290–305.

105. See Mousnier, "Etat et commissaire. Récherches sur la création des intendants des provinces (1634–1648)," first published in 1958 and reprinted in *La plume, la faucille et le marteau,* pp. 178–99. Arguing against Hanotaux, who minimized the importance of reforms in the intendancy in the 1630s, Mousnier shows that only then did the *intendant* change "from a reforming inspector to become an administrator," permanently installed in every generality.

106. Barbier, "Intendants de province," p. 433.

107. A.M. Châlons-sur-Marne, BB21, fol. 262 (July 1641).

108. B.N. Clairambault 950, fols. 156–59; edict of February 1692.

109. The eleven major *gouvernements* were the ones continuously occupied since the start of the sixteenth century, and all but one were on the frontier. They were: Brittany, Normandy, Picardie, Champagne, Burgundy, Lyonnais, Dauphiné, Provence, Languedoc, Guyenne, and Ile-de-France. Artois was normally attached to the *gouvernement* of Picardie, Brie to Champagne, Forez and Beaujolais to Lyonnais, and Gascony to Guyenne. Men who were appointed *gouverneur* during the absence or minority of someone else are not counted. See 130 below.

110. The proportions represented in the table are proportions of samples rather than of the total, because it was not possible to determine where every governor was born, died, and was buried. The samples are, however, large. Of the 142 governors, birthplaces are known for 110 (77 percent), death places for 133 (94 percent), and burial places for 126 (89 percent). In the case of burials, some governors ordered their hearts and sometimes their entrails buried apart from the rest of their bodies. Hence there were some cases calculated as one-third, or one-half, or two-thirds of a burial in Paris.

111. Sully, *Mémoires,* pp. 521–22.

112. M.-A. Millotet, *Mémoire des choses qui se sont passées en Bourgogne depuis 1650 jusqu'à 1668,* ed. C. Muteau, *Analecta divionensia* (Dijon, 1866), pp. 3–4. I owe this reference to Mr. Stuart Johnson, a former student, of Yale University.

113. M. Bordes, *L'administration provinciale et municipale en France au XVIIIe siècle* (Paris, 1972), pp. 25–26; G. Hanotaux, *Histoire du cardinal Richelieu,* 6 vols. (Paris, n.d.), 4:317–19; Treasure, *Cardinal Richelieu,* p. 171; J. Shennan, *Government and Society,* p. 62.

114. D'Avenel, *Richelieu,* 4:126–29.

115. M. Prestwich, "The Making of Absolute Monarchy (1559–1683)," in *France; Government and Society,* ed. J. Wallace-Hadrill and J. McManners (London, 1957), p. 108; Hanotaux, *Histoire du cardinal Richelieu,* 4:317.

116. A. Lublinskaya, *French Absolutism: The Crucial Phase, 1620–1629* (Cambridge, 1968), p. 244; see her theory of the new nobility epitomized in "Les Etats généraux de 1614–15 en France," *Album Helen Maud Cam,* 23 (1960): 213–45.

117. Zeller, "L'Administration monarchique"; Bordes, *Administration provinciale,* pp. 24–25, follows this argument. There is no space here to challenge this argument adequately. What seem to me to be the vulnerable assumptions are, first, Zeller's tendency to think that once parlements intervened in some administrative area, they set an immutable and irreversible precedent, and second, his belief that governors' obvious power in the civil wars was "political power" as distinct from administrative authority. In fact governors reassumed control over

many administrative activities that parlements had intervened in prior to 1560: supervision of municipal elections, grain trade, censorship, town defenses, royal finances, etc.

118. A governor is considered an heir of his predecessor if he was his son, grandson, brother, nephew, brother-in-law, or son-in-law.

119. Daffis to Forquevaux, 9 June 1573, printed with many other letters of Forquevaux in *Annales du Midi*, 5 (1893): 95–96.

120. M. Hurault, *Quatre excellens discours sur l'estat present de France* (Paris, 1593), p. 24 (B.N. 8°La²⁴1).

121. In 1692, 102 provincial *lieutenants* were created as venal officers, and they had already been created in two provinces: Brittany and Normandy. In 1696, *gouverneurs* were created as venal officers for all *villes closes*. See B.N. Clairambault 950, fols. 156–59; edict of Feb. 1692 and the accounts on fols. 181–92 (6 Oct. 1700); and B.N. (*imprimés*) F23616 (154), edict of Aug. 1696.

122. See A. Longnon, "L'Ile-de-France. Son origine, ses limites, ses gouverneurs," *Mém. de la Soc. de l'hist. de Paris et de L'Ile-de-France* 1 (1875): 41–42; Sully, *Mémoires*, p. 523; D'Estrées, *Mémoires*, p. 411; F. du Val, *Mémoires*, pp. 105, 139; Richelieu, *Mémoires*, 1: p. 253; F. du Val, *Mémoires*, p. 66; and A. Péricaud, *Notes et documents pour servir à l'histoire de Lyon*, p. 106, at year 1585 (B.N. Rés. Lk⁷ 4335). All memoirs cited are the Joseph Michaud and J.J.F. Poujoulat editions.

123. B.N. FF 4810, fols. 67–83, anon., "Advis au Roy pour le changement de tous les gouverneurs généraux et particuliers de province et places fortes de France" (n.p., 1626); J. Leschassier, *Maladie de la France*; C. Loyseau, *Les Oeuvres*; R. Miron, *Harangue faicte au roy*, pp. 44–45; M. Molé, *Mémoires*, ed. Aimé Louis Champollion-Figéac, 3 vols. (Paris, 1844), 1:35; *Recueil des cahiers généraux*, 4:89, 188–89, 307.

124. It was usual throughout this period for *gouverneurs* of major provinces to have the title "lieutenant general," while other agents held only the title of "lieutenant general." This is not counted as pluralism in these calculations.

125. Richelieu's first cousin, Charles II de la Porte (his mother's nephew) received the governorships of the town and citadel of Nantes, of Port-Louis, and of Brest, a lieutenant-general post of Brittany, and the *survivance* to the provincial *gouvernement*. Charles' father-in-law, François de Cossé, became lieutenant general of Brittany and governor of Hennebon, Quinperle, and, for a time, Port-Louis. Richelieu's nephew, François de Vignerot, gained the *survivance* to three of Richelieu's other governorships: those of the town and citadel of Havre and the *bailliage* of Caux in Normandy.

126. E. Pasquier, *Oeuvres*, 2: col. 1131.

127. C. Loyseau, *Les Oeuvres*, p. 345.

128. Two first presidents of the Parlement of Grenoble were appointed lieutenants general of Dauphiné in 1590 and 1592. In 1598 the post went back to a sword nobleman, Lesdiguières himself. Charles de Neufville-Villeroy, lieutenant general of Lyonnais, is a debatable case; he pursued a military career but had robe parentage. He became *gouverneur* of Lyonnais in 1612.

129. Declaration of 18 July 1648 in O. Talon, *Mémoires*, ed. Joseph Michaud and J. J. F. Poujoulat (Paris, 1857), pp. 250–52.

130. Since this essay was written, two fine books have appeared with chapters on the governors under Richelieu and Mazarin: Richard Bonney, *Political Change in France under Richelieu and Mazarin, 1624–1661* (Oxford, 1978), chap. 13; and Sharon Kettering, *Judicial Politics and Urban Revolt in Seventeenth-Century France: The Parlement of Aix, 1629–1659* (Princeton, 1978), chap. 4. In discussing the relations between governors on the one hand, and *intendants* and Richelieu on the other, both books put the emphasis on conflict rather than on cooperation. The difficulties and real ambiguities in determining who held certain governorships may be illustrated by several differences between my findings and those of Richard Bonney. Bonney (pp. 292, 293) considers d'Enghien to have been the governor of Burgundy in 1643 although he held this title only "during the absence" of his father, Condé, whom I consider the governor (Harding, *Anatomy*

of a Power Elite, p. 221). Bonney (p. 287) considers d'Elboeuf the governor of Picardie until 1633, although he points out that the charge had been "temporarily" transferred to Chevreuse in 1631. On the basis of the provisions in A.D. Somme I B 20, fol. 69, I see no reason why Chevreuse should not be considered the governor from 1631 to 1633 (Harding, p. 226). We also disagree on whether d'Elboeuf was restored in 1644 (Bonney, p. 293) or 1643 (Harding, p. 227, on the basis of A.D. Somme I B 24, fol. 27); on whether Condé became governor or lieutenant general of Guyenne in 1638 (Bonney, pp. 289–90, 292; Harding, pp. 223, 289, n. 13); and on whether Conti became governor of Champagne in 1644 or 1647. I consider Conti's brother, d'Enghien, to have been governor from 1644 to 1647 (Bonney, p. 293; Harding, p. 222; see M. Poinsignon, *Histoire de la Champagne et de la Brie*, 3 vols., 3d ed. [Paris, 1974], 3:149 and sources cited).

# The Journal
# of the House of Lords
# for the Long Parliament

## ELIZABETH READ FOSTER

*The Moving Finger writes; and, having writ*
*Moves on: nor all your Piety nor Wit*
*Shall lure it back to cancel half a Line*
*Nor all your Tears wash out a Word of it.*
The Rubaiyat

The record of the House of Lords during the years 1640–49 has been sadly and shockingly mutilated. King and parliament after the return of Charles II officially forgot or "put in utter oblivion" certain events of the reign of Charles I and of the years since his death.[1] The House of Lords went further and altered the record of what had happened.

The clerk of the parliaments, John Browne, had kept a record in three ways. He compiled a parliament roll for the regnal year 16 *Car.* I;[2] he arranged for the preparation of books of orders and ordinances, warrants and judgments;[3] and he roughed out a journal of the proceedings of the House of Lords.[4] Browne's parliament roll was a straightforward transcript of public acts, essentially a statute roll. His books of orders and ordinances, warrants and judgments, registered the orders and judgments of the upper

House, and the orders and ordinances of both Houses until 8 January 1648/49. It was the journal (3 November 1640–6 February 1648/49), the fullest account of proceedings, which was seriously damaged. The purpose of this essay is to examine the journal in detail, the way it was composed, how the Lords altered it, and why.

The journal of the Long Parliament was not the kind of journal which former clerks, Robert Bowyer (clerk from 1610 to 1621) and Henry Elsyng (clerk from 1621 to 1635), had prepared with care.[5] It was not even in physical appearance "the great parliament book"[6] of the reign of James I, lovingly engrossed on parchment, corrected and verified. The record of the House of Lords in the Long Parliament was made by a clerk of different personality, interests, and experience from those of his predecessors. He worked at a different time, when the House was not only seriously divided but also busy with work of government administration and problems of war, in addition to more familiar judicial and legislative tasks.

Both Bowyer and Elsyng had been Keepers of the Records in the Tower, devoted to the history of parliament, and experienced in its ways. Bowyer had sat as a member in the lower House before becoming clerk in the upper. Elsyng had served as his assistant in the Lords as early as 1614, long before he took over the clerical responsibilities himself. A profound regard for the record infused their work, a regard which sorted nicely with the increasing concern of the lords themselves, who in 1621 had appointed a subcommittee to view the journals. The "great parliament" books were the result—a splendid series of volumes prepared by the clerk from notes taken in the House by himself and his assistants, carefully redrafted later, examined by a committee of lords, recopied on parchment and finally checked once more by the clerk or his assistant.[7]

John Browne, who became clerk in 1638, took over a proud tradition of record keeping and a well-organized parliament office. He could rely on the experience of John Throckmorton, assistant clerk since 1621. However, Browne himself—so far as is known—had never served in any capacity in parliament. He had not Bowyer's familiarity with the king's records, nor Elsyng's training on the floor of the House. A member of the Middle Temple, he was son-in-law to Sir Thomas Crewe, formerly Speaker of the House of Commons, and godson to the Recorder of London. His father had been a Grocer, his uncle a Merchant Taylor. Though he had legal training, he was probably more comfortable with men of business than he would have been with men who studied parliament, either ancient or modern.[8]

John Browne's first parliament (the Short Parliament) met in the spring of 1640. In performing his duties, he sensibly tried to follow the pattern laid down by Bowyer and Elsyng. He made rapid notes, while the House was sitting.[9] These with the addition of other materials he later redrafted into a coherent account, or draft journal, which was checked by the Lords' subcommittee for the journals, whose signatures appear on successive pages.[10] The final version, or original manuscript journal, was engrossed on parchment. Perhaps it was verified by the clerk, but no indication remains that this was so.[11] Browne served his initiation in a difficult parliament. Much was debated, little decided. An experienced man might well have been puzzled what to record, and Browne, who had probably never been on the floor of the House, did not understand what was going on around him nor the kind of notes he should take.[12] He ultimately produced a respectable volume for the parliament—the last of a series in parchment, the last to include the full list of lords summoned, with those present marked "p."[13]

By the time the Long Parliament met in November 1640, John Browne had learned more about his job. He continued to take notes in the House himself, in notebooks or on single sheets.[14] An assistant clerk also continued notes in the House, "minute books," of which an incomplete series has survived.[15] The assistant was responsible for listing lords present,[16] and for registering orders and decisions of the House. He often took down the names of committee members and sometimes also quite a full account of proceedings.[17] John Browne's notes were usually brief. Robert Bowyer, who had originally kept a full diary of debate when a member of the House of Commons, had continued, as clerk of the parliaments, to write down all he could get, for his own use if not for the House. Henry Elsyng had also made full notes. He shared Bowyer's thirst for knowledge of parliaments past and present, and at the beginning of his career as clerk was not sufficiently confident to decide quickly what should be recorded and what should not.[18] John Browne, on the other hand, during the Long Parliament, took down very little more than he actually used in composing his draft.

Only two stages of Browne's narrative for the Long Parliament have survived—his own notes taken while the House was sitting and the account (referred to as the journal or original journal) composed from those notes and the notes of his assistant, an account which corresponds to the draft journal of earlier years. Probably this second stage of Browne's narrative is all that was ever made. It is in paper, written rapidly, with marks of reference in the margin for the assistant who later entered documents at

large. Sometimes these entries have been made in a space provided;[19] often they are grouped together at the end of a day's
proceedings. Sometimes the appropriate documents have simply
been laid in, not recopied. For example, Browne has included the
drafts of ordinances as they came from the House of Commons,
changing the date at the head and crossing off the signature of the
clerk of the Commons. He wrote "Agreed" to indicate the Lords'
vote, and scratched out the phrase "Lords' concurrence."[20] Browne
was busy. He took the quickest way to finish his work. Probably
he completed his narrative promptly, a few days after the proceedings had occurred which it recorded.[21] In the first months of the
Long Parliament, signatures of members of the subcommittee for
the journals appear on Browne's pages at regular intervals.[22] After
June 1641, all traces of work by the subcommittee disappear for a
long time. There is a reference to the subcommittee in March
1643/44 and again in April 1644.[23] Signatures of members of the
subcommittee reappear in the margin of the account of proceedings for November and December 1646 and for January and March
1646/47. The final signatures are beside the account for 21 September 1648.[24] These volumes, composed by Browne from notes
taken in the House and checked at intervals by the lords, are the
volumes so seriously damaged after the Restoration. These are
also the volumes which have been imperfectly edited and printed
as the *Journals of the House of Lords*.[25]

There is some evidence to suggest that in the early years of the
parliament, John Browne intended to make a further version of
the journal, as his predecessors had done. He had made such a
"finished" version for the Short Parliament.[26] He would do so
again in the more leisurely days after 1660, though his copy
would be in paper and not in parchment.[27] A second indication
that a further version was planned may be found in the renumber-
ing of committees in order of precedence, as if to assist a
copyist.[28] Browne has also written numerous directions to the
assistant to whom he delegated the job of transcribing documents
into his journal. "Enter the order which is to be drawn up by the
lords committees." It has been written in above.[29] Symbols or
letters of the alphabet indicate where documents should be entered. These directions remain in the journal even after the proper
entries have been made, and have not been deleted as one would
expect in a finished version.[30]

A third indication that yet another version was planned is the
matter of the "presents," or record of attendance. Registration of
attendance had always been an important function of the journal.
Attendance during the Long Parliament was kept regularly, as it
had been before, by the assistant clerk in the House, the excuses

of absent lords being sometimes noted by John Browne, sometimes by his assistant.[31] From 6 November 1640 to 21 September 1643, the "presents" has not, however, been transferred from the assistant's minute book to the next stage of the journal. The clerk had neglected to add these data from the minute book to his own notes when he made up the draft examined by the Lords' subcommittee.[32] Did both he and the lords assume that this would be done later in the usual "finished" version? After September 1643, the examining subcommittee had apparently temporarily ceased its work. Browne, being a realist, had by this time probably come to recognize that there might never be another, more finished version, and he incorporated the "presents" in his draft.

From 22 September 1643,[33] the "presents" appears fairly regularly in the journal until the journal itself comes to an end in February 1649. The "presents" is not a complete list of those summoned, marked "p.", but a list of those actually in the House on a given day. Doubtless, since attendance was low, this was a more practical way to keep the record. Even the strict order of precedence (formerly greatly prized) has been abandoned.[34]

The omission of the "presents" is a useful indication that yet another version of the journal may have been contemplated in the first years of the Long Parliament. It is not, however, conclusive. Even so careful a clerk as Henry Elsyng in the relatively peaceful times of the 1620s had occasionally forgotten to transfer the "presents" from his assistant's book to his own final version. He included a full list of lords, but did not check off those who were present.[35] The fact that Browne left out the full list and the "presents" for such a long period of time and then incorporated it consistently may be significant. Elsyng made an error. Browne seems to have been following a specific plan, which in 1643 he abandoned.

John Browne's journal for the Long Parliament, whether intended as a draft or as a final version, was, by earlier standards, unfinished. Even after Browne began to include the "presents," he has occasionally omitted it. He neglected to enter the name of the Speaker on certain occasions.[36] He did not record all the readings of ordinances. One must rely on endorsements made on the documents themselves.[37] The assistant has not always carried out the clerk's direction, "Here enter it."[38] Clearly Browne did not check his work. Blanks in ordinances left for the words "Lords and" have not always been filled in.[39] Nor have proceedings invariably been recorded on the days on which they occurred.[40] Only part of a letter from Sir Thomas Fairfax, which was to have been entered in the journal, has been included.[41] An assistant has seriously botched an entry for 25 April 1644.[42] Browne's instincts were not the instincts of a man who had worked with records. It did not trouble him to record lords' titles in a mixture of Latin and English, to amend an ordinance from the House of Commons to read like an ordinance from both Houses.[43] His concern was to get the job done. Neither his temperament nor the time at his disposal led him to recheck his or his assistants' work, and the work of the subcommittee for the journals became sporadic. By 1643 it seems evident that Browne and his assistants had abandoned the custom and expectation of producing a finished version of the journal. They had the necessary papers from which the House could work. They had a record of attendance. They had a record of decisions, and they had prepared a subject index for certain volumes of their journal.[44] Perfection of the record itself did not, in times of trouble, nor to a clerk of Browne's nature, seem essential.

In other ways, of greater significance, Browne's journal differs from those that went before. Robert Bowyer, clerk of the parliaments in the reign of James I, composed the journal of an undivided House. Factions there certainly were, bitter divisions of opinion, expressions of animosity or of reproach on the floor. But Bowyer, departing from earlier practice, reflected none of this in the journal—no votes, no debate, no angry or intemperate words.[45] The record was of a House united, its battles fought, its decisions made, its animosities resolved. Henry Elsyng, who succeeded Bowyer, only occasionally recorded a vote. In 1628 the petition concerning foreign nobility was read twice and "generally assented unto by all, except the Earl of Denbigh."[46] John Browne recorded votes more frequently.[47] At the request of the lords, he also entered formal dissents and protests. These entries begin in 1641/42 with volume 19 of the original journal. The lords did not actually sign either their dissents or protests until 1644 (original journal, volume 31). Even after the lords began to sign entries in the journal, many dissents continued to be entered in the clerk's hand alone. In volume 41 (26 February 1646/47–27 May 1647) and volumes 44 and 45, all protests have been signed by the lords. In later volumes, signatures and clerical entries both appear.[48] Though debates and quarrels were not recorded in the journal, nor in such notes of the clerk as we have, votes, dissents, and protests, all registered at the request of the lords themselves, clearly showed and were intended to show a divided House. The temper of the times, the march of events, the desire of individual lords to record their votes, dissents, and protests and to disassociate themselves from decisions of the House, together with the inclination of the clerk himself, had all worked to destroy an earlier concept of the journal. Even Bowyer could hardly have composed an account reflecting a united House in a period so distracted.

Despite these changes, the significance of the journal was still very great. In 1641 the king desired that his letter asking mercy for Strafford should be registered in it. A grave accusation against the attorney general was that he had caused charges against Lord Kimbolton and five members of the lower House to be entered in the clerk's book. The question of how Littleton, Lord Keeper, had voted on the militia ordinance was settled by perusing the journal.[49] Orders and ordinances were entered at large, recognizances registered.[50] Finally the Lords after the Restoration paid the ultimate compliment—they eradicated from the journal what they decided should not be there.[51]

Shortly after the king's return to England in May 1660, the House of Lords, which had been abolished in 1649, was restored and reconstituted. John Browne reappeared as clerk and once more took custody of the journals, which had been protected by a special "act" of the lower House.[52] In July the Lords ordered the Committee for Privileges to peruse the journal, "that those things which are derogatory to the honour of the King, and the Queen, and the Peers, may be reported severally to the House, that the same may be expunged out of the Books."[53] Fortunately what the committee accomplished was limited. An entry on 3 January 1643/44 concerning the impeachment of the queen has been scratched through, obliterated from the manuscript of the Lords journal and marked "vacated" in the margin.[54] In two other instances the House required the Committee for Privileges or its subcommittee for the journals to alter the record: the account of the impeachment of nine lords in 1642, and the order that peers created at Oxford should not sit in the House. The judgment in the case of the impeachment was to be "repealed, adnulled, and made void," a subcommittee of the Committee for Privileges to "take care to see the said judgement vacated." The phraseology of the assistant clerk, taking notes later in committee, was stronger—the judgment was to be "expunged," an important distinction. No alteration has, in fact, been made in the original journal; but the judgment has been deleted from the Book of Orders and Ordinances.[55] The direction that the subcommittee should cancel, null, and make void the order of 30 October 1646 excluding peers created at Oxford seems to have been neglected. The order stands as originally written.[56] The initial effort to vacate or to expunge items derogatory to king, queen, and peers had not seriously injured the journal.

The real damage occurred later in the account of the impeachment and attainder of the earl of Strafford. In 1663 an act of parliament, doubtless obtained through the efforts of Strafford's son, who sat in the House, "repealed, revoked and reversed" the attainder of the first earl. It further provided "that all records and proceedings of parliament relating to the said attainder be wholly cancelled and taken off the file, or other ways defaced and obliterated, to the intent the same may not be visible in after ages, or brought into example to the prejudice of any person whatsoever."[57] Four years later, on 21 November 1667, the Lords ordered the subcommittee for the journals to implement this section of the act and to raze the record.[58] In December Strafford's son was added to the Committee for Privileges and its subcommittee for the journals, which was scheduled to meet the following day to execute the order of the House.[59] Nothing was done for two years. In February 1669/70, the House again referred the matter to the Committee for Privileges.[60] On 3 March the Committee for Privileges debated its authority. Nine peers were satisfied that the House had empowered them to give directions for deleting the account of proceedings concerning Strafford from the journals. Two peers were not. The committee ordered the clerk of the parliaments, or some of his assistants, to go through the pages for 3 November–14 November 1640. On 14 March the clerks were told to proceed farther and make deletions from 19 November to 8 December inclusive.[61] Two weeks later, the House reiterated its order to raze the journal. The Committee for Privileges directed that a subcommittee should "see the books crossed"—"to mark what is to be obliterated."[62] By 5 April the subcommittee, having reached the account of 23 March 1640/41, returned for further instructions. In some places, they found, Laud, Ratcliffe, and others were involved. "Upon which the committee directed only to put out so much as related particularly to the Earl of Strafford and that the clerks obliterate what is crossed and those particular passages relating to the Earl of Strafford, not spoiling the sense of the said orders."[63] A week later, the House ordered the Committee for Privileges "to perfect the obliterating" as the first business after adjournment.[64]

The House, the committee, its subcommittee, and possibly the clerks had acted with admirable reluctance. Nevertheless, pages and pages of the journal had first been scratched through, and then, in some instances, totally obliterated.[65] This was not a matter of marking "*vacat*" in the margin. This was not "making void," "adnulling," and drawing a line through an order or judgment. This was "expunging," obliterating, wiping out forever, "utter oblivion."

In 1698 the House discovered that a mistake had been made. A committee reported that proceedings concerning the *impeachment* of Strafford should not be regarded as obliterated. The act of 1663 and the orders based upon it referred only to *attainder*. The clerk should so indicate in the journals. This he, or the subcommittee for the journals, has done, going through page by page and noting *"stet."*[66] In 1768, by order of the House, the account of these proceedings concerning impeachment was recopied, and interleaved in the original journal.[67] Belatedly the Lords repaired some of the damage that had been done; but the journal had been brutally disfigured. The material concerning Strafford's attainder was never restored.

There had been a curious inconsistency in the whole performance. An act to reverse an attainder presupposes an attainder; yet the deliberate destructive process, also provided for in the act, had been directed to wiping out all record of attainder. The action was so extraordinary and the vandalism so shocking that we must perforce try to understand it and come to terms with it.

The Lords had always determined what was appropriate to include in their journal. In 1621 they had struck out an account of unseemly words spoken on the floor of the House when Lord Arundel reminded Lord Spencer that Spencer's ancestors had herded sheep.[68] In 1626 the earl of Mulgrave and Lord Say had made the novel suggestion that material giving details of the charges against the duke of Buckingham could be entered in the journal and afterwards deleted if Buckingham should be cleared.[69] On certain occasions, the Lords had selected which proceedings of parliament should be used for a precedent, and which should not. When the House of Commons had gone beyond its powers in punishing Edward Floyd in 1621, the Lords had ordered that "the proceedings . . . be not, at any time hereafter, drawn or used as a precedent . . ." They had similarly resolved that words in the preamble to the subsidy act in 1624 should not be construed as lessening the jurisdiction of one House or adding to that of the other.[70] It was a step from such concepts and practices—though a very long step—actually to alter the record of what had occurred.

Several proposals had been made during the years 1641–49 to "vacate" or "obliterate" entries in the journal of the Long Parliament. Certain items have been crossed through, others rendered illegible. In March 1641/42, the Common Council of London asked that the Lords' votes damning a petition presented in February as a breach of privilege "may be obliterated." The offensive petition remained in the journal. There is no indication that any "vote" has been deleted, but the request is in itself interesting.[71] In May and June 1644, an affidavit and an order have been "vacated" by order of the House. Both have been crossed through.[72] In September 1644 and January 1644/45 one section of the journal, concerning a complaint by the earl of Denbigh against certain men of Warwickshire, has been deleted without comment; other sections have been totally obliterated, again without comment.[73]

The House ordered that all orders and proceedings concerning Lord Maguire should be "vacated." In the original journal, part of the day's proceedings for 22 January 1644/45 has been deleted, with a note in the margin "vacated by order of this House 23 of Jan. 1644." A section of the proceedings for 23 January, presumably also concerning Lord Maguire, has been totally obliterated.[74] In December 1647, a page and a half of the original journal was obliterated by order of the House.[75] In February 1647/48, three pages have been cut out and two obliterated without explanation.[76]

Throughout the years 1641–49, sometimes silently, sometimes on order of the House, items in the journal were "vacated" or "obliterated." The process observed in the years following the Civil War had its roots during the war period and perhaps earlier and was to continue long after. In 1670, at the suggestion of the king, entries concerning the case of *Skinner* v. *The East India Company*, which had caused a prolonged quarrel between the Houses, were expunged from the journals of both.[77] In 1680, proceedings against four peers (Buckingham, Salisbury, Shaftesbury, and Wharton) were removed from the journal of the upper House by vote of the Lords "that they may not be drawn into a precedent for the future."[78] Protests and the reasons for protests were similarly obliterated.[79] The House of Commons during the Long Parliament, Commonwealth, Protectorate, and early years of the Restoration treated its journal in the same way. By order of 6 January 1645/46, the judgment against Henry Marten, who had been expelled from the House in 1643, was to be "annulled, and made void, and rased out of the book."[80] The vote taken on 9 June 1649 to fill the seats of secluded members was obliterated on 21 February 1659/60. There are other instances.[81] In 1660 William Prynne procured the removal of the oath of fidelity to the Commonwealth.[82]

From this variety of examples, several different ideas emerge. If a House or both Houses together had reversed a previous decision, we might reasonably expect that the record would register this fact. If an order had been withdrawn, it would be so indicated. If an obligation had been fulfilled, a recognizance would be cancelled. It would be sufficient, in any record, to make a note in the margin or to draw a line through the appropriate passage, with an indication of why this has been done. Such was the normal practice in courts of law. On plea rolls one will find a line drawn through a judgment with *"vacat"* in the margin if in fact the case has been reversed. But the record of the case itself still stands. To record the reversal of a case of which there is no original record seems an absurdity.

A dramatic scene occurred in the upper House on 27 February 1640/41. The clerk has described it at some length and in unusual detail: "The Ship-Writs," he wrote, "and the Warrants for issuing them forth, the extrajudicial Opinion of the Judges therein both first and last, the Judgement given in Mr. Hampden's Case, and the Proceedings thereupon in the Exchequer-chamber concerning Ship-money, and likewise all the extrajudicial Opinions inrolled in the Chancery, Kings Bench, Common Pleas, and Star-Chamber, were all brought into this House, by the Master of the Rolls, the two Lord Chief Justices, Lord Chief Baron, and the Chief Clerk of the Star-chamber." All made three obeisances before they came to the Bar, and three more within the Bar. The records were first laid on the Lord Keeper's woolsack and then given to the clerk of the parliaments, who took them to his table. The House ordered that "a *vacat* should be entered, in open court, upon the said judgement, warrants, and enrollment, for ship-money. . . . And that all the rolls be razed cross with a pen, and subscribed with the clerk of the parliament's hand; all which was done accordingly, in open court, presently."[83] This was a clear, if extraordinary, demonstration of the way a court—in this case, the High Court of Parliament—registered the reversal of a decision. On some occasions this was the procedure less dramatically followed in altering the journal of the House of Lords. At other times, the record has been obliterated. Did a court ever act in this way, completely removing a record? Were there other activities connected with Parliament itself which will help to explain such actions?

In the courts a case, before or after it was heard, could be and sometimes was taken "off the file." Though still legible, the record was in effect destroyed—an English bill in Star Chamber, for example, was carefully slit in several places with a knife.[84] "Nothing," said a member of parliament in 1621, "is more ordinary than for the Chancellor or Master of the Rolls to take off the file bills that are scandalous, though the parties consent not."[85] In 1645 the House of Lords had ordered that proceedings against Prynne, Bastwick, and Burton in the courts of Star Chamber and High Commission "shall forthwith be forever totally vacated, obliterated and taken off the file, in all courts where they are yet remaining, as illegal and most unjust, against the liberty of the subject, the law of the land, and Magna Carta, and unfit to continue upon record."[86] Similarly a few months later in February 1645/46, the Lords voted that the sentence against John Lilburne in the Star Chamber was "illegal, unjust, and against the liberty of the subject . . . the sentence to be null and vacated, and to be taken off the file." This was very much the language to be used concerning Strafford's attainder: to "be wholly cancelled and taken off the file, or other ways defaced and obliterated."[87] A judgment which was reversed should remain on the record. Otherwise the reversal would be inexplicable. A judgment taken off the file was not "vacated" but removed from legal memory, of no effect in law, and at least symbolically destroyed. In the case of Prynne, Bastwick, and Burton, in the case of Lilburne, and indeed in the case of Strafford, the order of the House provided for taking the record off the file and for obliterating it.[88]

Documents or records have been destroyed for other reasons. A physical, ceremonious attack on the written or printed word was not unusual in the seventeenth century. It had had a long history, running back at least to the medieval Inquisition, and would persist far into the twentieth century with Adolf Hitler's burning of books. In 1642 the Lords ordered that a petition from certain citizens of London should be burnt by the common hangman. A letter from Lord Paget was to suffer the same fate, though spread at large in the journal. The Lords' purpose was primarily to indicate disapproval, not to eradicate. Several times in 1645, 1646, and 1647, the House ordered that scandalous books should be burnt.[89] In 1670 an unpopular speech was burnt, and in 1675 a pamphlet.[90] These lurid symbolic acts were the way a community or part of a community could vent its wrath or register its disapproval. Surely at the same time, by implication, the destruction of documents and books emphasized their importance. They might be scandalous, contemptible, worthy only of destruction by the common hangman, but destroyed they must be.

How do these ideas, how do these acts of destruction and obliteration, affect the journal of the House of Lords? To what purpose have we examined the nature of the record, the way it was made, the character of the clerk, and the attitude of the House itself? Can we now summarize with greater understanding what had happened and why the journal is as it is?

The journal of the Long Parliament was not the same kind of journal which had been kept for earlier years in the Stuart period. Even its physical appearance was different. A hastily composed volume in paper, written in several hands, sometimes including documents copied in full, sometimes with documents merely laid in, the journal of the Long Parliament more closely resembled the "draft journal" of previous clerks than it did the finished, engrossed journals on parchment for the period 1603–40. John Browne may well have intended to produce a more finished record for the Long Parliament. However, from all available evidence, he did not do so. In the beginning of his clerkship, the House continued to examine and approve his journal; later this was less regularly done. In other ways the journal had changed. Though conscious of his own dignity as clerk,[91] Browne was not by experience or by inclination a student of parliament. He rarely dwelt on points of procedure or troubled himself about niceties of expression in compiling his account.[92] He had much to do, and the most important thing was to get it done. He wrote a basic outline of each day's proceedings, marking places where his assistant should flesh it out with copies of documents. He does not seem to have checked to ascertain whether the work had been done correctly or done at all. Browne's journal, still in the nature of a draft, invited revision, or at least made it seem less drastic than would have been the case with a finished, engrossed volume.

Browne's work no longer reflected the philosophy which had guided Bowyer and the House in designing the journal of James's parliaments. It was no longer possible, or even desirable, to write the journal of a united House. The Lords themselves insisted on a record of their dissents and protests—a record of their differences. It was natural that a journal which had recorded the struggles of the Civil War period should also record by deletions and obliterations the changes brought by the Restoration. The record of the House of Lords for the period 1640–49 was not immutable because the decisions of the House (so bitterly protested when they had been made) did not stand.

The House continued to exercise the power to reverse judgments in King's Bench on appeal by writ of error. It assumed the power also to declare that judgments had been illegal and to vacate them (as in the Ship Money case) or to vacate and obliterate the record of a judgment (as in the cases of Prynne, Bastwick, Burton, and Lilburne). Similarly the House overthrew its own decisions during the Long Parliament and afterwards, during the Restoration, vacated or obliterated the record of them. Thus Browne's journal of the parliament, as it emerged from the Restoration, reflected not only a House divided but a House which attempted to cut itself off from certain decisions it had made in the past, resolving that they should not stand nor be used as precedents. To wipe them out of the journal was also a way of expressing rejection and disapproval, as one burnt heretical books or scandalous documents.

The journal for 1640–49 would never be called a "great parliament book." Roughly written, incomplete, unrevised, unchecked, and sporadically examined, it was later brutally disfigured in an attempt to reinstate Strafford and to protect the dignity of king, queen, and peers. It is interesting and understandable that the Lords should have thought that all of these ends could be achieved—in some measure—by the alteration of their journal. Although the practice is initially horrifying to historians, it was neither inconsistent with the Lords' other activities nor entirely novel to change the record by deleting what in retrospect had become objectionable. The journal of the Long Parliament which has survived is not, then, always a record of proceedings in the House. It is sometimes a record of those proceedings which the House in later years continued to approve.[93]

## *Notes*

1. An Act of Free and General Pardon, Indemnity and Oblivion (12 *Car.* II, c. 11).

2. Public Record Office (hereafter P.R.O.), C65.194, C65.195, C65.196. The roll is in three parts and actually includes public bills to which the royal assent was given in 16, 17, and 18 *Car.* I (see *Statutes of the Realm*, 11 vols. [London, 1810–28], 5:178 n.). Henry Scobell, after the House of Lords had been abolished, prepared another roll for the parliament, relating the trial of Charles I (House of Lords Record Office, hereafter H.L.R.O., Parchment Collection, 3 March 1650/51. See *The Manuscripts of the House of Lords*, vol. 11 (new series), *Addenda 1514–1714*, ed. M. F. Bond (London, 1962), Introduction, pp. xviii–xix).

3. H.L.R.O., Books of Ordinances, Book of Orders and Warrants, Books of Orders and Judgments.

4. H.L.R.O., Original Lords Journal, vols. 15–47.

5. Elizabeth Read Foster, *The Painful Labour of Mr. Elsyng. Transactions of the American Philosophical Society*, vol. 62 (Philadelphia, 1972), pp. 21–24.

6. This phrase occurs in H.L.R.O., Committee for Privileges, Minute Book no. 2, 21 Nov. 1667, p. 31.

7. Foster, *Painful Labour of Mr. Elsyng*, pp. 6–7, 13, 28. Elsyng referred to a scene in the House in 1610 at which he was present (Henry Elsyng, *The Manner of Holding Parliaments in England* [London, 1768], p. 97).

8. Maurice F. Bond, "Clerks of the Parliaments, 1509–1953," *English Historical Review* 73 (1958): 84; "The Formation of the Archives of Parliament, 1497–1691," *Journal of the Society of Archivists* 1 (1957): 153–57. For information concerning Browne's personal history, I have relied on the research of Mary Edmond, available at the House of Lords Record Office (see H.L.R.O. Memorandum, no. 61, Appendix 1). The suggestion concerning Throckmorton I owe to John Sainty.

9. H.L.R.O., Braye 16; Braye 95 (Osborn Collection, Yale University, available in photographic copies at H.L.R.O.).

10. H.L.R.O., Manuscript Minutes, vol. 6. The use of the term "manuscript minutes" in this instance is somewhat confusing. Subsequent minute books for this period are not the work of the clerk recasting notes at leisure, but books of notes kept in the House by an assistant. For the signatures of lords who examined the book (in one instance, Browne's note of their names), see the proceedings of 16 Apr., 25 Apr., 2 May 1640.

11. H.L.R.O., Original Lords Journal, vol. 14.

12. See Esther S. Cope, ed., *Proceedings of the Short Parliament of 1640*, Camden Society, fourth series, vol. 19 (London, 1977). Miss Cope has guided my thinking on these points.

13. In recording attendance for certain sessions in the reign of Edward VI, the clerk has entered the full list of lords summoned and marked those absent "ab.", rather than those present "p." (see *Journals of the House of Lords* [London, 1767–, hereafter cited as *LJ*], 1:317–88).

14. H.L.R.O., Braye 17, 18, 19, 20, 22, 23, 24, 25. Browne's notes for the period 29 April–9 May 1642 have been bound in the front of H.L.R.O., Original Lords Journal, vol. 21, where they may be found on pp. 1–132. They are wrongly described as an "incorrect duplicate" in *LJ*, 5:56n. Browne's notes may also be

found in H.L.R.O., Main Papers, H.L., 8 June; 3, 20, 25, 29 July; 5 Aug.; 8, 12 Sept.; 2, 6, 11, 19, 24, 27 Oct.; 7, 13, 22 Nov.; 4 Dec. 1643; 15 Dec. 1645; 19 July 1647. Browne's notes for 25 April–1 May 1660 are in H.L.R.O., Braye 9. There are other notes by Browne in Braye 95 in the Osborn Collection, Yale University, for some proceedings in 1641, more fully covered by his notes in Braye 18, 19, and 20.

15. Volumes 2, 5, 8, 9, 11, 14, which are now numbered 7, 8, 9, 10, 11, 12 (H.L.R.O., Manuscript Minutes).

16. All manuscript minutes contain the "presents"—the list of lords actually in the House, not a full list of those summoned, marked "p." Usually the list is in several columns (three before the departure of the bishops), by benches, but not in order of precedence within the column. Occasionally precedence has been indicated by numbers (H.L.R.O., Manuscript Minutes, vol. 9, 24 Mar. 1642/43).

17. See, for example, the account of Strafford's impeachment on 22 Mar. 1640/41, the cancellation of the judgment in the Ship Money case on 27 Feb. 1640/41 (H.L.R.O., Manuscript Minutes, vol. 7), and procedural details in the trial of Laud (Manuscript Minutes, vol. 10, 13 Nov. 1643).

18. Elizabeth Read Foster, *Proceedings in Parliament 1610,* 2 vols. (New Haven, 1966), 1:xxii, xxiv–xxvi, xxviii–xxx. Foster, *Painful Labour of Mr. Elsyng,* pp. 22–24.

19. H.L.R.O., Original Lords Journal, vol. 25, p. 10.

20. For examples, see H.L.R.O., Original Lords Journal, vols. 21, 22, 23 passim.

21. H.L.R.O., Original Lords Journal, vol. 44, 28 Dec. 1647. A page and a half has been obliterated and marked in the margin "put out by vote of the 30 December 1647," which probably indicates that the entry had already been made before 30 December. The Standing Order that dissents must be entered "the next sitting day" may have put pressure on the clerk to prepare promptly his draft of certain days' proceedings (see n. 48 below). "Sunday is the day they transcribe, which on the workdays they cannot attend" (P.R.O., SP 16/481/42, 17 June 1641).

22. H.L.R.O., Original Lords Journal, vols. 15, 16. The subcommittee had also examined the journal for the Short Parliament (see n. 10 above).

23. *LJ,* 5:450; 6:502.

24. H.L.R.O., Original Lords Journal, vols. 39, 40, 41, 47.

25. The printed Lords *Journal* does not always indicate what has been crossed through in the original journal. See, for example, H.L.R.O., Original Lords Journal, vol. 15, 10, 11, 12, 17, 19, 23 Dec., where passages have been crossed through but included without comment in *LJ,* vol. 4. See the reference to Browne's notes in *LJ,* 5:56 n. (n. 14 above).

26. H.L.R.O., Original Lords Journal, vol. 14.

27. H.L.R.O., Braye 27, is Browne's draft journal, 8 May 1661–20 February 1662. The original Lords journal for the same period represents the final version which was printed. From November 1640 to February 1649, it was the draft journal which was printed, no further journal having been completed. Bishop Nicolson commented in 1702, "The Journals in paper keep better than in vellum" (Diary of Bishop Nicolson, 11 Dec. 1702. Through the courtesy of Geoffrey Holmes and Clyve Jones I have used the typescript now at the Institute of Historical Research, London. A photocopy of Nicolson's diary is available at the H.L.R.O.).

28. H.L.R.O., Original Lords Journal, vol. 23 (22 Sept. 1642); vol. 44 (10 Dec. 1647).

29. H.L.R.O., Original Lords Journal, vol. 16 (12 Apr. 1641).

30. H.L.R.O., Original Lords Journal, vols. 22, 23, 24. Some of these directions have been included in the printed *Journal* (*LJ,* 6:658 and elsewhere).

31. Luke Owen Pike, *A Constitutional History of the House of Lords* (London, 1894), p. 128. For examples of the record of excuses of absent lords, see H.L.R.O., Manuscript Minutes, vol. 10 (27 Oct. 1643); H.L.R.O., Main Papers, H.L., 7 Nov. 1643. Attendance lists were not always accurate. Some discrepancies may be found between the lists in H.L.R.O., Main Papers, H.L., 14 May 1641 and 18 June 1641, and those in the *Journal.* Scholars working later in the century have also noted inaccuracies. See Godfrey Davies and Edith L. Klotz, "The Habeas

Corpus Act of 1679 in the House of Lords," *Huntington Library Quarterly*, 3 (1939–40): 469–70; E. S. DeBeer, "The House of Lords in the Parliament of 1680," *Bulletin of the Institute of Historical Research* 20, no. 59 (1943):24–25.

32. I discount Rogers' suggestion that omissions were for fear of reprisals from the king and a desire for secrecy (James E. Thorold Rogers, *A Complete Collection of the Protests of the Lords*, 3 vols. [Oxford, 1875], 1:xiii, xviii).

33. H.L.R.O., Original Lords Journal, vol. 28.

34. *LJ*, 6:229; H.L.R.O., Original Lords Journal, vol. 28. There are a few omissions: 4 Oct. 1643 and 29 Nov. 1647, for example. For the neglect of precedence in recording the "presents," see *LJ*, 6:235, 236, 240, 254, 261. On the importance of the record of precedence, see Elizabeth Read Foster, "Procedure in the House of Lords during the Early Stuart Period," *Journal of British Studies* 5 (May 1966): 64–65.

35. *LJ*, 3:781–878.

36. 10–13 Dec. 1642.

37. For examples, see H.L.R.O., Main Papers, H.L., 8 Apr. 1644 (ordinance for continuing the excise); H.L.R.O., Main Papers, H.L., 3 Apr. 1645 (Browne has failed to record the first reading of the ordinance for discharging members of both Houses from all offices, military and civil).

38. For examples, see *LJ*, 5:103, 107, 157, 256, 419, 683.

39. *LJ*, 5:328.

40. According to the manuscript minutes (H.L.R.O., Manuscript Minutes, vol. 2), the order for exempting peers' houses from billeting was read on 3 December 1644. It was entered in the Lords *Journal* on 4 December (*LJ*, 7:87. See also H.L.R.O., H.L., Main Papers, H.L., 3 Dec. 1644.

41. Cf. H.L.R.O., Main Papers, H.L., 30 Jan. 1642/43; *LJ*, 5:579–80.

42. Cf. H.L.R.O., Main Papers, H.L., 25 Apr. 1644; *LJ*, 6:527–28.

43. Latin and English have been intermixed in the titles of peers (*LJ*, 6:233, 252).

44. See H.L.R.O., Original Lords Journals, vols. 15, 16, 17, 18, 19.

45. Foster, *Proceedings in Parliament 1610*, 1:xxvi. For the practice of recording dissenting votes in the Tudor period, see Rogers, *Complete Collection*, 1:v–vii.

46. Foster, *Painful Labour of Mr. Elsyng*, p. 27; *LJ*, 4:31.

47. *LJ*, 8:499; 9:70, 150, 199.

48. One might expect to find lords' signatures in the notebooks Browne had with him in the House or in the manuscript minutes of the assistant clerks, since they are not in the journal or in the protest books at this time. There are no signatures in the minute books. All entries in Browne's notebooks have been made by Browne himself, or an assistant, not by the lords, and have been renumbered in order of precedence (H.L.R.O., Braye 20, 22C, 23, 24, 25). The Standing Orders (1641/42) provided that lords "shall make their . . . protestation, or give direction to have their dissents entered into the Clerk's Book, the next sitting day of this House" if the protestation or dissent is to be valid (*Manuscripts of the House of Lords*, vol. 10 (new series), ed. M. F. Bond [London, 1953], p. 11). In 1689, certain lords met before the sitting of the House to enter their dissent, "which could not be done yesterday, the Journal-Book not being made up" (Alan Simpson, "notes of a Noble Lord, 22 Jan. to 12 Feb. 1688/9," *English Historical Review* 52, no. 205 [1937]: 95. For this period, Rogers worked for the most part from the printed *Journal* and has assumed that the lords signed their protests when this was not, in fact, the case (Rogers, *Complete Collection*, 1:xxi, xxiv).

49. *LJ*, 4:245; 5:11, 127–28, 134–35.

50. H.L.R.O., Original Lords Journal, vol. 15; *LJ*, 4:115, 190.

51. James I had done the same thing to the Commons journal when he tore out the protestation in 1621.

52. *Journals of the House of Commons* (London, 1803–; hereafter *CJ*), 6:132, 168.

53. *LJ*, 11:93.

54. *LJ*, 11:93; *LJ*, 6:364 and H.L.R.O., Original Lords Journal, vol. 29, 3 Jan. 1643/44, pp. 162–64.

55. *LJ*, 11:14; H.L.R.O., Committee for Privileges, Minute Book no. 1, pp. 5, 42; H.L.R.O., Original Lords Journal, vol. 22, pp. 154–58; H.L.R.O., Book of Orders and Ordinances, vol. B2, pp. 721–24.

56. *LJ*, 11:50; H.L.R.O., Original Lords Journal, vol. 39; *LJ*, 8:551.

57. 14 *Car.* II, c. 29.

58. *LJ*, 12:143. In November 1667, the House debated whether Strafford's impeachment should be used as a precedent in the proceedings against Clarendon. Those who spoke against Clarendon's commitment said "that E. Strafford's precedent was not to be mentioned because made void by the Act for repeal of his attainder." Others maintained that the precedent had not been vacated by the act "which only condemned the Act of Attainder not the proceedings before that Act, which were legal and regular" (Bodleian Library, Rawlinson MS. A 130, 12 Nov. 1667). The trial of Strafford was later used as a precedent for the trial of other peers (H.L.R.O., Committee for Privileges, Minute Book no. 2, pp. 161–64; *LJ*, 13:584–85).

59. 6 Dec. 1667 (*LJ*, 12:159).

60. 23 Feb. 1669/70 (*LJ*, 12:293).

61. 3 Mar. 1669/70 (H.L.R.O., Committee for Privileges, Minute Book no. 2, pp. 63–64); 14 Mar. 1669/70 (ibid., p. 66).

62. 28 Mar. 1670 (*LJ.*, 12:329); 29 Mar. 1670, 5 Apr. 1670 (H.L.R.O., Committee for Privileges, Minute Book no. 2, pp. 69–70).

63. H.L.R.O., Committee for Privileges, Minute Book no. 2, p. 70. The bill of attainder was brought into the upper House on 21 April 1641 (*LJ*, 4:223).

64. *LJ*, 12:347.

65. H.L.R.O., Original Lords Journal, vols. 15, 16.

66. *LJ*, 16:341–42; H.L.R.O., Original Lords Journal, vols. 15, 16.

67. *LJ*, 4:88 n. This was doubtless done in connection with the arrangements for printing the journal.

68. Foster, *Painful Labour of Mr. Elsyng*, pp. 23–24. Samuel Rawson Gardiner, ed., *Notes of the Debates in the House of Lords Officially Taken by Henry Elsyng . . . A.D. 1621*, Camden Society, o.s. 103 (London, 1870), p. 73.

69. Samuel Rawson Gardiner, ed., *Notes of the Debates in the House of Lords . . . 1624 and 1626*, Camden Society, n.s. 24 (London, 1879), p. 204. The final decision was that the "aggravations" should not be entered, but delivered to the clerk "to be kept by him close from all, save from the members of this House" (*LJ*, 3:630).

70. *LJ*, 3:119, 408.

71. H.L.R.O., Main Papers, 18 Mar. 1641/42 and *LJ*, 4:651–52; 24 Feb. 1641/42, *LJ*, 4:609 and H.L.R.O., Original Lords Journal, vol. 20.

72. The deletions have been noted in the printed *Journal*: 31 May 1644 (*LJ*, 6:574); 13 and 14 June 1644 (*LJ*, 6:590–91); H.L.R.O., Original Lords Journal, vol. 31.

73. H.L.R.O., Original Lords Journal, vol. 31 (13, 14 Sept. 1644; 15 Jan. 1644/45).

74. *LJ*, 7:153; H.L.R.O., Original Lords Journal, vol. 32, pp. 319, 328. There is no indication in the printed *Journal* of what has been done in either case.

75. H.L.R.O., Original Lords Journal, vol. 44 (28 Dec. 1647), and marked "put out by vote of the 30 December 1647." For the order, see *LJ*, 9:618.

76. H.L.R.O., Original Lords Journal, vol. 44, 1 Feb. 1647/48 at p. 549. Pages 551–52 have been obliterated. There is no indication to this effect in the printed *Journal*.

77. *LJ*, 12:238–47; Pike, *Constitutional History*, p. 282.

78. For the order, see H.L.R.O., John Relfe, Book of Orders, 1710, p. 67; *LJ*, 13:664. For deletions, see *LJ*, 13:39ff.

79. H.L.R.O., Parliament Office Papers 354, Precedent Book, pp. 33–34; H.L.R.O., John Relfe, Book of Orders, 1710, p. 739.

80. *CJ*, 4:397; H.L.R.O., Original Commons Journal, vol. 25 (16 Aug. 1643); *CJ*, 3:206.

81. See, for example, 9 June 1649, 5 Jan. 1659/60 (both obliterated by order of 21 Feb. 1659/60), and 25 Jan. 1659/60 (obliterated by order of 2 Mar. 1659/60), H.L.R.O., Original Commons Journal, vols. 30, 49, 50.

82. David Ogg, *England in the Reign of Charles II*, 2 vols. (Oxford, 1962), 1:26.

83. *LJ*, 4:136, 173.

84. I am grateful to Thomas G. Barnes for explaining this procedure to me and for the reference to P.R.O., STAC 8/49/21 (*Sir John Bowyer* v. *James Brierlie et al.*), where both bill and answers have been slit through, and to P.R.O., STAC 8/49/22 (*James Brearley* v. *Sir John Bowyer*), where the bill has been mutilated. Both bills in these cross-suits are endorsed with a note that they were cancelled by order of the court, 8 May 1612.

85. The case under discussion was that of Sir George Marshall. Secretary Calvert reported to the House of Commons that the king "is well pleased that the bill be taken off the file and the proceedings in Chancery damned to oblivion." Sir Edward Coke preferred that the record be taken off the file only on consent of the parties and "upon a motion in open court." The Master of the Rolls offered to remove the record himself. Ultimately the House issued an order that all proceedings in the case should be taken off the file (Wallace Notestein, Frances Helen Relf, Hartley Simpson, eds., *Commons Debates 1621*, 7 vols. [New Haven, 1935], 5:123–26).

86. *LJ*, 7:352. Prynne, Bastwick, and Burton later petitioned the House of Lords. There was some doubt, they reported, how estreats and processes should be cancelled. Their prayer was that the cancellation should be carried out as had been done with ship money. The Lords ordered that Star Chamber records concerning the three should be brought in and vacated (H.L.R.O., Main Papers, 13 Dec. 1645; *LJ*, 8:39).

87. *LJ*, 8:165; 14 *Car.* II, c. 29.

88. According to Sir Francis Bacon's account, on the accession of Henry VII, "for honour's sake, it was ordained by parliament, that all records wherein there was any memory or mention of the King's attainder should be defaced, cancelled, and taken off the file." At the same time, Spedding noted, the act by which the marriage of Elizabeth Woodville had been declared illegitimate was reversed without being read, "that the matter might be and remain in perpetual oblivion for the falseness and shamefulness of it." The original was removed from the rolls, burned, and all copies destroyed. "History of King Henry VII," in *The Works of Francis Bacon*, ed. James Spedding et al., 7 vols. (London, 1870), 6:38, 51n.

89. *LJ*, 4:652; 5:152; 8:504, 615, 645–46.

90. *The History and Proceedings of the House of Lords from the Restoration in 1660 to the Present Time*, 8 vols. (London, 1742), 1:109; *LJ*, 13:13.

91. See Browne's answer to the complaint of John Poyntz *alias* Morris (*LJ*, 9:229), which involved a forged act of parliament. There is a great deal of material about this affair in the Main Papers of the House of Lords, 1647 and 1648 (11 May, 25 May, 2 Nov. 1647; 26 Aug., 25 Nov. 1648).

92. Cf. Elsyng's many drafts and anxious questions to the committee for the journal (Foster, *Painful Labour of Mr. Elsyng*, pp. 26–27).

93. I regret that Paul Christianson's article, "The 'Obliterated' Portions of the House of Lords Journals Dealing with the Attainder of Strafford, 1641," *English Historical Review* 95 (1980), was not available in time for me to use it.

# Community and Class: Theories of Local Politics in the English Revolution

## DAVID UNDERDOWN

The great debate over the social causes of the English Revolution of the 1640s has now run its course. Whatever may be thought of the original hypotheses advanced by R. H. Tawney, his critics, and his successors, there will be few to deny that out of the interpretative turmoil of the 1950s and 1960s has emerged a far more sophisticated understanding of the relationship between social and political change in the century before 1640.[1] Not that all the loose ends have been tied up in a single universally accepted orthodoxy: historians, happily, never allow this to occur. One of the most difficult problems for all the protagonists was to show precisely how the social forces they identified determined the behavior of men in 1640, 1642, or 1648—to bridge the gap between theory and events. For this reason among others, the publication in 1966 of Alan Everitt's *Community of Kent and the Great Rebellion* marked an important step forward.[2] Everitt, clearly, had been strongly influenced by the debate over the gentry; in some respects his work was a logical extension of Tawney's "rising gentry" thesis. The key to the revolution, Everitt has argued in this and other publications, is to be found in the nature of the local gentry community.

Everitt was, of course, not the first to lift English local history of this period out of the parochial antiquarianism that had so often beset it. Competent, professional studies of counties in the civil war began to appear in the 1930s: Mary Coate on Cornwall, A. C. Wood on Nottinghamshire, for example.[3] There had also been brilliantly suggestive essays like the first chapter of Sir John Neale's *Elizabethan House of Commons*, A. H. Dodd's analysis of the Welsh committees, and Peter Laslett's article on the Kent gentry.[4] Laslett, indeed, anticipated Everitt in defining the "county community" as the intellectual base of local consciousness; he did not, however, apply the concept systematically to politics, or assert the priority of local over national issues, as Everitt was to do. Meanwhile the "gentry" debate sharpened perceptions of the Court-Country polarity in English history, and persuaded historians to examine more carefully the structure of local politics and administration. A timely response was Thomas G. Barnes's study of Caroline Somerset, which identified a community of gentry that corresponded very closely to the Everitt model.[5] But it was above all Everitt's work that refined the "county community" concept to explain both the nature of local politics and the persistent tension between Westminster and the localities during the revolution. The county community has thus become the orthodox model for analyses of English regions and counties in the seventeenth century.

But the Everitt scheme of local politics is not the only one that has been proposed, and even if it were, we should have to admit that no single model can adequately encompass the bewilderingly contradictory responses of provincial Englishmen to the great Stuart upheaval. For Everitt himself has insisted on the remarkable diversity of English counties: each with its unique history, economy, social structure, and community values, each with a different set of relationships with its neighbors and with the larger realm. How is anyone who wishes to study the whole as well as the parts to make sense of this diversity? We ought to try, unless we are content to take refuge in a barren nominalism that shuns generalization altogether. It is certainly too early to attempt to synthesize the output of the new breed of English local historians and arrive at a general theory of local politics. But it may be useful to undertake the less awesome preliminary task of examining the various models that have been proposed, seeing what they explain and what difficulties they raise, and thus mark out lines of further investigation by which these and other hypotheses might be tested.

At the heart of the county community model is the assumption that each county had its own distinctive status hierarchy and its own political culture. To be sure, a national community was developing in both respects, but Everitt does not see this as a contradiction, for heightened senses of county and national identity often went hand in hand.[6] But during the century and a half since the establishment of the Tudor peace, the cohesion and vitality of the counties had been increasing more rapidly than those of the nation, the county community "gaining ground at the expense of other local groups and of the state."[7] Secure in the tight bonds of kinship and neighborhood, the gentry of such counties as Kent and Suffolk gave their first loyalty to their immediate community. Though they saw no contradiction between this and their larger loyalties to crown and kingdom, in times of crisis they were always apt to protect the interests of neighbors threatened by the power of the state. "Their primary sphere of activity . . . was the local community: their 'country' was the shire."[8]

It is easy to see the relevance of this to the revolution, or, as Everitt prefers to call it, the Great Rebellion. County communities across the land had been united in opposing the centralizing intrusions of Charles I's government and the imposition of an alien court religion. In 1640 they were united in welcoming the Long Parliament's measures of reform. But by 1642, confronted with Pym's appeal to the people against the king, and with Puritan pressure for a root-and-branch church settlement, the communities split asunder and civil war resulted. When they split, however, it was into three groups, not two. In Kent, especially, an overwhelming majority of the gentry stood fast by their localism, strove for peace and reconciliation, and were always neutral at heart even if the intimidating presence of military power made them appear to be nominal Parliamentarians. Only two small groups at opposite ends of the spectrum were politicized in national terms, and they tended to be drawn from recently established or insecure families rather than from the indigenous, ancient gentry more typical of the community. The Cavalier handful were soon driven out of the county, leaving the clique of Roundheads under Sir Anthony Weldon to govern the rest.

Throughout Everitt's account of Civil War politics echoes the continuing tension between Westminster centralization and the local communities' stubborn desire for autonomy. For the gentry soon found that the Whitehall pressures under which they had writhed in the 1630s were as nothing compared with the awesome powers appropriated by the parliamentarian state under the necessities of war. At first Weldon and his allies tried to protect their county's quasi independence, resisting the subordination to a regional association that their Suffolk counterparts were better able to swallow. But wittingly or unwittingly they became the tools of Westminster. As the localist moderates realized this they withdrew from the county committee, leaving Weldon with nowhere to turn but Westminster, and few local supporters beyond a scattering of Puritan enthusiasts. By the time the New Model Army was formed in the spring of 1645, Weldon's group already "looked to the state, and thought nationally."[9]

After the war the process continued. High taxes, a standing army, and the control of local government by Weldon's ruthless (and socially upstart) committeemen provoked a conservative reaction and eventually the explosion of 1648. In Fairfax's triumph at Maidstone Everitt sees not so much the victory of Roundheads over Royalists as that of "the nation-state of England over the 'county-state' of Kent."[10] Facing the almost total recalcitrance of the old community, Parliament now governed through whatever local allies it could find, mostly men from outside the network of traditional governing families. The result was even greater centralization under the Commonwealth and Protectorate, further subordination of the local community to "the community of the realm."[11] Herein lay the revolution's failure, for in the end the tenacious traditionalism of the localities was too strong for a central government lacking any legitimacy but the sword. It was through the recovered unity of the county communities that Charles II was restored.[12]

It will be apparent from this summary that Everitt is not much interested in ideology, in the Civil War as a conflict over principles of government, religion, or the nature of society, except insofar as these affected relations between the state and the localities. Weldon's opposition to the court before 1640 is dismissed as devoid of any philosophical basis, his vague Puritanism attributed merely to "feuds with his neighbours." His adherents are regarded as similarly unmotivated, except by their consuming "desire of rule."[13] It was ambition, not political principle or zeal for "Godly reformation," that enabled the Weldonians (Everitt's fondness for this nonpolitical term is significant) to overcome their own dislike of centralization. The state alone could perpetuate their local authority.

A second striking characteristic of Everitt's approach is its concentration on the elite. People below the rank of gentry scarcely figure in the analysis; when they do, it is as part of a silent unconscious mass. Divisions in Kent are gentry divisions. Thus, Everitt explains the Parliamentarians' failure to establish a stable base of support by noting that the county gentry had opted by more than six to one for neutrality or royalism.[14] Claims of popular support for Parliament are rejected as mere propaganda, Roundhead petitions ruled out as "parrot-petitions" drafted in London, with no backing in Kent outside the clique of Puritans and self-interested leaders.[15] The way politics works in Everitt's scheme is vertical: from the top down.[16]

The family who set out to control the shire must first of all secure the adherence of its group of cousins and friends amongst the greater county gentry, and they on their part that of their kinsmen and neighbours amongst the parochial gentry of the shire; finally, all in turn must obtain the allegiance of their tenants and labourers. In this way, the rival family galaxies which fought the elections of 1640 were gradually built up.

The central assumption is that we are dealing with a patriarchal "society of orders," unified by vertical community loyalties, a conception of society corresponding to that proposed by Roland Mousnier for France.[17] And as in Mousnier there is the further assumption that the outlook of the elite can be regarded as identical with that of the whole. No room is left for the effective expression of opinion by the yeomen and lesser people of the shire.

Everitt's conception of local politics assumes not only a rise of the gentry, but also the logical corollary, a decline of the aristocracy. On the eve of the revolution, such counties as Kent, Suffolk, and Northamptonshire were dominated by communities of gentry; the influence of their great families—Sackvilles, Howards, and Comptons—was at least temporarily in eclipse.[18] But there are some recent signs of a tendency to question Lawrence Stone's impressively sustained thesis of a nobility in crisis, and it has been suggested that, on the contrary, the roots of aristocratic power were little affected by the social and economic developments of the previous century. Conrad Russell has drawn attention to the "overwhelming evidence for tne Parliamentarians' dependence on aristocratic leadership." James Farnell has gone even further, characterizing the entire parliamentary leadership, from Pym to Sir Henry Vane, as virtual puppets controlled by such noble patrons as Bedford, Say, and Wharton.[19] And Paul Christianson proposes to replace the entire "Whiggish" Tawney-Stone paradigm with one based on the unshaken strength of hierarchy and the Great Chain of Being.[20]

Now, if national politics were dominated by the peerage, we should naturally expect to find that local politics were too. So far there has been no headlong flight from Everitt's gentry community toward a more aristocratic political universe. However, Clive Holmes's study of the Eastern Association bears some traces of a move in this direction, at any rate for the county of Essex.[21] Holmes questions the Everitt thesis at a number of points, re-

jecting the conventional wisdom about East Anglia's supposedly
unique socioeconomic unity and its unusually pervasive Puritanism. The region, he shows, was not unanimously parliamentarian: recurrent royalist and neutralist outbreaks had to be
suppressed, often by forces brought down from London.[22] Indeed,
Holmes directly challenges Everitt's case for localism as the determinant of county politics, proposing instead a "complex and
tension-ridden dialogue" between Westminster, the Association,
and the separate county committees—between state, region,
and shire—with most of the real initiative coming from
Westminster.[23]

There are county communities in Holmes's East Anglia, but
apart from Suffolk they seem to possess less coherence and vitality than Everitt's model community of Kent. And the East Anglian gentry were as indecisive in action as their brethren of Kent:
hence the constant intrusion of Westminster. The exception was
Essex, where through the territorial power of the earl of Warwick
the county was organized for Parliament far more effectively than
the rest of the region. Warwick had systematically presented
Puritan clergy to livings and lectureships, encouraged county officials (many of them appointed by him) to resist Ship Money and
other exactions of the 1630s, and used his great clientage connection to promote a stream of petitions favorable to Parliament in
the months before the war. When war came, Warwick's control
over the militia and the ministers was decisive: Essex appeared
for Parliament overwhelmingly and with enthusiasm. This,
Holmes argues, was less the result of the countrymen's "zeal to
the Parliament" than of their "love to the Earl of Warwick."[24] In
the absence of powerful peers capable of providing effective leadership, the responses of the other East Anglian counties were
fumbling and half-hearted. Even in Essex, when Warwick gave up
his command in November 1642, the militia forces he had raised
quickly disintegrated.

Holmes thus advances two modifications of Everitt's localist
model: a much greater role for Westminster power and national
issues, and the existence of aristocratic power as a major variable.
Everitt, one suspects, would be unlikely to quarrel with Holmes's
assessment of Warwick's role: it simply happens that few other
English counties in 1642 possessed so overpowering an aristocrat.
Indeed, Holmes's conception of politics is almost as elitist as
Everitt's. The outlook of the populace below the gentry receives
little attention, and such popular outbreaks as are recorded—the
disorders of the late summer of 1642, for instance—are viewed
mainly in terms of the gentry's reaction to them.[25]

Clearly something is missing from both the original county

community model and this aristocratic variant: some attempt to analyze systematically the relations between the gentry leaders and the lesser men—yeomen, husbandmen, craftsmen—who were their constituents. Now, it is possible for historians to ignore these people or to regard them as mere cyphers, untouched by the explosion of preaching, the spread of literacy, the whole religious and political ferment of the previous century. This is precisely the view of the English rural lower orders—as a static, deferential mass—taken by Peter Laslett in a book published at about the same time as Everitt's.[26] But much has been written since 1965 to expose the limitations of this view. A start has been made on the study of education and literacy. Carl Bridenbaugh and others have reminded us that running his own affairs in manor courts and parish vestries was part of the ordinary Englishman's common experience. Derek Hirst has demonstrated the extensive participation by men of small property in the electoral process before 1640: like the gentry, they naturally tended to think in local rather than in national terms.[27] In the light of this evidence, and that of the village studies we shall encounter later in this essay, analyses of local behavior that are confined to the landowning class cannot be completely convincing.

There is in fact no compelling reason why the county community must be defined as only the community of an elite. Indeed, one of the most successful applications of the concept, John Morrill's study of interregnum Cheshire, gives it much greater depth by paying attention to the county's lesser men.[28] Morrill begins with an analysis of the Cheshire gentry similar to that of Everitt for Kent. He finds an equally stable elite, a similar kind of politics based on family connection and patronage, a similar preference for neutrality when war threatens. Cheshire too has its powerful county boss, Sir William Brereton, who takes over when war reveals the other local oligarchs' lack of resolution, and who governs in alliance with men from outside the old elite. Like Weldon, Brereton has to rely on support from Westminster to overcome his relative weakness among the leading Cheshire gentry: like Weldon he is an agent of centralization. In the wartime polarization that he helps to provoke occurs "the temporary triumph of the Westminster viewpoint" over that of the county community, just as it does in Kent.[29]

But there are differences. In the first place, Morrill finds more social and ideological content to the dispute between Brereton and the Cheshire moderates than Everitt found in the corresponding struggle in Kent. Brereton's appeals to the people, his cultivation of sequestration committees at the hundred level, and his close ties with religious Independents like Samuel Eaton offended the old community elite just as much as his importation of West-minster authority. Brereton's priorities enabled him to accept the risks of social disruption in the single-minded pursuit of military victory—victory that was the essential preliminary to political and religious reform. On this showing, Brereton and his allies were inspired by something more than a simple "desire of rule."[30] Secondly, as already noted, Morrill's conception of the county community is broader than Everitt's through his inclusion of the lower social groups. Morrill argues that Puritanism was widely distributed throughout the county, not confined (as Everitt claims for Kent) to a few towns and clothing villages. For this and other reasons, the Cheshire yeomen and husbandmen tended to side with Parliament, and much of Brereton's strength derived from his popularity among the Puritan freeholders.[31] Above all, Morrill shows that Parliament's victory stimulated "a new self-awareness of the village communities," evident in greater popular participation in parish government (both secular and ecclesiastical), and a more self-confident demand for the reform of social abuses.[32]

It might perhaps be supposed that the undoubted differences between Kent and Cheshire society account for these contrasting analyses: that Everitt could not examine popular consciousness in Kent because it did not exist there at anything like the same level as in Cheshire. Another observer takes a different view. In his recent study of Kent society and politics, Peter Clark convincingly argues for a widespread Puritan-parliamentarian sentiment among the lower orders.[33] Having described socioeconomic, religious, and political tensions before 1640 that somewhat modify Everitt's rosy picture of the county, Clark can more easily account for the continuation of these tensions during the revolutionary decades. His brief survey of Civil War Kent thus relies less heavily on selfish cliques of power-seekers using imported military force to advance themselves. The election of the opposition partisan, Augustine Skinner, as knight of the shire in February 1642 was only one among many symptoms of a more radical outlook among the lesser freeholders than among the gentry. Clark also makes much more of the spread of radical Puritanism in the 1640s in the Weald and some of the urban centers.[34] The county community concept, brilliant as it was in Everitt's original formulation, is thus susceptible to further refinement. Indeed, it gains rather than loses when it is enlarged beyond its gentry base.

At the opposite end of the interpretative spectrum is the Marxist model of class politics. Instead of Everitt's regional or county consciousness as the determinant, we have class consciousness; instead of communities of gentry as the instruments of action (or inaction), we have the "middling sort," the bourgeoisie. The most persuasive exponent of this thesis is, of course, Christopher Hill, all of whose works contain a powerfully unified conception of 1640–60 as England's bourgeois revolution, a conception sustained by impressive scholarship. But Hill is a general, not a local, historian, and I know of no Marxist account of the politics of any specific English local community in this period. There are, however, some clues as to how a Marxist historian approaches the subject in the writings of Brian Manning. Although Manning's concerns do not require him to study any single region in the depth exemplified by the Everitt school, his work is a useful starting point for an assessment of the Marxist view of local societies during the English Revolution.[35]

In Everitt's England political life is confined to the county community elites. In Manning's England, on the other hand, the gentry play a negative or counterrevolutionary role, and the real source of historical change is found in the "middle sort of people." The poor (among whom Manning includes journeymen and laborers as well as paupers) are again seen as either apolitical or servile, but the middle sort display "a hostility towards the nobility and gentry . . . which converted constitutional, political and religious issues into class conflicts."[36] Now whatever may be thought of Manning's class analysis, it must be conceded that it rests on an impressive demonstration of the extent of earlier social tensions. The grievances of West Riding clothiers, the struggles between peasants and landlords, and the riots in the fen and forest districts may or may not be sufficient to explain the behavior of these regions in the Civil War, but Manning's argument for their relevance deserves to be taken seriously.[37]

Popular support for Parliament was strongest, Manning shows, in areas where there existed a strong middle class, independent of both landlord and large employer through a combination of agricultural and industrial employment. Thus, the small clothiers of the West Riding gave their district a more parliamentarian tone than was evident in broadcloth Wiltshire, where large employers with dependent laborers were the rule. Other industrial districts were equally militant—for example, the metal-working towns and villages of the Birmingham area, where, again, "smallholding handicraftsmen" were the key element.[38] As for agricultural England, Manning finds the greatest Roundhead zeal in the fen and forest regions, with their independent peasantry and their recent history of riot against drainage and disafforestation. In all regions, agricultural or semi-industrial, the middle sort, the "godly people," rallied behind the ideological banner of Puritanism. The king's greatest strength, correspondingly, lay in the parts of England where a more traditional economy survived, and where the bonds of deference enabled great aristocrats to call out their client gentry and tenants. But even here, Manning argues, the lords relied more on threats against the recalcitrant than on any sense of genuine loyalty.[39] It is a far cry from the smooth, contented system of hierarchy in Everitt's Kent.

Manning's greatest difficulty is the one that confronts any historian who imposes modern class categories on a preindustrial society. His evidence of bourgeois enthusiasm for the godly cause in the West Riding and similar areas in 1642 and 1643 is impressive, and it is impossible to doubt the existence of a rudimentary sort of class consciousness in some of these semi-industrial communities. But this is not the whole story, for communities of this kind were very different from those of more traditional, agricultural England. Manning, of course, recognizes this and presents some intelligible reasons why most English peasants did not support the revolution. They were, he thinks, still imprisoned in their localism, often resentful of a particular abuse by an oppressive landlord, but not yet conscious of general class grievances against the whole system. The wealthier yeomen in fact benefited from that system economically, and enjoyed modest political influence in their roles as jurymen, petty constables, churchwardens, and the like. Even the poorer peasants had no wish to destroy manorial structures that gave some protection to their rights and were part of a world of at least semi-benevolent paternalism.[40] Traditional agrarian communities were therefore hostile, or at best neutral, toward a Parliament that stood for change. Only in the fen, forest, and industrializing regions can we expect to find a bourgeoisie that identified its interests with Westminster.

This contrast between class-conscious independent communities and unawakened traditionalist ones is familiar, and seems to work fairly well during the first year or two of the Civil War. After 1644, however, it runs into serious difficulties, as will be apparent from a brief consideration of the most widespread popular protest movement of the entire revolutionary period, the rising of the Clubmen. The episode still awaits a definitive modern study, but the central facts can be quickly summarized.

Beginning in December 1644 and continuing throughout the next year, in a huge arc from Sussex to Devonshire and north from Dorset to Shropshire, nearly all the counties of southern and western England were engulfed at various times by popular neutralist outbreaks.[41] Armed with clubs, pitchforks, and an occasional fowling piece, the yeomen and husbandmen organized to protect their homes and properties from the depredations of Cavaliers and Roundheads alike. It is hard to get a clear sense of the Clubmen's political and social outlook because their behavior was so often opportunist—taking the winning side in the hope of getting the war over quickly—and because they were exposed to infiltration and influence by both of the warring factions. Their manifestoes were written for them by lawyers and clergymen, their leadership taken over by minor local gentlemen. The largest Club group in Dorset and Wiltshire was lured into the Cavalier camp before being smashed by Cromwell in August 1645. The biggest group in Somerset drifted into a parliamentarian alliance by the time of Fairfax's attack on Bristol a month later. Both of these lapses from neutrality may in part have reflected local opinion, but it is clear that neither group was completely autonomous.

So the actions of the Clubmen were not necessarily spontaneous expressions of the outlook of the rural lower orders. Still, by their very willingness to defend the integrity of their communities they were taking a political stance. And with due allowance for the rhetoric of their legal or clerical draftsmen, it was a consistently traditionalist stance, from whatever kind of community they came. A good many of the Clubmen's manifestoes have survived, from the one adopted by "the inhabitants of all the Northwest part of the County of Worcester" at Woodbury Hill on 5 March 1645, to the Berkshire declaration at Compton Down on 12 August.[42] Time after time they reaffirm the four points of the Protestation of 1641, subscribed by the whole kingdom before its unhappy division: to defend "the true reformed Protestant religion," the king's "royal person and estate," "the power and privilege of Parliaments," and "the lawful rights and liberties of the subjects."[43] Repeatedly they echo the four points of the Wiltshire and Dorset declaration issued at the end of May 1645, which again included the defense of the Protestant religion, of law, liberty, and property. And they define the "Protestant reformed religion" as that existing in the purer times of Queen Elizabeth and King James.[44]

These are generalities, but the point is that they are not revolutionary generalities. And the conservatism of the Clubmen is as evident among those from the more economically independent fen region of central Somerset or the clothing parishes in the north of the county as among those from the more traditionalist sheep-corn economies of Dorset and downland Wiltshire; among those who were in the end drawn to Parliament's side as among their more royalist counterparts. Humphrey Willis, leader of the parliamentarian Clubmen of Somerset, demanded that the four Wiltshire-Dorset articles be proclaimed in every parish church; his attachment to the traditional order is clear in all his later utterances.[45] A group of New Forest Clubmen declared themselves obedient subjects of Parliament. But they left "those high affaires of State, concerning Religion, Lawes, and Government, to be agitated in their proper Sphere, they being mysteries above the capacity of un-knowing multitudes."[46] A possibly more royalist body in Sussex protested against the encouragement of mechanic preachers and the public employment of "men of sordid condition" instead of "gentlemen of worth, birth and integrity, and knowne amongst us."[47]

The Club outbreaks were vertically organized, combining all levels of local society from lesser gentry to poor farmers in a move to defend the integrity of their communities against external threats. Some of the conservatism of their manifestoes may have been foisted on them by their spokesmen. Yet if the countrymen had wanted revolution they could have behaved as their fellows in the industrial districts—Manning's middle sort—had done in 1642 and 1643, could have come out actively for a forward policy of Puritan reformation. They did not do so.[48] Popular royalism can be explained as the enforced response of a deference society, the compulsory enlistment of the lower orders in the cause of their landlords. The Club movement, featuring men of small estates acting in opposition to their politicized superiors, cannot be disposed of in this way. Nobody *made* the Clubmen turn out in the thousands who came to their swarming, disorderly gatherings. No doubt most were motivated only by the immediate goal of protecting hearth and home, and understood little of the conservative political program that was devised for them. But they accepted it, were prepared to demonstrate and sometimes even fight for it, with more vigor than they had shown for either king or Parliament.

The Marxist model of local political behavior is useful in that it reminds us that the English Revolution was not simply a collision between groups of peers and gentry operating in a social vacuum. But the analysis is most valid for places in which industrial or commercial development had produced something resembling a class society: in the towns—London above all—and in areas with mixed industrial and agrarian economies. It is less easily applied to the wider world of rural England. Even in the fens and forests the vertical ties of community still determined the behavior of ordinary Englishmen far more compellingly than any hypothetical sense of class. To regain the path to that elusive goal of a general theory of local politics in the revolution, we must retrace our steps to Everitt's starting point. We must then make a further exploration of these fens and forests.

At the very outset of *The Community of Kent*, Everitt noted how remarkably dissimilar were the histories and social structures of the English counties. Nevertheless, in his original model of community politics there are relatively few variables, and so it is fairly easy to make comparisons between counties, especially as Everitt provides a superb methodological example. Investigating kinship groups, distinguishing between indigenous and recently arrived families, establishing the political hierarchy of the county: these are essential steps whatever one's view of the autonomy of the lower ranks of society. To explain differences in the behavior of counties in the Civil War, Everitt appeals mainly to variations in the relative antiquity of the gentry. Thus, the fact that in Kent nearly three quarters of the gentry were indigenous (established there before Tudor times) helps to explain the strength of localist opposition to Parliament; that only a third of the Suffolk gentry had such deep roots accounts for that county's more parliamentarian complexion.[49] Another variable is the relationship between a county's gentry and its aristocrats. In spite of having recently undergone a striking period of mobility (a large proportion of its gentry were new arrivals), Northamptonshire was politically fairly quiet during the civil war, whereas nearby Leicestershire, with a much more stable gentry, was the scene of constant faction. But Leicestershire had long been torn by the rivalry of the Hastings and the Greys, each trying to attract a gentry following. In Northamptonshire, on the other hand, there was no serious challenger to the Comptons to split the gentry into factions. The royalist earl of Northampton was easily overcome by a bloc of the new parliamentarian families.[50]

With its relatively small range of variables, the county community thesis seems to make the task of devising a general theory of local politics in the civil war a manageable one. But if we go on to insist, as both Everitt in his more recent work and other agricultural historians have done, that the variables are almost infinite—related to economic and geographical differences over small areas of even the same county—then proposing a general theory becomes difficult indeed. Yet in spite of (or perhaps because of) its baffling complexity, the "local-particularist" approach characteristic of Joan Thirsk, Everitt's later work, and the school of local historians associated with the University of Leicester offers some promising lines of investigation.

At the heart of the local-particularist model is the series of contrasting social and economic types that we have already en

countered in a different form when considering Brian Manning's
work: the "field-pasture" dichotomy.[51] In the field areas—the
regions of arable farming that covered much of southern and
eastern England—the traditional pattern of largely unenclosed
villages still prevailed. It was, to be sure, being transformed by the
trend toward capitalist farming in such counties as Wiltshire,
with bigger farms in severalty producing for the market.[52] But
even where this happened, the old settlement pattern remained
substantially unchanged: the nucleated village, grouped around
church and manor house (often with a resident squire), the whole
structure tightly bound by kinship and custom, and by readily
available mechanisms of social control. In the dairying or cattle-
grazing districts, and even more obviously in the fen and woodland areas, there was a very different pattern of settlement.
Villages tended to be more scattered, with several small hamlets
to a parish or isolated family farms working enclosed fields, and
to be less subject to strict manorial control. The inhabitants were
therefore more economically independent and more remote from
the authority of squire or parson. The forest villages, especially,
were often "open" settlements, unable or unwilling to prevent
immigration by newcomers. They thus tended to grow more
rapidly than the older, close-knit townships, and to become more
unstable, more vulnerable to high prices in bad harvest years. In
many places industrial employment, usually part-time, helped to
sustain this expanding population, exposing it to the vagaries of
the trade cycle, and detaching it even further from the less changing world of the common fields.[53]

The natural hypothesis to be derived from this form of analysis
is that popular support for Puritanism before 1640, and for Parliament during the war, is likely to have been stronger in the fen,
forest, and pasture regions than in the more traditionalist arable
districts. The combination of large parishes, weak manorial structures, strong traditions of common rights, and rapid population
growth might stimulate religious and political, as well as economic, independence.[54] Although no sufficiently detailed investigations of particular regions have been made from which firm
conclusions could be drawn, in a general way the evidence does
seem to support this hypothesis. The fens, woodland areas such
as the Kentish Weald and the Forest of Dean, and mixed agricultural and industrial districts like the clothing parishes of north-
east Somerset generally seem to have been markedly Puritan
before 1640 and strongly parliamentarian in the war. The distribution of post-1660 rural nonconformity also supports this
correlation between Puritanism and the forest or pasture type of
settlement.[55] Indeed, Everitt has suggested that the parliamen-

tarian armies were largely recruited from areas of this kind. No systematic attempt has been made to prove or disprove this, but the idea deserves investigation, as does Everitt's other suggestion that the older forest villages may have preferred the more traditional forms of Puritanism, while the newer, less stable heath settlements were characterized by a wilder kind of millenarianism. Here we are approaching the different conceptions of the Puritans as "masterless men" proposed by Michael Walzer and Christopher Hill; Hill makes the direct link between radical Puritanism and the fens and forests.[56]

We have already observed how attractive the field-forest antithesis can be for Marxist historians. Different geographical conditions produce different economic systems and hence different stages of class consciousness. Two important questions, however, still have to be answered. First, were the pastoral and industrial districts Puritan and parliamentarian because of their economies or because of their distinctive parochial and manorial structures? Secondly, was the more activist mentality of these places typically expressed in horizontal class terms or in vertical, local-community ones?

Some light has recently been thrown on the first question by Margaret Spufford's *Contrasting Communities*, a comparative study of three villages in Cambridgeshire. The book demonstrates the local-particularist method at a very close level of analysis, so much so that the conclusions are often hedged about by an impenetrable thicket of reservations about the quality of the evidence. Spufford's analysis of the mentalities of her peasant communities is also less than complete: she ignores politics and those aspects of popular culture that Keith Thomas has recently brought into prominence.[57] But her discussion of religion is very thorough. On her showing the most important determinant of the distribution of Puritanism was the strength of manorial control—weak or divided manorial structures with absentee lords tending to coincide with strong Puritan congregations—and this was a more decisive factor than anything relating to the field-forest contrast. However, much of the evidence on which this argument rests is from after 1660. One of her communities, Willingham, was a fen-edge village with the usual characteristics: more equal distribution of property, more plentiful commons, wider educational opportunities, and so on, compared with the field villages. There are some hints that before 1640 Willingham was more Puritan than the other settlements.[58]

Be that as it may, Spufford sets an example that needs to be widely followed. Many more comparative studies—as well as ones of single parishes, such as the one of Myddle, Shropshire, by

David Hey[59]—will be required before we can answer this question or the one about class and community with any confidence. On the latter point, the Clubmen episode suggests that class consciousness, when it existed, was so constricted by localism and so sporadic in appearance as to be of limited value to the historian in search of an explanation. But it need scarcely be repeated that the relationship between class, community, and nation is of great complexity, and this is not the place to embark on further discussion of it. The task of this essay has been not the impossible one of settling such questions, but that of examining the various models that historians have found useful and indicating some of the further lines of investigation that need to be pursued.

In the end what is needed is an approach which combines the careful analysis of elites characteristic of the county community school with the local particularism of the agricultural historians; which explores village communities with Spufford's painstaking detail, while taking account of the anthropological methods by which Keith Thomas has reconstructed popular culture; which recognizes class consciousness when appropriate, but does not make it the universal mechanism that it clearly was not. Formidable problems of evidence will have to be surmounted to distinguish the political outlook of the lower orders from that of their elite leaders, and perhaps these problems will be insurmountable. Yet the Clubmen's activities suggest that there may be possibilities of illumination even in less politicized communities than the industrial wood-pasture ones that figure more prominently in the record. There will be many puzzling exceptions to whatever general theory can be advanced, many contradictions. At this stage the field-pasture dichotomy appears likely to be the most immediately promising conceptual tool. What we need is to achieve a form of the *Annales* type of "total" history. Even in the well-tilled fields of the English Revolution there is still work to be done.

## Notes

1. Compare, for example, the surface account of Godfrey Davies, *The Early Stuarts 1603–1660* (Oxford, 1937), with the complex synthesis provided by Lawrence Stone, *The Causes of the English Revolution 1529–1642* (London, 1972), or by J. H. Hexter, "The English Aristocracy, Its Crises, and the English Revolution, 1558–1660," *Journal of British Studies* 8, no. 1 (November 1968): 22–78.

2. Alan Everitt, *The Community of Kent and the Great Rebellion 1640–60* (Leicester, 1966). Everitt had already advanced the "county community" hypothesis in earlier publications, notably "The Community of Kent in 1640," *Genealogists' Magazine* 14, no. 8 (1963), and in his introduction to *Suffolk and the Great Rebellion 1640–1660*, Suffolk Records Society, vol. 3 (Ipswich, 1960).

3. Mary Coate, *Cornwall in the Great Civil War and Interregnum, 1642–1660* (Oxford, 1933); A. C. Wood, *Nottinghamshire in the Civil War* (Oxford, 1937).

4. J. E. Neale, *The Elizabethan House of Commons* (New Haven, 1950), chap. 1; A. H. Dodd, *Studies in Stuart Wales* (Cardiff, 1952), chap. 4; P. Laslett, "The Gentry of Kent in 1640," *Cambridge Historical Journal* 9 (1948): 148–64.

5. Thomas G. Barnes, *Somerset 1625–1640: A County's Government During the "Personal Rule"* (Cambridge, Mass., 1961). Among other studies of the gentry of this period, note J. T. Cliffe, *The Yorkshire Gentry From the Reformation to the Civil War* (London, 1969), which, however, is not explicitly based on the county community concept.

6. A. M. Everitt, *The Local Community and the Great Rebellion* (Historical Association Pamphlet G.70, 1969), p. 5.

7. Everitt, *Suffolk*, pp. 33–34.

8. Ibid., p. 7.

9. Everitt, *Kent*, p. 151; see also pp. 139, 145–46, 149.

10. Ibid., p. 16.

11. Ibid., p. 14. For a different view of local politics under the Protectorate, see David Underdown, "Settlement in the Counties 1653–1658," in *The Interregnum: The Quest for Settlement 1646–1660*, ed. G. E. Aylmer (London, 1972), pp. 165–82.

12. Everitt, *Kent*, chap. 9.

13. Ibid., pp. 134–35.

14. Ibid., p. 118.

15. See, for example, ibid., pp. 86–87, 95, 104, 107.

16. Ibid., p. 70; and see also p. 83.

17. Roland Mousnier, *Peasant Uprisings in Seventeenth-Century France, Russia, and China*, trans. Brian Pearce, (New York, 1972), esp. chap. 1. The applicability of Mousnier's thesis to England is considered by C. S. L. Davies, "Peasant Revolt in France and England: a Comparison," *Agricultural History Review* 21 (1973): 122–34.

18. Among the counties Everitt has dealt with, Leicestershire is perhaps an exception: Everitt, *Local Community*, pp. 15–16, 18.

19. Conrad Russell, ed., *The Origins of the English Civil War* (London, 1973), Introduction, p. 7; James E. Farnell, "The Aristocracy and Leadership of Parliament in the English Civil Wars," *Journal of Modern History* 44 (1972): 79–86. See also the articles by Paul Christianson and Farnell in *Journal of Modern History* 49 (1977): 575–99, 641–60.

20. Paul Christianson, "The Causes of the English Revolution: A Reappraisal," *Journal of British Studies* 15, no. 2 (Spring 1976): 40–75.

21. Clive Holmes, *The Eastern Association in the English Civil War* (Cambridge, 1974).

22. See, for example, ibid., pp. 54–55.

23. Ibid., chap. 1, and p. 4. See also Holmes, "Colonel King and Lincolnshire Politics, 1642–1646," *Historical Journal* 16 (1973): 451–84.

24. Holmes, *Eastern Association*, pp. 19–22, 26, 34–48.

25. Ibid., pp. 36, 43–44.

26. Peter Laslett, *The World We Have Lost* (London, 1965).

27. See, for example, among many other possible citations, R. S. Schofield, "The Measurement of Literacy in Pre-Industrial England," in *Literacy in Traditional Societies*, ed. Jack Goody (Cambridge, 1968), pp. 311–25; Lawrence Stone, "Literacy and Education in England 1640–1900," *Past and Present* 42 (February 1969): 69–139, and "The Educational Revolution in England, 1560–1640," ibid. 28 (July 1964): 41–80; Margaret Spufford, "The Schooling of the Peasantry in Cambridgeshire," in *Land, Church and People: Essays Presented to Professor H. P. R. Finberg*, ed. Joan Thirsk (Reading, 1970), pp. 112–47; Carl Bridenbaugh, *Vexed and Troubled Englishmen 1590–1642* (New York, 1968), esp. pp. 240–51; Derek Hirst, *The Representative of the People? Voters and Voting in England under the Early Stuarts* (Cambridge, 1975).

28. J. S. Morrill, *Cheshire 1630–1660: County Government and Society during the English Revolution* (Oxford, 1974). Another attempt to extend the county community can be found in David Underdown, *Somerset in the Civil War and Interregnum* (Newton Abbot, 1973).

29. Morrill, *Cheshire*, p. 69, and in general, chaps. 2–4.

30. Ibid., pp. 147–67, 173.

31. Ibid., pp. 22, 78–79, 82–84, 132–34; Everitt, *Kent*, p. 126.

32. Morrill, *Cheshire*, chap. 6.

33. Peter Clark, *English Provincial Society from the Reformation to the Revolution: Religion, Politics and Society in Kent 1500–1640* (Hassocks, Sussex, 1977). I am grateful to Mr. Clark for permitting me to read the later chapters of his book in typescript.

34. Ibid., chap. 13.

35. For this summary of Manning's views I have relied mainly upon his *The English People and the English Revolution 1640–1649* (London, 1976). See also his "Religion and Politics: the Godly People," chap. 3 of *Politics, Religion and the English Civil War,* ed. Brian Manning (London, 1973); and "The Peasantry and the English Revolution," *Journal of Peasant Studies* 2 (1974–75): 133–58.

36. Manning, *English People,* Preface, p. vi. See also "Religion and Politics," pp. 102–4, 107.

37. See esp. Manning, "Peasantry"; and *English People,* chap. 6.

38. *English People,* chap. 7; Manning, "Religion and Politics," p. 105.

39. Manning, "Peasantry," pp. 138–48; *English People,* chap. 8, esp. pp. 230–33.

40. Manning, "Peasantry," pp. 154–55; "Religion and Politics," pp. 109–10.

41. By far the best account of the Clubmen is that in J. S. Morrill, *The Revolt of the Provinces* (London, 1976), pp. 98–114, which appeared after this essay was written. Morrill's superb book is a brilliant attempt to confront, all too briefly, the problems discussed even more briefly in this essay. However, its tendency to depict community sentiment as almost universally localist and to gloss over regional variations in popular allegiance means that it is not quite the last word on the subject. Morrill provides full references for virtually all previous work on the Clubmen. Manning's *English People* curiously ignores them, though they receive much attention in his thesis, "Neutrals and Neutralism in the English Civil War" (Oxford D. Phil., 1957).

42. J. W. Willis Bund, ed., *Diary of Henry Townshend of Elmley Lovett 1640–1663,* Worcester Historical Society (London, 1920), 2:221–23; Historical Manuscripts Commission, *Portland MSS,* 1:246–47.

43. British Library (hereafter B.L.), E. 274, 24: *Kingdomes Weekly Intelligencer* 92 (18–25 Mar. 1645), pp. 736–37; *The Humble Petition of the Inhabitants of the County of Dorset* (8 July 1645); *Diary of Henry Townshend,* 2:222; Bodleian Library, Tanner MS. 60, fols. 196–200. The 1641 Protestation is printed in Samuel R. Gardiner ed., *Constitutional Documents of the Puritan Revolution,* 3d ed. (Oxford, 1906), pp. 155–56.

44. B.L., E. 286, 28: *Mercurius Civicus* 106 (29 May–5 June 1645), pp. 945–46; B.L., E. 287, 7: *Kingdomes Weekly Intelligencer* 103 (3–10 June 1645), p. 824; B.L., E. 288, 18: *True Informer* 8 (7–14 June 1645), pp. 59–60. B.L., E. 292, 24: *The Desires, and Resolutions of the Club-Men of the Counties of Dorset and Wilts* (12 July 1645); B.L., E. 300, 13: *A Copy of a Petition* (10 Sept. 1645).

45. B.L., E. 293, 33: *Continuation of the Proceedings of the Army . . . 11–19 July* (26 July 1645), p. 14. See also Underdown, *Somerset,* pp. 107, 118, 191.

46. B.L., E. 297, 4: *Heads of Some Notes of the Cities Scout* 4 (19 Aug. 1645), p. 2.

47. Bodleian Library, Tanner MS. 60, fols. 25, 251–55.

48. Except perhaps in north Somerset, where their parliamentarian stance was foreshadowed by their behavior in 1642: Underdown, *Somerset,* pp. 34–40, 106, 111–13. For Manning's conception of the Clubmen, see "Neutrals and Neutralism," chap. 6. He puts more stress on the revolutionary implications of the Clubmen's mode of organization than on what he concedes were their conservative demands, and attributes the presence of gentry and clergy among them to an upper-class attempt to control what would otherwise have been a serious threat to property.

49. Everitt, *Kent,* p. 36; *Suffolk,* p. 21. It might be noted, however, that the proportion of indigenous gentry in Norfolk was at least as high as in Kent (Holmes,

*Eastern Association*, p. 12). Norfolk may have been less parliamentarian than often supposed, but it was certainly a good deal more so than Kent.

50. Everitt, *Local Community*, pp. 15–18, 22.

51. Joan Thirsk, "The Farming Regions of England," In *Agrarian History of England and Wales: 1500–1640*, ed. Joan Thirsk (vol. 4 of *Agrarian History of England and Wales*, edited by H. P. R. Finberg) (Cambridge, 1967), chap. 1; Alan M. Everitt, "Farm Labourers," in ibid., chap. 7; Joan Thirsk, "Seventeenth-Century Agriculture and Social Change," in Thirsk, *Land, Church and People*, pp. 148–77.

52. See, for example, E. Kerridge, "Agriculture c. 1500–c. 1700," in *Victoria County History of Wiltshire*, ed. Elizabeth Crittall, vol. 4 (London, 1959), esp. pp. 57–58.

53. Thirsk, "Farming Regions," pp. 8–13; and "Seventeenth-Century Agriculture," pp. 152, 157–58, 165, 167–68; Everitt, "Farm Labourers," pp. 409–12, 424–25, 433–35. For an example of the concept's application, see V. H. T. Shipp, "Economic and Social Change in the Forest of Arden, 1530–1649," in Thirsk, *Land, Church and People*, pp. 84–111.

54. The survival into the eighteenth century of this tradition of independence and community solidarity in the forest villages has recently been brilliantly documented in E. P. Thompson, *Whigs and Hunters: The Origin of the Black Act* (New York, 1975).

55. Alan Everitt, "Nonconformity in Country Parishes," in Thirsk, *Land, Church and People*, pp. 178–99.

56. Everitt, "Farm Labourers," p. 463; "Nonconformity," pp. 192–93; Michael Walzer, *The Revolution of the Saints* (Cambridge, Mass., 1965); Christopher Hill, *The World Turned Upside Down: Radical Ideas during the English Revolution* (London, 1972), esp. chap. 3.

57. Margaret Spufford, *Contrasting Communities: English Villagers in the Sixteenth and Seventeenth Centuries* (Cambridge, 1974); Keith Thomas, *Religion and the Decline of Magic* (London, 1971).

58. Spufford, *Contrasting Communities*, part 3, esp. pp. 227–28, 246, 255–57, 262–63, 276–80, 283–84, 337, and chap. 12.

59. David G. Hey, *An English Rural Community: Myddle under the Tudors and Stuarts* (Leicester, 1974).

# The Residential Development of the West End of London in the Seventeenth Century

## LAWRENCE STONE

### The Growth of London

#### THE PHENOMENON OF GROWTH

One of the most striking phenomena of seventeenth-century Europe was the rapid growth, in size, political and cultural importance, and architectural distinction, of the great capital cities, such as London, Paris, Rome, Vienna, and Brussels. This growth was stimulated by a wide variety of factors, of which the remarkable demographic expansion of Europe was only one. Our best guess at present is that between 1500 and 1620 the population of England and Wales increased from less than two and a half million to nearly five million. Thereafter the rate of increase slowed down, and the total population is unlikely to have risen between 1620 and 1700 by more than about 10 percent: that is, from 4.8 million to 5.3 million.

If this two-stage demographic development of the nation is compared with that of London, it becomes apparent that the latter continued to grow rapidly with no sign of any slowdown after the middle of the seventeenth century. The result was a remarkable expansion of the built-up area, particularly to the west and the east (figs. 1 and 2). This growth far exceeded that of all other English towns, very few of which seemed to have increased in size disproportionately to the general population growth. The result was that an ever-increasing proportion of the total population, and an ever-increasing proportion of the urban population, found itself crowded into the metropolis of London. Evidence of the first trend is provided by the comparative figures, which suggest that between 1500 and 1700 London's population rose from 2 percent to 10 percent of that of England and Wales.[1] By 1700 one Englishman in ten lived in the metropolis (see table 1).

*Table 1.* Growth of London's population, 1500–1700

| Date | Greater London | England and Wales | Percentage |
|------|----------------|-------------------|------------|
| 1500 | 60,000 | 2,300,000 | 2% |
| 1600 | 225,000 | 4,300,000 | 5% |
| 1660 | 460,000 | 5,000,000 | 8% |
| 1700 | 550,000 | 5,300,000 | 10% |
| 1800 | 1,120,000 | 8,900,000 | 13% |
| 1900 | 6,590,000 | 32,500,000 | 20% |

The second trend, the growing concentration of the urbanized sector of the population in a single city, is illustrated by the fact that whereas in 1524 the population of London was equal to that of the six largest provincial towns, by 1680 it was equal to that of the sixty largest.[2] At that time Gregory King calculated that all other English towns with a population of over one thousand contained only 225,000 persons, so that by then two out of every three persons who could conceivably be described as urban dwellers lived in London. By 1660 London was already at least twenty times larger than any of its nearest rivals, Norwich, York, Bristol, and Newcastle, and by 1700 the difference must have been even greater.[3] By then London was not only the second largest city in Europe; it also contained the largest proportion of the population of any nation-state. Of the state capitals of early eighteenth-century Western Europe, only Paris exceeded it in size, and Paris contained less than 5 percent of the population of the nation, compared with London's more than 10 percent.[4] Both absolutely and relatively, London was a unique phenomenon for the seventeenth century, a city whose extraordinary growth requires careful explanation.

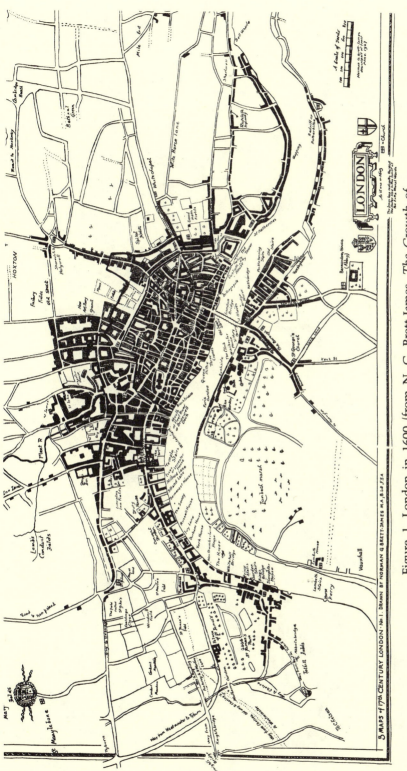

Figure 1. London in 1600 (from N. G. Brett-James, *The Growth of Stuart London* [London, 1935], p. 78. Reproduced by permission of G. Allen and Unwin Ltd.).

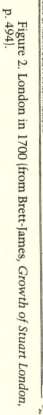

Figure 2. London in 1700 (from Brett-James, *Growth of Stuart London*, p. 494).

## IMMIGRATION

Deaths in London always greatly exceeded births, due to the unsanitary conditions prevalent in the crowded urban environment. Consequently the scale and character of London's expansion were dependent on immigration, not internal growth. This immigration consisted of three quite distinct social groups: a numerically very large influx of the drifting poor; a substantial but regulated flow of urban artisan apprentices, amounting in 1700 to about 1,900 a year;[5] and a small but highly significant movement, temporary or permanent, of landed and professional classes. The extent of vagrancy and the burden of poor relief suggest that a large mass of rootless unemployed first became a permanent feature of the English countryside in the sixteenth and seventeenth centuries.[6] There were many causes of this new phenomenon. Firstly, between 1500 and 1620 there was a very rapid growth of population, especially in the countryside, which in some districts was greater than could be absorbed by the demand for labor in the expanding area of cultivation and in the growing rural domestic industries. Decade by decade, villages grew in size, and decade by decade they still had a surplus of young people who were obliged to move elsewhere. Secondly, throughout the sixteenth and seventeenth centuries there was taking place a slow but steady change in land tenure, by which peasant copyholders or small freeholders were replaced by a few substantial tenant farmers employing considerable numbers of landless wage laborers. Thirdly, the demand for labor, both in agriculture and in rural industry, was intermittent and precarious;[7] and finally, in about 1620, industrial activity, especially in iron, coal, and cloth, moved into a period of prolonged near-stagnation. While other English towns grew in size—and grew, like London, by immigration—only one or two industrial centers seem to have expanded faster than the general level of population. It was London, and only London, which offered such varied opportunities for earning a living of sorts in domestic service with the middle and upper classes, in supplying them with a wide range of goods and services, in the proliferating service occupations of a great city, in craft and finishing trades, in house building, in handling the rapidly growing volume of overseas commerce, and in preying on the rich by theft or begging. It has been plausibly estimated that the growth of London between 1650 and 1750, despite the excess of deaths over births in the city because of disease, demanded a net annual inflow of 8,000 persons. This means that at least half the natural increase of the population of all England and Wales poured into London year after year throughout the century. When they arrived, the immigrants settled where they could, many of them on the marshy lands to the east of the city, where they created dense and dangerous slums without planning, sanitation, or police. A sample of 104 inhabitants of Whitechapel and Stepney between 1580 and 1640 reveals that only 14 percent were born in London or the suburbs, and that more than two-thirds came from more than fifty miles away. Only half of them had lived in the parish for more than ten years, so that it was a highly volatile community. Judging by tax records, at least a third of the population of most towns consisted of the abject poor on the very margin of subsistence, and the proportion was probably even higher in London, especially in these teeming, disease-ridden slums in the eastern suburbs along the river.[8]

The second immigrant group consisted of young men whose parents or guardians had sufficient funds to apprentice them to some London guild or company. Many settled down and joined the swelling ranks of the artisans in the city, while others returned again to the countryside to practice their craft, carrying with them the memory of city pleasures, tastes, and styles. In the first half of the seventeenth century the apprentices were drawn from a very wide catchment area, a surprising number coming from north of the Trent. By the end of the century, however, the recruitment pattern had changed, and the area of out-migration was increasingly concentrated in the southeast. This change may indicate either a contraction in the socially acceptable span of geographical migration; or a rise of alternative sources of urban employment in places like Birmingham and Sheffield; or a shift in the storm center of demographic pressure; or a combination of all three.[9]

The social consequences of this immigration are of the first importance. London took the pressure off the countryside by draining off its surplus population. This not only helped, along with an efficient and expensive poor relief system, to damp the fires of rural unrest; it also facilitated the processes of agrarian consolidation and enclosure which were essential preliminaries to the expansion of agricultural output. This output in turn made it possible to feed the city, so that late seventeenth-century England never experienced those catastrophic famines which continued to be the scourge of much of continental Europe up to about 1740. By 1700 English agriculture could feed a population that was double that of two hundred years before, and it could also sustain a significant and growing volume of grain exports.[10] Heavy immigration to London was thus one factor among many in maintaining relative social tranquility and stimulating an adequate supply of agricultural and industrial goods.

These were accidental and incidental consequences, but this

immigration made a more direct and positive contribution to the modernization of English society. The move to the city cut the immigrants loose from the constricting bonds of their kin and village community, and opened their eyes to a wider world. It may have plunged many of them into a life of poverty and squalor as grim as that described by Henry Mayhew over a century later, but it also seems that many, perhaps the majority, became more consumer-oriented, earned higher real wages, and were more literate and more politically articulate, than the country cousins they left behind them.[11] Finally, the congregation of so many people in one place created a demand for food which stimulated the growth of a specialized market economy in the countryside for up to eighty miles around.[12]

When all is said and done, however, the dynamo which drives a preindustrial city—and even London in 1700 must still be regarded as in a preindustrial stage—is not the labor of the working class but the wealth generated by the commercial and business classes and the consumer demand of a leisured aristocratic elite. The remarkable growth in the volume of trade, and particularly the colonial re-export trade, in the last half of the seventeenth century created a class of enormously wealthy commercial tycoons, and also greatly stimulated employment in the old city and downriver to the east. It has been estimated that by 1700 as much as a quarter of the population was employed in the port trades. Secondly, the tendency for growing numbers of the landed classes to spend some part of the year in the capital both created new employment for tens of thousands to minister to their basic needs and luxury cravings, and was the main stimulus for the development of urban architecture and urban planning. It is no accident that by far the fastest growth area in the seventeenth century was not the working-class housing along the river to the east of the old city, but the upper-class residential quarter upriver to the west.[13] For this reason the main thrust of this study is directed toward an understanding of the causes, nature, and consequences of urban development in the western suburbs.

## The Demand for Residential Housing

### THE NATURE OF THE DEMAND

The intense demand for high-quality housing in seventeenth-century London can best be explained by a threefold process: a great increase in absolute numbers of the gentry, a parallel increase in absolute numbers of the professional classes, and a growing tendency for both to converge on London, the former for part of the year, the latter as a permanent place of residence. The sixteenth and seventeenth centuries witnessed a striking rise in the numbers of those of upper-middling status and upper-middling wealth. The numbers of the titular gentry rose dramatically, those holding the title of esquire increasing from about 800 to 3,000, and those calling themselves gentlemen from about 5,000 to 15,000. At the same time, there was a remarkable increase of persons in trades and professions, particularly in the late seventeenth century, so that by 1700 Gregory King could reckon that they more or less equaled the landed classes both in numbers and in wealth.[14]

Within these growing classes there were five relatively distinct groups, each of which had different reasons for seeking housing in a residential district in the London suburbs. First, there were the magnates, mostly noblemen, who needed big houses for occupation and entertainment when they were in town in attendance at Court. In the sixteenth century these aristocrats demanded palaces to live in during their occasional visits to London, since they needed space to house their small army of retainers. By the eighteenth century, they traveled with few servants, and although they now spent more time in London than before, they were prepared to put up with a good deal of overcrowding in their town houses. It was their seats in the country upon which they lavished conspicuous consumption in buildings, gardens, parks, and lakes. In 1743 Horace Walpole complained that the nobility had abandoned the great urban palaces with extensive gardens of an earlier period and had "contracted themselves to live in coops of a dining room, a dark back room with one eye in a corner, and a closet. Think what London would be, if the chief houses were in it, as in the cities of other countries, instead of dispersed like great plums in a great pudding of country." Inspection of William Morgan's large-scale map of London and Westminster in 1682 shows that there were only about twenty-two great free-standing aristocratic palaces with gardens left, and by the time John Rocque did his new map in 1737, the number was down to ten. As a foreigner observed with surprise in the late eighteenth century, "Englishmen of rank continue to consider their estates their real residences, and their houses in London as a kind of pied-à-terre. Many who have revenues of £20,000 and more live in London with hardly a dozen rooms. Consequently, they and their numerous servants are rather crowded." In 1823 another foreigner made the same discovery: "Very few persons of rank have what we on the Continent call a palace in London. Their palaces, their luxury and grandeur are to be seen in the country." Arthur Young, on the other hand, was equally struck by the huge size of *hôtels* in Paris.[15]

Second, there were the county elite, baronets, knights, and squires, some of whom were courtiers based in London, but most of whom visited London only during the legal and social seasons, or when Parliament was sitting. In contemporary Paris, a richer member of this class would have built himself a substantial free-standing *hôtel* on his own land, to accommodate an extended family of relatives and servants that clustered around him. In seventeenth-century London a member of the equivalent class was content with the purchase or lease of a modest house in a fashionable terrace block. The leasing by Sir Edmund Verney of Middle Claydon of a double house in Covent Garden Piazza is a typical example.[16]

Third, there were the lesser parish gentry, who could not afford such a long-term investment, but merely wanted to be able to rent a furnished house for a few weeks or months in the odd year. This was a fairly numerous class, since not many gentry were London house-owners before the Civil War. Out of 800 Kent gentry, only 20 owned a house in London before 1640, although another 20 were Members of Parliament, another 30 were courtiers, and an unknown number came up to London from time to time. Although increasingly common before the war, the habit of visiting London was slow in forming among the lesser gentry and did not become a normal practice until after the Restoration. Lord Clarendon's father was a moderately substantial Wiltshire gentleman, but "from the death of Queen Elizabeth he was never in London, though he lived about 30 years after. . . . ; the wisdom and frugality of that time being such that few gentlemen made journeys to London or other expensive journeys, but upon important business, and their wives never."[17] This story seriously exaggerates the suddenness of the change of habit which was taking place gradually throughout the whole of the century, but it points to the fact that before 1640 it had affected only a limited section of the country gentry.

This conclusion is supported by an official survey made in 1632 of all gentry and above who were resident in London contrary to the recent royal Proclamation ordering a general return to the countryside. The survey covered both the old city and a wide belt of new suburbs to the north and west, and across the river in Southwark. Including wives and widows living alone in their own houses, the survey turned up 37 noblemen, 147 baronets and knights, and 130 esquires and gentlemen. This means that about one in four of the peerage, perhaps one in six of the baronetage and knightage, but less than one in a hundred of the squirarchy and gentry were then residing in London.[18]

This persistent provincialism was artificially prolonged in the mid-seventeenth century by three factors. The first was a revulsion against the growing stench and smog of the city as its growth in size outpaced its sewage and water facilities, and as it was heated increasingly—and indeed almost exclusively—by coal. The second was the thirty-year period of enforced exile from London, due first to fear of royal punishment for disobedience of the Proclamation in the 1630s, then to the civil wars of the 1640s, and finally to the absence of a royal court or cultural activities such as the theater in the 1650s. The third factor, which may well have been no more than a rationalization of the inevitable, was the intensification of the cult of rural life. Based on the writings of Horace and Virgil, this ideology took on new life between 1630 and 1660, as poets and publicists defined the ideal of the Happy Man as a cultivated gentleman living in peace and tranquility on his estate in the countryside.

Sir Thomas Fanshawe asked rhetorically in 1630:

> Who would pursue
> The smoky glory of the town
> That may go to his native earth.

His answer came in 1660, when there was a mass rush of nobles and squires back from the country to London to welcome Charles II and savor all the pleasures of luxurious urban life. The ideal of rustic living was transformed into the cultivation of sensual delights, the pursuit of willing nymphs in shady bowers.[19] But this was a pastime that could just as well, or probably better, be pursued in London.

In addition to these members of the landed elite who poured into London after 1660, there were the young gentlemen just down from the university or fresh from private tutoring at home, for whom some experience of the metropolitan scene was now regarded as an essential part of their education. In his late seventeenth-century treatise on education, Lord Clarendon wrote: "You see we have left the university at 17 years of age: and whatsoever you resolve to do, London must then be visited, and some time spent there in order to whatsoever is to be done afterwards." Some of these young gentlemen who studied the law occupied lodgings at the Inns of Court, but many others took up furnished rooms in the fashionable part of town. Finally, there were the courtiers, officials, and professional men whose duties tied them to London, and who therefore needed a permanent home in a respectable neighborhood near their place of work. This was a period in which the professions were in the painful process of acquiring gentlemanly status, and it was therefore particularly important for their members to establish their residence in the same quarter as the gentry and nobility.[20]

## THE ATTRACTIONS OF LONDON

During the course of the seventeenth century a number of developments took place which made visits to, and residence in, London more pleasant and attractive to the landed classes. In the first place the discomforts of the journey to and from London were eased by a very important innovation in transport technology. As late as the Elizabethan period most gentlemen were obliged to make the journey on horseback, an exertion which was often beyond the powers of women and the infirm, since it could last for up to a week. By the early seventeenth century, the heavy traveling coach, tightly slung on straps or chains, had superseded the horse or horse litter as a means of locomotion for the wealthy, and as a result it at last became possible for whole families, including women and children, the sick and the old, to travel considerable distances without too great discomfort. By the time Fynes Moryson was writing in 1617, the roads for thirty-five miles or so out of London were now kept in good repair, "sandy and very fair, and continually kept so by labour of hands." The combination of the light, loosely slung caroche and the smooth roadbed at last made the short pleasure excursion a real possibility for the wealthy Londoner. In 1685 John Verney urged his father Sir Ralph to refresh himself from the burdens of Parliament by taking a spin out to Highgate or Hampstead, and to take a walk in the country. For Londoners, a whole new field of leisure activity had at last opened up.

It was the gentry residing within fifty miles of London who were most deeply affected by these improvements in transportation. In the mid-seventeenth century the family coach of the Verneys rumbled up and down between London and the family seat at Claydon in Buckinghamshire, carrying the women and children to and fro. When it was not available, hackney coaches were hired by the day for the occasional trip. Finally, by the middle of the seventeenth century there appeared regularly scheduled stagecoaches connecting most towns to London. By 1681 the City was linked by stagecoach to 88 towns, and by 1705 to 180.[21] In about 1669 "flying coaches" were being brought into use, which greatly cut down the time. For example, by 1670 it was at last possible to travel by public transport from Oxford to London in a single day, without a night's stopover on the way. The Verneys were one of many families whose social life had clearly been transformed by the advent of the coach. Thanks to it, they were as closely linked to London in 1680 as they were to be for the next 150 years, until the advent of the railway again sharply reduced the importance of distance as measured by time, cost, and comfort.

On the other hand, this new instrument was effective only in the areas where there were roads fit for wheeled traffic, which apart from the main trunk roads means south and east of a line drawn from the Wash to Gloucester and from Gloucester to Weymouth. Off the main roads north and west of this line, the wheel was virtually unknown, or if known it could not be used. While the coach may have tied the landed classes of the lowland zone even more closely to London, it was therefore less effective in improving the lot of those who lived farther afield. Lord Cavendish, for example, spent six days in 1612 traveling down from London to Chatsworth. Moreover, the conditions in London itself remained very bad, for the cobbles and irregular paving stones made coach travel extremely uncomfortable. In 1700 Edward Ward reported that as soon as they got into London, "we were jumbled about like so many peas in a child's rattle, running, at every kennell-jolt, a great hazard of a dislocation."[22]

Concurrently with the development of the coach came the commercial carrier regularly transporting city luxury products, city fashions, and city news to the inhabitants of remote country houses. The carriers were in full operation by the early seventeenth century, so that in 1636 the earl of Newcastle could write reassuringly to his wife at home in Derbyshire: "if there be any matter of moment you shall be sure to hear it speedily; otherwise content yourself with carriers, and so will I."[23]

The trend toward London was further stimulated by another important development in communications in the late seventeenth century: the organization of an efficient public postal system along the main roads connecting all the major cities to London. By the early eighteenth century there were 182 deputy postmasters in England and Wales, and mail traveled at a speed of 120 miles a day, with three deliveries a week both out from and into London. This enormously speeded up the dissemination of London news, gossip, and fashions, which spread farther and more rapidly into the remote corners of the kingdom. In addition there was an extremely sophisticated mail system which linked the metropolis to its suburbs and neighboring towns. There were one main office and five sorting offices in London, employing a hundred sorters and messengers. Five hundred shops and coffee-houses acted as post-boxes. Mail was regularly collected from these boxes every hour in London and Westminster, every two hours in the suburbs, twice a day in towns near London, and once a day in remote towns. The delivery service covered all of London and Westminster and also dormitory towns on the periphery.[24]

So far from satisfying the craving for the latest fashion or the latest political news, this new development merely stimulated and spread the desire to hurry up to London to savor these pleasures at first hand. More and more wives of wealthy country squires found rural life intolerably boring and nagged their husbands into spending at least part of the year in London. As Lady Mary Wortley Montagu put it in 1712, "Very few people that have settled entirely in the country but have grown at length weary of one another. The lady's conversation generally falls into a thousand impertinent effects of idleness; and the gentleman falls in love with his dogs and horses and out of love with everything else." In 1733 Elizabeth Montagu took the same view. Her father "had the Hyp," complaining that "living in the country was sleeping with one's eyes open." Elizabeth correctly identified "one common objection to the country, one sees no faces but those of one's own family." Social visits were major expeditions fraught with hazards. A satirical description of 1807 could apply with even more force to 1707 or earlier.

> In the country how pleasant our visits to make,
> Through ten miles of mud, for formality's sake,
> With the coachman in drink and the moon in a fog,
> And no thought in our head—but a ditch or a bog.[25]

No wonder more and more women insisted on moving to London, at least for the worst winter months.

In London itself there were significant developments which made life more attractive for the upper classes. During the middle ages and the sixteenth century, transportation between London and Westminster was either by river, where boats were always available for hire, or on land on one's own horse. But by 1625 the first hackney coach had made its appearance at a stand set up in the Strand, midway between the City and the Court and in the heart of the fashionable quarter. Too costly for the general public, the hackney coach was patronized by members of the upper classes who either did not possess a coach of their own or had left it behind in the country. By the 1630s the city streets were so congested with hackney coaches and private vehicles that the crown attempted—unsuccessfully, of course—to license the former and to limit the number to fifty. Meanwhile, until the distances to be covered became so great that Hercules himself could no longer stand the strain, there was brisk competition from sedan chairs carried by porters. In 1636 Henry Peacham, who always had a keen nose for the latest issue, produced a pamphlet entitled "Coach and Sedan Pleasantly Disputing for Place and Precedence." By 1646 Lady Verney could complain that in London, "Coaches are most infinite dear, and there is no stirring forth without one or a chair." But the cost was indeed very high—Lady Verney was spending five shillings to six shillings a morning on coach hire in 1648 as she went about her husband's affairs—and the spread of the hackney coach in London was therefore entirely dependent on the growth of a wealthy clientele. Henry Verney summed up the predicament of all hard-pressed younger sons of gentry when he complained: "foot it in the dust I cannot, and coach hire is too dear for my purse." By 1725, however, internal transportation was both plentiful and cheap. De Saussure reported that there were then 1,000 hackney cabs and 300 sedan chairs, while some 15,000 boats were going up and down the river. His figures were not accurate, for in 1740 there were about 500 hackney cabs and 400 chairs, but the general impression was correct. Chairs were not too expensive by then, for they could be hired for a shilling an hour or a guinea a week.[26]

If it was getting easier for the rich to move about in London, despite the growing traffic jams, the residential areas of the town were also becoming more pleasant in other ways. It was not until the mid-seventeenth century that it became normal for fresh water to be piped directly into upper-class houses, and for sewage pipes to be laid to carry the refuse and night soil down to the river. This last was an important and expensive development, as we shall see, but it was one on which the health and amenity of the newly built residential areas depended. When Sir Edmund Verney took up the lease of a house in Covent Garden Piazza in 1634, the area had not yet been connected to a sewer, and he took the sensible precaution of reserving the right to break the lease if he found the stench too great to be endured. In that year four noble landlords banded together to put up the capital to run piped water from springs in Soho into St. Martin's Lane and Covent Garden, and to link the houses there to a main sewage pipe down to the river to carry off the wastes. In this area of residential development, the early 1630s were clearly an important period for improved sanitation. The tenants were insisting on this new amenity, and the landlords were obliged to supply it. By the late seventeenth century it had become standard practice for all new buildings in the fashionable areas like Golden Square and Leicester Square to be linked up to a main sewer provided by the ground landlords. Another development of this period was a provision in the leases that the builder supply a paved sidewalk in front of each house.[27]

Another great step forward in making life safer and more agreeable in the residential areas was the substitution of public oil lamps for private candles as street lighting. This revolution in lighting, with a fixed installation of lamps with reflectors, serviced by a private company contracted for by the corporation and paid out of rates, occurred between 1690 and 1740. In 1694 the Convex Lights Company contracted for London, and in 1704 the Conic Lights Company for Westminster. In 1736 a lighting rate was imposed, and the lamps were maintained all night all the year round. By 1739 there were 4,800 lamps, and by the 1750s some 15,000. The cause for this change was the growth of an active night life to amuse the wealthy. Taverns, coffeehouses, and ordinaries were crowded until a late hour and the public gardens at Vauxhall and Marylebone stayed open very late, while the theater did not begin until 6 P.M. Hackney coaches plied for hire until midnight to meet the growing demand.[28] Thus little by little, in entertainment, plumbing, sanitation, transport, and lighting, the amenities of life for the rich in the West End of London were steadily improving in the seventeenth and early eighteenth centuries.

During the course of the seventeenth century, therefore, four things happened. First there developed a significantly large leisure class whose demands for recreation, pleasure, and expert advice stimulated the growth of a whole range of specialized products and manufactures, imported goods and foodstuffs, and professional and technical services. The century saw the beginning of the age of leisure and of sophisticated urban consumption as a way of life for rather more than an insignificant handful at the top. Second, there took place improvements in communications, lighting, and urban sanitation, the combined result of which was to make London better known and more accessible, and also pleasanter and more healthful to live in.

Third, it came to be thought, not without some reason, that the saving on servants' wages which could be achieved by shutting up the country seat and moving to London would be sufficient to compensate for the very high urban rents and prices. In 1665 Edward Waterhouse reassured nervous country gentlemen that: "Taking one thing with another, as we vulgarly say, a family may live as handsomely and cheap in London as in any part of England; although rents are dear, and rates upon commodities and estates higher than in any other part, yet it is balanced by the little hospitality, fewness of servants, variety of food of all natures haveable with money in an instant, and in what proportion housekeepers please and the houses can spend."[29] This line of argument only became persuasive once the traditional moral obligation upon the gentry to dispense justice and offer open hospitality in the countryside had been at least partly eroded by the rise of a more commercial and more court-oriented culture. When the call of patriarchal duty no longer dominated men's minds, it was possible for county families to look at the problem of where to live in more narrowly selfish terms of pleasure and pain and more narrowly economic terms of profit and loss.

The fourth major change in the course of the seventeenth century was the growing monopoly achieved by London over the goods, services, and entertainment demanded by this enlarged leisured class at last freed from many of their rural prejudices and exposed to the full force of improved communications. London was the exclusive disseminator of political information and fashion in clothes, architecture, art, drama, music, and literature. Provincial culture at this level of sophistication was virtually nonexistent before the eighteenth century, and indeed some thought that the growing attractions of London were positively reducing it. Writing toward the end of the seventeenth century, Roger North ascribed the growth of alcoholism among the local gentry to the decline in amateur music-making, which in turn he believed was caused by "the now reigning humour of running to London." A century later, when this trend had reached its apogee, Thomas Gisborne summed up the role played by the capital city in English elite society:

London is the centre to which almost all the individuals who fill the upper and middle ranks of society are successively attracted. The country pays its tribute to the supreme city. Business, interest, curiosity, the love of pleasure, the desire of knowledge, the thirst for change, ambition to be deemed polite, occasion a continual influx into the metropolis from every corner of the Kingdom."[30]

In this respect the contrast with seventeenth-century France could not be more striking. There the monarchy was still peripatetic, spending long periods at Fontainebleau or in the Loire Valley before settling down a considerable distance outside the town at Versailles. The commercial capital of the country was not Paris but Rouen; the banking center was not Paris but Lyons. Much of the legal business was handled by the many provincial *Parlements* and commercial courts, and the many provincial assemblies attracted far more loyalty and attention than the very rare meetings of the *États Généraux*. Ever since the Renaissance in the early sixteenth century, a number of provincial towns had provided satisfactory cultural amenities for the local nobility, who had consequently built themselves town houses in them in which to spend the winters. In England, on the other hand, fashion, court, commerce, law, and politics were all being increasingly focused on a single city.

In the first place, London developed into the primary, indeed the only, center of elegant consumption in the island. In the first half of the seventeenth century there emerged a world of fashion in London, persons whose life revolved around clothes, pictures, sculpture, newsletters, books, and plays. Women in particular were attracted by this aspect of the metropolis, and bullied their husbands into renting a London house for part of the year. This fashionable aspect of London's attractions was further re-enforced by the fact that it was the only place where first-class professional advice could be obtained. If one wished to consult the most expert doctors, surgeons, or apothecaries, architects, sculptors, or painters, barristers, attorneys, or scriveners, bankers, financiers, or brokers, it was to London that one had to go. By the end of the century this centralization of technical services had gone so far that one Lancashire gentlewoman was sending her personal linen to be laundered in London, as the only place where it could be done to her satisfaction.[31] London was the center of litigation, and its predominance in this respect increased after the middle of the seventeenth century because of the abolition of the two local courts at Ludlow and at York, for Wales and the North respectively. This was an enormously litigious age, and no man of means was without his string of lawsuits which inevitably drew him up to London for several weeks in the year. To an increasing extent London also became the financial and credit capital of the country, the place to which was transferred the ever-growing volume of taxation, where joint stock companies were launched and operated, where the Bank of England functioned, and where mortgages could be raised or invested in. By the time of the South Sea Bubble in the early eighteenth century, stock-jobbing was "given as one of the principal causes of the prodigious conflux of the nobility and gentry from all parts of England to London, more than ever in former years."[32] London was also the seat of Parliament, an assembly whose pattern of work changed from brief and infrequent sessions at the beginning of the century, to regular annual sessions lasting several months by the end. Although attendance was far from regular, Parliament alone drew some 300 gentry and a substantial portion of the nobility to London from about November to April, and increased the demand for high-class accommodation. Finally, London was the home of the monarch and his court and administration, now more and more settled in the rambling palace complex at Westminster. As tax revenues mounted, and as the army and the bureaucracy expanded in the late seventeenth century, so the central government became the main dispensing agent for a growing mass of very lucrative patronage. To obtain a share of the jobs and the pickings for oneself, one's friends, or one's children, diligent lobbying and at least intermittent attendance at court at Westminster was virtually obligatory.[33] As a result of all of these attractions, the mere propinquity to London was sufficient to raise the price of land for over a hundred miles around.[34]

And so we have a remarkable paradox. On the one hand late seventeenth-century England was administratively the most decentralized country in Europe, in the sense that local government was firmly in the hands of local landowners, and that the fiscal and judicial powers of the central authority were fairly limited. On the other hand it was culturally, legally, economically, and politically the most centralized of all, in the sense that alternative provincial centers had hardly yet come into existence. In seventeenth-century England the lesser gentry of the shires despised and hated both Court and City, but they had as yet made little attempt to develop counter-attractions in the provincial capitals. They stayed at home in their isolated manor houses to drink and hunt, to gamble and grumble, to run the district and manage their estates.

It is certainly true that by the early seventeenth century there was developing a "county community" of local gentry, who were increasingly accustomed to assemble in the county town, dining together and organizing parties and other social events on the occasion of the three annual assizes, when the London judges came on circuit to convey royal wishes to the county and dispense royal justice. During the seventeenth century a handful of gentry began to acquire houses of their own in the local town, and some of the inns began to provide large rooms for the occasional meetings of the gentry on the days of the assizes or the local horse race.[35] But the prevalence of endemic and recurrent plague in towns must have acted as a serious deterrent to urban living, until it became apparent that the outbreak of 1665 was the last fling of the disease. Consequently, it was not until the eighteenth century that the lesser local gentry in substantial numbers began to pass the winter in their own town houses in the provincial towns, and so to create an urbanized provincial social life of their own. At York, which was the nearest thing to a second capital, only the Fairfaxes and the Ingrams owned town houses in the early seventeenth century, although others may have rented them. By 1736 York's historian Drake could remark, "What has been and is the chief support of the city at present is the resort to and residence of several country gentlemen with their families," but his own evidence makes it clear that this was a relatively recent development.[36] Among the inhabitants of Bristol, which was the second largest provincial city in England, there was in 1696 not a single baronet or knight of landed stock among the resident householders. All of the nine baronets and knights who lived in the city were local men who had worked their way up to the top of the economic and political ladder as merchants, mayors, or sheriffs. The only titled members of the landed classes of whom the city of Bristol could boast were two widows of knights, who had presumably retired to the town after the death of their husbands and the takeover of the family seats and estates by their sons.[37] Lincoln's experience was similar, for it was not until the early eighteenth century that the gentry began to build town houses up on the hill around the Cathedral Close, that horse racing began, and that an assembly room was built.[38] At Norwich, which was the largest provincial city in England, there resided in 1663 only a Bacon, a Hobart, and an Earle, and none of them was the head of the family. There was not a single man with a title living in the city, for the huge old palace of the dukes of Norfolk was now divided up and sublet. Even at the end of the century, as at the beginning, it was a center only of occasional gatherings of gentry for a few days at a time, for the assize week, county elections, the annual fair, and so on. A few owned houses, but most rented them for the occasion.[39] Smaller county towns were even slower to develop into social centers for the gentry, and in sleepy Warwick only the Archers of Umberslade owned a town house in 1661.[40] Comfortable town houses were certainly being built in places like Bristol, York, St. Albans, and Lincoln, but they were almost all owned by urban rentier "pseudo-gentry" or "town-gentry" as well as by the business oligarchy. They were not lived in by country gentry as a second residence. The only exception to this generalization about provincial towns in the seventeenth century seems to have been Durham, which in 1639 was described as full of gentry, "being the London (as it were) of those northern parts which extend as far as Berwick."[41]

Although there is some evidence that by the late seventeenth century some of the local gentry were beginning to buy as well as rent houses in the local county towns, it was not until the early eighteenth century that the necessary institutional amenities such as assembly rooms, ballrooms, bowling greens, and coffeehouses began to appear. If one looks at a town like Colchester, it was not until the 1730s that quarterly assemblies were held, which did not become monthly until the 1750s. Concerts and balls followed in the 1760s, when the first permanent theater was built, and by the late eighteenth century there were two or three circulating libraries. It was only in the 1760s that Margate acquired "a fine assembly room, a good tavern, a coffee house and a billiard table."[42]

When Defoe carried out his tour of England in the early 1720s, the commercialization of leisure activities in the province was only just beginning. Defoe loved to identify the commercial bourgeoisie with the gentry, and his social categorizations have therefore to be treated with some caution. While he could find nothing on the subject worthy of comment in places such as Bristol, Gloucester, Warwick, Northampton, or Norwich, there were a few centers where a local polite society was clearly beginning to form. At Winchester the local clergy and gentry "are gotten into that new fashioned way of conversing by assemblies." Bury St. Edmunds was a town "most thronged with gentry, people of the best fashion, and the most polite conversation." Maidstone was "a very agreeable place to live in, where a man of letters and of manners will always find suitable society both to divert and to improve himself." Derby and Shrewsbury also were singled out as budding social centers for the local gentry, and we know that Ipswich was another. But the number of county towns where this was happening was still limited, and the evidence strongly suggests that it was a development of very recent origin.[43] The kind of cultural amenities found in the provinces by John Byng and François de la Rochefoucauld on their tours in the 1780s—the clubs and the coffeehouses with the latest newspapers, the assembly rooms and tearooms, the repertory theaters and concert halls, the bowling greens and horse races—were nearly all developments of the previous eighty years, and few of them had existed a century earlier.[44] As late as 1700 there was really no satisfactory alternative to London as a social center for the sophisticated upper gentry and their wives during the long northern winter.

## RESIDENTIAL SEGREGATION

In view of the growing wealth and prestige of the London merchant elite in the late seventeenth century, it might have been supposed that they would desert the City and settle down as neighbors of the gentry and aristocracy in the new residential areas in the western suburbs. In fact, however, they did no such thing, and up to the very end of the seventeenth century— and indeed beyond—there was very little infiltration of city merchants into the western suburbs, which remained an exclusive preserve of professional men, courtiers, and the landed classes. Indeed there is reason to believe that the degree of residential segregation between the monied and the landed classes actually increased rather than diminished in the course of the seventeenth century. In the late sixteenth century, many noblemen owned palaces along the Strand, while others still lived in town houses within the city walls, cheek by jowl with aldermen, tradesmen, and artisans. This was a situation that only began to change toward the middle of the seventeenth century. In 1638 there were still living in the City and Liberties fifteen nobleman and their ladies, one ambassador, and thirty-four nonaldermanic knights, some of them government contractors and officials like Sir Henry Spiller or Sir William Russell, some of them royal officials like Sir Robert Heath, others mere landed gentry like Sir Thomas Richardson.[45] This distribution of the landed classes is supported by the survey of 1632.[46] Of the 184 men and women resident in London and the suburbs in that year who were of the status of knight or above, 61, or just one-third, were still living in the old City. The rest were scattered about the suburbs, mainly in the western sectors down to and including Westminster. By 1695, however, all this had changed. The nobility had all moved away to the west, and of those above the rank of esquire few were left within the City except some aldermanic or merchant knights.[47]

The landed classes were thus leaving the City in the seventeenth century, but the merchants were not moving westward with them. Of the twenty-four aldermen of London elected between 1629 and 1639 and still alive in 1638, certainly fifteen and probably nineteen were still living in the City. Since the record is only 90 percent complete, some of the missing aldermen may well have been living in the parishes with defective returns. Of the forty-five aldermen of London elected between 1687 and 1701 and alive in 1695, thirty-one were residing within the walls and a further six in the immediately adjacent suburbs. These City residents included seven directors of the Bank of England, one governor, and two deputy governors of the East India Company, a deputy governor of the Levant Company, and a warden of the Goldsmith's Company, so that this is not a roll of financial and political second-raters. A directory of nearly two thousand London merchants and bankers of 1677 offers further proof that hardly any of the monied elite lived in the western suburbs. Only 4 percent lived in the West End at all, and they were mostly in the already decayed area of King Street, Queen Street, and the eastern side of St. Martin's Lane. There was only one in Lincoln's Inn Fields, one in Covent Garden, and two in Bloomsbury. Not a single one of the thirty-three merchant knights, however, lived in this district. The conclusion that merchants did not reside in the fashionable western suburbs in the seventeenth century is supported by the records of tenancies, which have been preserved for the west side of St. Martin's Lane, Covent Garden, Lincoln's Inn Fields, Golden Square, and St. James's Square.[48]

Confidence in this generalization is strengthened rather than weakened by the very few exceptions about which we know something. In 1672 the great merchant financier Sir John Banks purchased a house in Lincoln's Inn Fields. But Banks, who up to now had been content with a series of City houses, was a special case. For fifteen years he had been building up a great landed estate, including a country house; he had been made a baronet eleven years before; he had always sedulously avoided all City offices; he had modeled his consumption patterns on those of the lesser nobility; and he had sought companionship amongst the virtuosi of the Royal Society and the gentlemen of the House of Commons. In a word, he was exceptionally rich, exceptionally uninterested in the power politics of the City, and exceptionally single-minded in his aspirations to break into the exclusive world of the squirarchy.[49] Banks was the first of his kind, and it was not until the early eighteenth century that we find any imitators. No merchants dared to take a house in St. James's Square before the great banker Sir Richard Child in the reign of Queen Anne, and he had already established himself in polite society and was shortly to be made an earl. A more significant turning point came in 1717, when Sir James Bateman took up residence in the square in the year of his mayoralty, apparently the first mayor of London to live outside the city walls.[50] He was a man at the very end of a long and prosperous commercial career, who already had his eye on the viscountcy which was to be granted to his son and heir eight years later.

Despite these one or two exceptions, the weight of evidence strongly suggests that as late as 1700 the community of trade and finance, and the community of politics, the professions, and pleasure were living in separate enclaves. As late as the 1780s, foreigners were still commenting on this division: "Two towns many miles apart could not be more different from each other than the City and the west end of London. . . . The West Londoners are derided by the inhabitants of the City for their idleness, their love of luxury, and their fondness for French manners; but the West Londoners amply repay the derision by despising the City Englishman as an uncouth animal who sees merit only in money."[51]

The degree to which the coffeehouses and the clubs mitigated this social differentiation is still an open question. The clubs certainly seem to have been almost exclusively composed of nobles, gentry, professional men, and literati, and the memberships of such different societies as the Kit-Kat Club, the Royal Society, and White's all support this conclusion. A century later, things had hardly changed, and Count Gronow, reminiscing about club life in 1814, remarked: "the members of the clubs of London, many years since, were without exception belonging to the aristocratic world." A man like Pepys, on the other hand, with a good education and high ambitions, and holding a government office which brought him into business relationships with both politicians and merchant contractors, seems to have bridged both worlds in the coffeehouses and elsewhere. But Pepys was an exceptional man in an exceptional position, and it would be very unwise to use his experience to generalize about the social cohesion of life in London in the late seventeenth century. Well-informed contemporaries certainly thought that there was a clear-cut social division between the City and the West End, and in 1714 Addison wrote: "When I consider this great city in its several quarters and divisions, I look upon it as an aggregate of various nations, distinguished from each other by their respective customs, manners and interests. The Courts of two countries do not so much differ from one another as the Court and the City in their peculiar ways of life and conversation. In short the inhabitants of St. James's, notwithstanding they live under the same laws and speak the same language, are a distinct people from those of Cheapside, who are likewise removed from those of the Temple on the one side and those of Smithfield on the other by several climates and degrees in their way of thinking and conversing together." Steele thought the City divided socially into three, "the very different nations of Cheapside, Covent Garden and St. James's."[52]

If this analysis is correct, it raises intriguing questions about the degree of social interaction between money and land, and suggests that contacts in London may have been less close than has hitherto been supposed. The psychological impact upon the gentry of the intermittent experience of urban life was mitigated by strict social segregation: in London, as in the countryside, the landed classes lived among their own kind, in what was known in the early eighteenth century as "the polite end of the town."[51]

## The Supply of Residential Housing

During the late seventeenth century there therefore developed a growing demand for housing in London for exclusive occupation by the professional and landed classes. To meet this demand there was a striking growth of residential building whose features must be explained in terms of conflicting pressures from a series of independent forces. From an examination of the records of the major urban property owners, notably the Cecils Earls of Salisbury, the Wriothesleys Earls of Southampton, and the Russells Earls of Bedford, it is possible to draw some fairly secure conclusions about the location, financing, and planning of high-quality residential housing in London in the seventeenth century.[54]

## LOCATION

There were two reasons why the upper classes should spread out to the west of the old City rather than in other directions. The first was the prevailing wind. The conversion of London from wood to Newcastle coal for its fuel supply meant that for many months in the year smog conditions were as bad as they were to be in the days of Dickens or Conan Doyle, and probably worse than they are today. Evelyn complained of the "Hellish and dismal cloud of sea-coal" which was responsible for the fact that "Cattharr, phthisicks, coughs and consumptions rage more in this one City than in the whole earth besides." It was the land surveyor and statistician William Petty who drew the obvious conclusion about the expansion of fashionable London: "It must be westward, because the winds blowing near 3/4 of the year from the west, the dwellings of the west end are so much the more free from the fumes, steams and stinks of the whole easterly pile; which where seacoale is burnt is a great matter." It was a happy chance that the river also flowed from west to east, carrying the sewage and garbage of the rich away from the residential districts and down past the slums of the city and the eastern suburbs. The sewage and garbage of the poor sloshed to and fro with the tide, but were never carried far enough upstream to offend the eyes or nostrils of the inhabitants of the west end of town, where the river was still sufficiently free from pollution to support salmon, some of them allegedly up to eight feet in length.[55]

The second and decisive factor was the presence upriver of Westminster, and it was between Westminster and the City that the housing development took place, in an area ideally situated for easy access to the main centers of attractions for this upper-class clientele (figs. 3, 4, and 5). To the east was the City, containing the center of finance at the Royal Exchange, and the center of gossip and information and books at St. Paul's Cathedral. It was also the place where one had to go to buy luxury articles like wines, silks, jewelry, plate, and furniture. On the western boundary of the city, just south of the area of development, were the Inns of Court, where worked the lawyers, attorneys, and scriveners whose services were needed for assistance in the endless litigation, for the conveyancing of property, and for the drawing up of marriage articles and settlements. To the southwest was the royal palace of Westminster, housing not merely the monarch and the court, but also both Houses of Parliament and the law courts, crowded in and around Westminster Hall. Finally, across the river in Southwark lay the pleasure area with the theaters, bear-baiting rings, and brothels. The land between the City and Westminster

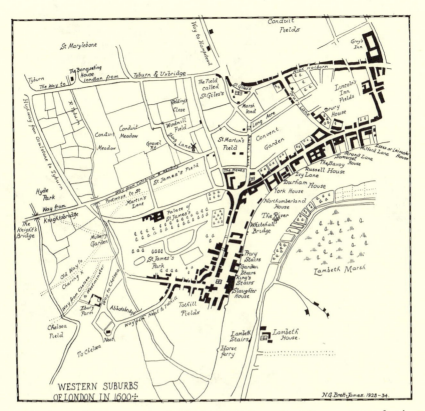

Figure 3. The western suburbs in 1600 (from Brett-James, *Growth of Stuart London*, p. 132).

was still open fields in 1600, except the south side of the Strand, between the street and the river, which was already fully occupied by a string of aristocratic town houses of considerable size (fig. 3). Between Lincoln's Inn on the east, the Strand and St. James's Park on the south, and High Holborn and St. Giles on the north lay a considerable stretch of open ground, conveniently situated for rapid access to all the main centers of attraction for upper-class society, and also upriver and upwind of the city and the impoverished eastern suburbs, and so relatively healthy and fresh.

In the long run, however, the desire to preserve an exclusive residential neighborhood was thwarted by the inexorable westward thrust of the lower classes of London, who year by year moved further and further into areas which had originally been designed for, and inhabited by, their betters. In the first half of the seventeenth century, the great nobility lived in the Strand, and courtiers, knights, squires, and professional men crowded around Lincoln's Inn Fields and the earl of Bedford's Covent Garden and

Figure 4.
West Central London
in 1682
(Morgan Map;
reproduced by
courtesy of
Mr. Harry Margary).

up the earl of Salisbury's St. Martin's Lane (fig. 4). In 1664 there were twenty-one peers living in this highly fashionable neighborhood. By the end of the century, however, this area was fully built over, and was evidently deteriorating (fig. 6). The combination of a rush of nobles, courtiers, and officials back to the revived Restoration Court, and the decay of the old residential area in or near the Strand created an acute shortage of upper-class housing in the early 1660s. It was to meet this demand that the earls of Southampton and St. Albans conceived the plans for Southampton (later Bloomsbury) Square and St. James's Square. The latter supported his application for a grant from the crown in 1663 with the valid complaint that "the beauty of this great town and the convenience of the Court are defective in point of houses fit for the dwellings of noblemen and other persons of quality." Once the new housing developments were begun, the great nobles moved north and west and with them went the officials and courtiers, knights and squires, who moved out into Southampton Square, Golden Square, King (later Soho) Square, and Leicester Square (fig. 4). As they left, they freed their houses for subdivision and occupation by lower social strata. According to Edward Ward, the site of Salisbury House was in 1700 the home of whores, coiners, highwaymen, pickpockets, and housebreakers.[56] In the early eighteenth century, the Strand and Covent Garden were still lived in by professional men, artists, doctors, and the like, but the world of fashion was gone, and pockets of slums had grown up in between the more respectable housing.

This westward and northward march was greatly facilitated by the fact that most residents held leases for terms of years rather than freeholds. In order to move, few had to sell on a falling market; the majority could wait until their leases ran out, and then move on. This mobility was further encouraged by the frequency of subletting. The building lessees often sublet to others if they did not wish to live in the house for the full thirty-one or forty-one years. Moreover, great noblemen thought nothing of letting their palaces to other great noblemen, some of whom, like the Manners Earls of Rutland, spent the whole of the seventeenth century in town houses rented from their friends. After the middle of the century, noble owners often subdivided superfluous sections of their palaces in the Strand and let them off to gentry and officials, reserving for themselves only what space they needed.[57] And when the demand for housing changed at the end of the seventeenth century, they did not hesitate to pull down the old family town house, replace it with rows of tenements, and build themselves a new house in a more fashionable quarter. Between 1674 and 1718 there came tumbling down nearly all the great

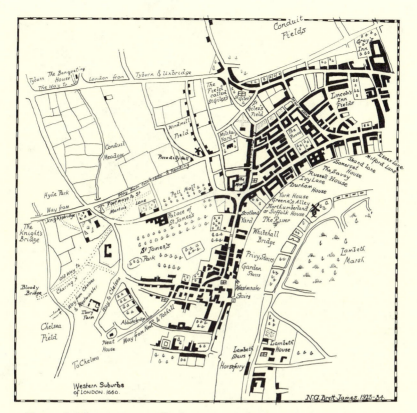

Figure 5. The western suburbs in 1660 (from Brett-James, *Growth of Stuart London*, p. 354).

palaces in the Strand area: Salisbury House, York House, Exeter House, Beaufort House, Norfolk House, Essex House, Hungerford House, Stanhope House, Wallingford House, and Bedford House. In the City itself the last houses, Elgin House and the Barbican, also came down. In 1682 a correspondent passed on the rumor that Albemarle House, Leicester House, Newport House, and Worcester House, which were situated a little north of the Strand, were also being pulled down.[58] It was the end of the aristocratic age of the Strand.

Even after they had moved to St. James's Square or Golden Square, the nobles still seemed incapable of settling down, and the big houses there changed hands with remarkable frequency in the late seventeenth and early eighteenth centuries.[59] These families tended to cling to their country seats through thick and thin, since they were centers of little political and social empires, and since they were the prime foci of ancestral loyalties. But their town houses seem to have generated surprisingly little family pride and affection or desire for continuity. This psychological disassociation of the family from the town house was greatly

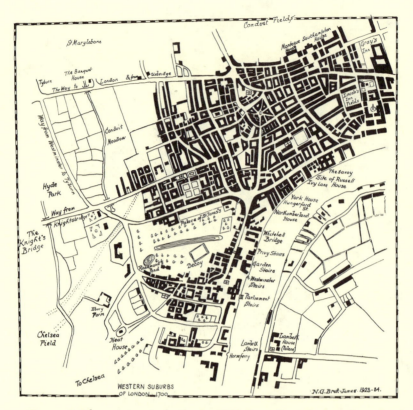

Figure 6. The western suburbs in 1700 (from Brett-James, *Growth of Stuart London*, p. 366).

encouraged by the leasing system, which further stimulated mobility from house to house.

## FINANCING

To understand the economic arrangements for urban development of west-central London in the seventeenth-century it is necessary to take into account the interests and aspirations of three distinct groups: the potential occupants of the houses; the crown; and the landlords, who were mostly noblemen. The forces driving the middle and upper classes into this area of London have already been described. What they wanted was exclusive residential housing of moderate size and at reasonable cost in what was currently considered a fashionable quarter in a healthy district with easy access to the main centers of upper-class business and pleasure. But between their needs and those of the ground landlords stood the state, which throughout the whole of the early and middle years of the seventeenth century attempted, without much success, to control, and indeed to prevent, the expansion of London.[60] What made these efforts futile was the relentless flow of immigrants into London, and the crown's ambivalence about its own objectives and motives. Basically, it was opposed to the further expansion of London, and in particular to the influx of the poor and the consequent growth of plague-ridden and unruly slums. Towards better-class housing, however, its attitude was more uncertain, wavering between outright prohibition for fear of subsequent subdivision, controlled regulation, and frank exploitation of growth for fiscal profit. In practice, both James I and Charles I seemed to have pursued the two latter objectives more wholeheartedly than the first, and both were fairly willing to grant building licenses, at a price, to aristocratic friends and acquaintances. One of the reasons why so much building at this time was on property held by noblemen and courtiers was that lesser men found it far more difficult to obtain a license.

A perfect example of the way the crown played cat-and-mouse with noble developers, although ultimately letting them proceed with their plans, is the experience of the earl of Bedford in building the Covent Garden Piazza. In July 1630, just as the project was getting under way, the crown reissued its proclamation absolutely prohibiting all new building in London. Six months later it sold Bedford a license to build, in return for a payment of £2,000. But, perhaps by accident, the drafting office of the attorney general failed to follow instructions and include in the license a pardon for previous "contempts and offences" against the proclamation. This offered the new attorney general in 1634 the chance to sue Bedford in Star Chamber and have him fined a further £2,000. After this Bedford was left in peace to continue his building of the Piazza, but it is perhaps hardly surprising that he economized on the proposed bronze statue of the king.[61]

The third and last interest group involved comprised the ground landlords who owned the freehold. A good deal of the land to the west of the old City had been locked up in the hands of the church until the Reformation, but most of it subsequently passed to the greater nobility, on whom fell the responsibility, and the opportunity, for directing urban development in this area. Their most important motive was naturally to increase their revenues, for many of these aristocratic developers were financially hard pressed. Agricultural improvement was slow, laborious, and liable to run into tenant obstruction and accusations of antisocial behavior, so that there was every incentive to turn instead to urban development. Because of their high-consumption life-style, nobles were personally short of ready cash, and had to allow the capital to be put up by others. But to maximize income, they wanted to keep up the social level of the quarter, and therefore to retain some control over size, quality, material, aesthetic appearance, and use of the houses built. Just as in aristocratic investments in privateering against enemy shipping, the lust for glory and the hope of profit were inseparably intertwined. By raising both the aesthetic and the social standards of his development, the nobleman might reasonably hope to increase the value of his property.

And so the first half of the seventeenth century saw the spread of urban development under aristocratic direction, in Drury Lane by the earl of Clare and Lord Craven, in Covent Garden by the earl of Bedford, and in St. Martin's Lane by the earl of Salisbury (fig. 6). The area was planned to meet the needs of the middling class of gentry, lawyers, and professional men, and was therefore at first very unlike the Marais in Paris, with its mixture of aristocratic palaces and artisans' workshops. Care was taken to stipulate in the leases that the houses should be of a certain size and comfort, and that they should not be used as places of work by artisans and tradesmen. Both in St. Martin's Lane at the beginning of the century and in Cecil Street at the end, the earls of Salisbury did what they could to preserve a gentlemanly standard of housing. Only in the development of Salisbury Street in the 1670s did the second earl's judgment falter, in attempting to crowd too many houses on too narrow a site, a lesson which was remembered when it came to planning Cecil Street a generation later. As for the New and Middle Exchanges, which were enclosed bazaars for shops and stalls catering for the luxury trades, they depended for their clientele on the existence of an upper-class residential area nearby. Since shops were forbidden in the building developments, there had to be somewhere for the inhabitants to buy finery, and the answer in the seventeenth century, as in the twentieth, was a multiple store or shopping center under a single roof.[62]

Since the financial objective of the noble landlords was to increase income without contributing capital, they nearly always resorted to the device of the building lease. The only important exceptions to this generalization were Salisbury's New Exchange and a small part of Bedford's Covent Garden, which were built by the ground landlords, and St. James's Square, the mansions around which were each built by the purchaser of the freehold. The Covent Garden project was described by its promoter as "houses and buildings fit for the habitation of gentlemen and men of ability." St. James's Square was specifically designed in 1662 by the entrepreneur (the earl of St. Albans) and by the ground landlord (Charles II) as a place of residence for the highest noblemen and politicians in the land. The earl soon found that men of this wealth and quality "will not build palaces upon any terms but that of inheritance." As a result, in 1665 the king was obliged to grant him the freehold, and he in turn was obliged to sell the freehold to the prospective builders, either noblemen or speculators.[63] But this was a case of men building not houses but small palaces, on frontages ranging from fifty to one hundred and thirty feet in width. Investment of capital in bricks and mortar on this scale had perforce to be carried out on freehold property.

Normally, however, the cost of building was borne by the prospective inhabitant or a speculative building contractor who took a thirty-one to forty-one year building lease of the empty site from the landlord. The extreme prevalence of this arrangement may have been partly due to the nature of the demand, the temporary and transient quality of so many of the residents, particularly of the gentry, who wished to rent rather than own a house. But the decisive factor was the nature of the supply. When development began, most of the available ground was owned by big noble landlords. They alone had the political influence to obtain building licenses from the crown, but they were unwilling to sell the freehold and yet were unable to find out of their own resources the capital for construction. The peculiar nature of both supply and demand thus worked in the same direction, to stimulate an urban development based on large freehold properties developed through the ground lease, with the obligation to build in a certain way placed on the lessee.

Since these noble landlords owned such very large blocks of property, they were able to plan on the generous scale of a Covent Garden or a Southampton Square, rather than allowing piecemeal development that rapidly degenerated into slums (plates 1 and 2). Moreover, they had a clear financial incentive to maintain the value of their property by preserving the architectural and social levels of development, and they therefore often imposed on the building lessees very rigorous conditions both for construction and for subsequent use. When the duke of Bedford's steward gave evidence before a Select Committee of the House of Commons in 1886, he was undoubtedly pleading a special case, but his words have nonetheless a ring of truth: "the existence of those large estates, well laid out and well cared for and well looked after because they have got one united freeholder, the freeholder of the entire area, is, in a manner of speaking, the salvation of London."[64]

An odd feature of the building lease of the seventeenth century was the very short duration of the term compared with the ninety-nine-year building lease current in the nineteenth and twentieth centuries. In the early seventeenth century, the standard term seems to have been thirty-one years, which did not leave the lessee much time to recover his capital investment. One

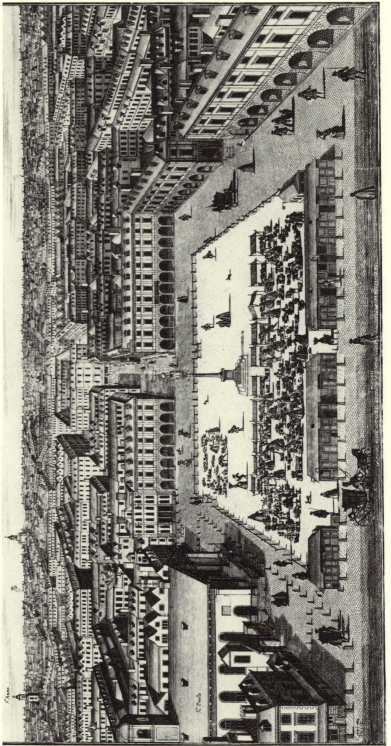

Plate 1. Covent Garden in about 1720 (engraving by Sutton Nicholls in Crowle's extra-illustrated vol. 6 in the British Library).

Plate 2. Bloomsbury Square in 1754 (from J. Stow, *Survey of London*, ed. J. Strype [London, 1755]).

may suspect that this term was the current one when buildings were of wood and therefore fairly cheap, and indeed within a decade or so of shifting over to brick the normal term rose to forty-one years or more. By the end of the seventeenth century, it had risen again to sixty-one years, and by the nineteenth century it was eighty years or more.[65]

The effects of these very short terms in the early seventeenth century may well have been unfortunate, for it seems likely that they inhibited architectural enterprise. In the late eighteenth century a foreign visitor certainly attributed the architectural modesty of London housing to the prevalence of the ground lease.[66] His argument is supported by the fact that parts at any rate of the four most striking and aesthetically ambitious undertakings of the seventeenth century—the New Exchange, the Covent Garden Piazza, St. James's Square, and Southampton Square—were not built on the leasehold system but were financed by the owners themselves. It also seems likely that the short building lease encouraged jerry-building, run up by lessees who were anxious to get a quick return on their capital before their leases ran out. In Saint Martin's Lane the houses seem to have needed to be largely rebuilt every thirty years or so, and in a parliamentary debate in 1677 a Member complained that three or four houses fell down and had to be rebuilt every year in the Covent Garden area. The extension of the term from thirty-one to forty-one years or more may have had a salutary effect in encouraging more substantial building, but even so it was said that at least a hundred lives were lost by the collapse of badly constructed houses in London in the course of the eighteenth century.[67]

The ground-lease system also stimulated the emergence of the speculative builder, whose function was to provide the risk capital and entrepreneurial skills for urban development. Having leased a whole street from the landlord, he could then do one of three things. He could act merely as the middleman, dividing the plots and leasing them individually to smaller speculative builders or tenants; or he could divide up the plots, lease them to tenants, and then build on their behalf to suit their requirements; or he could divide up the plots, build all the houses himself on speculation, and then go out to look for tenants. If he did the last, he was both the financier and the entrepreneur who planned and managed the operation, borrowed the money, and shouldered all the risk. The first such man we hear of was John Roper, who was building along Holborn in the 1590s on lease from the earl of Southampton. The next was William Newton, who was responsible in the 1630s for the development of a uniform row of elegant terraced houses, Portugal Row, along the south side of Lincoln's Inn Fields. In Queen Street, Newton varied his tactics. Here he actually purchased the land, laid out the plots, fixed on the architectural design of the frontage, and then let the plots to individual builders to erect houses either on speculation or for specific clients. The result was "the first uniform street, and the houses are stately and magnificent." Another example is Captain William Rider, who in the 1650s built and rebuilt Newport Street on a forty-one-year lease from the earl of Salisbury, who himself had a ninety-nine-year lease from the ground landlord.[68]

The greatest speculative builder of the century, however, was Dr. Nicholas Barbon, who flourished in the post-Restoration era and was responsible for a good deal of the development of the West End of London. He helped the earl of St. Albans to develop St. James's Square, and he specialized in the redevelopment of the old palaces along the Strand and elsewhere. He leased the properties from their aristocratic owners, pulled the palaces down, and covered the sites and their extensive grounds with middle-class housing: thus, he took over Essex House for the earl of Essex, York House for the duke of Buckingham, and Devonshire House for the earl of Devonshire. He also developed urban property near Holborn on lease from the Bedford Corporation and Rugby School.[69]

The financial result to the landlord of this policy of urban construction through the building lease was that the profits tended to be long postponed, and to move in sudden dramatic jumps as leases fell in some thirty or forty years after the initial development. On the other hand, there is no doubt that for the fortunate few who owned property in west-central London, there were enormous profits to be made which significantly affected the family fortunes. Let us look at a few examples. Soon after it was finished, the optimistic lessee of the New Exchange was paying the earl of Salisbury £1,000 a year, as a result of which urban rents constituted 15 percent of the latter's total rental. Within a few years, however, the revenues from the Exchange had fallen sharply, and while they slowly recovered in the thirties, and while the rents from St. Martin's Lane continued to grow, total receipts from London rents on the eve of the Civil War were still much what they were in 1612, and only amounted to 11 percent of a much shrunken landed estate. But by 1648 the startling rise in income from St. Martin's Lane as the building leases fell in resulted in a 50 percent rise in London income, which more than doubled again by 1677 thanks to the subdivision of Little Salisbury House, the prosperity of the New Exchange, the initial wild success of the Middle Exchange, and the development of

Salisbury Street. Thereafter the only major growth came from the demolition of Great and Little Salisbury Houses and the Middle Exchange complex and their replacement by new housing, and from the expiry of the building leases in Newport Street to the north of St. Martin's Lane. As a result, by 1720 London rents had swelled to over £3,200 and amounted to 37 percent of the old Cecil estate, now much diminished by rural sales to pay for debts. This was the high point, however, since the area was slowly sinking in social esteem in the eighteenth century, and so far as can be seen the London rental had fallen considerably by 1765. Despite these vicissitudes, it is difficult to avoid the conclusion that fortunate purchases of undeveloped or unexploited suburban properties at an early stage, and their subsequent shrewd management, played a critical, even a decisive, part in buoying up the tottering fortunes of the Cecils in the late seventeenth and the early eighteenth centuries.[70]

Equally striking was the growth in the importance of London rents in the finances of the Wriothesleys earls of Southampton. As late as 1624 they were only contributing rather over £100 out of a gross rental of £2,500, but from 1630 onwards the profits of London development rose spectacularly, so that on the death of the third earl in 1667 they brought in over £3,000 out of a total landed income of about £8,500.[71] By the middle years of the seventeenth century urban rents were clearly as important to the Wriothesleys as they were to the Cecils. After the Bloomsbury site passed by marriage from the Wriothesleys to the Russells, it grew increasingly profitable, its rental rising from £2,100 in 1701 to £3,800 in 1732.[72]

Nor were Salisbury and Southampton the only noblemen to turn their west London properties into a gold mine in the seventeenth century. The first and greatest architectural extravaganza of the age was the earl of Bedford's Covent Garden Piazza, constructed in the 1630s on the Italian model of Livorno and surrounded by arcaded terraced housing, his own city palace, and a spectacular Tuscan church designed by Inigo Jones (Plate 1). Bedford was a rare example of a noble entrepreneur who put his own money into urban building. He spent about £13,000 in building the church and three model houses, and by 1660 he was drawing at least £2,000 a year from the Covent Garden and Long Acre Estate.[73] How great was the increase in the late seventeenth century we do not know, but between 1701 and 1732 there was a growth in receipts of £800 a year, some of it from the thriving fruit market, some of it from urban development on the site and gardens of Bedford House.[74] In the first half of the seventeenth century many other noblemen were doing the same things. The earl of Clare was developing Drury Lane to his great profit, and the earl of Leicester was building round Leicester Fields, while the earls of Dorset, Worcester, and Northampton were exploiting the pressure for lower-class housing in the city.[75] In the latter half of the century there was development by the duke of Beaufort in Beaufort Buildings, with a rent of over £1,000 by 1714, and by Lord Hatton in Hatton Gardens, with a rent of £2,300 by 1711. In 1676 the London rent-roll of the earl of St. Alban's in St. James's Square and elsewhere came to over £4,000.[76]

## PLANNING AND AESTHETICS

In matters of planning and aesthetics, a significant influence was that of the crown, for all the Stuart kings had high architectural ambitions for such building as they allowed to take place. It was a proclamation of 1615, perhaps penned by James himself, which best revealed his hopes: "As it was said of the first emperor of Rome that he had found the city of Rome of brick and left it of marble, so We, whom God hath honored to be the first of Britain, might be able to say in the same proportion that we had found our City and suburbs of London of sticks, and left them of brick, being in material far more durable, safe from fire, and beautiful and magnificent."[77] The aesthetic ambitions of the Stuarts were based on the rapidly expanding English brick industry, and their most persistent, and ultimately most successful, efforts—aided not a little by the great fire of 1666 which destroyed so much of the old wooden city—were directed toward encouraging the construction of uniform housing in that material. These royal ambitions coincided with similar, if less strongly felt, desires of many of the aristocratic landlords. Just as they aspired to architectural distinction in their country houses, so too some of them were anxious to bring glory upon themselves by instigating aesthetically noteworthy urban development schemes, by laying out handsome squares and streets which were usually given family names.[78]

In terms of its influence on architectural style, the most important phase of royal activity was between 1625 and 1640, when a commission effectively under the direction of Inigo Jones exercised wide powers of control over the amount, quality, and style of urban development in the metropolis. It was partly to meet the requirements of a royal proclamation of 1625, and partly to satisfy his own desire for sound building structures and aesthetic harmony (which would add to property values), that on his Holborn site in 1629 the earl of Southampton was prescribing in his leases that the tenant was to build a house of brick 17 feet 6 inches wide and 34 feet deep, with three stories and cellars, each story 10 feet high, the facade avoiding all overhangs and cant windows.[79]

The most original and most architecturally ambitious project of the age was the Covent Garden Piazza, with its arcades running below its opulent terraced housing grouped round a huge square, with a church to the west and the earl of Bedford's palace gardens to the south (fig. 6 and Plate 1). The earl himself built three model houses in the early 1630s, and the building leases he granted for the rest contained the most detailed specifications about their external elevations on the piazza side and the materials for their construction. He also built the cellars all round; he constructed the church; and he had plans to erect a bronze statue of King Charles in the center of the piazza.

There is reason to think that this very ambitious and expensive plan was forced on Bedford by King Charles, encouraged, no doubt, by his Surveyor, Inigo Jones, as a *quid pro quo* for the granting of a building license. Charles and Jones were motivated by a desire to emulate the activities of the duke of Florence at Livorno, and those of the French king in the Place Royale and the Place Dauphine in Paris, while Bedford himself cannot have been insensible to the glory which would accrue from building a square of international fame. "Such buildings, and such a church, is the honour of the nation," argued one of his defenders in Parliament in 1657. The earl's architects, so far as can be seen, were perhaps Jones, and certainly Jones's associates Isaac de Caux and Edward Carter. A later submission to Parliament from Bedford's son explicitly stated that the Piazza was erected "by the speciall directions of the then King and his Council with much ornament and beauty and to a vast charge of your petitioner's father."[80] Thus, the introduction into London of both the brick terrace and the formal square owed much to the purposeful encouragement (although not the pocketbook) of the crown and its architectural adviser, Inigo Jones.

The two most architecturally ambitious developments after the Civil War, at Southampton Square (fig. 4 and Plate 2) and St. James's Square, were also conducted with the blessing, and perhaps with the active encouragement, of the crown. Foreign visitors were quick to compare the latter with the best French urban planning at the Place Royale in Paris and Belle Cour in Lyons.[81] There was considerable international prestige to be derived from a distinguished piece of urban planning in the seventeenth century, and contemporary sovereigns were well aware of this. Even when aristocratic ambition alone seems to have been responsible for a distinguished building, as in the cases of the earl of Salisbury's New Exchange and the earl of Southampton's square, it is not implausible to suppose that there was some degree of royal encouragement in the background. It is surely not without sig-

nificance that James I consented formally to open the New Exchange and that Southampton was the leading minister of the
crown when he was drawing up his plans. Even rather more modest schemes, such as those for the development of Leicester Fields
and Golden Square, the latter of which was intended to provide
"such houses as might accommodate gentry," had imposed on
them by the ground landlord the most detailed architectural specifications, in conformity with the regulations laid down in the
1667 Act of Parliament for the rebuilding of London.[82]

The result of these diverse pressures was that between 1630
and 1670 Covent Garden and Southampton Square had set the
example and had firmly established all the basic features which
were to dominate London's urban planning for another two
hundred years: the concept of the local community, in which
residential housing was supplemented by a church and a market;
the construction of residential housing around an open rectangu-
lar area, with streets running out at right angles along the axes;
and the formal rows of symmetrically fronted terrace houses with
basements for the servants and gardens running down behind to
stables and offices accessible from a mews (Plates 1 and 2). Both
arcaded pavements and the "shopping center" with many shops
under one roof also appeared briefly during the same period, only
to die out toward the end of the century; they were three hundred
years before their time.

The English system of royal licensing, aristocratic ownership
and control of large areas, and construction through tightly controlled building leases went a long way to divorce financial investment from architectural and planning design, and so helped
to prevent both reckless and haphazard exploitation of the land by
speculators and an unplanned growth of slum housing. On the
rare occasions when the planner and the financier were one, he
was usually a nobleman with ambitions for glory as well as profit.
Since the crown was usually penniless, London was deprived of
the splendid architectural achievements of a Henry IV in Paris.
Since the nobles operated on the nuclear rather than the extended
family system, they had no need for the huge, rambling multi-
apartment *hôtels* of the French aristocracy in the Marais in Paris;
they were content to live in smaller, more compact houses facing
directly onto the squares of Covent Garden, Bloomsbury, and St.
James's. Since so many squires were coming up to London for the
season from November to April, and since so high a proportion of
the nation's professional elites lived there, what was needed
above all was street after orderly street of upper-middle-class
houses in a respectable neighborhood. It was thus certain economic and political arrangements peculiar to England which

made residential development in London in the seventeenth century so segregated in occupation, so extensive in quantity, so modest in scale, so functional and socially conscious in planning, and so dignified but thoroughly unadventurous in aesthetics. The London square precisely fitted all these requirements.

## Conclusion

In 1700 London was different in its appearance from any other city in Europe. It was not merely that it was much bigger and played a more important role in all aspects of the life of the nation. Its social articulation was different, with its working-class slums to the east; its relatively humble but now—thanks to the great fire of 1666—solid brick housing in the City for the merchant community and the artisans and apprentices; and to the west the respectable terrace housing, arranged in squares and wide streets and paved and lit, for the accommodation of landed squires and professional men. It was unlike Amsterdam, which was dominated by ranks of substantial and architecturally pretentious houses overlooking tree-lined peripheral canals, which served their merchant and banker owners as places of residence, storehouses, and shops; it was also unlike Paris, dominated partly by the architectural and planning achievements of the crown—the Pont Neuf, the Louvre, the Place Royale, the Place Dauphine, and the Palais Royal—and partly by the rambling palaces of "les Grands" in their private *hôtels* in the Marais; and it was unlike Florence or Rome, dominated by the stunning architectural extravagances of enormously wealthy religious and secular princes. London's unique appearance in 1700 was the product of England's unique features: social segregation; political participation; an impoverished crown; the concentration of many functions in a single city; and an ideology that exalted life in the country.

## Notes

1. Estimates of the population both of the country and of London at this period differ considerably, and there is an area of uncertainty even for 1700. For some surveys of the material and some estimates see C. Creighton, *History of Epidemics* (London, 1965), 1: 472–74, 660; N. G. Brett-James, *The Growth of Stuart London* (London, 1935), pp. 495–513; D. V. Glass and D. E. C. Eversley, *Population in History* (London, 1965), pp. 183–204; P. E. Jones and A. V. Judges, "London Population in the Seventeenth Century," *Economic History Review* (1935); E. A. Wrigley, "A Simple Model of London's Importance in Changing English Society and Economy, 1650–1750," *Past and Present* 37 (July 1967): 44–45. The figures for 1800 and 1900 are taken from the 1951 *Census Report*.

2. W. G. Hoskins, "English Provincial Towns in the Early Sixteenth Century," *Transactions of the Royal Historical Society* 5th ser., 6 (1956): 5;

C. A. F. Meekings, *Dorset Hearth Tax Assessments*, Dorset Natural History and Archaeological Society (1951), pp. 108–10. This point was made, for a different conclusion, by A. Everitt in *The Agrarian History of England and Wales*, vol. 4, *1500–1640*, ed. Joan Thirsk (Cambridge, 1967), p. 479.

3. C. W. Chalklin, *The Provincial Towns of Georgian England* (London, 1974), pp. 3–25. In the 1660s York is estimated to have had a population of 11,000; Newcastle 13,400; Exeter 15,400; Bristol 26,000; and Norwich over 20,000. Meekings, *Dorset Hearth Tax Assessments*, pp. 108–9; *Victoria County History: City of York* (London, 1961), p. 162; R. Howell, *Newcastle-upon-Tyne and the Puritan Revolution* (Oxford, 1967), p. 9; W. MacCaffrey, *Exeter 1540–1640* (Cambridge, Mass., 1958), p. 12; Bryan Little, *The City and County of Bristol* (London, 1954), p. 327; C. M. Law, "Local Censuses in the Eighteenth Century," *Population Studies* 23 (1969): 90–93.

4. F. Dainville, "Un dénombrement inédit au XVIIe siècle," *Population* 7 (1952): 54; "Grandeur et Population des Villes au XVIIIe siècle," ibid. 13 (1958): 479.

5. D. V. Glass, "Socio-Economic Status and Occupations in the City of London at the End of the Seventeenth Century," in *Studies in London History*, ed. A. E. J. Hollander and W. Kellaway (London, 1969), p. 385.

6. E. M. Leonard, *Early History of English Poor Relief* (Cambridge, 1900), passim; A. L. Beier, "Poor Relief in Warwickshire, 1630–1660," *Past and Present* 35 (December 1966); W. K. Jordan, *Philanthropy in England, 1480–1660* (London, 1959), pp. 54–76.

7. A. Everitt, "Farm Labourers," in *The Agrarian History of England and Wales, 1500–1640*, pp. 396–99; D. C. Coleman, "Labour in the English Economy in the Seventeenth Century," *Economic History Review*, 2d ser., 8 (1956): 288–92.

8. D. Cressy, "Occupations, Migration and Literacy in East London, 1580–1640," *Local Population Studies* 5 (1970): 57; T. H. Hollingsworth, *Historical Demography*, (Ithaca, 1969), p. 87; Wrigley, "A Simple Model," pp. 46–47; L. Stone, "Social Mobility in England, 1500–1700," *Past and Present* 33 (April 1966): 23; East London History Group, "The Population of Stepney in the Early Seventeenth Century," *Local Population Studies Magazine and Newsletter* 3 (1969): 41–42.

9. Stone, "Social Mobility," pp. 31–32; Wrigley, "A Simple Model," p. 48, n. 9; Glass, "Socio-Economic Status," p. 387.

10. C. Wilson, *England's Apprenticeship, 1603–1763* (London, 1965), pp. 141–47; W. G. Hoskins, "Harvest Fluctuations 1620–1759," *Agricultural History Review* 16 (1968): 21–28; E. L. Jones, "Agricultural Change in England 1660–1750," *Journal of Economic History* 25 (1965): 1–18.

11. E. W. Gilboy, *Wages in Eighteenth Century England* (Cambridge, Mass., 1934), p. 241; Wrigley, "A Simple Model," pp. 50–51. By 1755 London marriage licences suggest that 92 percent of males and 74 percent of females could sign their names. There is reason to think that this abnormally high level of literacy also existed in the seventeenth century. Glass, "Socio-Economic Status," p. 388; Cressy, "Occupations, Migration and Literacy," p. 59.

12. Wrigley, "A Simple Model," pp. 55–58.

13. R. Davis, "English Foreign Trade, 1660–1700," *Economic History Review*, 2d ser., 7 (1954); D. C. Coleman, *Sir John Banks, Baronet and Businessman* (Oxford, 1963); R. Davis, *The Rise of the English Shipping Industry* (London, 1962), p. 392; M. J. Power, "East London Housing in the Seventeenth Century," in *Crisis and Order in English Towns*, ed. P. Clark and P. Slack (London, 1972).

14. Stone, "Social Mobility," pp. 24, 29.

15. *Horace Walpole's Correspondence*, ed. W. S. Lewis (New Haven, 1954), 18:315–16; John Roque, *Map of London, Westminster and the Borough of Southwark* (1737); L.C.C., *Survey of London*, 36 (1970): 306–7; for von Archenholz's comments, see R. Forster and E. Forster, *European Society in the Eighteenth Century* (New York, 1969), p. 18; H. L. H. von Pückler-Muskau, *Tour of England, Ireland and France* (London, 1823), p. 125; Forster and Forster, *European Society*, p. 580.

16. F. P. and M. M. Verney, *Memoirs of the Verney Family during the Seventeenth Century* (London, 1907), 1:67.

17. A. Everitt, "The County Community," in *The English Revolution, 1600–1660*, ed. E. W. Ives (London, 1968), p. 49; Edward, Earl of Clarendon, *The Life* (Oxford, 1857), 1:5.

18. Bodleian Library, Banks MSS., 62/1–35.

19. M.-S. Røstig, *The Happy Man* (Oslo, 1962), 1:13–287 passim.

20. Edward, Earl of Clarendon, *Miscellaneous Works* (London, 1727), p. 330; Stone, "Social Mobility," pp. 25–29.

21. J. Crofts, *Packhorse, Waggon and Post* (London, 1967), pp. 117–19, 125; F. P. and M. M. Verney, *Memoirs of the Verney Family during the Seventeenth Century*, 1:67, 179, 213, 359–60; 2:9, 140, 142, 181, 399; *Life and Times of Anthony Wood*, ed. A. Clark, vol. 2, *Oxford Historical Society* 21 (1892): 155.

22. J. Crofts, *Packhorse, Waggon and Post*, pp. 8, 109–124; Chatsworth, Hardwick MSS. 29; E. Ward, *London Spy Compleat*, ed. R. Straus (London, 1924), p. 151.

23. British Library, Loan MSS. 29/235.

24. J. Crofts, *Packhorse, Waggon and Post*, pp. 102–8; G. Miege, *The Present State of Great Britain and Ireland* (London, 1718), pp. 106–7, 161–62.

25. *Letters and Works of Lady Mary Wortley Montagu*, ed. Lord Wharncliffe (London, 1887), 1:72; E. J. Climenson, *Elizabeth Montagu, Queen of the Bluestockings* (London, 1906), pp. 11, 14, 16; *Catalogue of Political and Personal Satires in the British Museum*, 8:620, no. 10945.

26. J. Crofts, *Packhorse, Waggon and Post*, pl. 6; Verney, *Memoirs*, 1:69, 347, 357; 2:222; C. de Saussure, *A Foreign View of England in the Reigns of George I and George II* (London, 1902), pp. 166–69; University of Kansas, Spencer Library, MS. Q8.24; J. Macky, *A Journey Through England in Familiar Letters* (London, 1714), 1:107.

27. Verney, *Memoirs*, 1:67; Hatfield House, Accounts 157/3; 35/2; 137/7; *L.C.C., Survey of London*, 31 (1963): 139; 34 (1966): 425; 36 (1970): 31, 32.

28. M. Falkus, "Lighting in the Dark Ages of English History: Town Streets before the Industrial Revolution," in *Trade, Government and Economy in Pre-Industrial England*, ed. D. C. Coleman and A. H. John (London, 1976), pp. 255–56, 261.

29. L. Stone, *The Crisis of the Aristocracy, 1558–1641* (Oxford, 1965), pp. 555–57; E. Waterhouse, *The Gentleman's Monitor* (London, 1665), p. 297.

30. *Autobiography of Roger North*, ed. A. Jessop (London, 1887), p. 70.

31. T. Gisborne, *An Enquiry into the Duties of the Female Sex* (1797; London, 1806), p. 328; Stone, *Crisis of the Aristocracy*, pp. 387–92; *Crosby Records: A Cavalier's Notebook of William Blundell*, ed. T. E. Gibson (London, 1880), p. 135.

32. P. M. G. Dixon, *The Financial Revolution in England* (London, 1967), pp. 3–14.

33. Stone, *Crisis of the Aristocracy*, pp. 387–92; D. Defoe, *A Tour through England and Wales*, Everyman ed. (London, 1928), 1:326.

34. H. J. Habakkuk, "The Price of Land in England, 1500–1700," in *Wirtschaft, Geschichte und Wirtschaftsgeschichte*, ed. W. Abel et al. (Stuttgart, 1966), pp. 126–28.

35. A. Everitt, *Change in the Provinces: The Seventeenth Century*, (Leicester, 1969), p. 25; A. Everitt, "The English Urban Inn," in his *Perspectives in English Urban History* (London, 1973).

36. F. Drake, *Eboracum* (London, 1736), p. 240; *V.C.H., City of York*, pp. 208, 245–47.

37. *The Inhabitants of Bristol in 1696*, ed. E. Ralph and M. E. Williams, *Bristol Record Society* 25 (1968). The attempt by the editor to distinguish a "fashionable" quarter of high society and a business quarter of rich merchants collapses when it is realized that the baronets and knights are in fact all rich merchants.

38. J. W. F. Hill, *Tudor and Stuart Lincoln* (Cambridge, 1956), pp. 2, 4, 15, 17.

39. Public Record Office E. 179/154/701; P. Corfield, "A Provincial Capital in the Late Seventeenth Century," in Clark and Slack, *Crisis and Order in English Towns;* A. Hassall-Smith, *Country and Court: Government and Politics in Norfolk 1558–1603* (Oxford, 1974), p. 15.

40. *Birmingham Archaeological Society Transactions* 77 (1962): 101.

41. *V.C.H., City of York*, pp. 161, 245–46, 530; Herts. Record Office, Oldfield Drawings, passim (for St. Albans); *North Country Diaries*, vol. 1, Surtees Society 118 (1910): 7.

42. R. M. Wiles, "Provincial Culture in Early Georgian England," in *The Triumph of Culture: Eighteenth Century Perspectives*, ed. P. Fritz and D. Williams (Toronto, 1972); Everitt, *Perspectives in English Urban History*, pp. 113–20; A. J. F. Brown, "Colchester in the Eighteenth Century," in *East Anglian Studies*, ed. L. M. Munby (Cambridge, 1968), pp. 163–67; J. M. Biggins, "Coffee Houses of York, 1730–1830," *York Georgian Society* (1953–54); *Francis Letters*, ed. B. Francis and E. Keary (New York, 1901), 1:119.

43. J. H. Plumb, *The Commercialization of Leisure* (Reading, 1973); Defoe, *Tour through England and Wales*, 1:186, 49, 114; 2:156, 75; R. Halsband, *Lord Hervey* (Oxford, 1973), p. 37. For other accounts of the beginnings of cultural amenities in provincial towns near London in the first quarter of the eighteenth century, see Macky, *Journey through England in Familiar Letters*, 1:3, 56, 70, 78–79, 84; C. de Saüssure, *Foreign View of England in the Reigns of George I and George II*, p. 307. For an overview of the situation, see P. Borsay, "The English Urban Renaissance: the Development of English Provincial Urban Culture," *Journal of Social History* 5 (1977).

44. *Torrington Diaries*, ed. C. B. Andrews (London, 1934–38), 1:130, 227, 350; 2:63, 175; 3:235. F. de la Rochefoucauld, *A Frenchman in England, 1784*, ed. J. Marchand, (Cambridge, 1933), pp. 56, 147, 158, 162, 177, 242–43.

45. T. C. Dale, *The Inhabitants of London in 1638* (London, 1931).

46. Bodleian Library, Banks MSS. 62/1–35.

47. The statistics were compiled by checking the list of aldermen in A. B. Beaven, *The Aldermen of the City of London* (London, 1913), vol. 2, with the lists of city residents in T. C. Dale, *The Inhabitants of London in 1638* (London, 1931), and *London Inhabitants within the Walls, 1695*, ed. D. V. Glass, London Record Society, vol. 2 (1966).

48. *The Little London Directory of 1677* (London, 1863); Hatfield MSS. A 162/1, 3; G. Scott Thomson, *Life in a Noble Household 1641–1700* (London, 1937), pp. 79, 293, 295; D. C. Coleman, *Sir John Banks*, pp. 67, 123 (Coleman especially draws attention to "the complete absence of the well-known City names of the day in Lincoln's Inn Fields"); *L.C.C., Survey of London*, 20:40–41; 36 (1970): 96–97; A. I. Dasent, *The History of St. James' Square* (London, 1895), pp. 14–27; Wrigley, "A Simple Model."

49. Coleman, *Sir John Banks*, pp. 9, 43, 51, 67, 122, 123, 195–96.

50. Dasent, *St. James' Square*, pp. 161, 163.

51. Forster and Forster, *European Society*, pp. 16–17.

52. J. Timbs, *Club Life of London* (London, 1872), pp. 4, 15, 17, 20, 39, 47, 70, 71, 135, 137; *Reminiscences and Recollections of Count Gronow* (London, 1900), 1: 55; *The Spectator*, 403, 12 June 1712; R. Steele, *The Tender Husband*, ed. C. Winton (London, 1967), p. 14.

53. G. Rudé, *Hanoverian London, 1714–1808* (London, 1971), p. 209.

54. For the Cecils and Wriothesleys, see L. Stone, *Family and Fortune: Studies in Aristocratic Finance, 1500–1700* (Oxford, 1973), chaps. 3 and 8; for the Russells, see *L.C.C., Survey of London*, 36 (1970).

55. Brett-James, *Growth of Stuart London*, pp. 315, 508; *Life and Times of Anthony Wood*, ed. A. Clark, vol. 3, Oxford Historical Society 26 (1894): 330.

56. M. J. Power, "East and West in Early Modern London," in *Wealth and Power in Tudor England*, ed. E. W. Ives, R. J. Knecht, and J. J. Scarisbrick (London, 1978); Dasent, *St. James' Square*, p. 5; Ward, *London Spy Compleat*, p. 157.

57. Stone, *Crisis of the Aristocracy*, pp. 395–96.

58. *L.C.C., Survey of London*, 6:51, 96; 18:44, 57, 122, 123, 125, 126;

36 (1970): 207, 223; *H.M.C., Rutland MSS.*, 2:65; G. Miege, *Present State of Great Britain and Ireland,* p. 101.

59. Dasent, *St. James' Square,* App. A; *L.C.C., Survey of London,* 31 (1963): 143.

60. Brett-James, *Growth of Stuart London,* chaps. 3, 4, 12; T. G. Barnes, "The Prerogative and Environmental Control of London Building in the Early Seventeenth Century: the Lost Opportunity," *California Law Review* 58 (1970).

61. *L.C.C., Survey of London,* 36 (1970): 25–26, 32–33.

62. See Stone, *Family and Fortune,* chap. 3.

63. *L.C.C., Survey of London,* 36 (1970): 26; Dasent, *St. James' Square,* pp. 4–6, 11.

64. *L.C.C., Survey of London,* 36 (1970): 47.

65. For example, at Covent Garden (*L.C.C., Survey of London,* 36 [1970]: 29, 36, 37, 39, 45).

66. Forster and Forster, *European Society,* p. 19.

67. Brett-James, *Growth of Stuart London,* p. 308; J. P. Malcolm, *Anecdotes of the Manners and Customs of London during the Eighteenth Century* (London, 1808), p. 465.

68. Brett-James, *Growth of Stuart London,* pp. 157–59, 167. For a summary of the evidence on Newport Street up to 1640 see Stone, *Crisis of the Aristocracy,* pp. 361–63.

69. Brett-James, *Growth of Stuart London,* pp. 324–49. For other late seventeenth-century examples of the speculative builder see *L.C.C., Survey of London,* 31 (1963): 138–41; 33 (1966): 42; 34 (1966): 425, 428.

70. See Stone, *Family and Fortune,* chap. 3.

71. Ibid., pp. 228–30, 234, 237–38, 240.

72. G. Scott Thomson, *The Russells of Bloomsbury* (London, 1940), pp. 101, 302.

73. Stone, *Crisis of the Aristocracy,* p. 361; *L.C.C., Survey of London,* 36 (1970): 33, 34.

74. Scott Thomson, *Russells of Bloomsbury,* p. 302.

75. Stone, *Crisis of the Aristocracy,* pp. 361–62.

76. Badminton House, Beaufort MSS. 300.2.5; Northants. R.O., Finch-Hatton MSS. 2053; *L.C.C., Survey of London,* 29 (1960): 3.

77. Dasent, *St. James' Square,* p. 90.

78. For example, George St., Villiers St., Duke St., and Buckingham St.; or Cecil St., Cranborne St., and Salisbury St.; or Russell St., Tavistock St., and Bedford St.

79. Hampshire R.O., Wriothesley Deeds 306, 307.

80. *L.C.C., Survey of London,* 36 (1970): 26–31, 34; Woburn Abbey MSS. I owe this last reference to the kindness of Sir John Summerson. See also his "Inigo Jones," *Proceedings of the British Academy* 50 (1964): 170–82.

81. Dasent, *St. James' Square,* p. 6.

82. *L.C.C., Survey of London,* 31 (1963): 138–39; 34 (1966): 425. For illustrations of the specifications in the act, see T. F. Reddaway, *The Rebuilding of London after the Great Fire* (London, 1940), p. 80.

# The Problem of
# Ideological Adaptation

# Anxiety and
# the Formation of
# Early Modern Culture

## WILLIAM J. BOUWSMA

All men may be anxious; but it is commonly observed that some are more anxious than others, both individually and in groups. It is widely believed, for example, that our own age is a time of peculiar anxiety.[1] But though this impression may derive less from the considered views of professional historians than from the general distress of the later twentieth century, it is obviously a historical judgment; it implies that various moments in the past can be contrasted in terms of the degree of anxiety they exhibit.

But systematic elaboration of such contrast is difficult. "Anxiety" is itself a problematic term; and without some clear conception of its sources in the human personality, its dynamics, and its relation to other subjective states, we may well misread our evidence and above all misunderstand the relation between anxiety and objective experience. The study of historical anxiety therefore requires some special theoretical resources. But the empirical side of such investigation also presents unusual difficulties. Some degree of anxiety seems latent in the human condition, and various expressions of it can doubtless be discovered in every time and place. At the same time it seems unlikely that, outside of the laboratory, anxiety can ever be submitted to precise measurement. Accordingly, the judgment that one age or social group was more or less anxious than another can hardly be supported by the kind of hard comparative data that may be adduced for more objective phenomena. In dealing with matters of this sort we are therefore likely to find ourselves in the awkward position of basing essentially quantitative conclusions on patently qualitative evidence.[2] And we may find no evidence at all precisely where we most need it.

Nevertheless these problems have not deterred able historians from speaking about past anxiety. At least one distinguished scholar has used the term to characterize the later hellenistic world.[3] And it is notably present, at various levels of generality, in recent scholarship dealing with the transition from those centuries that were clearly "medieval" to those almost as clearly not. Historians of this important segment of the European past seem, in fact, to be discovering symptoms of a peculiar anxiety in many places. Origo and Bec have noted the heightened anxiety of Italian merchants, Lewis that of merchants in France, Dollinger that of German merchants; Herlihy has found it deeply embedded in the Renaissance family, transmitted from anxious mothers to their children.[4] Historians with larger purposes are meanwhile coming steadily closer to a general characterization of this as an age of special anxiety. The tendency is apparent in the excellent monographs of Douglass and Steinmetz on later medieval piety, and in the more general studies of Seidlmayer, Meiss, Becker, Delaruelle, Trinkaus, Oberman, Delumeau, Ozment, Dickens, and Walzer.[5] Garin speaks of the Italian Renaissance as "the beginning of an age of [subjective] torment," whatever it may have represented positively.[6] And Lynn White, Jr., broadly presenting the three or four centuries after 1300 as a time of "abnormal anxiety," has offered us a general interpretation of the period in these terms.[7] We seem to be reaching a point at which the general implications of this scholarship, based on both northern and southern Europe, on movements conventionally associated both with the later Middle Ages and with the Renaissance, and on every social group for which evidence is available, must be confronted more deliberately.

A rather different kind of pressure, less clearly the product of professional investigation, is impelling us in the same direction. There has been a remarkable tendency among recent translators into English, concerned to convey meaning from one time, as well as one language, to another, to read "anxiety" into a wide range of words or phrases in documents of this period. The transformation of the Latin *anxietas* into "anxiety" may occasion little surprise, though perhaps it should; in medieval usage *anxietas* signified a vague weariness or distress of heart, and came close to monastic *acedia* or even *tristitia*.[8] But the meaning of *anxietas* seems to have broadened by the sixteenth century, as we can learn from Calvin, that indefatigable translator of his own Latin into the vernacular. In his French *Institution*, Calvin variously rendered the *anxietas* of the Latin *Institutio* into *angoisse, destresse, frayeur*, and *solicitude*, and his Latin *solicitudo* (evidently a close synonym) could become either *solicitude* or *perplexité*.[9] By the time "anxiety" and "anxious" entered English in the sixteenth and seventeenth centuries (and that they did so at this time is of obvious interest here), they evidently already conveyed these various possibilities; and we can certainly forgive recent translators, themselves doubtless in some *perplexité*, at least a part of their freedom, even though it may occasionally raise an eyebrow. From Latin Petrarch's *cura* and the *distractio* of Thomas à Kempis can both emerge as "anxiety."[10] And a host of vernacular expressions come out similarly. The identification of the German *Angst* and *Anfechtung* with "anxiety" is sufficiently familiar, although, to be sure, Reformation scholars have been unusually conscious of the nuances of these more technically theological terms. But from the French, Commynes's *ce travail et misere* now appears as "their anxieties and their worries";[11] and a recent translation of Alberti's *I libri della famiglia* converts *maninconia, affanno, cura, sollecitudine, sospetto, perturbazione*, and *agonia di mente* indiscriminately into "anxiety," *buona diligenza* into "anxious attention," and *stare in paura* into "to be anxious."[12] From Spanish both *ansia* and *cuidado* emerge as "anxiety."[13] I do not propose to quarrel here with these renderings; I want only to suggest how, even by so apparently innocent a route, we are being led into strange new historiographical territory.

A further impulse behind our sense of the period after about 1300 as an age of unusual anxiety stems from the more benign impression conveyed by the culture of the twelfth and thirteenth centuries. In that earlier period, those men whose attitudes are accessible to us appear to have felt reasonably comfortable about human existence.[14] The prospects for mankind, both in this world and the next, seemed generally happy; the medieval schools could demonstrate, with increasing confidence, the intelligibility and friendliness of the universe; intellectuals were pleased to see themselves, though dwarves, as standing on the shoulders of giants; and men could hope that, in various walks of life, "the quality of our life should be improved."[15] The defects of the contemporary scene were not passed over (indeed selective attention to them was a sign of confidence), as we know from such popular works as the *Roman de la Rose;* but the essential quality of that work was its bold and exuberant naturalism, and even Dante could still believe in the power of intelligence and love to remedy the ills of existence. Generalized laments about the human condition abounded, like Innocent III's little treatise *De miseria* (though he had hoped to complement this with a more positive statement about life); but there seemed little specifically wrong with the times, much that was right, and much to look forward to.

Some caution is in order here. We know little directly about how, for example, merchants of the twelfth and thirteenth centuries felt about their lives; and it is hard to believe that existence in towns (a subject that will figure prominently in what follows) did not, from the beginning, generate profound inner as well as outer discomfort. It is even more difficult to assess the psychological condition of the vast rural majority. But even granting this, I think it would be a mistake simply to dismiss the optimism of high medieval culture as the invention of an isolated class of intellectuals. Medieval high culture was not altogether detached from its social context, as its hospitality to the more concrete world of Aristotelian thought would seem to demonstrate; and the combination of intellectual and pastoral concern in the great mendicant orders provided a two-way bridge between intellectual constructions and the needs of daily life. The result was that, though human problems might still be acute, men who addressed themselves to such general questions could still contemplate the future with relative confidence.

This positive attitude to the future in the high Middle Ages is of special significance because it is the key to a clearer understanding of the nature of anxiety. It reminds us that anxiety is a function of man's attitude to time. As the *Oxford English Dictionary* tells us, anxiety is "uneasiness or trouble of mind about some uncertain event." Man is anxious, therefore, because his existence extends into the *future,* and the future is inherently *uncertain.* This suggests that, since all human life unfolds in time, anxiety is in some degree inescapable, perhaps especially in the western tradition, with its peculiar sense of the significance of time. Chaucer's Knight understood the general element in human existence that gives rise to anxiety:

> It's good to keep one's poise and be protected
> Since all day long we meet the unexpected.[16]

The unusual anxiety of the period after 1300 is thus implicit in its novel concern with the passage of time, which found general expression in the familiar new historical consciousness of the Renaissance and was manifested more particularly in efforts to mark the flow of time with chronometers and to control its use by profitably filling the hours. The increasing reliance on clocks in later medieval and Renaissance Europe has been often remarked,[17] and their value celebrated. A fourteenth-century Milanese chronicler praised a new striking clock because it "marks off the hours from the hours, as is supremely necessary for all classes of men."[18] Calvin emphasized the utility of the sun, and Pascal that of his watch, for marking time.[19] And Petrarch hinted at the anxiety underlying the concern with time; time, as he wrote the emperor Charles IV, is "so precious, nay, so inestimable a possession, that it is the one thing which the learned agree can justify avarice."[20] Vergerio proposed that a clock be installed in every library, "that it may catch the eye of the reader, to warn him by the swift lapse of time of the need for diligence."[21] Rabelais's ideal teacher Ponocrates so arranged the schedule of his young pupil "that not a moment of the day was wasted."[22] But anxiety over the use of time was not confined to scholars. The anxious wife of the merchant Francesco Datini chided her husband for his misuse of time: "In view of all you have to do, when you waste an hour, it seems to me a thousand. . . . For I deem nought so precious to you, both for body and soul, as time, and methinks you value it too little."[23] This peculiarly modern concern would eventually find homely expression in *Poor Richard's Almanack*, but more was at stake here than "profit." For the proper regulation and use of time eliminated some of the uncertainty of life; it warded off, objectively, the blows of fortune, that comprehensive symbol of the uncertainty of life.

The fundamental relationship between the unreliability of fortune and human anxiety seemed, at any rate, obvious to contemporaries. So Alberti's Uncle Adovardo asked, quite rhetorically, "If a man is afflicted with so many anxieties, and always fears the instability of fortune . . . how can we consider him happy or call him anything but unfortunate?"[24] If the management of time suggested an objective means of escape from this predicament, Petrarch's *De remediis* (so popular also outside of Italy) promoted, at vast length, subjective remedies, chiefly along Stoic lines.[25] Machiavelli was following a similar direction of thought in proposing that although men "know not the end and move towards it along roads which cross one another and as yet are unexplored . . . they should not despair, no matter what fortune brings."[26] We have here further testimony to the general connection between anxiety and the uncertainty inherent in time itself as an inescapable dimension of life. Fortune expressed the radical untrustworthiness of the future.

But back of the future, beyond the limits of time as a dimension of each individual existence, lurks the uncertainty surrounding death. This is why, in some ultimate sense, all anxiety is anxiety about death,[27] and why the anxiety of this period, often when it was immediately focused on the use of time, tended to accumulate especially around death and judgment, the nameless horror beyond every particular danger. "It is sad," Thomas à Kempis wrote, "that you do not employ your time better, when you may win eternal life hereafter. The time will come when you will long for one day or one hour in which to amend; and who knows whether it will be granted?"[28] The peculiar obsession of Europeans with these matters from the fourteenth century onward has been of considerable interest to historians;[29] we seem to be dealing here with something more than a set of perennial platitudes. Death, both as a physiological process and as the entrance into a realm of final uncertainty, was surrounded, even more than fortune, though for the same reason, by a singular dread. For all his piety, Petrarch could not conquer his fear of death, which he described in obsessive and strenuous detail. *"Ubi sunt?"* he asked, and could only reply, "All has dissolved into worms and into serpents, and finally into nothing." He hated sleep because it reminded him of death, and his bed because it suggested the grave.[30] For Commynes death showed "what a petty thing man is, how short and miserable his life is, and how empty the differences between the great and the small, as soon as they are dead. For everyone is horrified by a corpse and vituperates it. . . ."

But the horror of death was compounded by a deeper anxiety over the uncertainty of judgment. "The soul," Commynes had concluded his little meditation on death, "must immediately go to receive God's judgment. Sentence is given at that very moment in accordance with the works and merits of the corpse."[31] Calvin spelled out the connection between this apprehension and the general anxiety of the age: "Where does death come from but from God's anger against sin? Hence arises that state of servitude through the whole of life, that is the constant anxiety in which unhappy souls are imprisoned."[32] Even laymen despaired over the mysteries of predestination and had to be advised to leave such matters to theologians.[33] The pains of Purgatory were sufficiently feared; Thomas More himself described them in grisly detail,[34] and the rich provided in their wills for masses to speed their souls to heaven: three thousand for a German merchant, ten thousand for Henry VII of England (who was prepared to pay above the going rate to insure their being said properly), thirty thousand for the emperor Charles V.[35] In the Medici Chapel in Florence, the massive figures of Michelangelo brooding over their solemn work, priests dropped with fatigue saying masses for their departed rulers.[36] But the fear of hell was infinitely worse. A popular catechism pictured the damned feeding on their own flesh and explained, "The pain caused by one spark of hell-fire is greater than that caused by a thousand years of a woman's labor in childbirth."[37] Nor were such fears alien to more refined minds. Petrarch described his thoughts of hell: "Terror grips my heart / Seeing the others I tremble for myself / Others urge me on, my last hour may be now."[38]

The peculiar guilt of this period is sometimes attributed to the confessional, but this seems at best a half-truth; the confessional was as much an expression as a cause of anxiety. Men submitted to its scrutiny because they were in desperate fear of appearing before God with a single sin left unrecognized and unabsolved. Even confessors sometimes shrank from so dreadful a responsibility, itself a source of unbearable anxiety.[39] And men often stayed away from confession because it gave no relief. Some looked instead to conscience, though this could be no more reassuring; for conscience, as Leonardo Bruni wrote, is a judge who "knows all" and "was present at every crime," and who "forces tears from you and compels you to weep among sacred things."[40] Luther, who had vowed to become a monk through "the terror and agony of sudden death,"[41] was eloquent on the inadequacy of conscience to relieve anxiety. To the guilty, he wrote, "all creatures appear changed. Even when they speak with people whom they know and in turn hear them, the very sound of their speech seems different, their looks appear changed, and everything becomes black and horrible wherever they turn their eyes. Such a fierce and savage beast is an evil conscience. And so, unless God comforts them, they must end their own life because of their despair, their distress, and their inability to bear their grief."[42]

The importance of these fundamental dimensions of the anxiety of this period is suggested by the attention given to the problem, both explicitly and implicitly, in the religious thought of the sixteenth century, among Catholics almost as much as among Protestants. The uncertainty we have identified as central to anxiety figured prominently in the Protestant indictment of later medieval piety, and conversely Protestants stressed the certainties implicit in their own understanding of the Gospel. For Luther the "fear, terror, and horror" of death were the peculiar work of the devil; and faith alone could produce that "comfortable certainty" he could not attain by himself.[43] For Calvin the terrible "anxiety and trepidation of mind" produced by honest self-examination, and the ignorance of providence that is "the ultimate of all miseries," could only give way before the "incredible freedom from worry about the future" that comes from faith. Scripture frees us from seeking "some uncertain deity by devious paths" and brings us to an "assurance that is not assailed by some anxiety." "Surely it is terrifying to walk in the darkness of death," he wrote; "and believers, whatever their strength may be, cannot but be frightened by it. But since the thought prevails that they have God beside them, caring for their safety, fear at once yields to assurance."[44] Saint Teresa described her own movement from a deep depression of uncertainty about God's favor to the recognition that "I might safely take comfort and be certain that I was in grace."[45] The personal intensity of both Protestant and Catholic piety in the age of the Reformation can only be understood against the background of the peculiar anxiety that it sought to assuage.

It is essential, to get at the ultimate meaning of anxiety, to notice first its attachment to the problems of time, death, and judgment. But anxiety also has other dimensions; as a diffuse condition of the personality, it can suffuse any area of experience. Indeed, it tends to seek out more particular and immediate expression, for, by providing itself with a local habitation and a name, it is therapeutically transformed into fear. Fear is distinguishable from anxiety by the specificity of its object; and because the object of fear is concrete and may be dealt with by some appropriate action, fear can be reduced or overcome. The effect of anxiety, on the other hand, is likely to be paralysis and depression. Yet the relationship between anxiety and fear remains close, for behind the fear of a particular danger always lurks, again, uncertainty about its eventual outcome. The close connection between these two states accounts for the fact that we encounter in this period not only anxiety about ultimate matters but also a peculiar capacity to be troubled, like Martha, about many things. The worries of this prototypical housewife can tell us, indeed, a good deal about the nature of historical anxiety. Mary and Martha (a point frequently made in a related connection) are two sides of the same existential coin. Mary represents the direct approach to human anxiety; she goes to its source. But Martha prefers to diffuse her anxiety among a variety of household tasks, with which she can immediately cope. We are here, perhaps, close to the psychological roots of the preoccupation of Renaissance moral and political discourse with the *vita activa*.

Europeans of the fourteenth century, and for some time thereafter, were thus both profoundly anxious and at the same time frightened by almost every aspect of experience. It is hardly necessary to review here the evidence of their pervasive fear;

historians are now discerning it in every sector of life. They have found it among rulers and merchants, and in every social relationship. It poisoned friendships and family ties, and even the sexual bond. The marriage bed itself now seemed less genial, as indeed we might expect; men who had learned a general distrust of life could hardly have been capable of a careless spontaneity in the most intimate realms of experience.[46] Anxiety also attended the pursuit of learning, which too often seemed only an occasion of further despair; the more one knew, the less sense the world made.[47]

Each of these particular concerns can doubtless be attributed to objective causes. Politics *was* a dangerous game, the pursuit of wealth did involve great risks, friends played false, treachery within families did occur, lovers could inflict deep wounds, the wisdom in books might indeed mislead and confuse. But it is not immediately obvious that much of this was not also true in the preceding centuries (or indeed in most centuries), and what is most striking about these expressions of distress is their inclusiveness. They arise in connection with every significant human activity. Indeed they may surround, with equal intensity and a mysterious poignancy, quite insignificant matters. Alberti could debate alternative solutions to the larger and more concrete problems of life, but he suggests that the same degree of anxiety could also surround its more trivial responsibilities, and with paralyzing effect. His uncles were radically upset by the "confusions, worries, and anxieties" of giving a dinner party, in which "upheaval and annoyance overwhelm you until you are tired before you have even begun your preparations"; and the difficulties of moving to a new house evoked in them "anxieties that afflict your mind and distract and disrupt spirit and thought."[48] Alberti seems to be reminding us that the problem of anxiety, the somber thread that runs all through his book, was, after all, more general and diffuse than any particular dangers could account for.

Historians have tended to attribute the peculiar anxiety of this period to the specific character, and above all the disasters, of European life after the beginning of the fourteenth century: to epidemics (and, of course, the Black Death!) more terrible than anyone could remember, to the uncertainties of a depressed economy, to the transition from a corporate to an individualistic society, to political disorder, to the contraction of Christendom in the East, to the disarray of the institutional church, to the pressures of the confessional, or to the novelties of rapid change. And evidence is not lacking that each of these experiences disturbed and depressed some men, from time to time and in varying degrees. But it is hardly demonstrable, however distressing these matters seem to modern historians, who can envisage them cumulatively and imagine their concentrated impact on themselves, that they had a similar effect on those who experienced them in the past. The men of our period engaged with them not simultaneously but separately and at intervals, and were rarely in a position to draw general conclusions about their meaning.[49] Nor is it clear that, had they been able to do so, they would have reacted much differently from men in earlier centuries to their own difficulties, which were not objectively insignificant. The diffuseness of the anxiety of our period suggests that the relationship of anxiety to particular disasters was incidental rather than essential. Explanation in these terms appears to neglect the distinction, and the relationship, between anxiety and fear.

Nevertheless it remains true that the malaise of our period was peculiarly its own. It must be seen as a historical phenomenon, and so it was considered at the time, when it became an essential component of a new historical consciousness. "*Now* the world is cowardly, decayed, and weak, / All goes badly," wrote Eustache Deschamps;[50] and it is this *now* that commands our attention: not simply life in general but the times, and above all what they might hold in store, were out of joint. Petrarch stressed the "present woes" that promised, if this were possible, worse to come: "*O tempora, o mores!*" he exclaimed.[51] "*Now* the study of holy eloquence and its professors suffer the laughter and derision of all," declared a French reformer about 1400.[52] Machiavelli denounced "the negligence of princes, who *have lost* all appetite for true glory, and of republics which *no longer* possess institutions that deserve praise."[53] Erasmus explained the spate of predictions of the world's end as a judgment on the particular conditions of the present age: "They say it's because men are behaving *now* just as they did before the Flood overwhelmed them."[54] Montaigne represented his own time as dull and leaden, all virtue spent.[55]

Implicit here, obviously, is comparison with a previous period when human affairs had presumably gone better, and with this comparison we begin to sense a contemporary explanation for the anxieties of the time that is somewhat different from the explanations favored by modern historians. There are hints of it in the town chronicles of fourteenth-century Italy, with their idealization of a simpler past,[56] as well as in Commynes, who believed that "our life-span is diminished, and we do not live as long as men did in former times; neither are our bodies as strong, and similarly our faith and loyalty to one another has been weakened."[57] The past now represented a lost ideal of peace, order, freedom, and above all brotherhood, in which men could exist without anxiety. The clue to the peculiar difficulties of the present thus seemed to lie in the deterioration of all social relationships; men had become anxious, contemporaries constantly repeated, because they had come to fear each other. "You are young," a Florentine merchant wrote one of his agents, "but when you have lived as long as I have and have traded with many folk, you will know that man is a dangerous thing, and that danger lies in dealing with him."[58] Everywhere one meets the charge that *now* men looked out only for themselves. "Men live among themselves in such a manner," wrote Luther, "that no consideration is given to the state or household . . . who does not see that God is compelled, as it were, to punish, yes, even to destroy Germany?"[59]

And the explanation for this novel egotism lies just below the surface of many expressions of contemporary anxiety: its cause was seen in the replacement of an agrarian by an urban society and in the attitudes and activities particularly associated with townsmen. A long tradition of antiurban sentiment lay behind this, nourished by both the Greek and the Latin classics, given substance by the medieval perception of towns as a disruptive intrusion into the old agrarian order, and finding expression in the Franciscan ideal of poverty. But by the fourteenth century there are signs that European observers were tending to regard towns as the cause of a general historical crisis and the source of their peculiar anxiety. Petrarch, adapting Juvenal, associated many of his worst moments with cities: with filthy, noisy and bustling Avignon and even with Venice, where, he reported, "wherever I go in full day a crowd of dogs drawn from the populace assails me noisily . . . they are innumerable, turbulent, and noisy, and they are plagued with endless worry because they cannot bite me."[60] Here, apparently, his anxiety was matched by that of those who surrounded him.

But towns provoked anxiety above all because they were greedy; townsmen preyed on others to benefit themselves, and this was what made them unreliable and dangerous, a threat to the general security of human existence. Even a merchant could lament that "where money is at stake or some personal interest, one finds no relative or friend who prefers you to himself and has not forgotten his conscience."[61] The rural victims of urban greed made particular complaint, as in the *Reformatio Sigismundi:* "Nowadays a man going to a city to buy or sell will come away saying 'They have cheated me.' Everything in the city is sold at too high a price."[62] "Nowadays," declared a Lutheran, "trading and bartering have brought our land to such a pass that a man, if he would save himself from ruin, is compelled to cheat, defraud, and lie to his neighbors, for he himself is deceived at every turn."[63]

"Nowadays." Again we are in the presence of a contrast, deeply felt, between a distressed present and a supposedly happier past, but also between man's present and his true home: *nostalgia* in its primary meaning. Ideally man should, and perhaps once did, reside in a garden: the more sophisticated garden in which Boccaccio's splendid youths found refuge from the horrors of plague-stricken Florence (itself a terrifying reality but even more potent as a symbol of the general malaise of urban life), or the primal garden where, as Luther remarked, Adam and Eve had lived "in the happiest security, without any fear of death and without anxiety."[64] Piety and brotherhood seemed to come more readily in the country, and radical intellectuals during the early years of the Reformation occasionally went to the land; Karlstadt bought a farm, wore peasant gray, tilled the soil with his own hands (at least for a while), and called on university students to follow his example.[65] Moralists like Bucer thought agriculture more virtuous than other pursuits,[66] a sentiment that would receive systematic application by the Physiocrats. Johann Agricola attributed the fall of Rome to its abandonment of its old ways in which "rulers and statesmen used to be summoned directly from the plow and the field" and "plain, honest, hardworking farmers aspired to honor and uprightness, not to riches."[67] Petrarch found only in the country the peace of mind favorable to the descent of his muse.[68] The genial host in Erasmus's "Godly Feast" marvelled at "people who take pleasure in smoky cities" when "the whole countryside is fresh and smiling."[69] Galileo is reported to have considered the city "the prison of the speculative mind" and his own thought liberated "only by the freedom of the countryside."[70]

We are evidently in the presence of an early formulation of the fruitful modern myth of *Gemeinschaft* and *Gesellschaft*. And there is much in this fragmentary contemporary diagnosis, however it differs from our own more particular explanations, to instruct us about the general causes of the anxiety in this period. Its foundation was, of course, partly a myth even then, as Hutten recognized in reminding the nostalgic Pirckheimer that in the countryside too "each day is filled with anxiety over what the morrow might bring."[71] Nevertheless it is true that much in urban life induced anxiety among those brought up in the country, as much of the urban population had been; since the death rate in towns tended to exceed the birth rate, even the maintenance of stable population in towns, and much more their growth, depended on substantial immigration from the country. For erstwhile peasants the proliferation of complex laws and bureaucracies meant the substitution of an external, coercive, and mystifying set of social controls for the old internalized sentiments of a simpler community. And the unusual mobility of the urban population meant also that, in cities, much of life was passed among strangers, potential predators, themselves made anxious by the novelty and insecurity of urban existence.

The needs of survival in this new environment and the increasing differentiation of economic and social roles compelled men to adopt specialized stances in relation to each other. A relaxed and candid self-exposure now became dangerous; human intimacy was inhibited by the need for vigilance in masking the true self. The villain of the Elizabethan and Jacobean stage was likely to be a dissembler, but so in some degree was the average *honnête homme*.[72] The conception of "friendship" was itself corrupted by self-interest; as a Florentine merchant remarked, "It is good to have friends of all kinds, but not useless men."[73] The making of friends now depended on the artful presentation of a carefully edited "image," and advice on this delicate operation became necessary. "If there is someone in your *gonfalone* who can help you and push you ahead," Giovanni Morelli advised his sons, "first try to become intimate with him, if possible, by means of marriage. If that is not practicable, then have dealings with him and his [relatives]; try to serve him, offer him aid, if you can do so without too much loss to yourself, when you see that he is in need; give him presents, honor him by inviting him often to dinner." Morelli cited the example of his own father, who had been skillful in these tactics: "And by such wise and provident means, he had so arranged matters that, in his time of great need, he had friends, and not only relatives, who gave him help and support."[74] Alberti's Uncle Adovardo advised that "to make friends it is necessary to study the gestures, words, customs, and conversations of others."[75] No wonder, then, that, as Commynes complained, "ours is indeed a miserable life, when we take such trouble and pains to shorten it by saying so many things which are almost the opposite of what we really think."[76] At the end of his life the disillusioned Poggio Bracciolini confessed that he now spoke "only with the dead, who do not lie."[77]

But urban life was also closer to the more ultimate sources of human anxiety. In cities time was experienced differently from in the country; change became a function not merely of the eternal rhythms of nature but of the unpredictable human will, and with the future always dependent on the actions of other men it became increasingly uncertain. Even death might seem more grim; it was now all too likely to occur among strangers or false friends, and without the prayers of a stable community.[78]

Are we, then, to substitute a more general social explanation of the special anxiety of this transitional age for the particular catastrophes on which historians have recently concentrated? Is the anxiety that seems to have hung over and darkened the lives of so many in this period, like smog, a direct consequence of the practical conditions of urban life? There is much to recommend this explanation; it directs us to the most general European developments to account for a general phenomenon, and it is suggested by contemporary testimony itself.

Yet this seems to me, however essential, not yet a sufficient explanation. For the problem here appears to lie less in the objective changes in the quality of European life that were, in any case, not altogether novel in the fourteenth century, than in the ability of Europeans to cope with them. Although the anxiety and depression of our period eventually declined, so that we can now see it as in this respect an unusual age in contrast not only to the medieval past but also (if a bit less clearly) to succeeding centuries, this can hardly be explained as a consequence either of the decline of cities or of a reduction in the rate of change. I think, therefore, that we must move to a deeper level of explanation: to the problem of man's ability to impose a meaning on his experience that can give to life a measure of reliability and thus reduce, even if it cannot altogether abolish, life's ultimate and terrifying uncertainties. The fundamental problem to which we must thus address ourselves appears to be the problem of culture and of its capacity to manage and reduce the anxiety of existence.[79]

Medieval culture was conspicuously successful in the performance of this essential task. Applying a common set of distinctions (like other cultures of the type described by anthropologists as primitive)[80] to all areas of human concern, notably such polarities as inside and outside, high and low, male and female, it was able at once to distinguish, to classify, and to relate all phenomena, and so to create an intelligible and coherent cosmos, apparently rooted in the eternal principles of nature itself, out of the undifferentiated chaos of raw experience. The phenomenal world could thus be reduced to a kind of orderly map; men could feel at home in it because they could distinguish one area from another by clear conceptual boundaries which were reflected in the structures of life as well as thought.

Thus medieval cosmology gave intelligibility to the universe as a whole by supplying it with an external boundary, and within it distinguished among its constituent parts. Bounding and distinguishing were fundamental to scholastic method, with its definitions (that is, conceptual boundaries), categories, and species. The sacred was clearly differentiated from the profane, *sacerdotium* from *imperium*. The various faculties of the human personality were similarly distinguished: soul and body; intellect, will, and passion. Human acts could be classified as virtuous or vicious, and the several virtues and vices were also unambiguously defined, and exploited to categorize and explain human behavior. Social identity depended on the boundaries between communities and classes, within which the individual was contained and at home. God was himself bounded by his intelligence, which guaranteed not only the immutability and intelligibility of the whole structure but also its ontological status. Boundaries were thus invested with numinous awe and surrounded by religious sanctions.

As a fully articulated system of boundaries, medieval culture was admirably suited to the management of anxiety. It provided well-defined areas of safety and focused the latent anxiety in the human condition at their margins. Anxiety was thus transmuted into a fear of transgressing the boundaries defining the cultural universe, and in various ways men could usually stay away from them.[81] They were safe in their communities or estates, or as long as the boundary between the sacred and profane was respected, or insofar as the soul was not contaminated by the body or reason by the passions, or in the performance of virtuous and the avoidance of vicious acts. They could even face death with greater confidence, not only because their latent anxiety could be released by the obligations of boundary maintenance, but also because the *viator* through and beyond this life could take his bearings from the boundaries that continually surrounded him, discover the true way, and above all know his direction. Dante may have strayed briefly from his path, but he was enabled to find it again.[82]

But certain peculiarities of the medieval system of boundaries made it appropriate only under special conditions. Above all it was based on the notion of absolute qualitative distinctions rooted in ultimate reality and therefore perennially applicable to human affairs. The system depended on the clarity of these distinctions, and it could not tolerate ambiguity. Thus it could remain plausible only as long as it was practicable for men to avoid transgressing its boundaries, for, although our response to experience is conditioned by culture, we also require a culture appropriate to experience and the needs of survival.

And it is at this point that the significance of urban life becomes apparent; the accumulating social changes of the later

Middle Ages eventually exceeded the flexibility of the inherited culture and forced men increasingly to violate the old boundaries. Lateral social mobility broke down the boundaries between communities; town walls still retained deep symbolic meaning in the thirteenth century but—I suspect for more than demographic or military reasons—seemed increasingly arbitrary and useless thereafter and gradually ceased to be built. Vertical mobility eroded the boundaries between classes; and we now begin to encounter disputes over precedence in ceremonial processions among socially ambiguous groups such as lawyers and university scholars.[83] The distinction between the sacred and profane was dissolving with the growing responsibility and dignity of lay activity and the secular state. The psychological boundaries by which the old culture had sought to understand the nature of man and predict his behavior were useless when he was no longer inhibited by the pressures of traditional community; and, experienced concretely in a more complex setting, human acts proved too ambiguous for neat ethical classification. Even the boundaries of the physical universe, so intimately linked to those in society and the human personality, were collapsing. No objective system of boundaries could now supply either security or effective guidance. When man still clung to the old culture, he seemed to have become, in spite of himself, a trespasser against the order of the universe, a violator of its sacred limits, the reluctant inhabitant of precisely those dangerous borderlands—literally no man's land—he had been conditioned to avoid. But his predicament was even worse if this experience had taught him to doubt the very existence of boundaries. He then seemed thrown, disoriented, back into the void from which it was the task of culture to rescue him. And this, I suggest, is the immediate explanation for the extraordinary anxiety of this period. It was an inevitable response to the growing inability of an inherited culture to invest experience with meaning.

There are hints that contemporaries themselves obscurely perceived their problems in these terms. Boundaries establish order by keeping each thing in its place, and the critics of cities were offended because, in them, confusion reigned. This is the deeper significance of the association of cities with dirt; with smoke, which obscures every visual boundary; perhaps even with noise, which intrudes on the inner life. Petrarch was nauseated by Avignon, "the narrow and obscure sink of the earth, where all the filth of the world is collected," with its "streets full of disease and infection, dirty pigs and snarling dogs, the noise of cart-wheels grinding against walls, four-horse chariots dashing down at every crossroad, the motley crew of people, swarms of vile beggars side by side with the flaunting luxury of wealth . . . the medley of characters—such diverse roles in life—the endless clamor of their confused voices, as the passers-by jostle one another in the streets."[84] The juxtaposition here of contamination and confusion is instructive. Filth, as Mary Douglas has pointed out, is culturally defined; dirt is matter out of place, and what may be unexceptionable when confined to the barnyard is noxious elsewhere.[85] Cities, as an anomaly in a traditional agrarian order, increasingly threatened to dissolve the patterns of a culture that had made the world comprehensible and comfortable, and accordingly they represented pollution and a reversion to chaos.

Petrarch's revulsion against cities has an ironic side, though it can be readily understood as expressing his apprehension of the consequences of his own onslaught against the old culture. For his attack on scholastic modes of thought radically challenged the principles underlying that culture. He repeatedly described scholastic efforts to identify the fundamental elements of reality in an orderly and systematic way, and so to define their boundaries, as "infantile babble"; "in total oblivion of the real basis of things," he maintained, the schoolmen "grow old, simply conversant with words."[86] What this charge amounted to, a charge in which Renaissance humanists were joined by a new breed of scholastics, and later by the Protestant Reformers, was that a culture once able to give an ontological foundation to the phenomena of human experience could no longer do so. It had lost touch with reality and become irrelevant; its definitions and boundaries could no longer supply meaning to life. The result was a crisis of confidence in the significance of human knowledge. For Salutati, "to speak properly, what to us is knowledge is really only a kind of reasonable uncertainty."[87] Pierre d'Ailly concluded "that the philosophy or doctrine of Aristotle deserves the name of opinion rather than science."[88] For Melanchthon the schoolmen "continually think up new and prodigious fancies and monstrous expressions by which, since they have no basis in reality, nothing can be understood."[89] Indeed the inherited culture had become positively mischievous since, though it still claimed, it no longer possessed, any ontological status. Thus, though the old culture was now seen to be clearly no more than a human invention, its practical demands, because they could no longer be satisfied, filled men with dread. As Calvin wrote of the schoolmen, "They torture souls with many misgivings, and immerse them in a sea of trouble and anxiety."[90]

The collapse of the old boundaries can be seen in many areas of cultural expression: for example, in the more fluid definition of nobility that we encounter in both humanists and Reformers, or in Nicholas of Cusa's conception of the infinite in which all polarities are reconciled and obliterated, or in the paradoxes of Luther, or in the new astronomy of the sixteenth and seventeenth centuries. An occasional thinker felt, in the presence of this disintegration, the exhilaration of freedom; this was its effect on Bruno:

There are no ends, boundaries, limits or walls which can defraud or deprive us of the infinite multitude of things. Therefore the earth and the ocean thereof are fecund; therefore the sun's blaze is everlasting, so that eternally fuel is provided for the voracious fires, and moisture replaces the attenuated seas. For from infinity is born an ever fresh abundance of matter.[91]

But infinity is not, for the majority of mankind, a comfortable habitat, as man's inability to live without culture would seem to attest; and Bruno's tragic fate testifies that his reaction to the new cultural situation was not only eccentric but profoundly threatening to his contemporaries. A more typical response to the implausibility and collapse of cultural boundaries was a frantic, if ultimately unsuccessful, effort to shore them up, of which the increasingly elaborate articulation of the old culture Huizinga noted in the fourteenth and fifteenth centuries, the regressive tendencies of later Renaissance Italy, and the more detailed application of the penitential system are examples.[92] Gerson proposed to cure the malaise of spiritual life by strengthening the boundary between theology and philosophy: "It is evident that although it surpasses philosophy, the teaching of faith has its predetermined boundaries in the sacred writings which have been revealed to us. One ought not dare define and teach anything beyond these boundaries."[93] Rulers were increasingly preoccupied with defining the boundaries of their states, which appeared the more plausible in the degree to which they could be attributed to "nature," that is, given a quasi-ontological status.

But none of these efforts was finally of much use, as Pascal in his radical honesty would testify at the conclusion of a long process of cultural disintegration. We may interpret his sensitivity to the frightening "eternal silence of these infinite spaces" as a metaphor for the larger cultural universe of which his new vision of the physical universe had become a part. Both had finally lost those old familiar boundaries by which men could orient themselves and find meaning, and human existence could be made tolerable now only if men could be distracted from reflecting "on what they are, whence they come, whither they go." "Ever drifting in uncertainty, driven from end to end," man, for Pascal, "feels his nothingness, his forlornness, his insufficiency, his dependency, his weakness," and "there will immediately arise from the depth of his heart weariness, gloom, sadness, fretfulness, vexation, despair." This was the terrible predicament that had come out of the cultural disintegration of the previous centuries:

When I see the blindness and wretchedness of man, when I regard the whole silent universe, and man without light, left to himself, and, as it were, lost in this corner of the universe, without knowing who has put him there, what he has come to do, what will become of him at death, and incapable of all knowledge, I become terrified, like a man who should be carried in his sleep to a dreadful desert island, and should awake without knowing where he is, and without means of escape. And thereupon I wonder how people in a condition so wretched do not fall into despair.[94]

Nevertheless Voltaire's incredulity as he confronted Pascal's vision of the human condition testifies that earthly palliatives for such general despair could be found.[95] From time to time, to be sure, Europeans have sought to recover the confidence of their medieval predecessors by insisting once again on the ontological basis of human culture. This, I take it, is the significance of both the Protestant and the Catholic Counter Reformations,[96] of the more absolutist tendencies of the Enlightenment, and of some recent authoritarian ideologies; our perennial nostalgia for the Middle Ages is perhaps a more innocent expression of the same impulse, which will doubtless continue to seek expression. But such attempts to resurrect the spirit of the old culture, however tempting, have so far proved incapable of meeting for long the need for cultural security. Relief would come rather from the gradual emergence of a new kind of culture, based on quite different principles, that was struggling to be born even as the old one disintegrated. The new culture of postmedieval Europe has often been described, with varying degrees of success; and I want in conclusion chiefly to suggest how it managed to reduce, though it could not eliminate, the terrible anxiety implicit in the disintegration of the medieval certainties.

The new culture of modern Europe was constructed on a quite different pattern of assumptions. It began with the recognition that culture is not an absolute but the creation of men, and therefore a variable and conventional product of changing conditions and shifting human needs. This change in the understanding of culture began in later medieval nominalism and Renaissance humanism, which collaborated, however unwittingly, in setting the West on a new path. For both movements language ceased to link the mind with ultimate reality and so to identify the objective boundaries defining existence.

Human culture was thus seen to consist simply in those matters that men (or a particular group of men) could agree on; its boundaries, having only a human character, could therefore no longer claim absolute respect.[97] Renaissance rhetoric was accordingly valued for its plasticity, its ability to flow into and through every area of experience, to disregard and cross inherited boundaries as though they had no real existence, and to create new but always malleable structures of its own. In both nominalism and humanism the word, now humanized, created its own human cosmos out of crude experience.

An important consequence of this humanization was a more modest approach to the kind of cosmos man could discern in chaos, that is, to the scope of culture. Since his culture was simply the product of his own creative impulses, it no longer seemed possible for man to make every dimension of reality permanently intelligible or to comprehend the whole under the same broad categories. The isolated proverb, the *pensée*, the familiar essay, became favorite vehicles for the transmission of human wisdom. The autonomous painting of modern art is a nice symbol of the new ways of culture formation; a painting is a distinctly bounded little universe, the product of deliberate choices among infinite possibilities, a little area of order separated by its own boundaries from the chaos without. Thus, in place of one overarching cosmos we now encounter a range of uncoordinated and often minuscule structures representing a limited order whose plausibility is only aesthetic or practical. A political construction, for example, could now no longer be justified by its conformity to the order of the heavens, a principle that had achieved few practical benefits, but only by its results. It should therefore also be apparent that this new culture is significant not only for its own novel characteristics but also for its new understanding of culture as such. It made possible the conception of *cultures*, each relative to its own time and place, as distinguished from *Culture*.

In addition, quantity now tended to be substituted for quality as the essential principle of orientation; more-or-less, which recognized no impassable boundaries between nothing and infinity, for the either-or suggested by the Aristotelian law of contradiction. The practical foundation for this development was supplied by the growing importance of numerical calculation to artisans and merchants; the numerical arts were the climax of a boy's education in mercantile communities, and their general value for the interpretation of experience was recognized. As the banker Giovanni Rucellai remarked of arithmetic, "It equips and spurs the mind to examine subtle matters."[98] Mathematical models broadly invaded fourteenth-century philosophy.[99]

That the practical resort to number implied a cultural revolution was by no means immediately clear, and its significance was for some time obscured by the sublimation of quantitative approaches to experience into a philosophical mathematics that sought to renew the ontological foundations of the crumbling traditional structure. In this view number became God's language in the book of nature. Salutati insisted on the indispensability of mathematics to theology; as another humanist proclaimed, "Mathematics raises us, prostrate on the earth, to the sky."[100]

But the growing reliance on measurement and number also provided a means of orientation when qualitative boundaries were disintegrating and all things had become, in a new sense, relative. The mathematician could begin at any point in the welter of the phenomenal world, by measurement in units of his own devising define its relation to other phenomena, and so, like the artist in words or in paint, describe an order in the universe (if not *the* order *of* the universe), in accordance with his chosen purposes. The practical meaning of the change is apparent in the new science of probability, for the calculation of probabilities might now present itself as man's best guide through an indeterminate universe. Montaigne, as part of his rejection of the inherited dogmatism that had so disrupted his world, proposed to base life instead on probability;[101] Pascal's notion of the wager applied the principle even to salvation.[102] For probability could provide some basis for choice when the old qualitative boundaries had disappeared and give some relief from the terror induced by "the eternal silence of these infinite spaces."

Pascal seems to have grasped the new situation in a general way, and there are hints of such general understanding elsewhere: for example, in Guicciardini's observation that fortune, that ubiquitous symbol of chaos in human affairs, is angry with those who seek to limit (that is, to impose boundaries on) her dominion.[103] The renewed emphasis on faith, among Catholics as well as Protestants, also reflects some insight into the new situation; a righteousness defined by works is a righteousness largely dependent on culture, and in this context justification by faith alone may be interpreted as a radical solution to the problem of the unreliability of culture. But of all the thinkers in the period of transition from medieval to modern culture, Nicholas of Cusa seems to have discerned most clearly what was happening and to have made the most positive attempt to establish human culture on a new basis. Nourished by both nominalism and humanism, he praised mathematics extravagantly, seeing in it a resource for the reorientation of thought to a universe no longer intelligible in traditional terms. For Cusanus the pursuit of ontological reality that had characterized western philosophy in the course of its long previous history had come to nothing. In cosmology, to which he gave particular attention, this meant that the notion either of a fixed center or an external boundary of the universe was illusory. But the point had larger implications; it suggested the indeterminacy of the entire phenomenal world, and the construction of man's conceptual universe became simply a project of the autonomous and creative human mind, and especially of its capacity for measurement. In this light all "reality" was essentially a function of the mathematical relationships between entities with which man, for reasons of his own, happened to concern himself.[104]

And this conception, applied by Cusanus most immediately to space, and eventually applied also to cartography by locating points on a grid of latitudinal and longitudinal parallels, was meanwhile becoming a general principle of cultural articulation. It was also applied, in much the same way, to time, so fundamentally related to anxiety. Time could no longer be a function of the natural and qualitative rhythms of day and night, the seasons, and the years; it was now shaped in accordance with human needs. The hours were numbered according to a conventional scale imposed on an intrinsically formless temporal flow, and their conventional significance was enforced by the ringing of bells. Their content was also practically defined: hours were designated for opening and closing one's place of business, for meetings with other men, for this task and that.[105] And once time, like money, could be measured, it became a precious human asset to be calculatedly exploited, as Alberti's Uncle Giannozzo solemnly advised his nephews, stressing also the novelty of the conception: "Keep these thoughts in your memory. . . . These are not sayings of the philosophers but, like the oracles of Apollo, perfect and holy wisdom such as you will not find in all our books."[106] This, in other words, was nontraditional wisdom.

Time quantified was, like money, related to power; and the same tendency to quantification now intruded itself into political thought in the guise of a concern with balance. Equilibrium became a primary category for analyzing the relations both of states and of the social forces within them; the maintenance of political stability was seen to depend on quasi-mathematical calculation and adaptation rather than on the preservation of a pattern of qualitative relationships. Machiavelli aimed to contain the dangerous energies of the various elements in Florentine society not by rigid boundaries but by systematic provision for their dynamic interaction, through which they might contain each other by the opposition of force to force. And the relativity in this new understanding of the political universe paralleled that in the new cosmology. It was a commonplace of political discussion that, because the structure of forces varies from people to people, every constitution, every set of laws, must suit the peculiarities of the situation to which it is applied.

Meanwhile, as the social cosmos too threatened to collapse into chaos; as qualitative distinctions in social status were gradually eroded by power, whose increase could be at least roughly measured; and as individuals, no longer defined and protected by traditional social categories, were left increasingly vulnerable to one another, a new set of boundaries was required to protect men from each other. The principle at work here would find expression in the ominous proposition that good fences make good neighbors, a symptom of the new culture that may usefully be contrasted with the open field system of medieval agriculture. And much of the worldly wisdom of the early modern age was directed to building fences. Its complementary emphasis on self-control and vigilance both kept the individual within the boundaries of his self-definition and guarded them against infringement by others;[107] this is the cultural significance of the famous bourgeois anal personality. It also helps to explain the deep revulsion, in this period, against begging. For the Alberti, "I beg" was a phrase peculiarly "hateful to a free man's mind"; whether represented by a wandering friar or a wretched layman, mendicancy posed a radical threat to individual autonomy and challenged the very basis of the new pattern of human relations.[108]

We also encounter hints of the new quantifying mentality in the definition of relationships among individuals. Where the absolute categories of status could no longer establish the relation of each individual to his fellows, men now defined themselves against each other by subtle processes of measurement. Life was a strenuous competition with others to become wiser, richer, more esteemed: a race in which one strove to surpass other men by as many paces as possible. "Honor" itself, the term by which Alberti's Uncle Lionardo evaluated success in life, ceased to be an absolute, to be contrasted with dishonor. He personified it as "a public accountant, just, practical, and prudent in measuring, weighing, considering, evaluating, and assessing everything we do, achieve, think, and desire."[109]

This attitude projected onto the social world that "bookkeeping mentality" often noted in the new mercantile culture, which served not only the needs of business but the deeper psychic needs of men inhabiting a newly problematic universe. Various human contrivances were developed to impose some pattern, when none was otherwise available, on the existence of the individual and his family: books for keeping mercantile accounts, systems for the filing of letters, records of the birth dates of children, plans for the orderly arrangement of household goods.[110] The value of such devices in meeting the immediate needs of life is obvious, but they also had a more profound significance. For the Alberti the keeping of family records had a moral quality; it reflected "the conscientiousness of a father." As Uncle Giannozzo informed his wife, "We should have order and system in all that we do."[111] This does not seem an altogether utilitarian principle.

By such devices postmedieval culture achieved substantial success in reducing anxiety. Its creation of new boundaries focused anxiety on their maintenance and converted it into relatively manageable fears: fear of being late or wasting time, which, translated into the modern work ethic, has been especially effective in holding at bay our more general uneasiness about the meaning of existence; fear that great social and political forces might, uncontained, break out and destroy the precarious balance that makes social existence tolerable; fear lest some relaxation of personal vigilance and control might jeopardize the boundaries that protect man from man; fear of losing out in the competitive business of life. The new culture taught men where to locate particular areas of danger and kept them busy shoring up the various barriers against chaos. And the general dissipation of anxiety by these means also reduced anxiety about death and judgment, the most serious symptom of the failure of the old culture.

The new culture could also reduce anxiety because its relativistic and quantitative principles gave it a measure of control over time. Flexible boundaries could accommodate to contingency and enabled men to construct legal instruments (notable among them wills, contracts, and various types of insurance) to control and shape the future. Practical reason could now impress Alberti as "more powerful than fortune"; planning now seemed "more important than any chance event." "Think well ahead and consider what you are going to need," his Uncle Giannozzo advised, evidently persuaded of the good results of such foresight.[112]

Various characteristics of the culture of early modern Europe attest to the decline of anxiety. One was a growing acceptance of cities, which found Italian expression in Leonardo Bruni's praise of Florence[113] and Botero's *Greatness of Cities*. And if antiurbanism can hardly be said to have died out (for the city has become a perennial symbol of the alarming complexities of modern life), Cowper's "God made the country, and man made the town" is at least no more representative of the eighteenth century than Dr. Johnson's relish of London life. The city was no longer necessarily a focus of anxiety, and Voltaire challenged Pascal's vision of the world as a "dreadful desert island" by pointing to the felicities of urban existence.[114]

But an even more fundamental symptom of the change in mood was the gradual decline of nostalgia for the past. The humanists of Italy began to locate the highest achievements of human civilization at the end rather than the beginning of its development;[115] Castiglione and Machiavelli both expressed reservations about the tendency of mankind to contrast the present unfavorably with the past;[116] writers of the later Renaissance—Pulci, Boiardo, Cervantes—ridiculed that chivalric heroism with which earlier generations had imaginatively identified themselves.[117] The Reformers, perhaps obscurely recognizing not only that Adam fell but that Jesus was betrayed in a garden, may have hinted at the same new conception of time. For Luther man could not be reformed—that is, restored to an earlier condition—but only forgiven;[118] and Calvin from time to time inveighed against the value of precedent as a barrier against change.[119] Hobbes's famous depiction of natural existence as "solitary, poor, nasty, brutish, and short" was, in context, a radical rejection of the nostalgic mentality of earlier generations, and implicitly a celebration of the new urban culture.[120] Man's true home was no longer in the past but increasingly in the future, whatever it might hold in store. And the growing belief in progress from the later sixteenth century onward attests that thoughts of the future were less and less accompanied by anxiety.

The redefinition of culture on the basis of the new principles was not completed in the early modern period, and the progressive substitution of fluid and relative for absolute and qualitative cultural categories has continued to disorient mankind and to release anxiety. We can see the continuation of the process in the emotional reaction to Darwin's attack on the fixity of species in the nineteenth century, and in the profound anxieties released more recently by the challenge to absolute distinctions of sex, an area in which (perhaps because it is peculiarly fraught with uncertainty) the principles of premodern culture have been unusually durable. And the new culture, precisely because of its own relativism, has never been more than relatively successful in the management of anxiety.

There were, certainly, problems that the structures of modern culture could not solve and might rather intensify. Its strategies, indeed, have sometimes themselves induced a peculiar anxiety, as Saint Teresa remarked about her own concern with the effective use of time. "If we find ourselves unable to get profit out of a single hour," she noted, "we are impeded from doing so for four. I have a great deal of experience of this. . . ."[121] Even more troubling consequences have come from the need of the individual to adapt to unpredictable circumstances and the changing expectations of others. The needs of survival in a problematic world have tended to alienate the public from any true self or, worse, to require the annihilation of the true for the sake of a social self. Thus, the relation between the boundaries of self-definition and any stable center of the personality have tended to become themselves problematic, and this has been the source of a peculiarly burdensome kind of anxiety in the modern world. Even the artist, his task no longer to discover and illuminate immutable truths but to create some relative cosmos from the chaos that surrounds him, may feel more terror than exuberance as he considers the contingency and fragility of his work. In spite of the impressive accomplishments of postmedieval culture, a higher level of anxiety was now to be a permanent feature of the West.

## Notes

1. As in Auden's *The Age of Anxiety*. For contemporary interest in anxiety, see Fred Berthold, Jr., *The Fear of God: The Role of Anxiety in Contemporary Thought* (New York, 1959).

2. We face here much the same problem as that confronted by Keith Thomas in his treatment of popular culture in *Religion and the Decline of Magic* (London, 1971); cf. his preface, p. x, on "the historian's traditional method of example and counter-example" as "the intellectual equivalent of the bow and arrow in the nuclear age." I am less confident than Thomas that models of scientific advance are applicable to historiography, and I suspect that "example and counter-example" will continue to be necessary to support many kinds of historical judgment, probably including those of greatest interest; but there is a serious methodological problem here.

3. W. H. Dodds, who took the title of his *Pagan and Christian in an Age of Anxiety* (Cambridge, 1965) directly from Auden. Also cf. the second volume of Theodore Zeldin, *France, 1848–1945*, which bears the title *Intellect, Taste and Anxiety* (New York, 1977).

4. Iris Origo, *The Merchant of Prato: Francesco di Marco Datini, 1335–1410* (New York, 1957), esp. her introduction, p. xi; Christian Bec, *Les marchands écrivains: Affaires et humanisme à Florence, 1365–1434* (Paris, 1967), pp. 127–28; P. S. Lewis, *Later Medieval France: The Polity* (London, 1968), pp. 242–45, 273; Philippe Dollinger, *La Hanse* (Paris, 1964), chap. 8; David Herlihy, "Some Psychological and Social Roots of Violence in the Tuscan Cities," in *Violence and Civil Disorder in Italian Cities*, ed. L. Martines (Berkeley and Los Angeles, 1971), p. 149.

5. E. Jane Dempsey Douglass, *Justification in Late Medieval Theology: A Study of John Geiler of Keisersberg* (Leiden, 1966); David C. Steinmetz, *Misericordia Dei: The Theology of Johannes von Staupitz in Its Late Medieval Setting* (Leiden, 1968); Michael Seidlmayer, *Currents of Medieval Thought*, trans. D. Barker (Oxford, 1960); Millard Meiss, *Painting in Florence and Siena after the Black Death: The Arts, Religion and Society in the Mid-Fourteenth Century* (Princeton, 1951); M. B. Backer, "Individualism in the Early Italian Renaissance: Burden and Blessing," *Studies in the Renaissance* 19 (1972): 273–97;

E. Delaruelle, et al., *L'Eglise au temps du Grand Schisme et de la crise conciliaire,* Histoire de l'Église, vol. XIV (Paris, 1962), vol. 2; Charles Trinkaus, *In Our Image and Likeness: Humanity and Divinity in Italian Humanist Thought* (Chicago, 1970); Heiko Oberman, *Forerunners of the Reformation* (New York, 1966); Jean Delumeau, *Naissance et affirmation de la Réforme* (Paris, 1965); Steven E. Ozment, *The Reformation in the Cities: An Essay on the Appeal of Protestant Ideas to Sixteenth Century Society* (New Haven, 1975); A. G. Dickens, *The English Reformation* (London, 1964); Michael Walzer, *The Revolution of the Saints: A Study in the Origins of Radical Politics* (Cambridge, Mass., 1965).

6. Eugenio Garin, *Science and Civic Life in the Italian Renaissance,* trans. Peter Munz (New York, 1969), pp. 2–3.

7. Lynn White, Jr., "Death and the Devil," in *The Darker Vision of the Renaissance: Beyond the Fields of Reason,* ed. Robert S. Kinsman (Berkeley and Los Angeles, 1974), pp. 25–46. The germ of this interpretation may perhaps be discerned in Huizinga's *Waning of the Middle Ages,* which H. Stuart Hughes has read, though Huizinga did not himself use such language, as a study in the management of "unbearable anxiety" (*History as Art and as Science: Twin Vistas on the Past* [New York, 1964], p. 54). But the notion seems also imbedded in Burckhardtian individualism; cf. the extreme case of Filippo Maria Visconti, whose personality is described in *The Civilization of the Renaissance in Italy,* trans. S. G. C. Middlemore (London, 1944), pp. 24–25.

8. Robert S. Kinsman, in *The Darker Vision of the Renaissance,* Introduction, p. 14. This medieval condition *may,* of course, be related to modern "anxiety."

9. This emerges from a comparison of passages in the recent translation of the *Institutes* by Ford Lewis Battles (London, 1961), where the word "anxiety" appears, with Calvin's own Latin and French. See especially II, viii, 3; III, ii, 17 and 23; III, xxiv, 6.

10. *Petrarch's Secret or The Soul's Conflict with Passion: Three Dialogues between Himself and S. Augustine,* trans. William H. Draper (London, 1911), p. 56; *The Imitation of Christ,* trans. Leo Sherley-Price (London, 1952), p. 28.

11. *The Memoirs of Philippe de Commynes,* trans. Isabelle Cazeaux, 2 vols. (Columbia, S.C., 1969–73), 1:230.

12. *The Family in Renaissance Florence,* trans. Renée Neu Watkins (Columbia, S.C., 1969), examples on pp. 49, 78, 58, 47, 88, 41, 191, 46, 54–55.

13. *The Complete Works of Saint Teresa of Jesus,* trans. E. Allison Peers, 3 vols. (London, 1950), 1:5, 75, 78, 257; *The Collected Works of John of the Cross,* trans. Kieran Kavanaugh and Otilio Rodriguez (Washington, 1973), pp. 88, 594, 619, 620.

14. The following generalizations are based on, among other works, M. D. Chenu, *La théologie au douzième siècle* (Paris, 1957); R. W. Southern, *The Making of the Middle Ages* (New Haven, 1953), and *Medieval Humanism and Other Studies* (New York, 1970); John Mundy, *Europe in the High Middle Ages, 1150–1309* (London, 1973); Jacques Le Goff, *Les intellectuels au Moyen Age* (Paris, 1957). The theological dimension of this optimism is particularly well described by Gerhart B. Ladner, "The Life of the Mind in the Christian West around the Year 1200," in *The Year 1200: A Symposium* (New York, 1975), pp. 4–6. That the *mentalité* even of peasants may have been relatively relaxed is suggested by Emmanuel Le Roy Ladurie, *Montaillou, village occitan de 1294–1324* (Paris, 1976).

15. In the words of Rolandino Passaggeri, quoted by Mundy, *Europe in the High Middle Ages,* p. 486.

16. "It is ful faire a man to bere him evene / For al-day meteth men at unset stevene" (lines 1523–24). I quote the modern English version of Nevill Coghill (London, 1960).

17. As most recently by Paul Lawrence Rose, *The Italian Renaissance of Mathematics: Studies on Humanists and Mathematicians from Petrarch to Galileo* (Geneva, 1975), p. 7. See more generally Carlo Cipolla, *Clocks and Culture 1300–1700* (New York, 1967).

18. Quoted by John Larner, *Culture and Society in Italy, 1290–1420* (London, 1971), p. 28.

19. Calvin, *Commentaries on the Book of Genesis*, trans. John King (Edinburgh, 1847), 1:84; Pascal, *Pensées*, no. 5 (in the arrangement in the translation of E. F. Trotter, [New York, 1941]).

20. *Epistolae familiares*, X, 1, trans. David Thompson, in *Petrarch: An Anthology* (New York, 1971), p. 101.

21. *De ingenuis moribus*, trans. William Harrison Woodward, in *Vittorino da Feltre and Other Humanist Educators* (Cambridge, 1897), p. 112.

22. *Gargantua and Pantagruel*, trans. Jacques Le Clercq (New York, 1944), p. 71.

23. Quoted by Origo, *Merchant of Prato*, p. 187.

24. Leon Battista Alberti, *Opere volgari*, ed. Cecil Grayson, 3 vols. (Bari, 1960–73), 1:77. I use the translation of Watkins, cited above, n. 12.

25. Nicholas Mann, "Petrarch's Role as Moralist in Fifteenth-Century France," in *Humanism in France at the End of the Middle Ages and in the Early Renaissance*, ed. A. H. T. Levi (Manchester, 1970), pp. 6–28.

26. *Discorsi*, II, xxix. I follow the translation of Leslie J. Walker (New Haven, 1950).

27. Cf. Peter L. Berger and Thomas Luckmann, *The Social Construction of Reality: A Treatise in the Sociology of Knowledge* (Garden City, N.Y., 1966), pp. 27, 101. For a penetrating discussion of this point in theological terms, cf. Peter Knauer, *Gott, Wort, Glaube: Ein theologischer Grundkurs* (Frankfurt a. m., 1973), p. 157: "If one's own transitoriness is the final certainty, this means that all earthly certainty is finally dependent on complete uncertainty." Knauer's extended remarks on this point, a commentary on Hebrews 2:14ff., were called to my attention by the Reverend Frederick McGinness, S. J.

28. *Imitation*, pp. 58–59; cf. p. 66: "Always remember your end, and that lost time never returns."

29. See, for example, Huizinga's *Waning of the Middle Ages;* the works by Seidlmayer, Meiss, and White cited above, n. 5; Alberto Tenenti, *Il senso della morte e l'amore della vita nel Rinascimento: Francia e Italia* (Turin, 1957); T. S. R. Boase, *Death in the Middle Ages: Mortality, Judgment and Remembrance* (London, 1972).

30. *De otio religioso*, in Thompson, *Petrarch: An Anthology*, pp. 153–54: *Epistolae familiares*, XIX, 6, quoted by Renée Neu Watkins, "Petrarch and the Black Death: From Fear to Monuments," *Studies in the Renaissance* 19 (1972): 215.

31. *Memoirs*, 2:433.

32. Commentary on Hebrews 2:15, in Calvin's *New Testament Commentaries*, trans. W. B. Johnston, 12 vols. (Grand Rapids, 1963), 12:31.

33. Douglass, *Justification in Late Medieval Theology*, p. 176; Susan Snyder, "The Left Hand of God: Despair in Medieval and Renaissance Tradition," *Studies in the Renaissance* 12 (1965): 41.

34. Cf. Dickens, *The English Reformation*, pp. 5–6.

35. Seidlmayer, *Currents of Medieval Thought*, p. 141; Dickens, *The English Reformation*, p. 12.

36. For this function of the Medici Chapel, see L. D. Ettlinger, "The Liturgical Function of Michelangelo's Medici Chapel," *Mitteilungen des Kunsthistorischen Institutes in Florenz* 22 (1978): 287–304.

37. Quoted by Ozment, *The Reformation in the Cities*, p. 28.

38. Quoted by Watkins, "Petrarch and the Black Death," p. 209.

39. See Douglass, *Justification in Late Medieval Theology*, p. 153, for the case of Geiler.

40. Quoted by Charles Trinkaus, "Italian Humanism and the Problem of 'Structures of Conscience,'" *Journal of Medieval and Renaissance Studies* 2 (1972): 28.

41. Letter to his father, 21 Nov. 1521, in *Luther: Letters of Spiritual Counsel*, ed. Theodore G. Tappert, Library of Christian Classics, vol. XVIII (London, 1955), p. 259.

42. *Lectures on Genesis*, ed. Jaroslav Pelikan, 8 vols. (St. Louis, 1958–66), 1:287.

43. Letter to Hess, Nov. 1527, in *Letters of Spiritual Counsel,* pp. 237–38.

44. *Institutes,* II, viii, 3; I, xvii, 11; I, xvii, 7; I, vi, 1; III, ii, 17; III, ii, 21. I use the translation of Ford Lewis Battles (London, 1960).

45. *Life,* in *Works,* 1:236.

46. J. G. A. Pocock, *The Machiavellian Moment: Florentine Political Thought and the Atlantic Republican Tradition* (Princeton, 1975), p. 28, offers interesting remarks on the anxiety of rulers. For merchants, see n. 4 above. The vast literature of the period on friendship, a common concern of Petrarch, Commynes, Erasmus, Montaigne, and Bacon, among others, suggests that this aspect of life had become a problem; cf. Lionel Trilling, *Sincerity and Authenticity* (Cambridge, Mass., 1971). On sexual anxiety, see Herlihy, "Psychological and Social Roots of Violence," p. 134, and J. R. Hale, "Violence in the Late Middle Ages: A Background," in Martines, *Violence and Civil Disorder,* pp. 28–29. The ancient commonplace that denied the delights of love to the busy man was revived, as in Donne's "Break of Day": "The poor, the foul, the false, love can / Admit, but not the busied man."

47. Cf. Petrarch: "Shall I pride myself on much reading of books, which with a little wisdom has brought me a thousand anxieties?" (*Secretum* in *Opere,* ed. Giovanni Ponte [Milan, 1968], p. 482); I follow the Draper translation, cited above, n. 10. See also Thomas à Kempis, *Imitation,* p. 28, and Alberti, *Opere volgari,* 1:247. In these illustrations, as in others presented here, one can detect echoes from such classical sources as Seneca; but the point, it seems to me, is that their Renaissance readers found them eminently relevant to their own predicament.

48. *Alberti, Opere volgari,* 1:161, 182.

49. These reflections were stimulated by an unpublished paper of my colleague Gene A. Brucker, "The Problem of Death in Fourteenth-Century Europe."

50. Quoted by Huizinga, *Waning of the Middle Ages,* p. 36. The italics here and in what follows are mine.

51. *Epistolae familiares,* XI, 7, and XIII, 6, in Thompson, *Petrarch: An Anthology,* pp. 107, 119.

52. Nicolas de Clamanges, quoted by Lewis, *Later Medieval France,* pp. 294–95.

53. *History of Florence,* trans. M. Walter Dunne (New York, 1960), p. 47.

54. In "Cyclops, or the Gospel Bearer," *The Colloquies of Erasmus,* trans. Craig R. Thompson (Chicago, 1965), p. 422.

55. In "Du jeune Caton," *Essais,* ed. Maurice Rat, 3 vols. (Paris, n.d.), 1:259–63.

56. See C. T. Davis, "Il Buon Tempo Antico," in *Florentine Studies,* ed. N. Rubinstein (London, 1968), pp. 45–69; and, for the general point, Harry Levin, *The Myth of the Golden Age in the Renaissance* (Bloomington, 1969). Huizinga has much on this point, passim.

57. *Memoirs,* 1:169.

58. Francesco Datini, quoted in Origo, *Merchant of Prato,* p. 68.

59. *Lectures on Genesis,* 2:65.

60. Letter to Boccaccio, 13 Mar. 1363, in *Lettere senili,* ed. Giuseppe Fracassetti (Florence, 1892), 1:69–70.

61. Quoted in Bec, *Les marchands écrivains,* p. 60.

62. In *Manifestations of Discontent in Germany on the Eve of the Reformation,* ed. Gerald Strauss (Bloomington, 1971), p. 21.

63. Johann Agricola, in ibid., p. 119.

64. *Lectures on Genesis,* 1:62.

65. See Jaroslav Pelikan's remarks in connection with Luther's attack on this movement, ibid., 1:211.

66. *De regno Christi,* trans. Lowell J. Satre, in *Melanchthon and Bucer,* ed. Wilhelm Pauck, Library of Christian Classics, vol. XIX (London, 1969), pp. 339–40. Similar sentiments were expressed by Luther in *To the Christian Nobility of the German Nation,* Art. 27, items 2–3.

67. In *Manifestations of Discontent,* p. 119.

68. Cf. *Secretum,* p. 488.

69. *Colloquies*, p. 48.

70. Cf. Garin, *Science and Civic Life*, p. 83.

71. Letter to Pirckheimer, in *Manifestations of Discontent*, p. 194.

72. There is much on this point in Trilling, *Sincerity and Authenticity*.

73. Datini in Origo, *Merchant of Prato*, p. 115.

74. Quoted by Gene A. Brucker, *The Civic World of Early Renaissance Florence* (Princeton, 1977), pp. 22–23.

75. *Della famiglia*, p. 297.

76. *Memoirs*, 1:265.

77. Quoted by Nancy S. Struever, *The Language of History in the Renaissance: Rhetoric and Historical Consciousness in Florentine Humanism* (Princeton, 1970), pp. 165–66.

78. Cf. Jack Goody, "Death and the Interpretation of Culture: A Bibliographic Overview," in *Death in America*, ed. David E. Stannard (Philadelphia, 1975), p. 7.

79. Students of an analogous transition in the modern world provide some support for this conclusion. The novel anxiety appearing among the populations of the new cities in developing countries seems to be a result not so much of the new urban experience directly as of the loss of a traditional culture. So Ari Kiev, *Transcultural Psychiatry* (New York, 1972), pp. 9–10, summarizes his conclusions: "Particularly stressful . . . is the loss of culture that is experienced by the educated yet still semi-primitive marginal African, who has become a member of a partially urbanized and Westernized society. Having renounced his old culture, yet so far having failed to assimilate the new, he is particularly prone to malignant anxiety. . . . The migration to the city removes the group protection, the psychological 'prop' of the African; he therefore finds himself psychologically isolated and vulnerable."

80. See especially Claude Lévi-Strauss, *The Savage Mind* (Chicago, 1966), passim; and Mary Douglas, *Implicit Meanings: Essays in Anthropology* (London, 1975), esp. p. 57.

81. For my understanding of culture as a mechanism for the management of anxiety, I am indebted to Berger and Luckmann, *Social Construction of Reality*; Clifford Geertz, *The Interpretation of Culture* (New York, 1973); and above all to Mary Douglas, *Purity and Danger: An Analysis of Concepts of Pollution and Taboo* (London, 1966), and *Natural Symbols* (London, 1972).

82. I am here applying the conception of religions as maps through and beyond life developed in John Bowker, *The Sense of God: Sociological, Anthropological and Psychological Approaches to the Origin of the Sense of God* (Oxford, 1973). Bowker's idea of "compounds of limitation" is also relevant to the argument here.

83. Cf. Traiano Boccalini, *Ragguagli di Parnasso e scritti minori*, ed. Luigi Firpo, 3 vols. (Bari, 1948), 1:177–80.

84. *Secretum*, p. 516.

85. Especially in *Purity and Danger*.

86. *Secretum*, p. 458.

87. Quoted by Jerrold E. Seigel, *Rhetoric and Philosophy in Renaissance Humanism* (Princeton, 1968), p. 74.

88. Quoted by Le Goff, *Les intellectuels au Moyen Age*, p. 154.

89. In Quirinus Breen, *Christianity and Humanism: Studies in the History of Ideas* (Grand Rapids, 1968), p. 57.

90. *Institutes*, III, iv, 1.

91. Quoted by Alexandre Koyré, *From the Closed World to the Infinite Universe* (New York, 1958), p. 44.

92. For the later Renaissance, see my "Changing Assumptions of Later Renaissance Culture," *Viator* 7 (1976): 421–40. On the penitential system, cf. Ozment, *Reformation in the Cities*; and Thomas N. Tentler, *Sin and Confession on the Eve of the Reformation* (Princeton, 1977).

93. In Jean Gerson, *Selections*, ed. Steven E. Ozment, *Textus minores*, vol. 38 (Leiden, 1969), p. 41.

94. *Pensées*, nos. 206, 72, 143, 146, 131, 692.

95. *Lettres philosophiques*, no. 25.

96. On the conception of a *Protestant* Counter Reformation, cf. Delumeau, *Naissance et affirmation de la Réforme*, pp. 360–61, though it is here interpreted rather narrowly as a reaction against Calvinism. Nietzsche understood the phenomenon more deeply as a repudiation of the original Protestant opposition of faith to reason: i.e., to the structures of human culture; cf. Walter Kaufmann, *Nietzsche*, 3d ed. (New York, 1968), pp. 352–53.

97. The general point is succinctly stated by Struever, *Language of History*, esp. pp. 44–45.

98. Quoted by Michael Baxandall, *Painting and Experience in Fifteenth-Century Italy* (Oxford, 1972), p. 94. Baxandall is especially useful for the general importance of mathematics in Italian urban culture. See also Rose, *Italian Renaissance of Mathematics*, chap. 1, on mathematics in humanist education, and Larner, *Culture and Society in Italy*, p. 28, for general remarks on the growing importance of quantification in Italy. But the point was already touched on by Burckhardt, *Civilization of the Renaissance in Italy*, p. 46.

99. Cf. Damasus Trapp, "Augustinian Theology of the 14th Century." *Augustinianum* 6 (1956): 148.

100. Cited by Rose, *Italian Renaissance of Mathematics*, pp. 12, 16.

101. In "Apologie de Raimond Sebond," *Essais*, II.

102. *Pensées*, nos. 187, 233. Pascal also denounced (though recognizing its influence) the "probabilism" of Jesuit casuistry in no. 917: "Take away *probability*, and you can no longer please the world; give *probability*, and you can no longer displease it." The relationship of Jesuit probabilism to the new mathematics is far from clear; cf. Benjamin Nelson, " 'Probabilists,' 'Anti-Probabilists' and the Quest for Certainty in the 16th and 17th Centuries," *Actes du Xme congrès international d'histoire des sciences* (Paris, 1965), 1:269–73. But even here habits of numerical calculation seem to be at work. On the history of probability theory and its peculiar importance for "modern" culture, see Ian Hacking, *The Emergence of Probability* (Cambridge, 1975).

103. *Ricordi*, C20.

104. For my understanding of the significance of Cusanus, in addition to Ernst Cassirer's classic *Individuum und Kosmos in der Philosophie der Renaissance* (1927), I owe much to the doctoral dissertation of Ronald Levao, "The Idea of Fiction and the Concept of Mind in the Renaissance" (Berkeley, 1978), chap. 1.

105. Cf. Bec, *Les marchands écrivains*, p. 318.

106. *Della famiglia*, p. 170.

107. Ibid., pp. 293–94, for an example of this general concern.

108. Ibid., p. 54.

109. Ibid., p. 151.

110. On the systematic mentality and the concern for accuracy reflected in mercantile records, see Armando Sapori, *The Italian Merchant in the Middle Ages*, trans. Patricia Ann Kennen (New York, 1970), pp. 29–31, 105; and for a hint of the more general significance of these qualities cf. the advice of a Venetian merchant to his son that he should frequently review his records because "he who does not frequently review his expenditures believes what is not true" (quoted in James C. Davis, *A Venetian Family and its Fortune, 1500–1900* [Philadelphia, 1975], p. 26).

111. *Della famiglia*, pp. 119–20, 239.

112. Ibid., pp. 9 (prologue), 237.

113. See Hans Baron, *The Crisis of the Early Italian Renaissance*, rev. ed. (Princeton, 1966), esp. pp. 191–211.

114. As in part 6 of *Lettres philosophiques*, no. 25.

115. Noted by Struever, *Language of History*, p. 152.

116. In their epistles to the second books, respectively, of *Il Cortegiano* and *Discorsi*. Cf. Huizinga, *Waning of the Middle Ages*, p. 80.

117. Cf. Huizinga, *Waning of the Middle Ages*, p. 80.

118. Cf. Steven E. Ozment, "The University and the Church: Patterns of Reform in Jean Gerson," *Medievalia et Humanistica*, n.s. 1 (1970): 121, which

uses this point to bring out the essential difference between medieval and Protestant conceptions of reform.

119. As, for example, *Institutes*, epistle, and III, v, 10.
120. Cf. Levin, *Myth of the Golden Age*, pp. 30–31.
121. *Life*, in *Works*, 1:69–70.

# Madness and Civilization in Early Modern Europe: A Reappraisal of Michel Foucault

## H. C. ERIK MIDELFORT

Historians everywhere have begun to pay close attention to the history of the poor and the downtrodden, the laboring classes and the dangerous classes, even the mad, or mentally ill, who pose peculiar challenges and difficulties. By examining the impact of Michel Foucault, whose book *Madness and Civilization* is perhaps the single best-known study of mental illness in early modern Europe, I hope to discuss some of these difficulties.[1] I also hope to discuss some of the literature in the field, including the history of medicine, which has displayed a myopic bias toward modern problems, and a Whig point of view that countenances only those progressive movements culminating in our own presumably happy time. This bias is pervasive in the history of psychiatry because many of its practitioners lack training in history and write from a complacent and unquestioning position, often after years of medical practice.[2] The resulting history is all too often a form of hero-worship, the singling out of prescient men who made "advances."[3] These great men mysteriously managed to transcend the limitations of their age and to approach the insights of our own age, thereby becoming "fathers" of their particular field. Rival medical historians have spilled a good deal of ink in vain paternity suits between alleged fathers; and all too often the argument boils down to finding the really humane doctors of the past. Instead of concentrating on the growth of method, or of knowledge, as is common in the history of science, the Whig historians of psychiatry seem to have praised their subjects only because they were humane.[4]

The best historians of madness have always avoided these pitfalls, but the field as a whole remains hostile to a nonprogressive, non-hero-worshiping history. One sad example is the recent massive history of madness by Werner Leibbrand and Annemarie Wettley, two erudite medical historians who approached their history from a topical and philosophical point of view.[5] Their detailed and profound book has had no perceptible influence on other histories of madness since it appeared nineteen years ago, and may unfortunately prove to be a mere relic of German idealist history. Perhaps one can anticipate a happier future for the recent survey of medieval madness by Judith Neaman.[6] Her breezy essay exposes in numerous ways a continuation of medieval attitudes toward the insane down to today, thereby throwing out a challenge of some importance for the history of psychiatry, one that forcefully emphasizes a vast continuity beneath the chatter of superficial changes.

Despite the flickering hopes that such recent accounts raise, by far the most audacious and learned challenge to the medical Whig tradition is Michel Foucault's *Folie et déraison: L'Histoire de la folie à l'âge classique.*[7] This work, written by a philosopher often identified as a structuralist, was an immediate success, despite grumblings on the part of some reviewers. For one thing, it stood the medical tradition on its head by debunking the heroes, and by showing how we got into the psychiatric mess we are in. Foucault, in other words, wrote an antiheroic and antiprogressive history, which at times seems close to what one could term Tory history, a romantic chronicling of decline from some previous age of greatness. But he did much more than simply invert an encrusted orthodoxy, for he connected the history of madness to the history of civilization and society, suggesting withal a structural approach to history aimed at penetrating beneath the facade of superficial variety to the underlying order that men in any age impose on their perceptions.[8]

The first and most obvious impact of Foucault's work was among the opponents of traditional psychiatry, especially the antipsychiatrists in Britain, R. D. Laing and David Cooper, who had already begun to regard institutional psychiatry as a hoax and forced confinement as a crime.[9] From sharply differing points of view, Erving Goffman and Thomas Szasz in the United States had also come to distrust the mental hospital.[10] For them, Foucault provided historical legitimation by debunking the origins of modern institutional psychiatry. As the same time, by continuing to develop as a philosopher, and by making *L'Histoire de la folie* integral to his philosophy, Foucault has also influenced speculative and philosophical pursuits.[11] Although Anglo-Saxon readers have often objected to his obscure, arrogant, sensationalist, and opaque form of discourse, which by his own admission is a "labyrinth into which I can venture . . . in which I can lose myself,"[12] his philosophy may well become a major force among self-consciously avant-garde intellectuals. But rather than get lost in Foucault's labyrinth, we can perhaps learn to live, at least temporarily, with a double truth. Following the medieval Averroists, I would like to suggest that something may be true in philosophy but not necessarily so in history; or, to use less provocative language, that Foucault could be right about language and the human condition, but wrong about the route by which we have arrived where we are. In this way the historian can hope to make his own peculiar contribution even if he does not reevaluate the foundations of epistemology or provide a new analysis of mind. I am strengthened in this proposed division by the fact that many of Foucault's readers seem to regard him as a historian and often extract historical details from him even as they object to the medium in which he has embedded them.[13]

Considered as history, Foucault's argument rests on four basic contentions. The first, and in some ways the most picturesque, is the forceful parallel between the medieval isolation of leprosy and the modern isolation of madness—a parallel that has been accepted by many and that rests on two suggestions made by Foucault: (1) that when leprosy disappeared from western Europe, it was replaced by venereal disease and then by madness as the one human defect men refused to contemplate or to deal with on a day-to-day basis,[14] and (2) that many lazar houses remained empty until filled with the mad two centuries later.[15]

Second is Foucault's contention that in the late Middle Ages and early Renaissance the mad led an "easy wandering life," madness having been recognized as part of truth. Even when ejected from a town, the mad were not shut away.[16] Or if a town did lock up some of its mad, as Foucault briefly concedes, it placed them in gate towers or other "liminal" positions symbolic of the medieval awareness of the mad limits of its world.[17] Around 1500 Foucault claims that the ambiguity and constant presence of madness became an obsession. "Madness and the madman became major figures, in their ambiguity: menace and mockery, the dizzying unreason of the world, and the feeble ridicule of men."[18] In popular literature, in the painting of Bosch and Bruegel, in festivals, "in learned literature too Madness or Folly was at work, at the very heart of reason and truth," and the late medieval fascination with death became, by a slight variation, a fascination with madness. "What is in question is still the nothingness of existence, but this nothingness is no longer considered an external final term, both threat and conclusion; it is experienced from within as the continuous and constant form of existence."[19]

According to Foucault, that is, madness had become the image of man's secret, sinful nature but also the image of wisdom itself. Since humanists and artists used "folly" as a critical tool for attacking the vices and vain pretensions of their day, the basic symbol of that age, and the title of Foucault's first chapter, is the ship of fools—a ship representing all the world crowded with various sorts of madness and folly. Far from being merely a theme for painters and poets, the ship of fools had, in Foucault's view, a real existence. He regards it as a common means by which fifteenth-century Rhenish towns dealt with their mad. Foucault expounds beautifully the link of liminality that men made between water and madness and conjures up the wonder of townsfolk watching the arrival of the latest ship of fools.[20] Slowly in the course of the sixteenth century, however, the tragic and disturbing dimensions of madness gave way to the rational and moral critique of the humanists; yet, even in this form, madness was only displaced, and scholars like Montaigne and Charron continued to place madness at the heart of reason. "For the truth of madness is to be inside reason."[21] Thus, the Renaissance basically made clear what had been implicit in the Middle Ages. Madness was still accepted as part of truth and life; it was a time "in which the man of madness and the man of reason, moving apart, [were] not yet disjunct."[22]

The third major contention of Foucault is that this openness disappeared in the Age of the Great Confinement, beginning in the mid-seventeenth century. As Christian critics of folly overwhelmed the tragic vision of both painters and writers like Shakespeare and Cervantes,[23] some thinkers, Descartes, for example, even began to regard madness as "impossible."[24] The awareness of madness at the borders of life withered as men began to conceal, lock up, repress, and confine the mad, as they did beginning with the "Great Confinement" in France, an attempt under Louis XIV to eliminate begging by confining the poor in "general hospitals," where they were to receive food and rudimentary care in exchange for light work. Foucault emphasizes that these general hospitals soon existed all over France, and that they came to house a motley assortment of criminals, aged, orphans, prostitutes, the poor, the mentally defective, and the mad.

Instead of regarding such persons as basically dissimilar, society now lumped them together because of their common refusal (or inability) to work. Foucault sounds a Marxist note, observing that the new bourgeois order would not tolerate the absence of the basic bourgeois virtue: "good," hard work.[25] Thus, madness was reduced to a form of immorality or scandal rigorously to be excluded from the life of moral and rational men. A similar development took shape in Germany with the spread of *Zuchthäuser,* and Foucault implies that the English workhouses were no different. On this view, the madness confined was not yet a mental illness or even a medical problem of any sort. It was simply man as animal, without reason and often healthier and stronger (and more dangerous) than his more rational brethren. Even hostile critics have accepted this view of matters.[26]

The fourth and final contention posits a transition to madness as mental illness, in which Foucault examines the work of the reformers, Tuke and Pinel, and concludes that they "invented" mental illness. By turning to "moral therapy," the reformers succeeded, that is, in making guilt one of the prime weapons in the arsenal of the physician. By learning to dehumanize and control the insane in asylums, they also seized power as arbiters of sanity, thereby cutting off all hope for continuing the dialogue between reason and unreason, however attenuated that dialogue had become since the seventeenth century.[27] It is at this point that many historians and critics have drawn back in horror. Only the antipsychiatrists have eagerly embraced Foucault's version of the invention of mental illness.

Taken as a simplified summary of Foucault's great work, these four arguments have been undeniably influential. Authors who would not dream of accepting Foucault's philosophy or all four of the arguments here described have not hesitated to call his book "brilliant."[28] The vast new quagmire of scholarship entitled *World History of Psychiatry* often cites Foucault as an authority.[29] And Werner Leibbrand, one of the authors of the ill-fated book on *Wahnsinn,* did not flinch from calling Foucault's works indispensable for the historian of medicine.[30]

Even scholars who oppose Foucault's antiheroic construction have been willing to grant his insight in areas other than those under close scrutiny; and because Foucault divides his history into three broad periods, it is not surprising that at least three kinds of reaction have developed. Happiest, perhaps, have been the medievalists, for they have found in Foucault an unexpected defender. In his pages they can ignore the frequent cruelty of medieval society toward the mad, emphasizing instead its open-ness to folly and unreason. With Foucault, they can shunt re-sponsibility for harsh treatment off to the age of the Great Con-finement.[31] The Dutch scholar, H. H. Beek, for example, cites Foucault with evident relief to show that a less religious and less humane attitude toward the mad came only after the Middle Ages.[32] Or to cite another example, a recent history of medicine in medieval England glows with pride over the "kindly and toler-ant" attitude usually shown toward unbalanced people, and notes with dismay that "it was to be a long time before this attitude returned, for the later history of Bedlam shows how callous the public could become."[33]

For historians studying the modern period since 1800, however, Foucault has usually been more of a threat than a help. They have either ignored him or found his work too abstract, too angry, or too difficult to be of much use.[34] Some of them have persisted in seeing the reforms of the nineteenth century as one example of the rising tide of humanitarian reform at work throughout soci-ety. Others have reexamined the work of Philippe Pinel without so much as mentioning the challenge thrown down by Foucault.[35] Only a few have taken the challenge seriously, and begun the sort of detailed work through which general assertions can be effec-tively tested.[36] This common reluctance to take Foucault seri-ously may have something to do with the ideological commit-ment of modern historians, who do not generally regard their own epoch as the savage wasteland of dehumanized silence that Foucault describes. But whatever the reason, the situation poses real problems for the historian of early modern Europe. On the one hand, medievalists have agreed that real cruelty toward the insane began after 1500. On the other hand, historians of modern medicine and psychiatry are equally agreed that the late eigh-teenth and early nineteenth centuries saw the first effective ef-forts at relieving the miserable plight of the mad. Early modern Europe, in other words, has been scourged from two sides, by Foucault and his followers, and by the traditionalists. Unfortu-nately, it cannot be said that historians of early modern Europe have responded effectively. Some work has recently appeared on the treatment of madness in the eighteenth century, but much remains to be done. As for the sixteenth and seventeenth cen-turies, the waters are largely uncharted. Work is proceeding, how-ever; and a brief consideration of the literature may tell us how well Foucault's contentions hold up.

Probably the first point concerning the putative analogy be-tween medieval leprosy and early modern madness is that Foucault deliberately disregarded the way in which madhouses

developed from medieval hospitals, and especially from monasteries.[37] This becomes a point of some importance when one
tries to understand the rigid discipline of the eighteenth-century
general hospital or *Zuchthaus*. Moreover, research into the history of medieval leprosy may also force a refinement of Foucault's
monolithic image of rejection. One recent study has shown that
medieval lepers were treated with a mixture of fear and pity,
contempt and sympathy; that although they sometimes experienced open persecution, they also received good care.[38] Another
study of leprosy in medieval literature concludes that the disease
was both an emblem of sin and a living purgation. In other words,
far from banishing leprosy from all areas of life, medieval literature reflected a fascination with it. And because leprosy was often
confused with venereal disease, it was a condition that threatened
all expressions of lust. One may not be able to say that all lepers
were banished to a living death in remote lazar houses,[39] but as a
model of social exclusion, the lazar house still stands as an ideal
type, the embodiment of a social attitude; the religious rituals
that accompanied confinement in a house of lepers were often
strikingly similar to the office of the dead.[40] Yet here Foucault's
parallel again is forced to bear more than it is able. For confinement to a madhouse or asylum did not involve the same kinds of
mortuary ritual or the same extinction of legal rights.

In the late Middle Ages and Renaissance, as recent work has
shown, many of the mad were in fact confined to small cells or
jails or even domestic cages, and not just to gate towers as
Foucault suggests.[41] It seems likely, indeed, that whenever a mad
person was considered a threat to others or to him- or herself,
society has dictated that the person be restrained, forcibly if necessary, and with chains.[42] The instances of harsh treatment of the
mad could be multiplied *ad nauseam*. Indeed, the Spanish friar
Juan Gilabert Joffre was so moved by the sight of a group of boys
insulting and stoning a poor madman in 1409 that he decided to
found western Europe's first hospital for the mad at Valencia. The
story is noteworthy on two counts: first, because it is evidence
that not all elements of medieval society accepted madness as
part of life, and second, because it demonstrates that the founding
of mental hospitals did not wait for the "absolutist" or "bourgeois" repression of the seventeenth century.[43] Such hospitals
were a medieval Arab invention, which probably explains their
spread in fifteenth-century Spain and from there to all of Europe
in the sixteenth and seventeenth centuries.[44] Foucault is quite
wrong in suggesting that they were an invention of the early
nineteenth-century reformers. And though he tries to salvage his
point by drawing a distinction between shutting up (*enfermer*) the

mad and confining them (interner),[45] the crucial distinction is between small-scale and often ecclesiastical efforts to succor the poor, the aged, the sick, and the mad, and larger, often secular attempts to encompass all of the poor and to eliminate begging.

The problem is not only that the poor mad were confined or hospitalized before the seventeenth century. That would be embarrassing but not devastating if late medieval men did have that other way of dealing with the mad, the ships of fools that Foucault puts on such elaborate display. Rather the central problem is that serious researchers have never found any mention of real ships of fools. There are references to deportation and exile of mad persons to be sure, and instances in which towns gave poor, mentally afflicted persons enough pocket money to last until they reached home. Occasionally the mad were indeed sent away on boats.[46] But nowhere can one find reference to real boats or ships loaded with mad pilgrims in search of their lost reason. The sources cited by Foucault merely prove that cities sometimes used boats to get rid of a difficult mad person;[47] and at that, there is only one known instance of a madman's having been set adrift on a boat, and it is quite possible that the intention was to drown him, since certain German laws of the fifteenth century introduced the death penalty for stubborn cases.[48] Foucault's rhapsody on the power of water takes on new meaning in light of these brutal episodes.[49]

But even if the mad were often treated roughly, even if they were frequently hospitalized or jailed, and even if they were not set aboard the Narrenschiffe, does it not remain true nonetheless that madness was regarded as part of medieval life and truth? To this question a kind of answer has begun to emerge. A literary scholar, Penelope Doob, has detailed the connection made by most medieval commentators between madness and sin, concluding that, generally speaking, madness was considered either a consequence of sin, a purgation, or a test of one's virtue.[50] Medieval thinkers may not have accepted madness any more than they accepted sin, but they accepted the reality of both; and many more of them were obsessed with sin than were obsessed by or even interested in madness. Then, too, Beek's marvelous book examines some of the other implications of the religious context within which mental illness was understood. Pilgrimage was a thoroughly common remedy for madness (and other afflictions), and other spiritual aids, including exorcism, were widely used as well.[51] According to the Spanish medical historian Pedro Laín Entralgo, the connection between sin and sickness has been extremely resilient in western culture: "It is not rare that a 'spiritual malady' in the moral sense goes on to become a 'spiritual malady' in the medical sense.''[52] Foucault is aware of this point; he mentions religious interpretations of madness but does not modify his general conclusion that madness was seen as cosmic tragedy by medieval and Renaissance artists.[53] By underestimating the force of sin as a source of horror and madness, he grossly exaggerates the Renaissance dialogue with madness.

When Foucault turns to literary treatments of folly and madness, he is on more solid ground, but his spirited treatment of Sebastian Brant, Erasmus, and the humanist tradition of folly as moral critique appears one-sided in light of recent investigations, which show that Brant and Erasmus had divergent goals in mind and that humanism cannot be reduced to naive moralism.[54] Barbara Könneker's study in particular contains some very stimulating speculation about why Brant's *Narrenschiff* became such an instantaneous success. She insists that the basic idea was the identification of sinful mankind with a "colorful host of court fools and shrovetide fools with their ridiculous and grotesque postures, leaps and dances;''[55] and that this was the idea that caught the fancy of the age rather than any deep concern with madness, melancholy, or mental disturbance.

It would be wrong, however, to conclude that madness everywhere encountered only criticism and abuse. Among some of the Renaissance humanists, the melancholy malady was cultivated as a pathway to spiritual growth or to genius. Relying on the pseudo-Aristotelian *Problem* (XXX, 1), many Renaissance scholars concluded that all true geniuses were afflicted with madness and melancholy. The researches of Klibansky, Panofsky, and Saxl have made the revival of this idea during the Renaissance well known.[56] And a recent dissertation has examined the religious, emotional, poetic, and philosophical reasons for cultivating the melancholy humor, which had become a fashion by the end of the sixteenth century, Yet this rise of melancholy was accompanied by a rising resistance to melancholy as well, from medical, Stoic, and religious points of view.[57] Thanks to them, the atmosphere was so contentious as to make one doubt whether the humanists' attitudes toward mental illness can be reduced to a single response as Foucault suggests.[58]

Which brings us to the Great Confinement. On this topic a great deal of material has recently come to light as scholars dig into the voluminous institutional records of the *ancien régime*. But one fact stands out; namely, that the *grand renfermement* was aimed not at madness or even at deviance, but at poverty. It was only the poor-mad, the poor-deviant, the poor-criminal, and the just plain poor who were sent to the general hospitals of Germany and France. Foucault says nothing directly to the contrary but often implies that the general hospitals confined not just the poor, but all persons who affronted bourgeois sensibilities.[59] His argument, to be precise, is that the confinement represented a bourgeois attempt to repress and regulate the poor; and here one must emphasize a feature that Foucault notices but does not fully assimilate. These general hospitals, having originally been built on monastic lines by reformers who thought in monastic terms,[60] combined the main features of the monastic environment: asceticism, work, morality, obedience, and supervision. And just as monasteries frequently cared for the sick, the aged, the mad, the orphans, and the poor, so too did the general hospitals. Lumping such diverse groups together was not a classical innovation prompted by bourgeois reverence for work or by a new *episteme*, but an echo of a long ecclesiastical tradition of dealing with misery and dependence.[61] Indeed, the various groups of poor were not usually housed together indiscriminately, as if there were no difference between orphans and the senile, but were generally separated into wards or floors or even separate buildings.[62] The classical innovation, if there was one, was the massive attempt to compel the poor to enter institutions originally set up on a voluntary basis.[63] And this attempt has more to do with absolutism and centralization than with bourgeois inspiration.[64]

In another instance, too, Foucault invites misinterpretation. He implies that the mad were shut away like lepers, that general hospitals were not medical institutions in any sense, and more remarkably that the mad were not even considered ill. In fact, many mentally disturbed persons in eighteenth-century Paris came first to the Hôtel-Dieu, where they took a six-week cure, after which they often went home. If they showed no improvement, they might repeat the six-week cure. Only then were they eligible for the lunatic wards of Bicêtre (for men) or Salpêtrière (for women).[65] And according to Sebastien Mercier, at least, many improved enough to be discharged even from those two hospitals, even though they had been set aside as incurable.[66] Here, too, general hospitals seem to have followed the monastic inspiration of custodial care, redemption, or rehabilitation as opposed to the sepulchral model of the leprosarium.

Moreover, recent research has shown the dangers of extrapolating from an idea, as Foucault does, without sufficient attention to chronological or regional differences. Klaus Dörner has paid close attention to these variables and has produced a large, tough-minded, inspired history of the way the poor-mad came to public attention in western Europe.[67] By devoting nearly equal attention to England, France, and Germany, Dörner could see the crucial "lags" or difficulties in the development of three different societies; by examining social conditions generally before looking at the fate of the mad, he came up with the first genuine social history of psychiatry. In other words, where Foucault is often content to speak of the classical experience, Dörner emphasizes the differences between the English, the French, and the German experience with madness. In so doing, he has been joined by Martin Schrenk, who stresses the way in which German psychiatry took off along different lines from that of France and England, even while attempting to imitate and assimilate French and English psychiatry,[68] and by other scholars, who have begun to emphasize how numerous purely private madhouses became, especially in England. This was a development that Foucault completely overlooked, and that again poses problems for his assumption that confinement of the mad by the state was uniform all over Europe.[69]

Nor is Foucault's periodization free of problems. Though he conveys the impression that the age of confinement of the mad coincided with the age of confinement of the poor, the political and economic failure in confining the poor was evident by the late eighteenth or early nineteenth century, but it was only then that the confinement of the mad really got under way. To take only a couple of examples, it is clear that England experienced a dramatic rise in confinements during the nineteenth century.[70] English asylums everywhere filled up much faster than the best estimates had projected; and it seems likely that as asylums became available, the definition of madness itself broadened to include the "awkward and inconvenient of all descriptions."[71] In France the picture seems to be much the same.[72] In the United States, the rate of admissions of patients to hospitals for mental disease went from 3.0 per 100,000 to 18.6 per 100,000 between 1831 and 1860. In the next hundred years the rate of admissions jumped to over 200 per 100,000.[73] Canadian statistics show a similar rise.[74] With regard to madness, therefore, we are witnessing the end of the age of confinement only now, as drug therapy and community mental health centers increase in popularity at the expense of in-patient hospital care.[75]

So far as concerns Foucault's fourth contention, that the reforms of the late eighteenth and early nineteenth centuries amounted to the invention of mental illness, it is here that his philosophical framework blends most perfectly with his history,[76] and that the empirical historian must tread most cautiously. Foucault frequently implies that prior to the nineteenth century madness was not a medical problem but was regarded either as a condition having its own truth or as a reduction to brute animality.[77] Stated so boldly, the assertion seems deliberately preposterous.[78] What is basically true is that before 1800 medical men quite uniformly tried to relate all mental disturbance to underlying somatic conditions. To that extent there was no *purely mental* illness until psychiatry subsequently divided itself into two bitter factions, the somatic and psychic (or moral).[79] In turning to the work of Tuke and Pinel as presented by Foucault, it seems only fair, therefore, to interpret Foucault as meaning that they and their reforms created a *mental* illness whose medical treatment was really *moral* repression, the attempt to foster guilt in a patient by setting standards and punishing him for any transgressions.[80] Some of Foucault's followers have gleaned precisely this message.[81] But it, too, is a polemical distortion.

Take Foucault's assessment of William Tuke and Philippe Pinel. Neither of them was the hero that medical hagiography has made him out to be. A German scholar has recently taken Foucault to task for creating the false impression that only the skilled intellectual archeologist (Foucault) can detect the full repression of Tuke's Retreat, when in fact accurate quotation of the source in question would have made the point without further delay.[82] It has also become clear that Tuke did not use only the force of judgment, the ever-watchful eye of supervision. He also emphasized the importance of diet, exercise, climate, and surroundings, all of which were echoes of the earlier medical practice of treating mind and body together. Furthermore, recent scholars have demonstrated that in England, at least, moral therapy was far from crucial in the medicalization of mental illness. Indeed, English physicians of the early nineteenth century, regarding moral therapy quite correctly as a lay threat to medical monopoly, a kind of treatment that was distinctly nonmedical, waged a strong and ultimately successful campaign to coopt or assimilate the new psychiatry of Tuke and Pinel.[83] Here then is a discontinuity, or at least a wrinkle, in the case for continuity between Tuke and our own age that Foucault tries to make.

With regard to Pinel, Foucault similarly clouds the perspective, first, by accepting the story of Pinel's liberating the mad of Bicêtre from their chains and then by showing how hollow that liberation really was.[84] Careful research has cast doubt on Pinel's famous gesture, showing that it may never have taken place at all and that far too many historians have remained content with the platitudes of psychiatric tradition.[85] The most far-reaching criticism of Foucault's view of Pinel, however, stems from recent scholarship that documents Pinel's explicit debt to earlier English theoreticians and to classical antiquity. Far from standing in a new environment governed by new rules (a new *episteme*), Pinel clearly felt himself in continuous dialogue with the Hippocratic-Galenic tradition of Aretaeus, Celsus, and especially Coelius Aurelianus.[86] If, as Hayden White has argued, the aim of Foucault is to "disperse" the elements of our cosmos, to "defamiliarize" us with the past, to emphasize the large discontinuities in history, then it is clear why he must deny the kinds of continuity, dependence, and debt that traditional historical scholarship often affirms.[87] It is also clear that recent research is making Foucault's task ever more difficult.

What we have discovered in looking at *Madness and Civilization* is that many of its arguments fly in the face of empirical evidence, and that many of its broadest generalizations are oversimplifications. Indeed, in his quest for the essence of an age, its *episteme*, Foucault seems simply to indulge a whim for arbitrary and witty assertion so often that one wonders why so much attention and praise continue to fall his way. The answer rests only partly on his erudite brilliance and on his standing as the man who "relaunched philosophy in France single-handed."[88] In the history of medicine, his importance rests not so much on his general philosophy as on his attempt to recast the shape of medical history, to present a history of medicine that does *not* proceed relentlessly toward the present, and to explore the deepest meanings of madness and the underlying structures of knowledge within a given period.[89] The execution of this important task is not so easy as some of the bedazzled followers of Foucault seem to assume, though neither is it so unimportant as many orthodox and self-contented historians of medicine suggest. If we are to have a structural, unheroic history, we must recognize the major flaws that run through much of Foucault's work. First, we will have to learn to rethink the historical periods of our past; it is one of the strangest aspects of Foucault's perceptions that for all his iconoclasm, he continues to uphold the firm concepts of the Renaissance, the Classical Period, and the Modern Age. Second, we will have to learn to work with structures of mind that do not pretend to underlie all of the thinking, or even all of the best thinking, of an age. There is too much diversity in any one period, and too much continuity between periods, for the relentless quest for the elusive *episteme* to prove ultimately useful. Moreover, in trying to extract or apply Foucault's method, we will have to remain aware of the need to control the force of intuition, to leave our arguments open to falsification.[90] Foucault runs into problems when he extrapolates the structures of the present back into the past, though it is not clear whether such empirical observations can be of use of philosophers.[91] Historians, however, should not conclude that a catalogue of Foucault's errors vitiates his whole enterprise, for he still has much to teach us: namely, the necessity of reading omnivorously and of reading closely; the necessity of probing behind a verbal facade to the emotion or unconscious intention within; and the need for a history of mental structures that dares to imagine discontinuity as well as continuity. If a disciplined intuition can grasp these things, our confrontation with the past will continue to be a (self-) critical encounter.

## Notes

1. Translated by Richard Howard (New York, 1965).

2. For a general survey (with 188 bibliographical footnotes) see George Mora, "The History of Psychiatry: A Cultural and Bibliographic Survey," *International Journal of Psychiatry* 2 (1966): 335–55.

3. For a recent example, see Aubrey Lewis, *The State of Psychiatry: Essays and Addresses* (London, 1967); for an able expression of the merits of this view, see George Mora, "The Historiography of Psychiatry and Its Development: A Re-Evaluation," *Journal of the History of the Behavioral Sciences* 1 (1965): 43–52; see also George Mora, "Historiographic and Cultural Trends in Psychiatry: A Survey," *Bulletin of the History of Medicine* 35 (1961): 26–36. For an excellent survey of problems in the whole subject, see Oswei Temkin, "The Historiography of Ideas in Medicine," in *Modern Methods in the History of Medicine*, ed. Edwin Clarke (London, 1971), pp. 1–21.

4. Gregory Zilboorg declared that "the history of psychiatry is essentially the history of humanism"; he is quoted approvingly by George Mora in his essay "From Demonology to the Narrenturm," in *Historic Derivations of Modern Psychiatry*, ed. Iago Galdston (New York, 1967), pp. 41–73, at p. 46. For this point see also Galdston's introduction to the volume. See also Ernest Harms, *Origins of Modern Psychiatry* (Springfield, Ill., 1967), p. 6. For a useful critique of psychiatric history and of the sterile clash between attackers and defenders of the mental hospital, see Gerald N. Grob, "Rediscovering Asylums: The Unhistorical History of the Mental Hospital," *Hastings Center Report* 7, no. 4 (August 1977): 33–41.

5. Werner Leibbrand and Annemarie Wettley, *Der Wahnsinn: Geschichte der abendländischen Psychopathologie* (Freiburg, 1961). For another, more modest example, see the provocative and excellent study of Esther Fischer-Homberger, *Hypochondrie. Melancholie bis Neurose: Krankheiten und Zustandsbilder* (Bern, 1970). Similarly, a fairly recent work combining erudition and anthropological perspectives has gone nearly unnoticed: Basil Clarke, *Mental Disorder in Earlier Britain: Exploratory Studies* (Cardiff, 1975).

6. Judith S. Neaman, *Suggestion of the Devil: The Origins of Madness* (Garden City, N.Y., 1975).

7. Paris, 1961. I cite the augmented second edition (Paris, 1971).

8. See especially the expansion of these ideas in Foucault's *Les mots et les choses* (Paris, 1966), translated as *The Order of Things: An Archeology of the Human Sciences* (New York, 1972).

9. R. D. Laing, "The Invention of Madness," *New Statesman* 73 (16 June 1967): 843; Robert Boyers and Robert Orrill, *R. D. Laing and Anti-Psychiatry* (New York, 1971), see especially pp. 238–39.

10. Erving Goffman, *Asylums: Essays on the Social Situation of Mental Patients and Other Inmates* (Garden City, N.Y., 1961); Thomas Szasz, *Ideology and Insanity: Essays on the Psychiatric Dehumanization of Man* (Garden City, N.Y., 1970); Szasz, *The Manufacture of Madness* (New York, 1970). Recently Szasz has angrily attacked Laing and antipsychiatry; see his "Anti-Psychiatry: The Paradigm of the Plundered Mind," *The New Review* 3, no. 29 (August 1976): 3–14, reprinted in his *Schizophrenia: The Sacred Symbol of Psychiatry* (New York, 1976).

11. See, e.g., Maurice Cranston, "Michel Foucault," *Encounter* 30, no. 6 (June 1968): 34–42; Hayden V. White, "Foucault Decoded: Notes From Under-

ground," *History & Theory* 12 (1973): 23–54; anonymous, "The Contented Positivist: M. Foucault and the death of man," *Times Literary Supplement* (London) 69 (2 July 1970): 697–98. Jean-Claude Guédon presents a sharp refutation of Hayden White's view of Foucault in "Michel Foucault: The Knowledge of Power and the Power of Knowledge," *Bulletin of the History of Medicine* 51 (1977): 245–77. For other criticism aimed at the philosophical level, see, e.g., Jean Piaget, *Structuralism* (New York, 1970), pp. 128–35; and the response of Michael Peters, "Extended Review of Foucault, *Madness and Civilization*, and Piaget, *Structuralism*," *Sociological Review* 19 (1971): 634–38.

12. Foucault, *The Archeology of Knowledge* (New York, 1972): 17. For the place of *Madness and Civilization* in his later philosophy, see *Archeology of Knowledge*, pp. 14–16, 47, 65, 157, 179. Even his most devoted followers admit difficulty in understanding Foucault; see Laing, "Invention of Madness."

13. See George Rosen, *Madness in Society: Chapters in the Historical Sociology of Mental Illness* (New York, 1969): 154–58, which leans rather heavily on Foucault, *Histoire de la folie*, pp. 41–53, without any acknowledgment. Note also the naive work of Barbara Frances Bird, "The Concept of Madness in the Dramatic Literature of Seventeenth-Century France" (Ph.D. diss., Florida State University, 1973). The author attempts to use Foucault as a "primary guide" to her subject but seems to misconstrue Foucault's arguments.

14. The section on venereal disease was cut from the abridged edition of *Histoire de la folie*, which served as the basis for the English edition. Perhaps Foucault no longer felt that venereal disease was strictly parallel to leprosy and madness.

15. *Madness and Civilization*, p. 3.

16. "Les fous alors avaient une existence facilement errante. Les villes les chassaient volontiers de leur enceinte; on les laissait courir dans des campagnes éloignées, quand on ne les confiait pas à un groupe de marchands et de pèlerins." *Histoire de la folie*, p. 19; *Madness and Civilization*, p. 8.

17. *Histoire de la folie*, pp. 20–22: "la situation liminaire du fou."

18. *Madness and Civilization*, p. 13.

19. Ibid., p. 16.

20. Ibid., p. 8.

21. *Histoire de la folie*, p. 46.

22. *Madness and Civilization*, p. x.

23. Foucault cut this section from the abridged editions, making the "mutation" from the Renaissance to the seventeenth century seem much sharper and more inexplicable than it seemed in the original edition. Since Foucault has subsequently developed a theory of cultural mutations that cannot be explained, these cuts from the original edition may be an attempt to bring his early book into line with his later thinking. Cf. *Histoire de la folie*, pp. 37–47; and White, "Foucault Decoded," pp. 50–51.

24. In the original edition Foucault had an interesting discussion of Descartes, *Histoire de la folie*, pp. 56–59; this discussion is continued as a critique of Derrida's view of Descartes in the excursus added to the second full-length edition: "Mon corps, ce papier, ce feu," *Histoire de la folie*, pp. 583–603.

25. In the second edition of the full *Histoire de la folie*, Foucault added a non-Marxian consideration of this point: "La folie, l'absence d'oeuvre," pp. 575–82.

26. See, e.g., Peter Gay in *Commentary* 40, no. 4 (October 1965): 93–96.

27. The power of physicians has become a matter of continuing concern to Foucault, who frequently sympathizes with anarchism: "Power is evil, it is ugly, it is poor, sterile, monotonous, dead; and that over which power is exercised is fine, it is good, it is rich"; Foucault, "Interview: Non au sexe roi," *Nouvel Observateur* (12 March 1977), p. 113. "If I wanted to pose in the garb of a somewhat fictitious coherence, I would say that this has always been my problem: the effects of power and the production of 'truth' "; Ibid., p. 105.

28. E.g., George Mora, "From Demonology to the Narrenturm," p. 47.

29. John G. Howells, ed., *World History of Psychiatry* (New York, 1975); see the authorities listed at the end of each chapter.

30. W. Leibbrand, "Das Geschichtswerk Michel Foucaults," *Sudhoffs*

*Archiv für die Geschichte der Medizin* 48 (1964): 352–59, dealing with *Histoire de la folie* and *Naissance de la clinique* (Paris, 1963).

31. See, e.g., Penelope B. R. Doob, "Ego Nabugodonosor: A Study of Conventions of Madness in Middle English Literature" (Ph.D. diss., Stanford University, 1970), p. 156. This dissertation was published in much briefer form as *Nebuchadnezzar's Children* (New Haven, 1974). I cite the dissertation because it contains much helpful medical literature omitted from the published version. But see Neaman, *Suggestion of the Devil*, for a trenchant reminder of medieval hostility and cruelty toward the insane.

32. H. H. Beek, *Waanzin in de middeleuwen: Beeld van de gestoorde en bemoeienis met de zieke* (Nijkerk, 1969). This little-noticed masterpiece should be translated into English. Its publisher, Callenbach, notes that an English translation was planned in 1969, but those plans clearly went awry. I am grateful to Charles H. Talbot for bringing the book to my attention.

33. Charles H. Talbot, *Medicine in Medieval England* (London, 1967), p. 185.

34. See Gerald N. Grob, *Mental Institutions in America: Social Policy to 1875* (New York, 1973), p. 42; David J. Rothman, *The Discovery of the Asylum: Social Order and Disorder in the New Republic* (Boston, 1971), pp. xvii–xviii; Norman Dain, *Concepts of Insanity in the United States, 1789–1865* (New Brunswick, N.J., 1964), pp. xii–xiii; idem, *Disordered Minds: The First Century of Eastern State Hospital in Williamsburg, Virginia: 1766–1866* (Williamsburg, 1971), p. 1.

35. Walter Riese, *The Legacy of Philippe Pinel: An Inquiry into Thought on Mental Alienation* (New York, 1969).

36. One of the best of these scholars is Andrew T. Scull, whose dissertation is an exceptionally powerful analysis: "Museums of Madness: The Social Organization of Insanity in Nineteenth-Century England" (Ph.D. dissertation, Princeton University, 1974).

37. A point made clearly by Martin Schrenk, *Über den Umgang mit Geisteskranken: Die Entwicklung der psychiatrischen Therapie vom "moralischen Regime" in England und Frankreich zu den "psychischen Curmethoden" in Deutschland* (Berlin, 1973), p. 17.

38. Huldrych M. Koelbing et al., *Beiträge zur Geschichte der Lepra* (Zurich, 1972), pp. 84–93.

39. Saul Nathaniel Brody, *The Disease of the Soul: Leprosy in Medieval Literature* (Ithaca, 1974), pp. 32, 55–58, 64–70.

40. Ibid., p. 65.

41. For a brief summary of much nineteenth-century literature, see Rosen, *Madness in Society*, pp. 139–50. For a celebrated example of the confinement of a mad poet, see William Boulting, *Tasso and His Times* (1907; reprint ed. New York, 1968), pp. 211, 242–49.

42. To take but one example, Roman law provided that dangerous *furiosi* be restrained with chains; *Digest* 1, 18, 14. For a Renaissance example of the same treatment, see Jason Pratensis, *De Cerebri Morbis* (Basel, 1549), p. 214. See also Neaman, *Suggestion of the Devil*, pp. 78, 126, 136.

43. See J. J. Lopez-Ibor in Howells, *World History of Psychiatry*, pp. 97–98.

44. Arslan Terzioğlu, *Mittelalterliche islamische Krankenhäuser unter Berücksichtigung der Frage nach den ältesten psychiatrischen Anstalten* (D.Ing. diss., Berlin, 1968); J. B. Ullersperger, *Die Geschichte der Psychologie und Psychiatrik in Spanien* (Würzburg, 1871), pp. 65 ff.; Norman A. Stillman, "Charity and Social Service in Medieval Islam," *Societas* 5 (1975): 105–16.

45. *Madness and Civilization*, p. 58; *Histoire de la folie*, p. 85.

46. Georg Ludwig Kriegk, *Ärzte, Heilanstalten, Geisteskranke im mittelalterlichen Frankfurt a.M.* (Frankfurt, 1863), pp. 16–18; Theodor Kirchhoff, *Grundriss einer Geschichte der deutschen Irrenpflege* (Berlin, 1890), pp. 9–32; Beek, *Waanzin in de middeleuwen*.

47. *Histoire de la folie*, pp. 18–24. The uncut French edition cites many more sources than the abridged versions.

48. Hermann Knapp, *Das alte Nürnberger Kriminalrecht* (Berlin, 1895), p. 13; for laws permitting execution of the insane, see Rudolf His, *Die Strafrecht des deutschen Mittelalters: Erster Teil, Die Verbrechen und ihre Folgen im allgemeinen* (Leipzig, 1920), pp. 66–68.

49. *Madness and Civilization*, p. 11.

50. Doob, *Nebuchadnezzar's Children*, passim.

51. Beek, *Waanzin in de middeleuwen*, pp. 10, 50.

52. Pedro Lain Entralgo, *Enfermidad y pecado* (Barcelona, 1961), p. 83.

53. For an attempt to follow Foucault in this argument see Robert S. Kinsman, "Folly, Melancholy and Madness: A Study in Shifting Styles of Medical Analysis and Treatment, 1450–1675," in *The Darker Vision of the Renaissance: Beyond the Fields of Reason*, ed. R. S. Kinsman (Berkeley and Los Angeles, 1974), pp. 273–320, at pp. 281–85. Kinsman, however, points out that the hospital motif replaced the ship motif in the first half of the sixteenth century, i.e., a full century before one might have expected the shift.

54. Barbara Könneker, *Wesen und Wandlung der Narrenidee im Zeitalter des Humanismus: Brant, Murner, Erasmus* (Wiesbaden, 1966), pp. 330–31; Walter Kaiser, *Praisers of Folly: Erasmus, Rabelais, Shakespeare* (Cambridge, Mass., 1963).

55. *Wesen und Wandlung*, p. 8; see also Thomas G. Benedek, "The Image of Medicine in 1500: Theological Reactions to *The Ship of Fools*," *Bulletin of the History of Medicine* 38 (1964): pp. 329–42.

56. Raymond Klibansky, Erwin Panofsky, and Fritz Saxl, *Saturn and Melancholy* (London, 1964).

57. Noel Lacy Brann, "The Renaissance Passion of Melancholy: The Paradox of Its Cultivation and Resistance" (Ph.D. diss., Stanford University, 1965), pp. 423–82. Brann's encyclopedic work has difficulty staying with a well-defined topic, but even so it should be better known to Renaissance scholars. Another dissertation documents the use of the Aristotelian-Galenic tradition to debunk Puritanism: Thomas Lester Canavan, "Madness and Enthusiasm in Burton's *Anatomy of Melancholy* and Swift's *Tale of a Tub*" (Ph.D. diss., Columbia University, 1970). On this topic see also Alan Mark Levensohn, "Swift Against Madness: The Early Years" (Ph.D. diss., Brandeis University, 1974), and Henry A. C. Forbes, "A Study of Religious Melancholy and Seventeenth-Century English Puritan Dissent" (Ph.D. diss., Harvard University, 1961).

58. Perhaps Foucault would argue that despite superficial differences, the "structure of knowledge" about madness in the sixteenth century was uniform.

59. *Madness and Civilization*, e.g., p. 45.

60. Ibid., pp. 59, 62.

61. Olwen H. Hufton, *The Poor of Eighteenth-Century France* (Oxford, 1974), pp. 139–59.

62. Dieter Jetter, *Zur Typologie des Irrenhauses in Frankreich und Deutschland, 1780–1840* (Wiesbaden, 1971), pp. 11–13, 76. But see Erwin H. Ackerknecht, "Political Prisoners in French Mental Institutions Before 1789, During the Revolution, and Under Napoleon I," *Medical History* 19 (1975): 250–55, for evidence that political prisoners were frequently held in both state and ecclesiastical (but not in private) hospitals.

63. Hufton, *The Poor*, pp. 139–42. See also J. P. Gutton, "À l'aube du XVIIe siècle: Idées nouvelles sur les pauvres," *Cahiers d'Histoire* 10 (1965): 87–97.

64. See Orest Ranum, *Paris in the Age of Absolutism: An Essay* (New York, 1968), pp. 195–292, for the argument that Paris actually retreated from the modern world of capitalism in the second half of the seventeenth century. See also Emanuel Chill, "Religion and Mendicity in Seventeenth-Century France," *International Review of Social History* 7 (1962): 400–425.

65. Jetter, *Zur Typologie*, p. 11.

66. Ibid., p. 12. For another example of the rehabilitative intention of the hospitals, see Cissie C. Fairchilds, *Poverty and Charity in Aix-en-Provence, 1640–1789* (Baltimore, 1976).

67. Klaus Dörner, *Bürger und Irre: Zur Sozialgeschichte und Wissenschaftssoziologie der Psychiatrie* (Frankfurt, 1969).

68. Schrenk, *Über den Umgang*, p. 4. Both Schrenk and Dörner see themselves as correcting the excesses of Foucault. For a good, clear analysis of the frequent ambivalence of eighteenth-century English writers toward the mad, see Max Byrd, *Visits to Bedlam: Madness and Literature in the Eighteenth Century* (Columbia, S.C., 1974).

69. William L. Parry-Jones, *The Trade in Lunacy: A Study of Private Madhouses in England in the Eighteenth and Nineteenth Centuries* (London, 1972). Eighteenth-century Paris had as many as eighteen private mental institutions; Ackerknecht, "Political Prisoners."

70. See especially Scull, "Museums of Madness," pp. 605–10.

71. Ibid., p. 612.

72. Howells, *World History of Psychiatry*, p. 135; cf. *Statistique de la France*, n.s., vol. 10: *Statistique Annuelle, Année 1880* (Paris, 1883), p. lxii. I owe this latter reference to the kindness of Marc D. Alexander, whose recent dissertation documents the rise of custodial asylums in the 1860s and after: "The Administration of Madness and Attitudes Toward the Insane in Nineteenth-Century Paris" (Ph.D. diss., Johns Hopkins University, 1976).

73. U. S. Bureau of the Census, *Historical Statistics of the United States: Colonial Times to 1957* (Washington, D.C., 1960), p. 38, Series B 271–274; *Historical Statistics of the United States. Continuation to 1962 and Revisions* (Washington, D.C., 1965), p. 7. See also Grob, *Mental Institutions*, pp. 371–72.

74. M. C. Urquhart and K. A. H. Buckley, *Historical Statistics of Canada* (Toronto, 1965), pp. 47–50.

75. See Michael Alfred Peszke, *Involuntary Treatment of the Mentally Ill: The Problem of Autonomy* (Springfield, Ill., 1975). Although in 1955 77.4 percent of all mentally ill patients in the United States were treated in in-patient centers, by 1975 that percentage had fallen to 27.9. At the same time, although state and county mental hospital populations have shrunk, the total hospitalized in general hospitals and community mental health centers has risen, so that the gross rate of hospitalization has risen slightly from 799 per 100,000 in 1955 to 847 per 100,000 in 1975. The biggest change in this recent period has been the explosive growth of outpatient facilities, which grew from usage by 234 patients per 100,000 population in 1955 to 2,185 patients per 100,000 in 1975. U. S. Bureau of the Census, *Statistical Abstract of the U. S.: 1977 (98th edition)* (Washington, D.C., 1977), p. 108, no. 167.

76. And here we find Foucault also most adamant. In *The Archeology of Knowledge*, p. 179, Foucault describes the invention of mental illness as the "linch-pin" of *Madness and Civilization*.

77. *Madness and Civilization*, pp. 40, 46, 65, 72–77.

78. The constant involvement of Renaissance and classical medicine with various kinds of madness hardly needs documentation. But for a good example, see Oskar Diethelm, *Medical Dissertations of Psychiatric Interest Printed Before 1750* (Basel, 1971).

79. Pedro Lain Entralgo has identified in a beautiful way the classical roots of western medicine's overwhelming somatic (or materialist) bias in *The Therapy of the Word in Classical Antiquity* (New Haven, 1970). See also L. J. Rather, *Mind and Body in Eighteenth-Century Medicine: A Study Based on Jerome Gaub's "De Regimine Mentis"* (Berkeley and Los Angeles, 1965).

For a brief introduction to the somatic-psychic controversy, see Erwin Ackerknecht, *A Short History of Psychiatry* (New York, 1959); Dörner, *Bürger und Irre*, pp. 241, 311–12; Schrenk, *Über den Umgang*, pp. 119–30; Riese, *The Legacy of Philippe Pinel*, pp. 9–13. For a recent historical treatment of moral insanity, see S. F. Fullinwider, "Insanity as the Loss of Self: The Moral Insanity Controversy Revisited," *Bulletin of the History of Medicine* 49 (1975): 87–101; and Vieda Skultans, *Madness and Morals: Ideas on Insanity in the Nineteenth Century* (London, 1975). For current thinking on mental illness as illness, see especially Peter Sedgwick, "Illness—Mental and Otherwise," *Hastings Center Report* 1, no. 3 (1973): 19–40; and Miriam Siegler and Humphry Osmond, *Models of Madness, Models of Medicine* (New York, 1974).

80. *Madness and Civilization*, pp. 243–52.

81. Laing, "The Invention of Madness"; Edgar Z. Friedenberg, "Sick, Sick, Sick?" *New York Times Book Review* (22 August 1965), p. 6.

82. Schrenk, *Über den Umgang*, p. 19.

83. Scull, "Museums of Madness," pp. 246–94; Peter McCandless, "Insanity and Society: A Study of the English Lunacy Reform Movement" (Ph.D. diss., University of Wisconsin, 1974); William F. Bynum, "Rationales for Therapy in British Psychiatry: 1780–1835," *Medical History* 18 (1974): 317–34.

84. *Madness and Civilization*, pp. 242–43.

85. Jetter, *Zur Typologie*, pp. 20–36; see also Schrenk, *Über den Umgang*, pp. 5, 18.

86. Schrenk, *Über den Umgang*, p. 18; Riese, *The Legacy of Philippe Pinel*, pp. 2–3.

87. White, "Foucault Decoded," pp. 51–53.

88. Anonymous review: "The Contented Positivist."

89. See the bewildered but favorable comments of Keith Thomas in "An Anthropology of Religion and Magic, II," *Journal of Interdisciplinary History* 6 (Summer 1975): pp. 91–109, at pp. 105–8; and the sharp critique of Jan Miel, "Ideas or Epistemes: Hazard versus Foucault," *Yale French Studies* 49 (1973): 231–45.

90. Even Foucault's most ardent admirers identify his method as intuition; David Matza, "Review of Foucault's *Madness and Civilization*," *American Sociological Review* 31 (1966): 551–52. The citation of numerous references is not exactly the same as disciplining one's intuitions, but Michael Peters exaggerates little in claiming that Foucault's erudition "is at least as authentic as anything one will find employed anywhere else to back up more orthodox theses in the history of ideas"; "Extended Review," pp. 636–37.

91. It is sometimes argued that one can hardly do otherwise than project present-day structures of perception onto one's vision of the past (e.g., Foucault's search for the history of repressive attitudes toward the mad), but "the systematic interconnections which constitute a 'structure' do not necessarily correspond to the sequence of actual stages by which the phenomenon itself came to be constituted." Although Michael Peters applied this criticism to Piaget, it applies to Foucault as well; "Extended Review," p. 636. These reflections bring us directly into the domain of one of J. H. Hexter's favorite topics.

# The Elizabethan Bourgeois Hero-Tale: Aspects of an Adolescent Social Consciousness

*LAURA STEVENSON O'CONNELL*

At the height of the golden age of Elizabethan poetry and drama, there arose a minor literary vogue that deserves the attention of historians concerned with the development of Elizabethan social consciousness. The vogue, itself neither golden nor poetic, was that of the bourgeois hero, the merchant or craftsman whose exploits were praised in order to dignify men of trade.[1] It was created by three of the most popular second-rate Elizabethan authors: Thomas Heywood, who claimed to have had a hand in the composition of two hundred plays; Richard Johnson, a London apprentice turned author whose works sold well throughout the seventeenth century; and Thomas Deloney, a silkweaver whose prose fiction remained popular for over a century after his death.[2] The vogue was continued by authors influenced mainly by Deloney's works: Thomas Dekker and William Rowley, each of whom wrote a play based on *The Gentle Craft, Part I;* William Haughton, who collaborated with several other dramatists in four plays based on *Thomas of Reading;* and Henry Robarts, a seaman and unsuccessful pamphleteer, whose novel *Haigh for Devonshire* was obviously inspired by Deloney's popularity.[3] Between 1591 and 1608, these authors and a handful of anonymous playwrights wrote nineteen works that dealt with the achievements of merchants, clothiers, craftsmen, and apprentices.

The bourgeois hero-tale, like its more aristocratic contemporary, Euphuistic prose fiction, was short-lived, although the continuing popularity of the best works of both sorts suggests that readers enjoyed them long after they ceased to be written.[4] Euphuistic fiction, however, has fared better in the long run than the bourgeois hero-tale; while literary critics still study Euphuism as an experiment in the elasticity of Elizabethan English, the bourgeois hero-tale has received little attention since 1935, when Louis Wright published *Middle-Class Culture in Elizabethan England*. Nor is the reason for this neglect far to seek. Wright believed that the bourgeois hero-tale, like the rest of the literature he studied, reflected the self-consciousness of a large Elizabethan middle class; but recent historians, having witnessed the controversy over the gentry, no longer believe that such a class existed.[5] Though the controversy resolved little about the rise or fall of the gentry, it did call attention to the difficulties that arose when historians divided preindustrial society into three Marxist classes and attributed the Renaissance, the Reformation, and the Civil War to the rise of the middle class. As J. H. Hexter pointed out in the course of the debate, the middle class had come to include merchants, gentry, yeomen, and even monarchs—any or all of these groups, depending on the whim of the historian. Properly speaking, Hexter argued, it ought to include only "merchants, financiers, industrialists, the town rich, the *bourgeoisie*"— a small fraction of Tudor society that was neither class-conscious nor powerful. So persuasive was Hexter's argument that in the years following his attack on the "myth of the middle class," historians discarded the Marxist paradigm, constructing instead new models of the Tudor social hierarchy that omitted the middle class altogether.[6] Wright's conclusions about the implications—and even the existence—of middle-class culture now became suspect; for if there was no large middle class in Tudor England, there can have been no literature written for it.

The problem, as even the most sceptical reader of *Middle-Class Culture* has to admit, is that many Elizabethan authors wrote books specifically appealing to the self-consciousness of merchants and craftsmen. There is, moreoever, no denying that the "town rich"—the oligarchies that monopolized civic government—encouraged such literary output directly by subsidizing popular authors and indirectly by founding grammar schools in all parts of England.[7] Finally, recent research has shown that the increased availability of education, coming at a time when many craftsmen were prosperous enough to send their sons to school instead of using their labor at home, caused a dramatic growth of literacy among men of trade. In the suburbs of London, for example, tradesman literacy rose from 31 percent in the 1580s to 69 percent in the first decade of the seventeenth century; during the same period, the literacy of tradesmen in Norfolk and Suffolk rose from 39 percent to 52 percent. In London, where almost all Elizabethan printing was done and where books were most easily available, 82 percent of the tradesmen were literate at the time the bourgeois hero-tale became popular.[8] Thus, even if there was no large middle class such as Wright described, there were bourgeois hero-tales, and there were tradesmen who could read them.

The message of the bourgeois hero-tale was simple: merchants, clothiers, craftsmen, and apprentices were as useful to the commonwealth as the aristocracy and the gentry. This was certainly true. Though the clothing trade had suffered a depression in the mid-sixteenth century, it was still England's primary industry. The loans of London merchants financed Elizabethan policy and the splendor of the Elizabethan court. In times of war, London's city fathers levied troops for the queen. And in the second half of the sixteenth century, newly chartered companies of great merchants increased England's power and prosperity by finding new markets for English goods.[9]

Curiously enough, however, the figures chosen for celebration in bourgeois hero-tales are praised for virtues having nothing to do with economics or the realities of mercantile service. The most popular figure extolled in the tales, for example, is William Walworth, the lord mayor of London who defended Richard II against the leader of the Jack Straw Rebellion in 1381.[10] All the authors praise Walworth's personal, chivalric service enthusiastically. In Richard Johnson's *Nine Worthies of London*, Walworth appears as an ancient warrior who does not shun "death, or grievous pain, / To follow him that is his sovereign." It is this hero, not the knights in the king's train, who wades into the crowd of jeering rebels and stabs their leader; it is the merchant, not the courtiers, who is "a light to all ensuing ages" because he does not "falter or refuse any peril to profit his country and purchase honor."[11] Honor is a strange commodity for a merchant to purchase, but in the play *The Life and Death of Jack Straw*, Walworth is similarly praised for attaining it. His "magnanimity" is carefully compared to that of the ancient Romans, and he assures Richard II that like Rome, London will be "such a storehouse still, / As not alone you shall command our wealth, / But loyal hearts." He adds, with emphasis on his quasi-feudal loyalty, "God

I praise, that with this holy hand, / Hath given me heart to free my prince and land."[12] London may be a storehouse, but London's mayor speaks the language of chivalry, not the language of the countinghouse, and it is his heroism that brings honor to his city.

Walworth's service was undoubtedly exceptional; most fishmongers do not have such an opportunity to prove they are the king's loyal vassals. But Walworth is not the only merchant praised for chivalric service in the bourgeois hero-tales. When Thomas Heywood wants to glorify merchants in *1 Edward IV*, he too places them in a heroic setting, devoting one act of the play entirely to the London business community's battle with the Bastard Fauconbridge and his rebels. The audience learns that

> whole companies
> Of Mercers, Grocers, Drapers, and the rest,
> Are drawn together for their best defense,
> Beside the tower . . .

ready to die for Edward's right to rule England. Heywood goes out of his way to show that the heroism of these men is not exceptional; the lord mayor urges his men to act as valiantly as "a hundred Walworths" in the coming fray, and the apprentices tell the rebels they are continuing the tradition of "memorable actions" performed by London's apprentices in the past.[13]

The heroes of the Walworth stories and Heywood's play are obviously designed to appeal to Londoners' "citizen pride."[14] But the service that is praiseworthy in fishmongers, mercers, grocers, drapers, and the rest is quasi-feudal service; merchants are shown to be as good as knights at the very things knights are supposed to do. This is puzzling to the modern reader, for he would expect civic pride to result in the glorification of merchants who were fundamentally different from knights, not social miniatures of the elite.

The works that celebrate the deeds of apprentices yield further insight into the social ideology of bourgeois hero-tales. These works are designed to appeal to the pride of adolescent merchants and craftsmen; and it is not surprising, therefore, to find that many of them demonstrate the virility of these young men, or that the demonstration is a military one.[15] It is surprising, however, to find that Elizabethan authors cannot cope with the figure of the low-born man who turns military hero.

To begin with, most of the "apprentices" in bourgeois hero-tales are actually princes in disguise. Crispianus, the chivalric shoemaker in Deloney's *Gentle Craft, Part I*, is the son of a king, as is his counterpart in Rowley's *A Shoemaker, a Gentleman*; the heroes of Heywood's *Four Prentices of London* are the sons of an earl. Furthermore, these aristocrats make no secret of their long-ing to give up trade and return to their "natural" vocations as warriors: Rowley's Crispianus volunteers to fight in the army, and Heywood's apprentices agree with their eldest brother when he sighs, "if I knew where to go to war, / I would not stay in London one hour longer."[16] This technique is supposed to show apprentices that noblemen admire their mettle; in the heat of battle, Heywood's Four Prentices long for the help of "honest Prentices" so that "the doubtful day's success we need not fear."[17] Socially, however, these apprentices are no more "bourgeois" than the heroes of chivalric romance who leave their humble homes upon finding that they are princes' sons; what they really show is that no amount of manual labor takes away an aristo-crat's native military ability.[18]

When the bourgeois tales concern the feats of real apprentices, they run into further difficulties. At one end of the spectrum, attempts to reconcile an apprentice's fictional heroism with his later factual life as a merchant are notably unsuccessful. In John-son's *Nine Worthies of London*, the reader meets the ghost of Christopher Crocker, a man "carrying in his brows the picture of Mars, and in his manners the majesty of a prince"; he turns out to be a vintner who says he spent his youth working hard so that his "master's purse might thrive." His diligence, he adds, won him the undying love of his master's daughter, but to make him-self worthy of her love, he went to France with Edward III, killed scores of enemy soldiers, and was knighted. Having thus proved that "a prentice (though but small esteemed) / Unto the stoutest never giveth way," he returned to London, settled down to trade, and married his boss's daughter.[19] It apparently does not occur to this warlike vintner (or to his creator) that a knighthood might be more than an assertion of virility, and that trade might not look quite so attractive to a knight as it had to a stout-hearted but lowly apprentice.

At the other end of the spectrum, the authors who do not try to reconcile chivalry with business write pure bombastic fantasy. The hero of the popular ballad "The Honour of a London Pren-tice," for example, is sent to Turkey by his master. Unaccount-ably, he sees fit to appear in a tournament, where he bravely kills the Turkish prince. The sultan throws the apprentice to two very hungry lions, and it appears that all is lost. But the boy saves the day by calmly reaching down the throats of both lions (simultane-ously, one assumes), tearing their hearts out, and throwing them to the sultan. This act of valorous impudence convinces the sultan that an English son-in-law is better than a Turkish son, and he gives his daughter to the honorable apprentice for a bride.[20] The reader never learns what happens to the commodities the apprentice had been sent to buy.

The chivalric praise of bourgeois heroes in these tales is perplexing to a modern reader. The merchant in full armor and the apprentice who tears out lions' hearts are comic figures, yet the stories in which they appear were very seriously written. It is essential to realize, however, that these tales juxtapose elements that we consider to be mutually exclusive, but that Elizabethans did not. Bourgeois hero-tales are the literary equivalents of sixteenth-century accounts kept partly in roman numerals, partly in arabic numbers; old and new systems of ideas sit side by side on a single page, somewhat uneasily, but with no specific sense of incongruity. In the episodes above, the authors are appealing to the pride of merchants and apprentices, but they make that appeal in the language (and the social ideology) of the elite. Though they wish to prove that merchants have a dignified tradition of service to the realm, the idea that *mercantile* service is dignified does not occur to them. The tales are designed to show that bourgeois heroes, *even though* they are merchants, are as brave as—or braver than—knights. At the same time, however, the chivalric motifs in the tales suggest that the old system of social values, which is precapitalist and based upon the ideal of a stratified, rural hierarchy, is being used to evoke the social consciousness of urban businessmen. The old terminology clearly does not fit its new role comfortably; the authors either abandon the attempt to praise businessmen for doing business or construct hybrid figures who wear armor in the countinghouse.

There is, however, one Elizabethan work that makes a serious attempt to reconcile chivalric motifs and bourgeois service—*Jack of Newbury,* the first novel of the best and most influential creator of bourgeois tales, Thomas Deloney. The hero of the novel is a famous and semilegendary clothier who lived in the reign of Henry VIII. Deloney adopts Jack's legend and enhances it by telling of his rise to fortune, portraying his mythical clothing establishment, and relating a series of tales that prove he is worthy of his wealth.[21] One of the first episodes in the book concerns Jack's loyalty to the king as it is expressed in military terms. When the Scots invade England in 1513, Jack (who is technically a yeoman) is required to bring six men to the field. Instead, he brings one hundred fifty, all dressed in "white coats, and red caps with yellow feathers," and he rides in front of them on a "goodly barbed horse," dressed in full armor. Most of the county elite admire Jack's showy contribution, but some envious gentlemen sneer that he is "more prodigal than prudent, and more vain-glorious than well-advised, seeing that the best Nobleman in the Country would scarce have done so much." A lord, they add, would of course know that the king often asks for troops, and so he "would do at one time as [he] might be able to do at another." Jack, however, denies that he is being ostentatious. Observing to Queen Catherine that the gentlemen are merely jealous because he has surpassed them in "hearty affection" to his king, he is careful to let her know that he, unlike the lord who counts the cost of service, will give everything he has to serve her:

Gentleman I am none, nor the son of a Gentleman, but a poor Clothier, whose lands are his Looms, having no other Rents but what I get from the backs of little sheep: nor can I claim any cognisance but a wooden shuttle. Nevertheless, most gracious Queen, these my poor servants and myself, with life and goods, are ready at your Majesty's command, not only to spend our bloods, but also to lose our lives in defense of our King and Country.[22]

The scene is still that of the Walworth stories and *1 Edward IV*: a monarch in need meets a businessman in armor and is assured of the businessman's undying loyalty. But Deloney, unlike the other authors, is not at all concerned with Jack's personal heroism; Jack's troops are in fact rendered unnecessary by the victory at Flodden Field. Instead of presenting Jack as a knight, Deloney portrays him as the mounted lord of a band of feudal retainers and then shows that the basis of Jack's lordship is not birth and land, but looms, shuttles, and sheep. This change in emphasis shifts the theme of the story from chivalry to social power. Deloney has shown that the clothing trade makes Jack the most powerful man in Berkshire; a man wealthy enough to raise Jack's army counts as a lord, not as a yeoman. The social implications of that revelation are disturbing; the country gentlemen are quite right to be upset.

Deloney, while perceptive in his mixture of chivalric and bourgeois motifs, has no radical social vision. Whatever the wider implications of the episode, it is *used* merely to prove that Jack is the king's loyal vassal. The language Deloney uses neither invites nor permits him to say that trade makes clothiers as a class more powerful than gentlemen as a class. He lets the matter rest when he has proved that a clothier's loyalty can be as useful as a lord's. It is possible, too, that he was disturbed by the social implications of the scene. None of his later heroes appear in a similar position of military power: the valorous shoemakers in *The Gentle Craft* are princes or courtiers, and the clothiers in *Thomas of Reading* leave war to their betters. Deloney seems to have turned away from the questions *Jack of Newbury* raised.

The military motif used in the praise of bourgeois heroes reveals the limitation of the authors' social consciousness most plainly; but further examination of the tales shows that all the episodes designed to appeal to merchant pride are similarly circumscribed by precapitalist assumptions. To begin with, when the authors want to assert the dignity of trade, they do not say that trade is good for the nation; they say that gentlemen think well enough of merchants to apprentice their sons to them. Thus, in *The Nine Worthies*, the mercer John Bonham informs the reader that his father was a knight, "yet thought no scorn / To place his son within a prenticehood."[23] Similarly, in Heywood's *Four Prentices of London*, the Earl of Bouloigne informs his daughter that her brothers "have no scorn" of their civic trades although they are of noble blood.[24] And in *The Gentle Craft, Part I*, Deloney promises to tell the reader about "worthy and renowned Kings, / and divers Lords and Knights also," who took up shoemaking in hard times and found shoemakers fine companions, a motif Dekker and Rowley adopt when they use Deloney as a source for their plays.[25]

Furthermore, the authors are eager to prove that a gentleman who enters trade need give up none of his aristocratic ideals, because merchants are not narrow misers who think only of cloth and spices, but dignified men with a tradition of aristocratic magnificence who (to all appearances) simply practice trade in their spare time. Thus, the adjectives applied to bourgeois heroes could be applied with equal ease to Elyot's governor. Henry Robarts, for example, praises the merchant William of Exeter as a man of "good behavior, charity, and good conscience," and he describes the other merchants as men of "liberal hands," generous housekeeping, "bounty, mirth and fellowship."[26] In Johnson's *Nine Worthies*, Thomas White appears as a man whose "liberal hand" has enriched all the "chief boroughs" of England; as lord mayor of London, he has "judged all causes right in each degree" and has never been "partial in the law."[27] Deloney's Simon Eyre is commended specifically for being "a good Master" to his men.[28] Benevolence, liberality, justice, care for servants—these are the virtues of Elizabethan bourgeois heroes.

The problem of how the bourgeois hero handles his money receives much attention in the tales, but praise for the proper use of wealth does not always take the form one would expect. Johnson's jest-book figure Old Hobson chides a servant for burying gold instead of putting it to use, in an ill-concealed plagiarism from an earlier jest-book (and the Parable of the Talents); but the servant is reprimanded not for lack of business enterprise but for "covetousness."[29] Jack of Newbury is careful not to spend more than one shilling a week on merriment, but this is a trick he has learned as a social defense—everybody borrowed from him when he lent money at the tavern, and so he stopped. Deloney assures the reader that Jack is not "at any time a churl of his purse," but a man who can "spend money with the best" and become "every gentleman's companion."[30] Jack's diligence and prudence, in short, do not prevent him from spending like a gentleman when the occasion demands it.

The reader of bourgeois hero-tales, in fact, may be pardoned for wondering why the occasion requires bourgeois heroes to spend money like gentlemen so frequently. The reason is not difficult to find: the tales are told in reaction to earlier literary portrayals of merchants as usurers and misers, and so it is essential for the authors to show that their heroes can be as magnificent as any governor. Here again, old values conflict with new social pride, for some authors find themselves obliged to praise gratuitous extravagance in order to show that merchants think nothing of money. Henry Robarts, for example, says the motto of his six west country merchants is "A straw for a peck of royals!" To prove it, he constructs an episode in which James, the factor of William of Exeter, defends the honor of Englishmen by gambling with a Spanish duke for a valuable jewel—and losing "not only all the wealth he [has] gained, but his Master's stock, and all the goods he [has] of other Merchants to deal for as factor."[31] William of Exeter takes the loss in good part, for he too accounts the honor of Englishmen higher than mere money. One cannot help noticing, however, that James's lack of avarice has cost his master a fortune. The same sort of extravagance appears in Heywood's *If You Know Not Me, You Know Nobody*, in which Sir Thomas Gresham buys an expensive pearl, powders it, and drinks it as a toast to the queen.[32] Like Robarts' gambling scene, this episode is supposed to show that merchants disdain loss; but the examples actually suggest that Heywood and Robarts expect a wealthy merchant to indulge in conspicuous expenditure on an aristocratic scale.

There was, fortunately, a happier method of demonstrating the wealth and magnificence of merchants than praising their ability to squander money with good grace. This was to show that a merchant could give a banquet that was literally fit for a king. In almost every bourgeois tale the hero gives a feast for his monarch—an episode that allows him to display both his loyalty and his financial ability to express it. In the hands of Johnson or Robarts, the banquet scene is simply a display of money, but in the hands of more thoughtful authors, the motif is used as a basis for social commentary.

In Dekker's *The Shoemakers' Holiday*, Simon Eyre, a poor shoemaker who has become lord mayor of London, gives a feast to which he invites all the apprentices of London and the king. Dekker uses the scene to imply that monarch, merchant, and apprentices are all equals in wit and good fellowship. Eyre is not defensive about his background; in fact, he calls attention to his lowly occupation with pride. As the king enters, Eyre asks him to pardon his "rude behavior," adding, with a play on words, "I am a handicrafts man, yet my heart is without craft." Assured that his boldness is in fact appreciated, Eyre expresses his loyalty in the rhetoric he uses in talking to men of all social levels; he tells his monarch that though he values his own beard at a king's ransom, he is willing to shave it off "and stuff tennis balls with it to please my bully king."[33] Eyre's familiarity does not limit the deference he feels for the king, but he is not self-deprecating. He thanks the king for coming to his "poor" banquet, but the fare he offers is "poor" only because nothing is worthy of the king's grace. Eyre uses his roughness to imply that the relationship between kings and merchants is so friendly that the merchant does not need to adopt the rhetoric of the court in the king's presence. The scene has a double significance. It shows that Eyre can live up to aristocratic standards of liberality, fidelity, and personal charm; but it also shows that Eyre is his own man as well as the king's, and it suggests that a monarch must appreciate a merchant for what he is.

In Heywood's *1 Edward IV* there appears a banquet scene that is more challenging in its attitude toward genteel virtues than Dekker's feast. The banquet is given for Edward IV by John Crosby, lord mayor of London, and it is carefully presented as the high point of Crosby's life. The audience is reminded that Crosby was a foundling, raised at a hospital, apprenticed to the grocers' company, and that he has finally risen to the mayorality and been knighted by Edward for his services against Fauconbridge. Although Crosby preens himself before the mirror while he waits for the king to arrive, looking forward to the banquet and reflecting upon his past life, he is no fawning parvenu. When Edward enters, Crosby welcomes him graciously, dismissing his role in London's defense as mere "duty, / Thereto obliged by true subjects' zeal," and thanking the king for gracing his feast. But the banquet that starts so ceremoniously ends in disaster; Edward meets Mistress Shore at Crosby's house and is so taken with her that he ignores the mayor completely. Finally, overcome by his feelings, he "starts from the table," says brusquely, "Thanks for my cheer, Lord mayor! I am not well," and leaves abruptly. Crosby is crushed ("Oh, God! here to be ill! My house to cause my Sovereign's discontent!"), but he remains loyal. Standing alone upon the stage with the untouched banquet heaped before him, he sighs that he wishes the king had been satisfied

> With the poor entertainment of his Mayor,
> His humble vassal, whose lands, whose life, and all,
> Are, and in duty must be always, his.[34]

Here, the "humble vassal" has displayed a far greater depth of fidelity than his overlord. The play does not judge Edward harshly, but this scene and the scene in which Edward seduces Mistress Shore suggest that Edward's courtly behavior, unlike the London citizen's loyal conduct, is merely a cover for what in Heywood's plays are consistently the greatest of faults—callousness and ingratitude.

In the hands of Deloney, however, the social commentary in the banquet scene takes on a truly challenging aspect. Like the other authors, Deloney uses the banquet to demonstrate the wealth and personal merit of his hero. He makes his point, however, by comparing Jack of Newbury to the greatest of Henry VIII's courtiers, changing the issue from fellowship and good manners to the proper use of wealth, status, and power. Again, by using the language of the elite to glorify his clothier, Deloney turns that language inside out.

The merchants in other bourgeois tales begin their feasts by showing their monarchs what loyal vassals they are. Jack takes a different approach; he does not entertain Henry VIII until the king has recognized him as a prince in his own domain. When he hears that Henry is in Berkshire, Jack dresses thirty of his men in livery and gives them swords. He dresses himself in a russet coat and slops, attire fitting his yeoman status. He and his men go to an anthill near the road along which Henry and his train are to pass, and pretend to defend it. The king sees them and sends a herald to ask who they are. Jack says that he is "poor Jack of Newbury, who being scant Marquis of Molehill, is chosen Prince of Ants." He adds that he is defending the Ants against the "furious wrath of the Prince of Butterflies." The king is amused, though he does not fully grasp the implications of Jack's pose; he sends for Jack to come speak with him. But Jack replies to the shocked herald: "his Grace hath a horse and I am on foot; therefore will him to come to me." Surprisingly enough, Henry comes, saying he is content to ride to this "Emperor of Ants, that is so careful in his government."

Once Henry has accepted Jack as an emperor, Jack becomes a humble vassal. Claiming that the arrival of the king has dispersed

his foes, he explains the war of Ants and Butterflies. The Butterfly, he says, was oppressing the industrious commonwealth of the
Ants, but the Ants dared not complain because of the Butterfly's
"golden apparel." Since nobody stopped the Butterfly, he became
"so ambitious and malapert, that the poor Ant could no sooner
get an egg into her nest, but he would have it away." Then the
Butterfly "assembled a great many other of his own coat, by
windy wars to root this painful people out of the land, that he
himself might be seated above them all." At this point, Jack prepared to withstand the Butterfly, until the king's arrival put all
the Butterflies to flight.[35] The Butterfly, of course, is Cardinal
Wolsey, whose wars have caused a depression in the clothing
industry; and Wolsey understands the allegory only too well.
Henry, however, is so delighted with Jack's tale and his loyalty
that he decides to visit Jack's establishment.

When the king arrives at Jack's house, he receives a present that
is both expensive and politically instructive. It is a golden beehive, out of which springs a "flourishing green tree" bearing
golden apples. Both tree and beehive are beset by serpents, but the
serpents are trampled down by two virtues. The virtues hold an
inscription that informs Henry that the icon is "the figure of a
flourishing Commonwealth: / Where virtuous subjects labor
with delight." The serpents, Ambition, Envy, and Treason, strive
to destroy the commonwealth, but Prudence and Fortitude destroy them. "Thus," the inscription concludes, "are they foiled
that mount with means unmeet, / and so like slaves are trodden
under feet."[36] Jack's present to Henry shows iconographically that
the tree of commonwealth is supported by the busy community
of clothiers. Both the clothiers and the commonwealth are threatened by the ambition of the serpentine Wolsey, who has risen to
power by improper means and who can be controlled only with
the help of the monarch's prudence and fortitude.[37]

Lest Henry should miss the meaning of his present, Jack gives
him a guided tour of his clothing establishment after a magnificent feast "served all in glass." Some historians have interpreted
this tour as a portrait—perhaps somewhat glorified—of a typical
sixteenth-century "factory."[38] Deloney, however, is not concerned with the working conditions of weavers and spinners; the
tour, like Jack's other pageants, is designed to show the king why
the Commonwealth of Ants deserves protection from the Prince
of Butterflies. And surprisingly enough, Deloney does not use the
tour to prove that the clothiers' diligence and thrift supports
the commonwealth whereas Wolsey's conspicuous expenditure
ruins it. The contrast between labor and extravagance is indeed
implicit in the scene; a reader familiar with Cavendish's *Life and
Death of Cardinal Wolsey* can easily compare Jack's fruitful

establishment with Wolsey's household of gaudily dressed cooks, ushers, servants, yeomen, and chapel processions of forty priests in matching copes. One may doubt, however, that Elizabethan readers would have made much of the contrast, even though Cavendish's work was familiar to many of them through the chronicles of Holinshed and Stow.[39] For a close reading of the passage reveals that Jack does not ask Henry to protect the realm from the idleness and display of the Butterflies, but from the social woes that are the result of the Prince of Butterflies' pride.

In the first room the king finds two hundred men working at looms and singing about the benefits of lowly estate; he remarks on their good cheer and gives them one hundred angels to spend on a feast. In the next room, Henry finds a great number of pretty spinners and carders contentedly singing about the treachery of a Scot; he casts them "a great reward." By the time the king has seen the fulling mills and the dye house, where more people are cheerfully working, he has learned the lesson Jack hopes to teach. He remarks at "what a great number of people were by this one man set on work," and he adds "that no Trade in all the Land was so much to be cherished and maintained as this, which (quoth he) may well be called, The life of the poor." The Nation of Ants deserves protection because it supports men and women who would otherwise be poor and unemployed.

But Jack can employ the poor only under certain conditions, and the last pageant Henry sees, put on by ninety-six poor children who make money by picking burrs out of wool, drives home that point. One of the children, dressed as Diana, presents the king with four prisoners: Bellona, goddess of war, and her three daughters, Famine, Sword, and Fire. All four are terrifyingly dressed, and Famine is described in particular detail. This is a plea of the poor for an end to Wolsey's "windy wars," which (as Deloney has carefully explained) cause depressions in the clothing industry and widespread unemployment among the families of the poor children. The children do not wish the king to end war at the expense of honor—they present him with two servants, Fame and Victory, and tell them to wait upon their prince forever. The pageant suggests, however, that the clothing industry cannot be "the life of the poor" unless the king realizes that the welfare of the Commonwealth of Ants is more important to England's well-being than the ambitious wars of the Prince of Butterflies. Impressed with the little play, the courtiers find a short-term solution to the problem of the poor children. The queen remarks that "God gives as fair children to the poor as to the rich, and fairer many times," and she, Henry, and the noblemen in their train acknowledge this fact by adopting all ninety-six children, giving them places at court, an education at the universities, or gentlemen's livings. The children are so worthy of promotion that all become "men of great account" in the realm.[40]

And so Jack has instructed his monarch in the duties of governance. He has shown Henry that a clothier can give as lavish a feast as any courtier in the realm, Wolsey included. He has taught the king that clothiers are important to the commonwealth because they set the poor to work. And he has suggested that the king should be a prince like Jack, who cares for his people and sees his position as a social obligation, not a prince like Wolsey, who uses his power only to heap further glories upon himself at the expense of the poor. But Jack has *not* taught Henry that he should change his social ideology. Deloney does not compare Jack to the aristocracy of birth, nor does he condemn courtiers per se; he never suggests that the king's court is extravagant and wasteful while Jack and his ants are diligent and thrifty. Jack's banquet, after all, is conspicuous expenditure at its height, and ninety-six of his workers are promoted to a life of leisure that Deloney unhesitatingly presents as being far better than any employment Jack can give them. Deloney carefully compares Jack only to a man who has risen from origins as humble as his own and forgotten that the *existing* social ideology thrusts responsibility upon men of wealth and position.[41] It is Wolsey's pride, not his idleness and extravagance, that makes him beggar the poor by conjuring up wars to win. And it is Jack's sense of justice and charity, not his belief in the intrinsic value of hard work, that makes him look out for the welfare of his weavers, spinners, and carders.

As Henry VIII leaves Jack's house, he wants to acknowledge the clothier's service by knighting him. But Jack, unlike Crosby, Walworth, and the heroes of *The Nine Worthies*, declines the offer. He asks to remain a "poor clothier" among his people, whose welfare he values more than "all the vain titles of Gentility":

for these are the laboring Ants whom I seek to defend, and these be the Bees which I keep: who labor in this life, not for ourselves, but for the glory of God, and to do service to our dread Sovereign.

Henry presses the honor on Jack, but Jack is firm. Honor, he says, makes men forget their origins,

and to the end I may still keep in mind from whence I came, and what I am, I beseech your Grace let me rest in my russet coat, a poor Clothier to my dying day.[42]

Accepting a knighthood would put Jack in Wolsey's category—that of a man who forgets social duty in the thirst for promotion.

There is, however, more in Jack's refusal than his desire to avoid the sin of pride. The phrases in which he denies himself honor recall all the incidents in which he has shown himself to be a prince. He asks to remain a "poor Clothier" in his "russet coat"; but it was "poor Jack of Newbury" who identified himself to the herald as Prince of Ants, and it was the man in the russet coat who refused to come when the king commanded. Jack asks to live among his people, but he describes them as his subjects: they are the ants that he *defends,* the bees that he *keeps.* To a man who is a prince in his own commonwealth, a knighthood is indeed a "vain title of gentility."

In describing Jack as a prince, however, Deloney speaks of the clothier's power and wealth in terms that were originally designed to describe power of a different sort, and this strains the meaning of the terms he uses. A man may be a "prince" not because the king has promoted him, but because his trade has made him powerful and independent. A man can have "subjects" who work for him at an industrial enterprise. The clothing trade is a "commonwealth" unto itself. By implication, then, social power (lordship, princeliness) depends not solely upon birth or royal favor, but also upon industrious commercial service and the great wealth that comes from it. Deloney is far from insisting that aristocracy of birth should be replaced by aristocracy of trade, but his presentation of the Prince of Ants gropes toward the suggestion that social power and pride could conceivably be determined by economic interest.

Jack of Newbury has frequently been called a typical bourgeois hero, a figure who exemplifies the excitement felt by middle-class Elizabethans at the power of money.[43] In fact, Jack is unique among bourgeois heroes because his power is *not* accompanied by a tangible rise in social status. Jack is also unique among Deloney's heroes. In *The Gentle Craft,* the apprentice-princes, poor boys who become wealthy, and businessmen who accept promotion as their due are very like the heroes in the works of Robarts or Johnson. The clothiers to whom Deloney returns in *Thomas of Reading* are not men of Jack's dimensions.[44] Indeed, Deloney seems consciously to have made them provincial so that they do not threaten the values of the elite. When these clothiers meet the king, one remarks sagely that he "had rather speak to his King's Majesty, than to many Justices of peace." When these clothiers give a banquet for the princes of England, one of them asks the cook to make a "good store of pottage," and another fails to attend because he has been strung up like a sausage on the rafters of an inn as punishment for trying to seduce the innkeeper's wife.[45] These men are wealthy and patriotic, but they are by their own admission "country folk," not lords or princes of industrial commonwealths.

In the three novels that followed *Jack of Newbury*, then, Deloney retreated from the sociological threshold he had been so close to crossing in his earliest one. And ironically, his less powerful, more ordinary heroes were adopted enthusiastically by the authors of later bourgeois hero-tales. *The Gentle Craft* was used as a source for two plays; *Thomas of Reading* influenced four plays (all of which are lost) and a novel. But the playwrights never touched *Jack of Newbury*—its social implications were apparently unstageable. The ideas in Deloney's most searching work remained unrevived and unexamined throughout the last years of the life of the bourgeois hero-tale.

Deloney died in the early months of 1600, and the bourgeois hero-tale lumbered to its death within the next seven years. During these years, there arose a new vogue of "citizen comedy," created by Ben Jonson and taken up by playwrights more skillful than Rowley and better at writing "finished," elegant plays than Heywood. The new comedy was about London citizens and was certainly concerned with the problem of social status, but it revived the very citizen villains the hero-tales had tried to replace. The year Deloney died, John Marston introduced the villainous usurer Mammon in *Jack Drum's Entertainment*; within a few months of the first production of Heywood's *If You Know Not Me, You Know Nobody*, Middleton revitalized the old plot of a gentleman's misfortunes at the hands of a usurious merchant in *Michaelmas Term*. And for the most part, merchants appeared on stage throughout the seventeenth century as avaricious men with aspirations to gentility.

There are many reasons why bourgeois heroes were eclipsed by citizen villains. Most simply, literary fashion changed. The comedy of Jonson, Middleton, Massinger, and Marston was satirical; it dealt with the foibles of all ranks of men, and it extended a sceptical view of society to its audience. In this scheme of things, citizens came off no worse than impoverished knights, indebted gentlemen, booby squires, and self-seeking servants; but the sophistication of the new comedy made the inflated praise of civic heroes look naive (as indeed it often was), and bombast quickly went out of favor. Furthermore, the creators of the new comedy poked fun at the unstylish playwrights who pandered to popular taste for bourgeois heroes, pointing out that the old comedy was written for men who could not possibly live up to its ideals.

A glance at the plays that satirize bourgeois hero-tales shows how perceptively the Jacobean playwrights ridicule the fantasy of Heywood, Johnson, and Robarts. In *Eastward Ho!* (1605), for example, Jonson, Marston, and Chapman present Touchstone, a diligent goldsmith whose morality is formed entirely by the time-worn aphorisms of John Heywood's *Proverbs,* but whose plodding imagination is touched by such bourgeois heroes as Walworth and Gresham. When Golding, Touchstone's apprentice, becomes an alderman's deputy, Touchstone eagerly looks forward to the time when he will be a civic hero like Whittington, see his deeds played "by the best companies of actors, and be called their get-penny."[46] But who is this worthy apprentice whose social ambition is to get actors a long run? No Jack of Newbury, but a man so miserly that he flinches at the thought of having a feast at his own wedding, insisting that "the superfluity and cold meat left" from the marriage of Touchstone's daughter will furnish his table "with bounty."[47] The virtue of magnificence is utterly beyond his imagination. The same is true of the citizens in Beaumont and Fletcher's *Knight of the Burning Pestle* (1607); they cannot understand a play that has the slightest complication of plot or character, but they want to see their stage-struck apprentice Ralph kill a lion, court a king's daughter, rescue prisoners from a giant, and die nobly at the end of a comedy. The popular plays over which they and citizens like them tyrannize, according to Beaumont and Fletcher, only encourage the childish dreams and bad taste of London theater audiences.

This kind of satire could not have killed the bourgeois hero-tale if it had been healthier. It did not, in fact, kill the popular taste for bourgeois heroes, as the continued popularity of *Jack of Newbury* and Heywood's *Four Prentices* (and the stage failure of *The Knight of the Burning Pestle*) proves. The satirists were merely instrumental in stopping the creation of tales that might very well have continued to bring profits to authors, printers, and actors alike—a fact that suggests the bourgeois hero died as much from internal weakness as from external attack.

The weakness of the bourgeois hero was not just that he was implausible; the heroes of chivalric romance were implausible, too. His ailment was the puzzling and potentially subversive nature of his achievement. The social consciousness of which he was the product was outgrowing the assumption that trade was necessarily ignoble and tradesmen were inferior to gentlemen; but it was not yet ready to shed the older assumptions completely. As the spokesman for this adolescent consciousness, the bourgeois hero asked perceptive questions about accepted social ideology. Was an apprentice who fought bravely as good as a knight? Could a wealthy clothier rival the power of Cardinal Wolsey? And if not, why not? Unfortunately, the terms in which the questions were cast prevented them from being answered thoughtfully. It was all too easy to point out that the tales were fantastic—there *were* no apprentices who tore out lions' hearts, no clothiers who owned a hundred looms. And the creators of the tales were helpless in the face of this charge, for though they could repeat stories of apprentice heroism and merchant banquets *ad nauseam*, they could not see that they needed to prove that trade had intrinsic merit. The idea was unthinkable; even Deloney failed to consider it. And so the bourgeois hero-tales continued to insist that men of trade were worthy members of the commonwealth because they could live up to the standards of the gentry.

The political and social events of the years following Deloney's death made the aspirations of bourgeois heroes seem more threatening than naive; for in the first nine months of his reign, James I created 1,161 knights.[48] The overgenerous distribution of knighthoods was far more dignified than the wholesale commerce in higher titles that began with Buckingham's period of influence. Yet it was shocking enough to a generation accustomed to Elizabeth's parsimony with honors, and it was the first dignity the crown allowed to be sold.[49] Gentility had long been a reward for "ancient riches," but now it was a reward for the possession of ready cash. Baptist Hicks bought a knighthood and continued to keep a shop in London; and the possibility that stories about heroic merchants could encourage other such financiers to pose as William Walworth or Simon Eyre added barbs to the pens already sharpened to attack the cheapened titles.[50] The satirists wrote play after play ridiculing the vulgarity of citizen taste, portraying London merchants as men who wanted to cheat their way into gentility, and pointing out that, contrary to what the bourgeois hero-tales had said, a merchant could not possibly adopt the honorable code of the elite. The bourgeois hero disappeared from the stage and from prose fiction. He lived on, fittingly enough, in ballad literature about heroic apprentices, an unchanging product of adolescent consciousness that appealed to generations of adolescents.[51]

When the bourgeois hero reappeared in the early eighteenth century, he was a spokesman for a social consciousness that had come of age. He had shed his respect not just for the gentry, but for the values of the gentry. Mr. Sealand, for example, the merchant in Steele's *Conscious Lovers* (1722), remarks testily that merchants

are as honorable and almost as useful as you landed folks that have always thought yourselves so much above us; for your trading, forsooth, is extended no farther than a load of hay or a fat ox. You are a pleasant people, indeed, because you are bred up to be lazy; therefore, I warrant you, industry is dishonorable.[52]

Six years later, Defoe echoes this remark in *A Plan of the English Commerce:*

If Usefulness give an Addition to the Character, either of Men or Things, as without doubt it does; Trading-men will have the Preference in almost all the Disputes you can bring: There is not a Nation in the known World, but have tasted the benefit, and owe their Prosperity to the useful Improvements of Commerce: Even the self-vain Gentry, that would decry Trade as a universal Mechanism, are they not every where depending upon it for their most necessary Supplies?[53]

In these works, the gentry are "lazy" and "self-willed." Men of trade have become "industrious" and "useful." Trade has become "honorable" and an "addition to the character" of tradesmen. Merchants and gentlemen are no longer compared in terms of the values of the elite; they are compared in terms of bourgeois values. The works of Defoe and Steele reveal the development of a language and a habit of mind that enable merchants to take pride in themselves as men of trade, not as social miniatures of the elite.

The consciousness visible in Elizabethan bourgeois hero-tales is less straightforward than the consciousness of Defoe and Steele. It is the peculiar mixture of social values that preceded the idea that men of trade were "conscious of themselves as something like a separate order, with an outlook on religion and politics peculiarly their own."[54] For the bourgeois hero-tale is a double phenomenon. It affirms, on the one hand, Lawrence Stone's observation that in Elizabethan England "the dominant value system remained that of the landed gentleman," in spite of the emerging " 'middle class culture' of educated artisans, small shopkeepers, and merchants."[55] On the other hand, it suggests that the value system of the elite was not adequate for a description of the social pride of men of trade; the professionally articulate Elizabethans who wanted to appeal to merchant consciousness had to experiment with the flexibility of the accepted value system, stretching it to fit men for whom it had not been designed. And so the popular authors of the bourgeois hero-tale labored to create a basis for what, a century later, had clearly emerged as middle-class pride—*before* "bourgeois virtues" of industry, thrift, and business acumen were considered praiseworthy attributes and *before* money-making was considered a dignified enterprise. This implies that the development of bourgeois values was a product of, not a precondition for, the attempt of urban businessmen to define themselves as a social group.

The social consciousness visible in the bourgeois-hero tales suggests, then, that the study of seventeenth-century social developments should not begin with the premise that there was little self-consciousness among merchants and craftsmen until there were bourgeois values to bind these groups together. It should instead begin with the realization that in the early seventeenth century, bourgeois pride was expressed in terms of the values of the elite, and by the end of the seventeenth century, it was expressed in terms of the values of the middle class. The Elizabethan expression challenged the idea that the elite had a monopoly on political talent, wealth, historical service, and social self-consciousness. The later expression challenged the assumption that making money was less dignified than spending money, and it implicitly questioned the elite's monopoly on both power and social ideology. Though the first consciousness developed into the second, they are fundamentally different, as is apparent when they are examined side by side.

It is beyond the scope of this essay to ask when urban businessmen shed their belief in the value system of the elite and defined themselves in terms of bourgeois values. Tentatively, however, it seems altogether possible that the change occurred after the events of the 1640s. The London oligarchy that remained loyal to Charles I, for example, was composed of men whose political consciousness was recognizably similar to that of the citizens in *The Nine Worthies of London* or *1 Edward IV;* but the consciousness of the merchants of "the moneyed interest" in the early eighteenth century was recognizably different.[56] The social turmoil of the Civil War and the years that followed it may have precipitated the development of a bourgeois value system.

Be that as it may, the ideology visible in the Elizabethan bourgeois hero-tale is interesting in its own right because it is so different from the bourgeois ideology that developed in the seventeenth century. It is difficult to grasp the sensibility of an Elizabethan author who cannot praise Jack of Newbury without making him act like a prince, or praise William Walworth without making him act like a knight. But that very difficulty should serve as a reminder that the context of Elizabethan social thought was different from that of later centuries. Even Elizabethan authors who engaged in trade, like Thomas Deloney or Richard Johnson, could not praise a man of trade without considering him in the context of aristocratic virtues. And although Deloney could see (or perhaps merely sense) that businessmen did not fit into this context, he could not separate the values of his clothier from the other values of traditional society. If the historian can feel the distance between the groping consciousness of Deloney and the clearly articulated position of Defoe and Steele, he can appreciate the anxieties and antagonisms that changing social ideology thrust upon both gentlemen and merchants in the seventeenth century.

## Notes

The composition of this article was assisted by a grant-in-aid awarded to me by the American Council of Learned Societies in 1975.

1. The tales discussed here were not the only works written about merchants and craftsmen during this period; praise and condemnation of merchants appeared in plays, poems, sermons, and handbooks throughout Elizabeth's reign. Bourgeois hero-tales are works of fiction, drama, or poetry that were written specifically to praise merchants' exploits.

A chronological list of these tales appears below. Drama is dated according to Alfred Harbage, *Annals of English Drama, 975–1700*, rev. by S. Schoenbaum (London, 1964). Following the title of each play is the date Schoenbaum considers to be the most likely for its first performance. Dates for ballads and prose tales are from *A Short-Title Catalogue of Books Printed in England, Scotland, and Ireland And of English Books Printed Abroad 1475–1640* (1st ed., London, 1946; 2d ed., vol. 2, revised by Jackson, Ferguson, and Pantzer, London, 1976). Where no author is cited, the work is anonymous. All titles are modernized.

*The Life and Death of Jack Straw.* 1591.
Richard Johnson. *The Nine Worthies of London.* 1592.
Thomas Deloney. *Jack of Newbury.* 1597?
——. *The Gentle Craft, Part 1.* 1597?
——. *The Gentle Craft, Part 2.* 1598?
——. *Thomas of Reading.* 1599?
[All estimates are from F. O. Mann's edition of Deloney's works.]
Thomas Heywood. *1 Edward IV.* 1599.
Thomas Dekker. *The Shoemakers' Holiday.* 1599.
Thomas Heywood. *The Four Prentices of London.* 1600.
Henry Robarts. *Haigh for Devonshire.* 1600.
William Haughton et al. *The Six Yeomen of the West.* 1601 (lost).
——. *2 Tom Dough.* 1601 (lost).
Haughton, Hathaway, et al. *1 The Six Clothiers.* 1601 (lost).
——. *II The Six Clothiers.* 1601 (lost—possibly not finished).
Thomas Heywood. *2 If You Know Not Me, You Know Nobody.* 1605.
*Richard Whittington.* 1605 (lost).
Richard Johnson, *The Pleasant Conceits of Old Hobson.* 1607.
William Rowley. *A Shoemaker, A Gentleman.* 1608.
Richard Johnson. *A Crown Garland of Golden Roses.* Two apprentice ballads. 1612.
William Vallans. *The Honourable Prentice: Or This Taylor is a Man.* Pamphlet, 1615.
"A Ballad in Praise of London Prentices." 1617.

2. On Heywood's dramatic career, see Gerald E. Bentley, *The Profession of Dramatist in Shakespeare's Time, 1590–1642* (Princeton, 1971), pp. 27–28. On the editions of Deloney's and Johnson's works, see Charles C. Mish, "Best Sellers in Seventeenth Century Fiction," *Papers of the Bibliographical Society of America* 47 (1953): 362–63.

3. The facts of Robarts' life are obscure. See Louis B. Wright, "Henry Robarts: Patriotic Propagandist and Novelist," *Studies in Philology* 29 (1932): 176–99.

4. John Lyly's *Euphues, the Anatomy of Wit* went through ten editions in the sixteenth century and ten more in the seventeenth. Mish estimates that Deloney's *Jack of Newbury* went through fourteen editions in the seventeenth century, while *Thomas of Reading* went through sixteen. The early editions of Deloney's works were read out of existence, and so no precise number of editions can be stated. See Mish, "Best Sellers," pp. 362–63 (Deloney) and p. 367 (Lyly).

5. See Louis B. Wright, *Middle-Class Culture in Elizabethan England*

(Chapel Hill, 1935), p. 2. While historians have rejected the idea of middle-class culture, literary critics have used the Marxist paradigm in their interpretations of the bourgeios hero-tale. Wright's social ideal appears, with a stronger Marxist bias, in L. C. Knights, *Drama and Society in the Age of Jonson* (1937; reprint ed., Harmondsworth, 1962). More recent works also assume that the tales, especially those of Deloney, are inspired by the "spirit of capitalism": see Walter Davis, *Idea and Act in Elizabethan Fiction* (Princeton, 1969), p. 252; and Max Dorsinville, "Design in *Jack of Newbury*," *Publications of the Modern Language Association* 88 (1973): 233–39. A partial exception to this rule is Kurt-Michael Pätzold, *Historischer Roman und Realismus Das Erzählwerk Thomas Deloney*, Sprache und Literatur: Regensburger Arbeiten zur Anglistik und Amerikanistik (Regensburg, 1972), chaps. 2–4; Pätzold deals with Deloney's mixture of new "bourgeois" values and older feudal ideology.

6. See "The Myth of the Middle Class in Tudor England" and "Storm over the Gentry," in J. H. Hexter, *Reappraisals in History: New Views on History and Society in Early Modern Europe* (1961; reprint ed., New York and Evanston, 1963). For new models of preindustrial English society, see Lawrence Stone, "Social Mobility in England, 1500–1700," *Past and Present* 33 (April 1966): 18–20; Peter Laslett, *The World We Have Lost* (New York, 1965), p. 38; and Paul Christianson, "The Causes of the English Revolution: A Reappraisal," *Journal of British Studies* 15 (1976): 57–60.

7. John Stow, the historian whose ever-expanding chronicles of London and England began the tradition of praising civic leaders, was subsidized by the Merchant Taylors' Company. See *A Survey of London by John Stow*, ed. Charles L. Kingsford (Oxford, 1908), 1:xxiv–xxv. Other merchants were patrons of the nonuniversity scientists, most of whom lived in London. See Christopher Hill, *Intellectual Origins of the English Revolution* (Oxford, 1965), chap. 2. On the foundations of grammar schools, colleges, and scholarships, see W. K. Jordan, *The Charities of London, 1480–1660*, pp. 248, 253.

8. David Cressy, "Literacy in Pre-Industrial Society," *Societas* 4 (1974): 234–35. "Literacy," in Cressy's study as in all studies of preindustrial literacy, means the ability to sign a document instead of making a mark. "Tradesmen" are all men of trade, without regard to their wealth. As one would expect, however, the members of the great companies, skilled artisans, and booksellers had a literacy rate of 94 percent in the period from 1580 to 1700. At the bottom of the hierarchy of trade, men in menial trades, like thatchers and bricklayers, had a rate of only 16 percent in the same period. In East Anglia, 64 percent of the weavers and tanners Cressy sampled in the period from 1580 to 1700 were literate; and roughly half the butchers, bakers, millers, tailors, blacksmiths, and shoemakers could sign their names. See David Cressy, "Education and Literacy in London and East Anglia, 1580–1700" (Ph.D. diss., Clare College, Cambridge, 1972), pp. 332–41.

9. P. J. Bowden, *The Wool Trade in Tudor and Stuart England* (London, 1962), p. xv; Frank F. Foster, "The Government of London in the Reign of Elizabeth I" (Ph.D. diss., Columbia University, 1968), pp. 12–13, 18–19.

10. Walworth's heroism was celebrated in all the Elizabethan chronicles, two plays, a lord mayor's show, a religious treatise, and three poems between 1565 and 1600. Recently, however, May McKisack has suggested that Walworth in fact endangered the king's life by losing his temper at a critical moment of negotiations. See *The Fourteenth Century, 1307–1399*, Oxford History of England, vol. 5 (Oxford, 1959), p. 413.

11. In *The Harleian Miscellany*, ed. William Oldys and Thomas Park, (London, 1811), 8:442, 444. All future references to *The Nine Worthies* are to this edition and volume. I have modernized the spelling in all quotations.

12. In *A Select Collection of Old English Plays Originally Published by Robert Dodsley in the Year 1744*, ed. W. Carew Hazlitt (1874–76; reprint ed., New York, 1964), 5:406, 413.

13. *The Dramatic Works of Thomas Heywood*, ed. R. H. Shepherd (1874; reprint ed., New York, 1964), 1:13–14, 17–18. (Hereafter referred to as "Heywood.")

14. Wright, *Middle-Class Culture*, chap. 2.

15. See Steven R. Smith, "The London Apprentices as Seventeenth-Century Adolescents," *Past and Present*, no. 61 (1973): 159.

16. Heywood, 2:172–73.

17. Ibid., pp. 192–93.

18. On the influence of chivalric romances upon "realistic" Elizabethan fiction, see Davis, *Idea and Act*, pp. 258–69.

19. *Nine Worthies*, pp. 454–55.

20. *Ancient Songs and Ballads, from the Reign of King Henry the Second to the Revolution, Collected by Joseph Ritson*, ed. by W. Carew Hazlitt, 3rd ed. (London, 1877), pp. 318–23.

21. *Dictionary of National Biography*, S.V. Winchcombe, John.

22. *The Works of Thomas Deloney*, ed. Francis Oscar Mann (1912; reprint ed., Oxford, 1967), pp. 23–24. Hereafter referred to as "Deloney."

23. *Nine Worthies*, p. 451.

24. Heywood, 2:168.

25. Deloney, p. 71.

26. Henry Robarts, *Haigh for Devonshire. A Pleasant Discourse of Six Gallant Marchants of Devonshire* (London, 1600) [sig. Dv], [sig. A4].

27. *Nine Worthies*, p. 450.

28. Deloney, pp. 131–32.

29. In *Shakespeare Jest-Books*, ed. W. Carew Hazlitt (London, 1864), vol. 3: "The Conceits of Old Hobson," pp. 44–45.

30. Deloney, p. 3.

31. Robarts, *Haigh for Devonshire* [sig. A4v], [sig. G4v].

32. Heywood, 1:301.

33. *The Dramatic Works of Thomas Dekker*, ed. Fredson Bowers (Cambridge, 1955), 2:84–87.

34. Heywood, 1:63.

35. Deloney, pp. 27–29.

36. Ibid., p. 29.

37. Max Dorsinville suggests that the icon compares Henry's commonwealth, which is beset by idle courtiers, to Jack's, "where pride in hard work is celebrated as the ideal life style" ("Design in *Jack of Newbury*," p. 235). But surely the point is that Jack's beehive supports the realm, whereas Wolsey's ambition threatens its destruction.

38. Peter Ramsey, for example, calls Jack's household an example of the few "large-scale establishments comparable to the factories of the Industrial Revolution," in *Tudor Economic Problems* (London, 1965), p. 88. For a critique of similar statements, see Laslett, *World We Have Lost*, pp. 153–54.

39. Raphael Holinshed, *Chronicles of England, Scotland and Ireland*, ed. Henry Ellis (London, 1807–8), 3:761.

40. Deloney, pp. 31–38.

41. Dorsinville suggests that Jack is "the epitome of the rising Elizabethan mercantile class that wishes to counterbalance the power of the courtiers" ("Design in *Jack of Newbury*," p. 236). But if Jack wants to replace anybody in Henry's esteem, it is not the courtiers of *noble* birth; Deloney carefully compares him to Wolsey and *only* to Wolsey. No other princely courtier in Henry's train is mentioned by name.

42. Deloney, p. 38.

43. See the exerpts from Dorsinville, above; Alexander Leggatt, *Citizen Comedy in the Age of Shakespeare* (Toronto, 1973), p. 14; Davis, *Idea and Act*, p. 252; and Herbert S. Donow, "Thomas Deloney and Thomas Heywood: Two Views of the Elizabethan Merchant" (Ph.D. diss., University of Iowa, 1966), p. 36.

44. The chronology of Deloney's novels is uncertain because all the early editions are lost. It is only probable, not definite, that *Thomas of Reading* was written after *The Gentle Craft, Part II*. See Deloney, p. 547.

45. Ibid., pp. 228, 229, 232.

46. *Eastward Hoe by Chapman, Jonson, and Marston*, ed. Julia H. Harris (New Haven, 1926), p. 67.

47. Ibid., p. 20. An excellent interpretation of this aspect of the play appears in Leggatt, *Citizen Comedy*, pp. 47–53.

48. Stone, *Crisis*, p. 74.

49. Ibid., p. 81.

50. *Dictionary of National Biography*, S.V. Hicks, Baptist.

51. See the chronological list of the tales, above, n. 1.

52. Richard Steele, *The Conscious Lovers*, in *Six Eighteenth-Century Plays*, ed. John H. Wilson (Boston, 1963), p. 105.

53. *A Plan of the English Commerce* (1728), the Shakespeare Head Edition of the Novels and Selected Writings of Daniel Defoe, vol. 10, (Oxford, 1927), p. 7.

54. R. H. Tawney, *Religion and the Rise of Capitalism* (1926; reprint ed., New York, 1954), p. 173.

55. Stone, *Crisis*, p. 39.

56. See Valerie Pearl, *London and the Outbreak of the Puritan Revolution: City Government and National Politics, 1625–43* (London, 1961), chaps. 3 and 4.

# Constitutional Uncertainty and the Declaration of Rights

### HOWARD NENNER

What is perhaps most remarkable about the political cataclysm of 1688 is that it generated no revolutionary momentum. Once James II had been driven from his throne and his crown offered jointly to the prince and princess of Orange, the Revolution had reached an end. The hold of the monarchy on political power had been dramatically loosened, but on 13 February 1689, with the prerogative largely intact, William and Mary ascended a still formidable throne. In consequence of the Revolution, a new equilibrium had been created; and, with the promise of its continuation, the familiar contest of king versus Parliament could be resumed.

Much of this is a recognizable story and accounts in large measure for the Whig assessment of these events as the splendid final chapter in the English struggle for constitutional government. The achievement was made to seem all the more impressive because of the technical—indeed, almost surgical—skill with which the operation was executed. Excised from the body politic was the tumor of absolutism, removed at the penultimate moment, just as it was to begin an irreversible metastatic course. As a happy result the constitution was not only saved; it was returned to its condition of "original" well-being. Thus could Macaulay report in a now famous passage of his *History* that whatever changes had to be effected in order to achieve the Revolution, they were very small:

Not a single flower of the crown was touched. Not a single new right was given to the people. The whole English law, substantive and adjective, was, in the judgment of all the greatest lawyers, of Holt and Treby, of Maynard and Somers, almost exactly the same after the Revolution as before it. Some controverted points had been decided according to the sense of the best jurists; and there had been a slight deviation from the ordinary course of succession. This was all; and this was enough.[1]

In this perspective the Revolution is glorious because it was so conservative. It was neither overreaching nor at any time out of control. It succeeded because it did nothing more than substitute a king who would honor the constitution for one who had endangered the rule of law. It went only so far as was necessary and no further. It did not innovate; it preserved!

In 1938 G. M. Trevelyan endorsed this view of the Revolution as the product of constitutional moderation and control. Calling into question the label "Glorious Revolution" because it suggested to him a quality of contemporary enthusiasm that he believed to be absent, Trevelyan suggested instead "The Sensible Revolution" as a description much more appropriate to the event. In 1688 and 1689, he asserted, there are no innovations, no new ideas; rather, "a new and happier turn is given to the old issues . . . by compromise, agreement and toleration. An heroic age raises questions, but it takes a sensible age to solve them."[2]

For these reasons the Revolution is easily understood as an exercise in restraint that, for all its drama, remains remarkably uncomplicated. The laws, liberties, and religion of Englishmen having been gravely threatened by a papist king, a Protestant deliverer is raised up—not, however, by the Lord alone, but with the aid of a specific invitation from the beleaguered kingdom. Assuming the direction of its own affairs, the political nation then confidently promulgates a comprehensive declaration of its rights, settles the crown in the same hereditary line (the "slight deviation" notwithstanding), and concludes that its work is done. Nowhere to be found are the excesses, the confusion, and the uncertainty usually associated with so monumental an event. Again Macaulay: "To us, who have lived in the year 1848, it may almost seem an abuse of terms to call a proceeding, conducted with so much deliberation, with so much sobriety, and with such minute attention to prescriptive etiquette, by the terrible name of Revolution."[3]

Indeed, what we have learned from the Whig tradition is that there was nothing in the Revolution that was terrible at all. How could there be, when the "proceeding" was "conducted" by men who knew precisely what needed to be done, who accepted the responsibility for doing it, and who did not allow themselves to be carried beyond the limits of the specific matters before them? Drawing upon the guiding precedents of law and history, they arrived at an appropriately narrow determination, one based squarely upon the facts of the particular case. Theirs was not so much an act of political aberration as a confident restatement of the constitution and a return to its principles. If it was properly to be styled a revolution, it would have to be in the more popular seventeenth-century meaning of the word, a cyclical return to a fixed and known point in the past, in this instance to a balanced government of king, Lords, and Commons.[4]

Macaulay and Trevelyan are, of course, right about the qualities of restraint and rectitude in the Revolution, even if their national sentiments inclined them to view the episode as a triumph of a peculiarly English sensibility. Moreover, their historiographical perspective is not exclusively English. In von Ranke's evocation of the Revolution, the scene is similarly dominated by those whose intellect allowed them "to comprehend and to satisfy the requirements of the moment with circumspection and great practical sense."[5] Yet whether these historians were correct in their characterization of a political nation in full possession of its collective wisdom, meticulously applying that wisdom to the crisis at hand, is another matter. Forebearance may just as often proceed from indecision as from resolution; and when all the seventeenth-century posturing is stripped away, there appears among those contemporary with the events of 1688–89 to have been a strong residue of constitutional uncertainty. Instead of sober, self-confident, and deliberate Englishmen providing "the still, small voice of prudence and wisdom that prevailed through the din,"[6] there would seem, in their place, to have been a nervous, self-conscious, and tentative political elite not quite certain of how far they might carry the implications of what they had already done.

Nor should this anxiety be surprising. If we can easily acknowledge the confusion and divisiveness that characterized parliamentary politics in the year immediately following the settlement of the crown upon William and Mary, it should be no more difficult to comprehend the insecurity of those two months before 13 February when there was neither a settled government nor a recognized king.[7] In the first instance there was the need to treat with William in an atmosphere of political and constitutional dislocation. From late December, following the king's successful flight to France, until mid-February, when William and Mary were placed on the throne, there was the continuing problem of how to legitimate political power in the absence of constitutional authority. On 22 December Roger Morrice encapsulated the dilemma when he recorded in his "Entring Book" that "the King had legall Authority, but the Prince they had invited had power &c. And there was another power tho it were very unwarrantable that the Mobile had."[8] More than a month later the situation was no better. There was still no collective agreement as to how, precisely, the crown should or could be settled, and Morrice, a clear partisan of William's cause, feared that if the matter were not settled soon there would be bloodshed. The problem, as he saw it, was the intransigence of the Tories, the army, and "the debauched party that cannot beare a Reformation."[9]

Yet it was more complicated than that. There was no easy way to overcome the scrupulous resistance of a large cross-section of the Convention to the placing of William on the throne and thereby doing violence to the principle of hereditary monarchy. The idea of a sovereign people electing its king was scarcely apparent at the time of the Convention, and still less was it acceptable.[10] While there were those few radicals among the Whigs in the Convention who were proponents of popular sovereignty, and a greater number who would have had the Convention act as a sovereign Parliament, most members remained unconvinced on both counts. Much more in evidence were those who worried whether anything done before such time as the crown was settled could in any way be considered constitutional. For that reason it was the advice of "the able Lawyers and most wise men" in December that William and Mary overcome their lack of constitutional authority by an act of assumption;[11] for "whoever assumeth the Title hath absolute authority to do all things that our Lawes impower a King to doe."[12] The advice was not heeded, but a responsive chord had been struck. Ultimately, those who would have retained James as king, those who were for Mary alone, and those who were solidly for William, all agreed that the political nation was acting with an uncertain and precarious authority. And almost all could agree with Halifax's judgment at the end of January that until the matter of the throne was settled, "there could be no Legall Process, nor no authoritative acts done."[13]

The anxious desire to resume a more certain basis for constitutional government proved, ironically, to be the greatest impediment to any constitutional change. There was no way for the political nation to take advantage of being temporarily without a king unless the Convention was ready to act as a sovereign body;

and this it was not prepared to do. To state with pride, as Macaulay did, that the whole English law remained almost unchanged was to be accurate, but was also to make a virtue of necessity. Contrary to the strong implication that the reasons for political restraint were to be found in a national satisfaction with existing law, the lesson of Stuart rule, and an important cause of the Revolution, was that the law was in considerable need of alteration if the monarchy was to be held to closer political account. Under James II the limits of the prerogative had been extended legally through the effective use of the judicial process. *Godden* v. *Hales* may have been politically unpalatable, but it was nonetheless constitutionally correct. The result was that the king was now legally free to dispense, in individual cases, with the penal effect of virtually any law; and despite the verdict of acquittal in the Seven Bishops case, the legality of the suspending power was, at the least, still defensible. There was, then, a high sense of importance about the need for constitutional repair, but by 13 February 1689, when the Convention surrendered its enormous potential for political leverage to its new king, that repair was yet to be effected. It is not entirely clear why such important work was left undone; why, in the light of the nation's recent experience, the Convention did not take advantage of its unique situation to arrogate to itself greater power. All that is certain is that the absence of another revolution for almost three hundred years has tended to make that question moot. Because all has worked out in the end, it has proved ultimately attractive to accept the Convention's forebearance as a testament to confidence rather than to paralysis.

What is more likely from the evidence is that in addition to its reluctance to accept sovereignty, the Convention suffered from an incapacitating fear of extending the Revolution too far, and thereby reviving the costly civil wars that had been laid to rest only one generation before. For this reason it tended to proceed anxiously and, at times, uncertainly. For a long time there was an overriding reluctance among Whigs and Tories alike to accept responsibility for the deposing of their king. The Revolution may well have been restrained, but it was, for all its forebearance, treason nonetheless, an implication that in the light of their recent history escaped the notice of scarcely any of the participants.[14] But to take notice of reality does not mean necessarily to accept it. Instead of admitting to revolution, they pretended to be responding to the unfolding of events. Like the common law, revolution might be declared, but it would not in this instance be made. For the brief life of the Convention, the reality of invitation, invasion, and insurrection was obliterated from the collective political consciousness, and alone in its place was the imposing figure of a despotic king who had first betrayed and then abandoned his people. James II had been undone by his own acts, without the need of any resistance from the kingdom. It is a maxim of state, Halifax was later to observe, "That a people may let a King fall, yet still remaine a people, But if a King let his people slip from him, he is no more King."[15] This was to be the enduring myth of the Revolution, one which led to the ironical truth that belief in nonresistance had not evaporated with the coming of the Prince of Orange. The doctrine, although empty of meaning by the time of the Convention, was neither to be abandoned nor closely examined until William and Mary were safely on the throne. The Convention, having established itself in the custody of the law, could now assure itself that although it was acting in a judicial capacity, it was acting without latitude or discretion; it was, according to settled legal procedures, interpreting the deeds of its misguided king—but, in so doing, it was in no way defying him.[16]

Equal in importance to the pretence of nonrebellion was the genuine uncertainty about the nature of the monarchy. To the extent that a comprehensive revolutionary purpose existed, it could do no more than focus upon the need to be rid of James and to see him replaced by a more responsible king. Beyond that there was no agreement, not only because there was a variety of conflicting political goals, but also because no one could be altogether sure of how much constitutional authority the Convention should dare to exercise. Monarchy itself was never in question; but how to justify the accession of a new sovereign during the life of James was another matter.[17] This is where the uncertainty and its attendant insecurity resided. Once James, by virtue of his own misdeeds, was held to have forsaken his crown, the important question was "who would be king—and by what right?"

The necessary answer was William of Orange by right of Parliament; but what, in February 1689, that meant about sovereignty and hereditary monarchy was far less clear to contemporaries than to later historians. Holdsworth, in one example of the prevailing historical view, interpreted the resolution in favor of a vacant throne as the clear and self-assured statement of a supreme Parliament. "The throne had been vacant," he wrote, "and Parliament had filled it. . . . It was a Revolution; and the people, through their representatives in Parliament, had assumed the right to make and unmake kings."[18] David Lindsay Keir was of the same opinion. Adopting the Whig perspective, he too recognized that little of any constitutional significance was changed by virtue of the Revolution, but this did not dissuade him from the view that the Convention represented "popular sovereignty in action." "Sovereignty in 1688," he believed, "was for practical purposes grasped by the nation."[19] Yet despite this historiographical confidence, it is doubtful whether the alteration in the succession suggested to Englishmen of the time that the right and title of their kings was now in the unqualified disposal of Parliament. If that had been the case, it is probable that there would have been a much more sweeping constitutional settlement. Men who can confidently assume the sovereign power to "make and unmake kings" can be presumed to be no less willing to tell their monarch precisely what he can and cannot do. Yet this did not happen. William came to the throne with a commanding prerogative, not because the political nation regarded the existing ill-defined prerogative as no threat to the constitution, but rather because there was no confidence in the Convention's right to abridge the powers of a king. Just as the political nation was not yet ready to admit to its responsibility for effecting the Revolution, so was it unconvinced that a Convention acting without a king might take unto itself the work of constitutional change. Whatever else it may have done, and whatever constitutional opportunities it may have had, the Convention was not to make a confident grab at sovereignty. It was not to seize the main chance.

At the center of the Convention's uncertainty was a hesitant approach to the Declaration of Rights. Had there been a greater confidence in its constitutional powers and a realistic admission of its role in revolution, there might have emerged from the Convention something other than a statement of grievances and rights only loosely connected to the proferring of the crown. The Declaration itself, after the ten days that were required to work it into acceptable form, might well have issued forth as more precise, specifying, for example, those uses of the dispensing power that were alleged to be illegal, and stating the exact intervals at which new Parliaments should be called. Instead, there was the condemnation of the dispensing power only "as it hath been assumed and exercised of late" and the assertion that "Parliaments ought to be held frequently."[20]

There have been several explanations offered for this imprecision, all significant, but none that allows for the Convention's collective uneasiness about what could be done constitutionally in the absence of a king. In Macaulay's still widely accepted analysis, it was simply that to "deal properly with matters so numerous, so various and so important" could easily take much more time than was thought to be available.[21] Yet the pressure of time as an explanation makes sense only if it is coupled with the Convention's self-perceived incapacity to act legally and effectively without a monarch. Otherwise it could have taken whatever time necessary to settle the constitution in a manner conformable to its needs and desires. Certainly there were members who were urging that the chance to do just that not be lost, that the Convention take the opportunity afforded both to choose and to secure the nation against a new king. Sir Robert Howard believed that "the Right is . . . wholly in the people, who are Now to new form themselves again, under a Governor Yet to be Chosen"; and Sir William Pulteney exhorted the Convention to recognize that "the Game is in our own hands."[22] To this end, particularly if there was any expectation of William's accepting a conditional throne, it would have been appropriate to make more specific what was meant by "frequency" and to provide machinery for enforcement. Indeed, in the early draft stages of the Declaration, when hope ran briefly ahead of doubt, it was reportedly proposed by the drafting committee that Parliament's "frequent sitting be secured" and that "the too long continuing the same Parliament be prevented."[23] Yet the most the Convention was willing to provide was a Declaration of Rights that allowed for no security of enforcement and that afforded no guaranty of monarchical compliance. As a consequence of surrendered opportunity for constitutional repair, William would ascend the throne with the prerogative virtually undiminished, a circumstance immediately lamented by politically suspicious Tories as well as by philosophically radical Whigs. The Tory Lord Mulgrave held it a mistake that "they did not mend the Constitution as well as Seem to restore it from its abuses . . . such opportunities seldome coming into the peoples hands."[24] And political reality appeared in total harmony with that appraisal. Within a fortnight of the accession of William and Mary, the Declaration receded from view and the politicians were back to exploring thoroughly conventional methods for bringing about frequent Parliaments. If the king's revenue could be effectively limited to three years, he would be under severe financial pressure to summon Parliament at least that often. In this regard the remarks of Sir John Lowther are especially suggestive. Lowther, in the debate on the revenue, attempted to minimize concern with the issue of frequency. It was not that he believed that any constitutional security had been provided by the Declaration of Rights. He appealed instead to "confidence" in William, the belief that William would be a king to call Parliaments often. "If I had thought him a man of that temper as not to call Parliaments," Lowther said, "I should never have ventured my life and fortune for him."[25] Yet at no time during the debate did Lowther or anyone else invoke the Declaration of Rights as an assurance of Parliament's frequent meetings. With the new reign only two weeks old, the Declaration was being regarded solely as an expression of political desire that placed no binding obligations on the crown. The Declaration's call for frequent Parliaments, then, was general and imprecise because there was nothing to be gained by making it anything more. The hard and familiar work of controlling the king could only be resumed when once again there was a recognized king in being.

A second explanation for the failure of precision is derived from that spirit of compromise which characterized much of the proceedings. According to this view there were areas of dispute between Whig and Tory that were allegedly irreconcilable, that no amount of time could hope to cure. In such an area was the dispensing power. Although the Tories had finally joined the opposition to James, they would not yield on the need to preserve the prerogative. From the moment James had gone they had tried to break the momentum of the Revolution and to prevent any further action that might alter the structure of the constitution. In addition, there were those, Whig and Tory alike, who believed that the *non obstante* should not be condemned categorically. In consequence of that belief, they would refuse to support any criticism of the dispensing power unless it was properly qualified.[26] It was not the dispensing power in principle that they found objectionable, but the way in which it had been abused by James and by Charles before him. The result was the compromise worked out between 7 and 12 February, which opposed the prerogative use of the *non obstante* only "as it hath been assumed and exercised of late."

That the Convention's criticism of the dispensing power, specifically, and its stand on the Declaration, generally, were the product of sensible compromise has proved to be an attractive basis for an interpretation of the Revolution. It is once more suggestive of that virtue which has been alleged to be peculiar to England, what Ranke called the "English intellect."[27] Certainly it is true that rather than a run of generalizations on the abstract rights of men, the list of claims that emerged from the Convention was closely tied to common assumptions about English law and history. The Declaration, in this light, could be likened comfortably to the case holding of a common law court. Conflicting political positions had first been heard, and then by a familiar process had been narrowly determined. This is one reason why Dalrymple, in the eighteenth century, found the "compromise" interpretation of the Declaration so appealing. "Political wisdom," he noted, "is founded more upon experience than theory: . . . all the improvements of the English constitution have arisen from applying remedies to ends that were felt, not to those which men thought they foresaw."[28] The same observation could just as easily have been made about common law jurisprudence, that it was remedial and specific, that it dealt with problems in being rather than with those that might someday arise. In a culture that had for so long been indebted to the mood of legal mind, this was in no way surprising.

Yet in the matter of the dispensing power, particularly, the inclination to compromise has to be understood as arising out of a failure of constitutional conviction. In the early drafts of the Declaration, the prerogative dispensing power was condemned categorically as illegal.[29] In the final version all that remained was the equivocal criticism of the dispensing power's use, and no denial, as before, of that power's existence. Here again was the most the Convention was prepared to do because of its collective unwillingness to condemn a constitutional instrument that was believed both to exist in law and to be useful in the application of justice. Despite the recent political abuses of the *non obstante*, there were compelling reasons to believe that the power resided in the prerogative and that if the power were to be partially abridged or totally denied it would have to be done by king in Parliament.[30] The result was a statement of objection to the recent use of the power and the implicit hope that once the crown was settled the issue might be addressed with profit. In this regard the Declaration of Rights operated as a visible underscoring of the desire for constitutional change—but no more. By the end of the year the issue would be effectively settled, but the division and confusion, even with respect to the more egregious suspending power, continued well past 13 February, when the Declaration and the crown were offered to the new king and queen.[31]

Another factor to be recognized in any compromise was William. From the end of December it was the prince of Orange who was in control of the government, who was increasingly sensitive to signs of republicanism, and who had made it quite plain that he was waiting impatiently upon events. Despite his repeated disclaimers of any design upon the English throne, William, by February, was the "heir" in fact, if not in law. It was for this reason that the wording of the Declaration had to be measured not only against time and constitutional scruples, but against the interests of William as well. In this interpretation of the Declaration's ambiguities, the Prince, presumably and understandably, could not be expected to acquiesce in anything substantially adverse to his own prospects. He would not willingly suffer any limitations on the crown that he was expecting soon to be his.[32]

The difficulty with this interpretation, as indeed with any

interpretation of William's aspiration and design, is that the dour and taciturn Dutchman was consistent in keeping his own counsel.[33] Yet we do know that William was obdurate in his view of monarchical power: he would not accept a role as his wife's gentleman usher, nor would he accept a place on the English throne without full executive power being vested in himself alone. To have asserted this position and then to have undercut it by accepting a crown hedged by conditions is suspiciously inconsistent. Nor does the balance of the evidence incline toward a conditional throne. In the first instance William studiously avoided any specific and unnecessary commitments. On the eve of the Convention's first meeting, the Prince was even understood to have refused a request for an express promise "that he would establish the Church of England according to law."[34]

In the specific matter of the Declaration of Rights William may ultimately have adopted the same position. Morrice, who was in favor of conditions, treated with contempt the attempt by the Lords as late as 8 February to defeat a movement toward a conditional crown, although he feared that such an effort would be successful.[35] What happened thereafter is unclear, except that some compromise acceptable to William, to those who favored conditions, and to those more constitutionally scrupulous was effected, and a bargain struck that satisfied all with an interest in the Declaration. Two days later, in fact, on 10 February, "things . . . began to look comfortable," a turnabout that Morrice supposed was due to William's receipt of assurances that the stipulations of the Declaration were not intended "for any snare to him. That they contained nothing in them but the known lawes."[36] But even those assurances were unnecessary, if Morrice is to be believed, because William allegedly responded that the furor was all for nought: he, William, did not care at all what conditions were set. He said that "he had never expressed his sense one way nor another. He came to preserve their Religion, their Lawes and their Liberties according to his Declaration, and so he desired to doe, and his sense in this case was what the Lords and Commons thought fit."[37]

Yet William did not, as demonstrated by the internal evidence set forth below, accept the Declaration as a condition of his throne. It is therefore probable that his ready acquiescence in "what the Lords and Commons thought fit" was based largely on the understanding that he would not be required to issue an express endorsement of the Convention's constitutional view. It is also likely that the Convention was dissuaded from insisting that William "sweare and signe to [the Declaration] before he . . . be crowned" because the legal effect of such a commitment was substantially in doubt.[38] As the lawyers had cautioned earlier, "If he signed this Stipulation antecedent it would be null, because what he did before he was king, would not oblige him after."[39]

Notwithstanding the evidence of constitutional doubt and the fact that the Declaration was understood by contemporaries to be of no binding effect until it was significantly translated into the Bill of Rights, the Declaration has been continuously accepted by historians as a contract, either express or implied, between the Convention, on the one hand, and William and Mary on the other.[40] In consideration of their acceptance of the Declaration, the prince and princess of Orange were accordingly proclaimed king and queen of England. The merit in this construction is that it salvages for the Declaration an important measure of legal and constitutional importance. Even though the Convention, before 13 February, had no standing to make law, it can still be argued that it made a broad assertion of constitutional fundamentals that William and Mary accepted as a condition of their throne. William, then, becomes king upon conditions that he is contractually bound to honor, and the Declaration is raised as proof of a great parliamentary victory. Not only have the lords and commons elected a king of their free choice; they have also told him by what standard he must rule. A divinely countenanced heritable monarchy has, by parliamentary intervention and control, become more manageable and less exalted. Or has it?

There is little firm evidence to suggest that this is what happened. Despite the long-held and little-contested thesis that William and Mary were obliged to accept the Declaration as a condition of their throne, the internal evidence inclines to the contrary. In the first place, it is unlikely that such a contractual arrangement between king and people would have been contemplated at precisely the same time as all mention of the social contract was conspicuously and deliberately removed from the Convention's early drafts. In the final version, as a concession to the scrupulous, the word "contract" is not mentioned at all. Second, and more important, the language of the Declaration is remarkably devoid of any contractual or conditional wording. The preamble begins with a recitation of James's actions alleged to have been illegal. Then there is the important statement of James's abdication and, accordingly, the vacancy of the throne. Next is a brief rehearsal of the material circumstances that have brought William and the nation into the present conjunction. And then, in cautious and conservative fashion, "as their Ancestors, in like Case, have usually done," there is "for the Vindication and Asserting their ancient Rights and Liberties," the Declaration itself, the now familiar general heads of proposal, the most that could be agreed upon by all concerned within the limits imposed by time.[41]

What follows next is singularly important because it is the bridge between the assertion of rights and the settling of the crown jointly upon William and Mary. It is here that it would be reasonable and likely, indeed necessary, for the statement of any conditions to be made. Instead, there is only what would be construed in law as the hope, and not the requirement, that a new monarch would heed the entreaties of the Declaration. Lords and commons might well "claim, demand, and insist upon, all and singular the Premises, as their undoubted Rights and Liberties," but at the critical moment of joining this assertion to the offering of the crown, there is a conspicuous failure of contractual vocabulary. Instead of legally simple and proper language to the effect that the Convention, in consideration of the prince and princess's recognition of these rights, as declared, do resolve to settle the crown upon William and Mary, there is only this:

To which Demand of their Rights they are particularly encouraged by the Declaration of his Highness the Prince of *Orange;* as being the only Means for obtaining a full Redress and Remedy therein.

Having therefore an entire Confidence, that his said Highness the Prince of *Orange* will perfect a Deliverance so far advanced by him; and will still preserve them from the Violation of their Rights, which they have here asserted; and from all other Attempts upon their Religion, Rights and Liberties;

The said Lords Spiritual and Temporal, and Commons assembled at *Westminster,* do *Resolve*

That William and Mary, Prince and Princess of Orange, be and be declared, King and Queen of England.[42]

Being "particularly encouraged" and "having . . . an entire Confidence" are not words that lawyers would choose carelessly or at random. In the vocabulary of the law, they are precatory rather than imperative terms. They convey a desire but impose no obligation. Certainly they are by no construction legally conditional.

From this point to the end, what remains is the important settling of the succession to the throne, the prayer that William and Mary accept the crown, and, finally, the substitution of new oaths for the old oaths of allegiance and supremacy, the purpose of which was to satisfy those subjects who were able to look upon their new sovereigns as *de facto* only.

As a consequence of the language of the Declaration, William and Mary were being offered a crown upon one possible condition only, that they accept a particular and somewhat irregular line of descent. It is even questionable whether this much was explicitly conditional, but it is possible that an implied contract might be constructed from the phrase following the granting and habendum clauses, that the "Lords Spiritual, and Temporal, and Commons do pray the said Prince and Princess of *Orange* to accept the same accordingly," and the account in the *Commons Journals* of the ceremony of offer and acceptance on 13 February, as follows:

The Clerk of the House of Lords, by Order of that House, read the Declaration to their Highnesses: Which being ended, his Highness made a short Speech in the name of Himself, and of the Princess his Consort: Wherein he declared their Acceptance of the Crown.[43]

Yet in Henry Powle's contemporary and official report of that speech, there is nothing to suggest that William took the Declaration of Rights to be anything more than a strong statement of opinion. Whatever the Convention's hopes for their manifesto's effect, William's response was an evasion of commitment hauntingly reminiscent of Charles I's reply to the Petition of Right some sixty years earlier. William made no explicit reference to the Convention's assertion of their ancient rights and liberties. Instead, he referred first to the offering of the crown as the "greatest Proof of the Trust you have in Us," which on behalf of the princess and himself, he thankfully accepted. Only then did he turn to a critical mention of the rights of the kingdom and say:

As I had no other Intention in coming hither than to preserve your Religion, Laws and Liberties, so you may be sure that I shall endeavour to support them; and shall be willing to concur in any thing that shall be for the good of the Kingdom.[44]

In this response to the Declaration, there is nothing more than the traditional coronation undertaking to govern according to the laws of the realm, which in itself would have been meaningful only if William had expressly accepted the Convention's construction of what the law was—and this he did not do.

On the basis of the evidence, an interpretation of the Declaration of Rights as "a precedent condition of William and Mary's accession"[45] is unwarranted. The document, instead, is a conservative declaration of the rights of the nation as the Convention wished them publicly to be seen. Quite consciously, anything believed to require new legislation was omitted. Being uncertain of its authority to alter the constitution, the Convention could proceed nevertheless to declare what it believed to be a vital catalogue of ancient rights. As long as new law needed the approval of the king, Lords, and Commons, nothing that the Convention might do without a king could have any legal bearing. But the Declaration, not being "introductory of new laws," was consciously in a different category.[46] Here the Convention might surmount its insecurity with no adverse result. It needed no authority for a declaration of ancient rights. All that it was advancing was a compendium of rights that, in law, if not in recent practice, was allegedly already in effect. It was saying, as it had throughout its proceedings, that the Lords and Commons assembled were competent to acknowledge the existing and applicable law. They would need the cooperation of the king to bring about legal change, but to interpret and declare the constitution were things they might do entirely on their own.

Nonetheless the Declaration of Rights is an important document because it summed up the grievances of the last two reigns and presented them to a new king in the hope of redress. But, like the Petition of Right, it turned out to be of no binding effect. William, like Charles I, agreed to govern by existing law, but he made no statement of what he understood that law to be. Nor, as we have seen, was the law clear to the drafters of the Declaration or the Convention at large. On the singularly important issue of the prerogative, particularly of its extent and limitations, Whigs and Tories differed among themselves as well as from each other, and most were in some way at variance with the judicially approved opinions of the last two kings. To expect William, then, to fall into line with a consensus view of the constitution was impossible so long as no consensus existed. All that did exist was a respect for a political ideal that masqueraded under the labels "ancient constitution," "ancient law," "ancient rights," and "ancient liberties." For these the respect was considerable and near to universal, an understandable phenomenon once it is recognized that the process was to select the ideal first and only then to accord it constitutional eminence by seeking its origins in a remote and undocumented past.[47] But this approach could never be without extensive problems so long as men would not agree on the particulars of a common ideal. The result in 1689, therefore, was all that it could be, a unilateral and indefinite expression of the ancient constitution—and nothing more.

If, then, the Declaration was not a contract of any kind, but an expression only of principle and hope—or even expectation—we may have to take a somewhat altered view of the Convention. We may no longer be able to accept the picture of a political nation, momentarily united in vision and decisive in crisis, imposing a consensus view of its constitution on a strong and obdurate king. We may have to recognize that men who could scramble arrogantly for preferment and place might nevertheless grope haltingly for the limits of parliamentary power. The result is a view of the Revolution that is similar in detail but different in focus from most other accounts. Instead of the transition from a divinely countenanced hereditary monarchy to a monarchy regulated and controlled by Parliament, the Revolution through mid-February 1689 should be seen to have accomplished nothing more than a change in the occupant of the throne.[48] Whatever this came to mean in the years immediately beyond, there was, in the Convention of 1689, no confidence in anything that could properly be called a legally secure constitution. There was undoubtedly a much greater measure of trust in William than there had ever been in James, and the fact of William's Protestantism meant that the internal threat of Romanism had been dramatically neutralized; but the expectations of a new constitutional balance had to be, and were, based upon no greater assurance than an anxious faith in William might somehow provide.

## Notes

1. Lord Macaulay, *The History of England from the Accession of James the Second*, ed. Charles Harding Firth, 6 vols. (London, 1913–15), 3:1310.

2. G. M. Trevelyan, *The English Revolution 1688–1689* (New York, 1965), pp. 3–4. Balanced modern accounts of the Revolution are in general agreement with the Macaulay-Trevelyan view that no major constitutional change was effected by the Revolution itself. For example, Jennifer Carter, in 1969, analyzed the impact of the Revolution upon the constitution and concluded that all important constitutional alterations are properly to be attributed to the twenty years following 1688–89. Jennifer Carter, "The Revolution and the Constitution," in *Britain After the Glorious Revolution, 1689–1714*, ed. Geoffrey Holmes (London and New York, 1969).

3. Macaulay, *History of England*, p. 1310.

4. See Vernon F. Snow, "The Concept of Revolution in Seventeenth-Century England," *Historical Journal* 1 (1962), especially the citation of Sir William Temple's *Essay on the Origin and Nature of Government*, in which Temple refers to the Restoration as a "revolution" by which "usurped Powers . . . give way . . . in favor of Ancient and Lawful Government" (p. 171).

5. Leopold von Ranke, *A History of England Principally in the Seventeenth Century*, 6 vols. (Oxford, 1875), 4:500.

6. Trevelyan, *English Revolution*, p. 4.

7. "It cannot be emphasized too strongly that the immediate aftermath of the Revolution was a period of weakness, confusion and something like demoralization." J. R. Jones, *The Revolution of 1688 in England* (London, 1972), p. 326. See, for example, the remarks of Col. Birch on 22 May 1689 during the parliamentary debate on the suspension of habeas corpus: " 'Tis said, 'now the Government is settled, no need of this'; but we all know that it is not settled yet; and before it will be better it will be worse. We are in a State of War, and worse than War. There is a great man on one side of the water, and King James on the other; and a Popish party, and another, in the midst of us; and this is a state of War, Sure." Anchitell Grey, *Debates of the House of Commons*, 10 vols. (London, 1763), 9:265.

8. Roger Morrice, "The Entring Book: Being an Historical Register of Occurrences from April An: 1677 to April 1691." Volume 2. Dr. Williams's Library, MS. 31. Q, p. 365. Morrice appears to have been paraphrasing the observations of Sir George Treby.

9. Morrice, "Entring Book," p. 446.

10. The fiction of a continuing hereditary monarchy was maintained throughout the meetings of the Convention, and beyond. Two weeks after William and Mary were "elected" to the throne, Sir George Treby, speaking in defense of the Lords and Commons having disposed of the crown, stated nevertheless " 'tis mighty plain that this Crown is an hereditary Crown." Grey, *Debates*, 9:116.

11. Morrice, "Entring Book," p. 382.

12. Ibid., p. 378. Morrice himself was in favor of William and Mary assuming the title, pp. 395–96.

13. Ibid., p. 449.

14. Note, for example, Serj. Maynard's observation in the Convention on 28 January: "I think if the King should come back every one that sits here now would be equally Criminall with any one that should attemt the King's life with a Dagger." Lois G. Schwoerer, ed., " 'A Jornall of the Convention at Westminster begun the 22 of January 1688/9,' " *Bulletin of the Institute of Historical Research* 49 (1976): 258. I am grateful to Professor Schwoerer for allowing me to see her transcript of the manuscript in advance of publication.

15. "Maxims of State, or Observation on government by the Late Marq. of H[alifax] 1694," British Library (hereafter B.L.), Sloane MS. 2680, fol. 9v.

16. J. P. Kenyon has demonstrated that the Whig ideology of contract and resistance entered very little into the resolution of events in 1688–89. J. P. Kenyon, "The Revolution of 1688: Resistance and Contract," *Historical Perspectives: Studies in English Thought and Society in Honour of J. H. Plumb*, ed. Neil McKendrick (London, 1974). The important inference to be drawn from Kenyon's study is that the Whigs who assumed custody of England's constitutional history after 1688–89 were not, at the time of the Revolution, in commanding control of the events themselves. See also J. P. Kenyon, *Revolution Principles: The Politics of Party, 1689–1720* (Cambridge, 1977).

17. Despite the differences of opinion on how best to settle the crown there was never any support for re-establishing a republic. "We will have a King," Morrice reports, "for the Lawes know nothing but the name of a King." Morrice, "Entring Book," p. 393.

18. W. S. Holdsworth, *A History of English Law*, 12 vols., 2d ed. (London, 1937), 6:230.

19. David Lindsay Keir, *The Constitutional History of Modern Britain since 1485*, 8th ed. (Princeton, 1966), pp. 269–70.

20. *Commons Journals* (hereafter cited as *CJ*), 10:28–29 ("The Declaration of the Lords Spiritual and Temporal, and Commons, assembled at *Westminster*," 12 February 1688–89); William Cobbett, *Parliamentary History of England* (London, 1806–20), 5:108–11; Public Record Office (hereafter P.R.O.) C212/18/1.

21. Macaulay, *History of England*, p. 1298.

22. Schwoerer, "Jornall of the Convention," pp. 251, 256.

23. Morrice, "Entring Book," p. 457.

24. "Humanum est Errare, or false Steps on both Sides: By the Earl of M[ulgra]ve: 1688." B.L., Harley MS. 6274, fol. 93.

25. Grey, *Debates*, 9:124.

26. The initial drafts of the preamble to the Declaration register, as the first specific complaint against James II, that the king sought to undermine the law "By assuming and exercising a Power of dispensing and suspending of Laws, and the Execution of Laws, without Consent of Parliament," *CJ*, 10:21 and 23. To this the Lords voted an amendment to add the words "as by consequence would subject all the laws to his will and pleasure." The amendment was rejected by the Commons and waived by the Lords on the twelfth. The reason for wanting the amendment was "Because the dispensing power in some cases has been exercised by many proceeding Kings without complaint," Historical Manuscripts Commission (hereafter HMCR), 12th Report, App. pt. VI, pp. 29–30.

27. Ranke, *History of England*, p. 300.

28. Sir John Dalrymple, *Memoirs of Great Britain and Ireland*, 2 vols. 2d ed. (London, 1774), 1:274.

29. The drafts of 7 and 8 February stated, "That the pretended Power of dispensing or suspending of Laws, or the Execution of Laws, by Regal Authority, without Consent of Parliament, is illegal." *CJ*, 10:22–23.

30. In March the Lords canvassed the judges on the location and validity of the dispensing power. A majority, following the lead of Chief Justice Holt, were of the clear opinion that the power resided with the crown. Others of the judges, however, were not entirely certain. HMCR, 7th Report, App., p. 759.

31. In May, during the debate over continuing the temporary suspension of habeas corpus, there were renewed discussions of whether the law should or could be suspended, and, if so, by whom, king or Parliament. Grey, *Debates*, 9:263.

32. This is the argument advanced by Lucille Pinkham, *William III and the Respectable Revolution* (Cambridge, Mass., 1954), pp. 234–35, and endorsed by Robert J. Frankle, "The Formulation of the Declaration of Rights," *Historical Journal* 17 (1974).

33. "The prince carries all things with that secresy that few no his Mind." E. Harley to Robert Harley, 7 February 1688/89. B.L., Add. MS. 40, 621, fol. 18.

34. Morrice, "Entring Book," p. 435.

35. Ibid., p. 463.

36. Ibid., p. 464.

37. Ibid., p. 465.

38. From the proceedings of 29 January, when the matter of drawing up "antient stipulations or State of the Constitution" was "referred to a Committee." Ibid., p. 445.

39. Ibid., p. 447.

40. The best case made for William and Mary's throne being conditionally tied to the Declaration of Rights is by Henry Horwitz, "Parliament and the Glorious Revolution," *Bulletin of the Institute of Historical Research* 47 (1974): 47–49. The only studies that have asserted a nonconditional throne in 1689 are Pinkham, Frankle, and Kenyon. See also my "The Convention of 1689: A Triumph of Constitutional Form," *American Journal of Legal History* (1966): 295–96.

41. *CJ*, 10:28–29.

42. Ibid., p. 29.

43. Ibid.

44. Ibid., p. 30.

45. Carter, "The Revolution and the Constitution," p. 42.

46. On 7 February Sir George Treby reported from the Committee a draft of the Declaration that provided for both the introduction of new laws and the declaration of ancient rights (*CJ*, 10:21–22). Yet on the following day (8 February), it was resolved in the House of Commons that "such Part of the Heads as are introductory of new Laws" be left out of the Declaration (p. 23).

47. J. G. A. Pocock, *The Ancient Constitution and the Feudal Law* (Cambridge, 1957).

48. The constitutional results in 1689 were remarkably consistent with Sir Robert Filmer's anticipation and resolution of a closely related problem. In *Patriarcha* (VI, "Of the Escheating of Kingdoms") Filmer argued that it might sometime happen that a royal line would fail and have to be replaced. At such time the "prime and independent heads of families" would convene to establish a new dynasty, but they would be absolutely precluded from placing any limitations whatever upon the crown.

# The Origins of the Calvinist Theory of Revolution

## QUENTIN SKINNER

The main question I wish to consider is when and where a recognizably modern justification of revolution first came to be articulated in early modern Europe—a justification that is recognizably modern in the sense of being secular in its premises and populist in its vindication of government by, as well as for, the people.[1] I hope it may be possible in this way to add a footnote to the classic analysis of the outbreak of the English Revolution supplied by Professor Hexter in *The Reign of King Pym*. The climax of Professor Hexter's story comes with the recognition by John Pym and other members of the "middle group" in the House of Commons that Charles I would have to be forcibly resisted.[2] But Professor Hexter is not concerned with the theoretical background to this momentous decision, since his main aim is to trace its practical effects on the later progress of the Parliamentary cause. So it may not be inappropriate to try to investigate a little further the origins and early development of the revolutionary ideas which the leaders of the "middle group" were able to invoke as they attempted to justify their sudden and dramatic assertion of the right to overthrow their lawfully constituted government.

The classic formulation of a fully secularized and populist theory of revolution in early modern Europe occurs in John Locke's *Two Treatises of Government*.[3] It may be most convenient, therefore, to begin by surveying the leading elements in Locke's account, as a prelude to asking when and where this canonical version of the argument in favor of active political resistance was first unequivocally stated in early modern political thought.

Locke's theory may be said to embody three fundamental contentions that serve to distinguish it from a number of earlier and less radical strands of revolutionary thought, and at the same time license us to describe it as having a wholly secular and populist character. The first is that the right of resistance to tyranny is taken to be lodged with the body of the people at all times, never being relinquished under any circumstances. At this point Locke is implicitly opposing a more conservative form of populism originally espoused by the Thomists, and later restated in the sixteenth century by such leading scholastic writers as Molina and Suárez. Suárez had argued that while the people may originally have been free, and in consequence able to choose their own form of government, the act of establishing a legal authority must have involved them "not in a delegation but rather in a form of alienation" of their rights, resulting in the creation of a genuine sovereign above the law, not a mere delegate of the sovereign people.[4] Locke argues on the contrary that the status of any ruler established by a free people can never be more than that of a trustee elected to administer and protect their rights. His contrasting conclusion is thus that "the community perpetually retains a supreme power" at all times over any rulers or magistrates it may agree to set up.[5]

Locke's next major point is that the possibility of resistance in cases of tyrannical government must be treated straightforwardly as a right. Here he goes beyond the theory of resistance originally developed in the sixteenth century by such Calvinist revolutionaries as John Knox in his *Appellation* of 1558. Knox had continued to view the establishment of political society in traditional religious terms as a creation of God himself. This had led him to insist that the people have a duty to God to ensure that they "promote to the uttermost" the reign of godliness in the commonwealth. He accordingly treated the lawfulness of resistance as part of the people's duty to uphold the law of God, on the grounds that God himself has always "approved and greatly rewarded such as have opposed themselves" to "the ungodly commandments and blind rage" of tyrannical governments.[6] Locke assumes on the contrary that the creation of political society merely reflects a decision on the part of the citizens themselves to set it up for their own purposes. This establishes his central contention that our rulers are not a direct gift of God, but are simply elected officials placed in authority by their own subjects in order to discharge a specific trust, that of administering justice and maintaining the peace. This in turn means, as he puts it in his chapter on "Tyranny," that any ruler who "exceeds the power given him by the law" automatically "ceases in that to be a Magistrate," and becomes nothing more than a tyrannical wielder of unjust force.[7] He thus concludes that any instance of a "breach of trust" on the part of a ruler must always make it legitimate for the people to resist—not as a religious duty, but rather as a moral right derived from the contractual basis of the ruler's authority. As he puts it in his concluding chapter, "The Dissolution of Government," our rulers in such circumstances simply "forfeit the power the people had put into their hands for quite contrary ends, and it devolves to the people, who have a right to resume their original liberty."[8]

The other important feature of Locke's theory of revolution is that the right of resistance is treated as the possession of each individual citizen, and hence of the whole body of the people viewed as a legal entity. Here Locke is carrying a stage further the justification of revolution that the so-called monarchomach, or "king-killing," theorists had originally worked out in the course of the French religious wars in the latter part of the sixteenth century. These writers had always been careful to exclude any suggestion that the right of resistance might be lodged with the whole body of the people. Although they begin by describing man's original condition as a free and nonpolitical state, they go on to argue that the people must be understood to have transferred the right of exercising their original sovereignty to some form of assembly set up to a represent their interests. As the author of the *Vindiciae contra Tyrannos* explains, "good government depends on a degree of order that cannot be maintained in a large multitude," so that it becomes desirable for the rights "granted and entrusted to the people as a whole" to be exercised on their behalf by certain "officers of the kingdom" rather than by the people themselves.[9] When the monarchomachs come to describe the contracts required to set up a political society, they accordingly emphasize that the signatories can only be the chosen ruler on the one hand and "the officers of the kingdom" on the other, without any direct intervention from the body of the populace.[10] This in turn means that when they defend the right of resistance against tyranny, they insist that this right can only be possessed, as the author of the *Vindiciae* puts it, by the officers to whom the people "have transferred their authority and power." It is only to these officers that the ruler has given his promise to rule justly; it is only they who may in consequence be said to have the right to "defend the commonwealth as a whole from oppression" if this promise is not kept.[11] This relatively cautious and constitutional form of revolutionary theory became the orthodoxy among radical political writers in England and Holland as well as in France throughout the upheavals of the early modern period. It is flatly contradicted by Locke, however, at the end of his chapter on "The Dissolution of Government." First he notes, in an evident allusion to the prevailing theory, that it is a "common question" to ask "Who shall be judge whether the prince or legislative act contrary to their trust?" Then he gives his own unorthodox and far more radical answer: "to this I reply, the people shall be judge," since the only proper "umpire" in such a fundamental dispute "should be the body of the people."[12]

I now turn to ask when and where this secular and radically populist theory of revolution was first articulated. One answer that has often been suggested is that it was originally developed in connection with the Calvinist-inspired revolutions of mid-sixteenth-century Europe. This contention has supplied the theme for a large number of important historical works, one of the more recent and remarkable of which is Michael Walzer's account of *The Revolution of the Saints*. Walzer begins his book by speaking of "the appearance of revolutionary organization and radical ideology" as one of the "startling innovations of sixteenth century political history." And he proceeds to argue that "it was the Calvinists who first switched the emphasis of political thought" from the figure of the prince to that of the revolutionary, and in consequence "formed the basis for the new politics of revolution."[13]

There are I think two aspects of this answer that no one would wish to challenge. There is no doubt, in the first place, that most of the leading protagonists of revolution in mid-sixteenth-century Europe were Calvinists, or at least took some trouble to present themselves as defenders of Calvinism. This is hardly surprising, since most of the political struggles to which the Reformation gave rise were struggles against the domination of the Catholic Church. This applies to the attempted revolutions in Scotland and England in the 1550s, as well as to the upheavals in Holland and France in the 1570s. The leaders of all these movements were professed Calvinists, and their leading ideologists were all prominent Calvinist intellectuals—Knox and Buchanan in Scotland, Ponet and Goodman in England, Beza and Mornay in France, and St. Aldegonde and William of Orange himself in the Low Countries.

The other point that is not in doubt is that, in connection with these revolutionary movements, the fully secularized and populist theory of resistance I have sketched was unequivocally stated by a number of Calvinist ideologists. It is true that the theory in its most radical form was less frequently affirmed in the course of the sixteenth century than is sometimes implied. We do not find it in the writings of the most famous Calvinist revolutionary of the age, John Knox, nor do we find it in the works of any of the Calvinist monarchomachs of sixteenth-century France. As we have seen, the monarchomachs remained unable to countenance the idea of revolution by the whole body of the people, while Knox continued to repudiate altogether the concept of a right, as opposed to a religious duty, of resistance. Nevertheless, we do find the idea that a right to resist remains lodged with the whole body of the people being advanced in several Calvinist treatises before the end of the sixteenth century, the earliest example being the Latin dialogue by George Buchanan entitled *The Right of the Kingdom among the Scots*.[14] This was written, as one might expect, in Scotland during the 1560s, in the immediate aftermath of the first successful Calvinist revolution.[15] Buchanan's treatise has not attracted a great deal of attention from the historians of early modern revolutions—it is never mentioned, for example, in Walzer's book. But it is arguably a work of major historical importance, for it is here (so far as I am aware) that one encounters for the first time an unequivocal statement by a Calvinist of the classic and most radical version of the early modern theory of revolution.[16]

Buchanan begins by stressing that political society is in no sense directly given by God. The State is a naturalistic construct, invented by men themselves for the improvement of their welfare and the greater security of their rights. The proof lies in the fact that man's original condition was not political in character. Originally men "lived in huts and even in caves," leading "a wandering and solitary life" and "moving about like so many aliens, having neither laws nor even any fixed abode."[17] It follows that any legitimate political societies now in existence must have arisen out of human desires and decisions, in consequence of the recognition that, as Buchanan expresses it, "some common benefit or utility" would thereby be secured that could not be attained in a solitary and nonpolitical life.[18] There is a singular absence in this account of the assumption—virtually universal amongst the Calvinist monarchomachs—that the people must swear a covenant with God at the formation of any legitimate commonwealth in order to ensure that it is based on the rule of righteousness. Buchanan simply concludes that the body of the people will consent to the election of a ruler and the inauguration of a law-making authority as soon as they come to recognize the sheer convenience of having "someone to deliberate and concern themselves with the affairs of each member of the community."[19]

This secularized account of the origins of political society is matched by a radically populist view of the proper relationship between government and the governed. Since the people are pictured as consenting to the establishment of the common-wealth essentially in order to secure (but not to alter) their existing rights, it follows that any ruler must have the status of an official (not an overlord) to whom the people, as Buchanan puts it, "assign the exercise of their law-making powers" solely as a matter of convenience.[20] There is no question of the people creating a sovereign who is *legibus solutus*, since as Buchanan insists "they prescribe to the king the form of his law-making powers" in advance. And there is no question of the people alienating or "transmitting" any of their rights in the act of establishing their king, since they are only electing a "minister" or representative to act "like a guardian of the public accounts."[21]

Finally, when Buchanan comes to the question of political resistance, he is led to endorse a populist and almost anarchistic view of the right of revolution. He has argued that the people only delegate and never alienate their original sovereignty to their elected rulers. So he is able to insist that "whatever rights the populace may have granted to anyone, they can always with equal justice rescind."[22] His first conclusion is thus that it must always be possible in the face of tyranny for the whole body of the people "to shake off any law-making authority they may have imposed upon themselves."[23] He has also implied, however, that the ruler has a duty to protect not merely the welfare of the community, but also the rights of its individual members. His other and even more populist conclusion is thus that the right of resistance against tyrannical government must be lodged "not merely with the whole body of the people, but even with each one of the citizens."[24]

Before we conclude, however, that there is no reason to doubt that this classic version of the early modern theory of revolution was first developed by the radical Calvinists in the middle of the sixteenth century, we need to ask whether the chain of reasoning I have now sketched originated with the Calvinists themselves, or whether they simply adopted it from some wholly different source. This further question can most simply be put as follows:

granted that the *men* who mounted and theorized about the revolutions of mid-sixteenth-century Europe were in general self-
proclaimed Calvinists, was it also the case that the *arguments*
they invoked were specifically Calvinist in provenance and
character?

One of the most influential of the recent studies to address
itself specifically to this question is, again, Walzer's *Revolution
of the Saints.* The main aim of his book is to show that the
revolutionary ideologies of early modern Europe were indeed
the product of a specifically Calvinist psychology and experience.
He treats the theories of political resistance espoused by the
Catholic political theorists in the course of the sixteenth century
as little more than a reiteration of medieval beliefs. Suárez is
taken as the paradigm of the Catholic outlook, and his view of
resistance is said to be that it constitutes nothing more than "a
temporarily necessary form of legal violence," which is brought to
an end as soon as order is restored.[25] This backward-looking attitude is then contrasted sharply with the "new politics" of Calvinism, a politics that is said to center on a far more revolutionary
attempt to "set legality and order aside" in order to accommodate
the theory and practice of "permanent warfare."[26] The outcome of
this contrast is an insistence that "the origins of radical politics"
are to be sought in a specifically Calvinist set of political beliefs,
since it is Calvinism that is said to have "taught previously passive men the styles and methods of political activity."[27]

It is arguable, however, that this view of the revolutionary Calvinists as the originators of a distinctive theory of radical politics
is founded on a misunderstanding of the way in which the discussion of revolutionary theory actually developed in early
modern Europe. Two major criticisms can, I think, be made of
Walzer's line of argument. The first is that his thesis as stated
involves a *non sequitur.* Even if we concede that the revolutionary theories of the Calvinists were in no way adopted from, but
are rather to be contrasted with, the assumptions of scholastic
thought, it still does not follow that Calvinist radicalism must
have been a product and conceptualization of a distinctively
Calvinist psychology and experience. There is clearly a further
possibility to be explored: the radical theories developed by the
Calvinists may have represented one instance of a more general
response by the leaders of the Reformation to the threat of persecution by the protagonists of the Catholic Church. What remains to be investigated is thus the possibility that the radical
political theory of the Calvinists may have originated with the
Lutherans, from whom the Calvinists may simply have adopted
some, at least, of their revolutionary attitudes and arguments.

It is easy to explain why this possibility has so often been over-looked. It has become one of the chief commonplaces in the study of early modern political theory that, as Walzer expresses it, Luther was "a political conservative," whose followers "turned away from politics and left the kingdom of earth, as Luther him-self wrote, 'to anyone who wants to take it.' "[28] But this ortho-doxy seems misleading in two important respects. The first is that neither Luther himself nor the other leading theorists of the Lutheran Reformation were ever consistent in adopting a con-servative political stance. When faced in 1530 and again after 1546 with the immediate threat of an imperial campaign designed to crush their church, they decisively abandoned their earlier postures of political passivity. They not only responded by vin-dicating the lawfulness of political resistance, but argued in terms of one of the major principles later taken up by the most radical of the Calvinist revolutionaries. They maintained, that is, that since all rulers are assigned their authority on condition that they insti-tute the rule of justice, it follows that any ruler who betrays this trust "ceases in that to be a Magistrate," as Locke was later to put it, and may thus be lawfully opposed as nothing more than a tyrannical wielder of unjust force.

This argument is clearly stated by Luther himself in his tract of 1531 entitled *A Warning to His Dear German People*. The warn-ing he issues is that the emperor may be planning to start a war—which indeed seemed likely at the time. Luther declares that if this happens it will no longer be possible to accept the emperor as a lawful magistrate. He will be acting with unjust force, since his conduct will be "built exclusively on force" and will rely en-tirely on "the power of the fist."[29] Once this characterization is established, the conclusion in favor of resistance readily follows. Luther announces that "if war breaks out," he "will not reprove" those who decide to resist these "murderers and bloodthirsty papists." He will "accept their action and let it pass as self-defence," since it will not in fact amount to an instance of rebel-lion against a lawful magistrate, but merely a case of repelling unjust force with force.[30]

This argument has sometimes been dismissed, even by those scholars who have pointed out that Luther appealed to it, as an uncharacteristic outburst in a moment of crisis, which failed to exercise any lasting influence.[31] But if we turn to the later theoretical writings of Melanchthon, Luther's chief lieutenant in the Wittenberg Reformation, we find the same line of argument being even more plainly set out. This happens most clearly in the second edition of his *Prolegomena* to Cicero's treatise on moral obligation, a work which Melanchthon originally published in 1530, reissuing it in a revised and much more radical form in 1542.[32] Melanchthon added a new section to this later edition in which he specifically dealt with the office of rulers and magistrates. His discussion opens with an extended account of "the natural instinct of self-preservation" implanted by God in beasts as well as men, through which "they are moved to the repulsion of unjust force." This "natural knowledge" is said to be "the testimony which God has given us for discriminating between justice and injustice."[33] It is then argued that the reason for instituting political society is to guarantee the rule of justice, and thus that the office of rulers and magistrates specifically excludes any right to inflict "manifest injury" on their subjects.[34] This in turn allows Melanchthon to state the crucial conclusion that "if the magistrate fails in his office" in this way, or "falls into acting in a criminal manner," then "it must be lawful" for the citizens "to repel this unjust force with force," using "whatsoever means they are able to call upon, including their own hands."[35]

Finally, the same revolutionary argument was restated by a number of later Lutheran theorists in the face of the emperor Charles V's attack on the Schmalkaldic League after 1546. The most important treatise to revive the same claims was an anonymous *Confession and Apology*, which was probably written by Luther's close associate Nicholas von Amsdorf, and was issued in German and Latin at Magdeburg in April 1550.[36] The second section of this tract takes as its point of departure the justification of resistance already offered by Luther in his *Warning* nearly twenty years before.[37] It is first emphasized that all the powers that be in the State are ordained to fulfill a particular office. It is then argued that since "the magistrate is ordained by God in order that he should be an honor to good works and a terror to the bad," it follows that "if instead he begins to be a terror to good works and to honor the bad," then "he cannot any longer be accounted" a genuine magistrate.[38] This again is taken to license the conclusion that anyone who resists such actions is not resisting a proper magistrate, but merely a wielder of unjust force who may be lawfully repudiated.

As I have indicated, there is a further way in which it is misleading to speak of Lutheran political theory as consistently pacifist in stance. To emphasize the conservatism of Luther and his followers is to imply that when the earliest of the Calvinist revolutionaries—such writers as John Ponet, Christopher Goodman, and John Knox—began to publish their radical political theories in the 1550s, this must have marked a complete break with the prevailing assumptions of Reformation political thought. This certainly appears to be Walzer's view in *The Revolution of the Saints,* and here he agrees with a large number of other scholars who have continued to endorse J. W. Allen's classic generalization to the effect that before the 1550s "the Lutherans and Calvinists alike preached with rather singular consistency a doctrine of non-resistance."[39] One difficulty with this account, as I have now sought to indicate, is that the leading Lutheran theorists in fact developed a revolutionary political ideology some time before any of the radical Calvinists began writing in the 1550s. A further difficulty, as I shall next seek to show, is that the earliest Calvinist revolutionaries, so far from breaking away from this background of Lutheran beliefs, at first largely contented themselves with taking over and reiterating the arguments in favor of forcible political resistance that the Lutherans had already developed.

This can clearly be seen, for example, in John Ponet's *A Short Treatise of Politic Power*, which first appeared in 1556, as well as in Christopher Goodman's *How Superior Powers ought to be Obeyed*, which was first published at Geneva in 1558.[40] Their point of departure is with the idea, already emphasized by Luther and Melanchthon, that all rulers are appointed to discharge a particular office. They are "ordained to do good, not to do evil," and are thus to be judged by their capacity "to punish the evil and to defend the good."[41] Both writers then proceed to consider the position of a ruler who, in Ponet's words, fails to fulfill the duties of his "office and authority" and attempts "to spoil and destroy the people" instead of protecting them.[42] Both endorse the conclusion already reached by the Lutheran theorists to the effect that such rulers cannot any longer be counted as lawful magistrates. If they "transgress God's laws, and command others to do the like," as Goodman maintains, "then have they lost that honour and obedience which otherwise their subjects did owe to them, and ought no more to be taken for magistrates."[43] These premises are then treated, again in the manner of the Lutheran theorists, as a basis on which to justify active political resistance. Ponet concludes that when we find our magistrates "abusing their office" and exceeding their bounds "notoriously," we are no longer obliged to submit to their rule, but ought rather to oppose them and ensure that they are "deposed and removed out of their places and offices."[44] Goodman repeats the same conclusion, claiming that when "kings and rulers are become altogether blasphemers of God and oppressors and murderers of their subjects," then "ought they to be accounted no more for kings or lawful magistrates, but as private men, and to be examined, accused, condemned and punished by the law of God."[45]

I now turn to my second criticism of Walzer's thesis about "the origins of radical politics." As I began by noting, one of the ways in which Walzer seeks to establish that the early modern theory of revolution was essentially a Calvinist invention is by arguing that there is nothing of a comparably "modern" and radical character to be found in the political writings of scholastic philosophers from the same period. So far I have sought to show that the conclusion of this argument does not follow from the premise, even if the premise is true. I now wish to suggest that the premise is in fact false, since I wish to point to an early sixteenth-century school of scholastic political theorists who clearly articulated the main principles of the theory of political resistance that was later restated by Buchanan, and still later enshrined in the *Two Treatises* of Locke. These writers have received little attention from historians of early modern thought, but it is the thesis of this essay that they need to be brought to the center of the stage if the story of the emergence of the modern theory of revolution is to be coherently told.[46]

Their arguments largely derive from two important strands of late medieval legal and political thought. One of these was the discussion among Roman lawyers of the conditions under which the infliction of violence need not be held to constitute an injury. Although Justinian's Code was often invoked by the defenders of an absolutist view of political obligation and rights, the *Digest* also offered a clear statement of the claim—later taken up by Lutheran as well as Calvinist radicals—that it is always legitimate to repel unjust force with force. This maxim itself appears in Book XLIII, where the jurist Cassius is cited for the view that force can always be repelled by force (*vim vi repellere licere*), since "this right is conferred by the Law of Nature."[47] The implications are most fully spelled out in the analysis of the *Lex Aquilia* in Book IX. The main example discussed is that of robbery with violence. If I kill a thief who is attacking me, I am said to be "free from liability," since "natural reason permits a man to protect himself from danger." And even if it is only my property rather than my life that is at stake, it may still be lawful to kill as long as I give fair warning.[48]

It is of course true that none of the jurists ever intended this justification of private violence to have any application to the public or political realm. But this was not enough to deter a number of political writers from adapting and extending the argument in such a way as to generate a theory of political resistance. Nearly two centuries before Luther and Melanchthon made their appeal to the maxim *vim vi repellere licere*, we already find William of Ockham arguing in the same fashion in his *Eight Questions on the Power of the Pope*. Discussing the jural relationship between the pope and the emperor in his second question, Ockham considers the parallel problem of the relationship between a kingdom and its king. He concedes that "the king is superior to his whole kingdom in the ordinary course of events" but adds that "in exceptional circumstances he may be inferior to the kingdom." This is said to be proved by the fact that "in cases of dire necessity" it is lawful for the people "to depose their king and keep him in custody." And this in turn is said to be justified by the fact that "the law of nature makes it lawful to repel force with force."[49]

The other and even more important basis for the development of radical scholastic ideas in the early sixteenth century was provided by the theorists of the Conciliar movement. At the time of the Great Schism at the end of the fourteenth century, Jean Gerson and his followers had adapted the Roman Law theory of corporations in such a way as to defend a thesis of popular sovereignty in the Church.[50] They had maintained that the highest power to govern the Church remains lodged with the General Council as the representative assembly of the faithful, and that the pope's *plenitudo potestatis* is merely assigned to him as a matter of administrative convenience. But they had also laid it down that the legal characteristics of the Church must be symmetrical with those of any other *societas perfecta*. So they committed themselves at the same time to the view that the highest law-making authority within a secular commonwealth must analogously remain at all times within a representative assembly of all its citizens. The implication is clearly brought out by Gerson himself at the end of his tract *On Ecclesiastical Power*, where he offers "to speak about the concept of politics" and "to describe the nature of the community established for the perfecting of this end."[51] He first insists that no ruler can ever be *maior* or greater in power than the community over which he rules. As in the Church, so in secular society, the ultimate authority must reside at all times in the body of the community itself, so that the status of its ruler can only be that of a "rector" or "minister," never that of an absolute sovereign.[52] He then infers that, since the people's representatives in effect install their rulers in office in order to protect their welfare, such representatives must retain the right to insist that the authority of any ruler remains dependent on his willingness to discharge the duties imposed on him. Any ruler worthy of the name must always govern "for the good of the commonwealth" and "according to the law." He is not "above" the community but a part of it: he is bound by its laws and limited by an absolute obligation "to aim at the common good in his rule."[53]

Early in the sixteenth century these legal and conciliarist ideas were revived and extended by a group of avowed followers of Ockham and Gerson at the University of Paris. The occasion for this development was provided by the fact that the French king, Louis XII, became involved in a quarrel with Pope Julius II in 1510, after the collapse of the League of Cambrai.[54] Alarmed by Louis' decisive victory over the Venetians in the previous year, Julius sought to repudiate the alliance he had formed with the French in 1508. Louis responded by appealing over the pope's head to a General Council of the Church, calling at the same time on the University of Paris to confirm his claim that the Church as a body possessed a higher authority than the pope.[55] The professors at the Sorbonne produced in reply a number of systematic works of political theory, defending the idea of popular sovereignty not only as a claim about the government of the Church, but also as a thesis about the location of political authority in the State.

The first and most radical exponent of this argument was Jacques Almain (c. 1480–1515), who was commissioned by the university to furnish its official reply to the king, and responded in 1512 with a treatise entitled *A Brief Account of the Power of the Church*. It seems that Almain may have won this commission as the result of a disputation he had already conducted in 1512 under the title *A Reconsideration of Natural, Civil and Ecclesiastical Power*, a work that later formed part of his *Exposition* of "the views of William of Ockham concerning the powers of the pope."[56] But the most important figure in these discussions was undoubtedly John Mair (1467–1550). Mair was Almain's teacher, probably collaborated with him in the writing of his *Brief Account*, and later went on to publish similar views about the concept of popular sovereignty,[57] outlining them first of all in his *Commentary* on the fourth book of Lombard's *Sentences* in 1516, and subsequently restating them in a more accessible style in his *History of Greater Britain* in 1521.[58]

Mair has largely been neglected by recent historians of political theory, but he is arguably a figure of pivotal significance in the evolution of early modern theories about popular sovereignty. He not only took up and developed the radical views already adumbrated by his two acknowledged masters, Ockham and Gerson, but also acted as a direct channel through which their ideas passed into the age of the Calvinist revolutionaries. When Mair began teaching theology at the Collège de Montaigu in the early years of the sixteenth century, one of his pupils there was Calvin himself.[59] Even more suggestively, when he returned to his native Scotland in 1518, one of the students he taught as professor of philosophy and divinity at the University of Glasgow was John

Knox.[60] And most suggestively of all, when he transferred to the University of St. Andrews in 1522, one of the young scholars who followed him there "to sit at his feet" was George Buchanan.[61]

For Almain as well as Mair the point of departure in the analysis of political society is the idea of the original freedom of the people. Mair offers the fullest account of man's natural liberty in the later editions of his *Commentary* on the fourth book of Lombard's *Sentences*. He agrees with Gerson that Adam enjoyed a paternal but not a political form of dominion, since there was no need for coercive authority in a sinless world.[62] So he reiterates— as Gerson had done—the patristic view that the need for secular communities must originally have arisen in consequence of the Fall. Wandering and congregating in different parts of the world, men found it expedient for their own protection "to constitute heads for themselves" and to set up "kingly forms of government." The origin of political society is thus traced to two complementary developments: the fact that God gave men the capacity to form such communities in order to remedy their sins; and the fact that men duly made use of these rational powers in order "to introduce kings" by "an act of consent on the part of the people" as a means of improving their own welfare and security.[63]

The chief corollary that Mair and Almain draw from this account is that no ruler established by a free people can ever possess absolute sovereignty, since he must originally have been installed on set terms to serve as a delegate or "minister" of the community. This doctrine is best summarized by Almain at the start of his *Reconsideration*, where he paraphrases the central section of his *Exposition* of Ockham's views about the proper relations between political society and the Church. He agrees that the capacity to institute "civil dominion" was originally granted to men after the Fall, and goes on to state what he takes to be five corollaries of this claim. The third and main one is that the "right of the sword" must remain with the body of the people at all times, and thus that the status of a ruler "can only be that of an official" appointed by the people.[64] It is conceded in the fifth corollary that "since it is not possible for the whole community to congregate," it is "appropriate that they should delegate this jurisdiction to a certain person or persons who are able to meet together regularly."[65] But it is still insisted in the fourth corollary that such persons can never be more than delegates, since "the power which the community has over its ruler" is one "which it is impossible for it to renounce."[66]

There are two implications of this view that Almain—who is more explicit and radical than Mair—is particularly anxious to emphasize. The first, which is evidently directed against the more conservative thesis of the Thomists, is that we cannot speak of any new rights of sovereignty being established with the inauguration of a commonwealth. The Thomists had insisted—and Molina and Suárez were later to repeat—that because no individual possesses the right of judicial execution, and because any ruler unquestionably possesses such a right, it follows that even though the people may originally have set up their own legal authorities, the act of doing so must have involved them in creating a power greater than themselves. Almain contends in effect that this doctrine is incoherent, on the grounds that "no one can give what he does not possess."[67] This leads him to argue—just as Locke was later to do—that since there is undoubtedly a right of judicial execution in any commonwealth, this must be due to the fact that a similar right already existed before the commonwealth was brought into existence—a right, as Locke was to describe it, to act as the "executioner of the law of nature" on one's own behalf.[68] This enables Almain to conclude that even "the right of the sword," the essential criterion of sovereignty, must originally have been possessed by the people, and must subsequently have been "conceded by them to their ruler" with the sole intention of securing its more efficient employment for the benefit of all.[69]

The other implication Almain is anxious to underline is that, since any legitimate ruler must be a mere delegate of the people, the act that the people perform in setting up a commonwealth can never be one that involves them in alienating any of their rights. The fullest statement of this claim occurs in the opening chapter of the *Brief Account*. Here again Almain appears to be opposing the more conservative outlook of the Thomists. They had characteristically argued—and Suárez, as we have seen, was later to reiterate—that when the people establish a political society, they must always alienate rather than merely delegate their original sovereignty. Almain argues on the contrary that "the power which the community possesses is one which it can never abdicate," any more than an individual can voluntarily relinquish his natural right to preserve himself. And this enables him to insist once again that "the power of the ruler in relation to such a community can never be greater than that of the holder of an office."[70]

Since Mair and Almain both picture the ruler as a mere "minister" of the people, elected on condition that he protect their rights, they both go on to argue that where a ruler fails to discharge this duty, he may lawfully be resisted and deposed. Almain insists at the start of his *Brief Account* that the community must always possess "such a power over its prince by the manner of its constitution that it is able to depose him if he rules not for the benefit but for the destruction of the commonwealth."[71] And Mair endorses the same revolutionary conclusion in his *Commentary* on the fourth book of Lombard's *Sentences*. Here he treats the right of political resistance, using a favorite and homely simile, as a straightforward corollary of his doctrine of popular sovereignty. Since any ruler is in effect an administrator, "who cannot have the same free power over his kingdom as I have over my books," it follows that "the whole people must be above the king and can in some cases depose him."[72]

Two features of this doctrine of resistance deserve to be particularly emphasized. One is that the argument is conducted in wholly secular terms. Since Almain and Mair both see the State essentially as a device for protecting the welfare of the people, they defend the lawfulness of resistance entirely as a moral right, bypassing the traditional language of religious duties. The other crucial feature of their argument is its radically populist character. The authority to exercise the right of political resistance is said to be lodged not merely with the leaders or representatives of the people, but also with the body of the people themselves. It is true that Mair is extremely hesitant and in consequence inconsistent at this vital point. When discussing the right of deposition in his *History*, he concludes his analysis by insisting that unless there has been "a solemn consideration of the matter by the three Estates," even a tyrannical king "is not to be deposed."[73] At an earlier stage in his argument, however, he maintains that even though "the chief men and the nobility who act for the common people" are normally responsible for checking an evil ruler, his power is ultimately "dependent upon the whole people." The far more radically populist conclusion he then appears to endorse is that "the whole people must be above the king and in some cases can depose him," and that "a people may deprive their king and his posterity of all authority, when the king's worthlessness calls for such a course, just as at first it had the power to appoint him king."[74] When we turn, moreover, to the younger and less cautious Almain, we find the same conclusion being endorsed with considerably greater confidence. The point is made with characteristic briskness at the start of his *Brief Account*. Since it is the members of the community who establish their rulers in order to protect their interests, it must be the community, Almain concludes, that retains the power to resist or depose a tyrannical ruler if he fails to discharge the duties he was originally elected to perform.[75]

The study of radical politics in early modern Europe has for some time been dominated by the concept of the "Calvinist theory of revolution." I have now sought to suggest that strictly speaking no such entity exists. The revolutions of sixteenth-century Europe were, of course, largely conducted by professed Calvinists, but the theories in terms of which they sought to explain and justify their actions were not, at least in their main outlines, specifically Calvinist at all. When the Calvinist George Buchanan stated for the first time on behalf of the Reformed Churches a fully secularized and populist theory of political resistance, he was largely restating a position already attained by the Catholic John Mair in his teaching at the Sorbonne over a half a century before. Mair and his pupils had bequeathed to the era of the Reformation all the leading elements of the classic and most radical version of the early modern theory of revolution, the version most familiar to us from the closing chapters of John Locke's *Two Treatises of Government*. It only remained for Mair's pupil Buchanan to take over the concepts and arguments he had learnt from his scholastic teachers and press them into service on behalf of the Calvinist cause.

Once this scholastic background is brought into focus, it may even appear that recent studies of Calvinist ideology have perhaps been asking the wrong question about the so-called Calvinist theory of resistance. They have tended to ask what could have prompted the Calvinists to develop their distinctive analysis and justification of revolutionary activity. It is arguable that they ought instead to have asked what prompted the Calvinists to appeal so extensively to the existing theories of revolution developed by their Catholic adversaries. The significance of this question lies in the fact that it hints at the possibility of a new view of the relationship between the ideology of the radical Calvinists and their political practice. Since Walzer, for example, thinks of their ideology as distinctively Calvinist, he sees it essentially as a means of self-definition and hence as a direct motive for their revolutionary behavior.[76] Once we see, however, how little of their ideology is distinctively Calvinist, we are bound to ask whether they may have been concerned not only with efforts at self-definition, but also with appealing to the uncommitted, seeking to reassure those who might be thinking of joining the cause, and above all attempting to neutralize as far as possible the hostile Catholic majority by showing them the extent to which revolutionary political actions could be legitimated in terms of impeccably Catholic beliefs.[77]

It would, of course, require a great deal of further research to test such a hypothesis about the reasons that may have led the Calvinists to make such extensive use of their enemies' arguments. But if we recall for a moment the situation in which the radical Calvinists found themselves, we may at least be able to make two points about the plausibility of such an argument. Characteristically the radical Calvinists were in a small minority, trying to promote illegal and subversive behavior, and confronting a hostile majority dedicated to claiming that their actions were wholly at odds with good and godly government. In such a situation it would not be surprising if the Calvinists were in fact motivated, at least in part, by a felt need to try to broaden the basis of their support, and to defuse as far as possible the denunciations of the Catholic majority. The second point is that if these *were* amongst their aims in developing their revolutionary ideology, it would have been rational for them to act in precisely the way in which they in fact acted. When they presented themselves as the exponents of a political theory already articulated by a number of leading Catholic philosophers, they were arguably adopting the best available means of preventing their Catholic enemies from simply dismissing their behavior as inimical to good government, as well as encouraging and reassuring the waverers and the uncommitted about the legitimacy of supporting the Calvinist cause. Perhaps this was in fact their own perception; and perhaps it is in this perception that we should be looking, in part, for the secret of their success.

## Notes

1. This essay is an attempt to present a brief epitome of an argument I have already tried to develop at much greater length (and in a somewhat different form) in *The Foundations of Modern Political Thought*, vol. 2: *The Age of Reformation* (Cambridge, 1978), especially in chaps. 2, 4, and 9. In writing this essay I have greatly benefited from discussions with Professor J. H. Burns about John Mair and with Professor Julian H. Franklin about the interpretation of radical Calvinism. My account of radical Lutheranism owes a great deal to a valuable dissertation by Richard R. Bernert, "Inferior Magistrates in Sixteenth-Century Political and Legal Thought" (Ph.D. diss., University of Minnesota, 1967). I am also very grateful to Clare Scarlett for checking notes and references, and to Stefan Collini, John Dunn, Susan James, and John Thompson for reading and commenting on earlier drafts. In quotations from original sources, all translations are my own, unless otherwise specified, and spelling and punctuation have been modernized.

2. J. H. Hexter, *The Reign of King Pym* (Cambridge, Mass., 1941), pp. 182–83. For the "middle group," see p. 47; for Pym's role in it, see pp. 62, 70.

3. In describing Locke's doctrine as wholly secular, I am of course referring only to his actual argument about the justifiability of revolution, not to its presuppositions. This is not to question the claim, which has been argued in a wholly convincing manner in John Dunn, *The Political Thought of John Locke* (Cambridge, 1969), that Locke's political arguments rest upon a natural theology that alone makes sense of them.

4. Francisco Suárez, *Tractatus de Legibus ac Deo Legislatore*, 2 vols. (Naples, 1872), 1:171.

5. John Locke, *Two Treatises of Government*, ed. Peter Laslett, 2d ed. (Cambridge, 1967), p. 385.

6. John Knox, "The Appellation of John Knox," in *The Works*, ed. David Laing, 6 vols. (Edinburgh, 1845–48), 3:481–83, 495, 496.

7. Locke, *Two Treatises*, p. 418.

8. Ibid., p. 430.

9. [Anonymous], *Vindiciae contra Tryannos*, in Julian H. Franklin, *Constitutionalism and Resistance in the Sixteenth Century* (New York, 1969), p. 150. For a discussion of the authorship of the *Defence*, see pp. 139 n. and 208 n.

10. *Vindiciae*, pp. 120, 154, 196.

11. Ibid., p. 195.

12. Locke, *Two Treatises*, pp. 444–45.

13. Michael Walzer, *The Revolution of the Saints* (Cambridge, Mass., 1965), pp. 1, 2.

14. All my references will be to the original edition: George Buchanan, *De Iure Regno apud Scotos* (Edinburgh, 1579). This is available in a modern facsimile reprint as number 80 of *The English Experience* (New York, 1969).

15. The fact that Buchanan first began to sketch this work late in 1567, although it remained unpublished until 1579, has been ingeniously established by H. R. Trevor-Roper, "George Buchanan and the Ancient Scottish Constitution," *English Historical Review* (Supplement 3) (London, 1966). But Trevor-Roper introduces an inconsistency into his argument by seeking to ascribe a "memorial" of 1571 to Buchanan, which he then describes as "the earliest extant formulation" of Buchanan's political theory. For a discussion of this and other difficulties in Trevor-Roper's analysis, see G. W. S. Barrow in *Annali della Fondazione italiana per la storia amministrativa* 4 (1967): 653–55.

16. There is at least one earlier tract that allows for resistance by the whole body of the people rather than merely by their elected representatives. This was published anonymously in French at Lyons in 1562, during the first of the religious wars, under the title *The Civil and Military Defense of the Innocents and of the Church of Christ*. The tract has not survived, so its claims can only be inferred from other sources. But it appears to have confined itself to religious arguments rather than appealing to the sovereignty and rights of the people. For a discussion of the tract, see Robert M. Kingdon, *Geneva and the Consolidation of the French Protestant Movement, 1564–1572* (Geneva, 1967), pp. 153–55. See also Vittorio de Caprariis, *Propaganda e pensiero politico in Francia durante le guerre di religione, 1559–1572* (Naples, 1959), p. 113 and note.

17. Buchanan, *De Iure Regno*, pp. 8, 9. Cf. J. H. Burns, "The Political Ideas of George Buchanan," *Scottish Historical Review* 30 (1951): 62–63. As befits a humanist, Buchanan holds to a Stoic rather than an Aristotelian view of the origins of political society. His account closely follows Cicero's discussion at the start of his treatise *On Invention*. See Cicero, *On Invention*, trans. H. M. Hubbell (London, 1949), pp. 5–7.

18. Buchanan, *De Iure Regno*, p. 9.

19. Ibid., pp. 9, 12.

20. Ibid., p. 25.

21. Ibid., pp. 32–33, 58, 62.

22. Ibid., p. 80.

23. Ibid., pp. 52, 62.

24. Ibid., p. 97. Cf. also pp. 61, 79, 81, and see also Burns, "Political Ideas," pp. 65–67.

25. Walzer, *Revolution*, p. 111 and note.

26. Ibid., pp. 111–12.

27. Ibid., p. 18. For a similar view see Hans Baron, "Calvinist Republicanism and Its Historical Roots," *Church History* 8 (1939): 31, 40–42.

28. Walzer, *Revolution*, pp. 23, 26. For a classic statement of the view that Luther was entirely committed to a doctrine of passive political obedience, see J. N. Figgis, *Political Thought from Gerson to Grotius, 1414–1625* (Torchbook ed., New York, 1960), pp. 73–93.

29. Martin Luther, *Dr. Martin Luther's Warning to His Dear German People*, trans. Martin H. Bertram in *Luther's Works*, vol. 47, ed. Franklin Sherman (Philadelphia, 1971), pp. 11–55, at p. 12.

30. Luther, *Warning*, p. 19.

31. See for example the accounts of Luther's *volte face* in 1530–31 in Pierre Mesnard, *L'Essor de la philosophie politique au XVIe siècle*, 3d ed. (Paris, 1969), p. 228, and in Hans Baron, "Religion and Politics in the German Imperial Cities during the Reformation," *English Historical Review* 52 (1937): 422.

32. Philipp Melanchthon, *Prolegomena in Officia Ciceronis* in *Opera Omnia*, ed. C. H. Bretschneider, 28 vols. (Halle/Brunswick, 1834–60), 16:533–680. For the publishing details, see pp. 529–32.

33. Ibid., p. 573.

34. Ibid., p. 574.

35. Ibid., p. 573.

36. The full title of the tract is [Anonymous], *The Confession and Apology of the Pastors and other Ministers of the Church at Magdeburg* (i.e., *Confessio et Apologia Pastorum et Reliquorum Ministrorum Ecclesiae Magdeburgensis* (Magdeburg, 1550). My ascription of the tract to Amsdorf is based on the fact that his name stands first in the list of Lutheran pastors who signed the tract at the end.

37. *Confession*, sig. A. 2a.

38. *Confession*, sig. F. 3a.

39. J. W. Allen, *A History of Political Thought in the Sixteenth Century*, rev. ed. (London, 1957), p. 103. For the suggestion that the radical Calvinists of the 1550s made a complete break with the earlier assumptions of Lutheran and Calvinist thought, see for example Winthrop S. Hudson, *John Ponet (1516?–1556): Advocate of Limited Monarchy* (Chicago, 1942), p. 126; Christopher Morris, *Political Thought in England: Tyndale to Hooker* (London, 1953), p. 155; Jasper Ridley, *John Knox* (Oxford, 1968), p. 171.

40. My quotations from [John Ponet], *A Short Treatise of Politic Power* (n.p., 1556) are taken from the facsimile version of his text that is printed— preserving the pagination of the original edition—at the end of Hudson's study of Ponet. (See n. 39 above.) Ponet's authorship can be inferred from the fact that the title page of the *Treatise* is signed "D.I.P.B.R.W."—i.e., "Dr. John Ponet, Bishop of Rochester and Winchester." Ponet attained the see of Winchester under Edward VI, was deprived under Mary, went into exile at Strassburg, and had his book published there in 1556, the year of his death. For these and other biographical details, see C. H. Garrett, *The Marian Exiles* (Cambridge, 1938), and Hudson, *Ponet*, pp. 36–90. My quotations from Christopher Goodman, *How Superior Powers ought to be Obeyed of their Subjects, and wherein they may lawfully by God's word be disobeyed and resisted* (Geneva, 1558), are taken from the original edition.

41. Ponet, *Treatise*, p. 26; Goodman, *Powers*, p. 190. Walzer contrasts Ponet's argument with Goodman's at this point, on the grounds that Ponet's concern with the duties of princes is "more profane than holy," whereas Goodman exhibits "virtually no social connections or sympathies," being wholly concerned with the obligation of rulers to uphold the true faith (Walzer, *Revolution*, pp. 102–3). The contrast seems overdrawn. Goodman as well as Ponet insists that our rulers are ordained "for our profit," with a duty "to obtain peace and quietness," to maintain "the preservation of the people," and "to see justice administered to all sorts of men" (pp. 36, 113, 118, 191). And Ponet no less than Goodman insists that the enactments of our rulers must never be "contrary to God's laws and the laws of nature" (pp. 22, 43).

42. Ponet, *Treatise*, pp. 100, 112.

43. Goodman, *Powers*, pp. 118–19.

44. Ponet, *Treatise*, pp. 104, 105.

45. Goodman, *Powers*, pp. 139–40.

46. On Almain, however, there is a useful paraphrase in R. W. and A. J. Carlyle, *A History of Medieval Political Theory in the West*, vol. 6: *Political Theory from 1300 to 1600* (London, 1936), pp. 241–47. On John Mair there are several important articles by J. H. Burns. See especially "New Light on John Major," *Innes Review* 5 (1954): 83–100. See also the valuable articles by Francis

Oakley, "On the Road from Constance to 1688: The Political Thought of John Major and George Buchanan," *Journal of British Studies* 1 (1962): 1–31, and "Almain and Major: Conciliar Theory on the Eve of the Reformation," *American Historical Review* 70 (1964–65): 673–90.

47. *The Civil Law*, trans. and ed. S. P. Scott, 17 vols. (Cincinnati, 1932), 9:311.

48. Ibid., 3:324.

49. William of Ockham, *Eight Questions on the Power of the Pope* (i.e., *Octo Quaestiones de Potestate Papae*) in *Opera Omnia*, vol. 1, ed. J. G. Sikes (Manchester, 1940), p. 86.

50. On the history of the Schism, see Alexander C. Flick, *The Decline of the Medieval Church*, 2 vols. (London, 1930), 1, esp. pp. 262, 271, 312. For Gerson and his followers, and their development of conciliar theories at this period, see especially John B. Morrall, *Gerson and the Great Schism* (Manchester, 1960). For the background of earlier conciliar ideas, see especially Brian Tierney, *Foundations of the Conciliar Theory* (Cambridge, 1955).

51. Jean Gerson, *On Ecclesiastical Power* (i.e., *De Potestate Ecclesiastica*), in *Oeuvres Complètes*, vol. 6: *L'oeuvre ecclésiologique*, ed. P. Glorieux (Paris, 1965), p. 247.

52. Gerson, *Ecclesiastical Power*, pp. 222, 226, 232, 247.

53. Gerson, *Ecclesiastical Power*, p. 247.

54. For the quarrel, see Olivier de La Brosse, *Le Pape et le concile* (Paris, 1965), pp. 58–59.

55. Hubert Jedin, *A History of the Council of Trent*, trans. Ernest Graf, 2 vols. (London, 1957–61), 1:32–34. The Council was summoned by Louis XII to meet at Pisa in May 1511. (It was at this point that the city of Florence, menaced by the pope's forces, sent representatives to persuade the French king to hold it elsewhere—an embassy on which Machiavelli served as one of the negotiators. See Augustin Renaudet, *Le Concile gallican de Pise-Milan: Documents Florentines (1510–1512)* (Paris, 1922), pp. 469–76.) For the dependence of the ensuing discussions of popular sovereignty by the French theorists (especially Almain and Mair) on the works of Gerson and his associates, see La Brosse, Part II, and Francis Oakley, *The Political Thought of Pierre d'Ailly: The Voluntarist Tradition* (New Haven, 1964), pp. 203–4, 213–15.

56. The *Reconsideration* (i.e., the *Quaestio Resumptiva, de Domine Naturali, Civili et Ecclesiastico*) forms the final section (fols. lxii–lxvii) of Almain's *Exposition* of Ockham (i.e., the *Expositio, circa Quaestionem Decisiones Magistri Gulielmi Occam, super potestate summi pontifici*). The whole *Exposition* was first published as item (iv) in a posthumous collection of Almain's works in 1518. See Jacques Almain, *Opuscula*, ed. Vincentus Doesmier (Paris, 1518), sect. iv., fols. i–lxvii. It was later published as a separate treatise (Paris, 1526). The most convenient version in which to read the *Exposition* (and the source from which I have made my translations) is in the appendix to the second volume of Jean Gerson, *Opera Omnia*, ed. Louis Ellies du Pin, 5 vols. (Antwerp, 1706). Here the *Reconsideration* is printed as a separate tract at cols. 961–76. Du Pin also republished Almain's *Brief Account* (i.e., the *Libellus de Auctoritate Ecclesiae* [Paris, 1512]), in the same appendix, at cols. 976–1012. Again, I have made my translations from this source.

57. For these and other biographical details about Mair, see Aeneas J. G. Mackay, "The Life of the Author," in John Mair, *A History of Greater Britain*, trans. and ed. Archibald Constable (Edinburgh, 1892), pp. xxxiii–xxxviii. For Mair's date of birth, see Burns, "New Light," p. 83.

58. I shall cite from John Mair, *A Commentary on the Fourth Book of Lombard's Sentences* (i.e., *In Quartum Sententiarum* [Paris, 1519]), and also from his *A History of Greater Britain* (i.e., *Historia Majoris Britanniae tam Angliae quam Scotiae* (Paris, 1521). Mair's *Commentary* was originally published in 1509. Mair first added his radical political arguments to the edition of 1516, republishing this version in 1519 and again in 1521. My translations are from the 1519 edition. Mair's *History* was translated and published by Archibald Constable in

1892 (cf. n. 57 above). My quotations from the *History* are taken from that edition.

59. Alexandre Ganoczy, *Le Jeune Calvin: genèse et évolution de sa vocation reformatrice* (Wiesbaden, 1966), pp. 39–41.

60. Ridley, *Knox*, pp. 15–16.

61. Burns, "New Light," pp. 85, 92–93.

62. Mair, *Commentary*, fol. ciib.

63. Ibid., fol. ciiia.

64. Almain in Gerson, *Works*, 2: col. 964.

65. Ibid., col. 965.

66. Ibid., col. 964.

67. Ibid., cols. 964, 978.

68. Locke, *Two Treatises*, p. 290; cf. Almain in Gerson, *Works*, 2: cols. 963–64.

69. Almain in Gerson, *Works*, 2: cols. 963–64.

70. Ibid., cols. 978–79, and cf. col. 964.

71. Ibid., col. 978.

72. Mair, *Commentary*, fols. ciib–ciiia.

73. Mair, *History*, p. 219. Cf. Oakley, "Constance to 1688," p. 18.

74. Mair, *History*, pp. 213, 214, 215; cf. *Commentary*, fol. ciiia.

75. Almain in Gerson, *Works*, 2: cols. 964, 977.

76. See for example the comments in Walzer, *Revolution*, p. 2, on the Calvinists as "moved by new and revolutionary ideologies."

77. For a general statement of this way of thinking about the relations of political thought and action, see my article "Some Problems in the Analysis of Political Thought and Action," *Political Theory* 2 (1974), esp. pp. 289–301.

tions die is a little-known branch of political science.[3] Perhaps
the revival of emphasis on this problem reflects the mood of our
own society since 1970; whether this is so or not, it is a problem
we do well to study. We shall not understand the way in which
the traditional constitution and the rule of the established elites
were challenged and changed during the 1640s until we understand how and why they were apparently restored in 1660, and
how far that restoration was apparent and how far real. We still
lack a good conceptual vocabulary for dealing with this problem;
the various attempts which have been made to determine how far
the restored order was more commercially oriented than the pre-
revolutionary are useful but by no means sufficient.

However, these are problems for historians; political theorists,
on the other hand, continue (rightly) to make assumptions in
their own work which they base on an understanding of what
occurred in seventeenth-century political thought. What Hobbes
said and what Locke said is still supposed to be important to our
understanding of our own political culture; what have the historians been doing to that? One must still begin by emphasizing
that we cannot study the first crisis period solely in terms of
Hobbes, or the second in terms of Locke; each period furnishes a
complex texture of thought which both provides the context for
Hobbes (or Locke) and proves to have functioned autonomously,
in ways which are important to us without necessarily including
Hobbes (or Locke) at all. Thus, our understanding of the thought
of the first crisis period must continue to focus very largely on the
enormously significant topic of that great explosion of quasi-
democratic antinomianism which we call Puritan radicalism for
short; and this is a subject which seems to have grown more
problematical as our understanding of it has deepened. We know
much more than we did twenty years ago about the workings and
inner logic of millennialism and antinomianism; one need only
mention the names of Norman Cohn, William M. Lamont,
Sacvan Bercovitch, and Christopher Hill in this connection;[4] and
we have moved away from the problem, much debated a generation ago, of how far religious perception was a mask for perception of material and social change, to the extent that we can now
see that, for the Puritan radical, spirit and matter were virtually
interchangeable terms, so that arguing for the primacy of the one
mode of thought over the other is like arguing about the chicken
and the egg. There is even a tendency to see this hylozoistic
spiritual materialism as the mainstream of radical thought, and
the scientific revolution of the Restoration period as, in ideological terms, a conservative reaction aiming at the separation of
spirit and matter in the name of authority and rational order.[5]

But there are problems here for those who wish to interpret Puritan radicalism as part of the consciousness of a revolutionary bourgeoisie: a radical antinomianism which is essentially part of the continuing protest of the Brethren of the Free Spirit seems to cut too deep into social and spiritual experience to be dismissible (even though it is partly explicable) as the ideology of discontented small tradesmen and craft-masters, and when one compares the earlier with the later writings of Christopher Hill—a major student of this subject—one seems to detect something like a shift from an Old Left to a New Left perspective. In his earlier works, Independents and Levellers appear as pioneers of an entrepreneurial and market society, much as they do in the interpretations of C. B. Macpherson; but as Hill continues his investigations of chiliasm and antinomianism,[6] we move left even of the Diggers, into the society of Seekers, Ranters, Familists, and Muggletonians, and the social setting is less that of a nascent bourgeoisie than that of the roving masterless men from the margins of craft and cultivation in a preindustrial society—social types who might appear at any time from the thirteenth to the seventeenth century, and who look more like intellectual equivalents of Eric Hobsbawm's *Primitive Rebels,*[7] or the "wandering braves" of early Mao, than the "industrious sort of people" about whom Hill has often told us. I do not doubt—knowing my Marxists—that a diligent attempt will be made to sort out the protobourgeois from the prebourgeois among the English radicals; and I do not doubt—knowing my seventeenth century—that this classification will not turn out to be very satisfactory. Writing as one no more committed than Hexter to a sequential class interpretation of history, I suspect that what we have found is the radical consciousness of Laslett's *World We Have Lost*—that of a patriarchal rather than a class society.[8]

A further set of problems in the interpretation of Puritan radicalism is created by that shift of emphasis from revolution toward restoration which furnishes the general background of this survey. If we are to organize our thinking around the fact that the first crisis period culminated in the apparent re-establishment of the traditional elites and the second in the confirmation of Whig oligarchy, we must look back at that marvelous explosion of radical consciousness which occurred around 1649 and ask where it all went to. It is very tempting to reply—we would all like to believe—that it went somehow underground in Restoration London, or in the English villages under the game laws, and resurfaced a century and a half later, in the era of Tom Paine and William Blake. There is a romanticism of the English Left which feels that this must have happened, and it is perfectly possible that it did; but neither the school of Christopher Hill, with their emphasis on the middle seventeenth century, nor the schools of George Rudé and E. P. Thompson,[9] with their emphasis on the late eighteenth, have yet brought to light evidence which enables us to speak very confidently about what happened to underground radicalism in the intervening period. What, after all, do we mean by "underground"? Where does popular or populist radicalism go in an era of repression? Is it kept going as an underground tradition by obscure articulate groups, or does it retreat into silence, to a level of subconscious or subarticulate potentiality, waiting to become actual again? If we are unsure which of these to look for, it is for lack of evidence rather than lack of theory.

But in a restorationist perspective—one in which the recovery of authority looks as important (if not as attractive) as the assertion of liberty—we find ourselves re-examining the radical tradition itself and asking what elements of authority may be found even there.[10] The reality of antinomian libertarianism is not to be denied; all the same, the origins of all Puritan political thought are largely to be found in the search for the godly magistrate, and there is a sense in which the true meaning of antinomianism was that the individual must be prepared to act as his own magistrate—which imparted a peculiar tension to the definition of the individual as family head, and to what the prophetic women of the Puritan sects thought about that.[11] The point is, however, that we must be prepared to find magisterial as well as radical elements at the heart of the antinomian tradition itself; even Gerrard Winstanley has been shown to be involved in the search for magistracy, and William Sedgwick—a friend but not an ally of Reeve and Muggleton—can be shown to have employed the antinomian scepticism of all claims to authority as a paradoxical justification of submission to whatever authority exists.[12] And this was Sedgwick's central and permanent position; we should not think that every antinomian retreated into quietism only after his radical and revolutionary impulses had been defeated. In a world of magistracy, the antinomian effect could start at several points and move in several directions, and this is to say nothing of the broader theoretical contention—one not limited to the seventeenth century—that it is impossible to assert even the most radical liberty without asserting some conception of authority at the same time. Even the Putney debaters, even George Fox, even Lawrence Clarkson, would have agreed unhesitatingly with this thesis.

The shift which I am trying to describe in our understanding of the first critical period can now be stated in another way. From William Haller to Christopher Hill, the emphasis has rested upon the idea of liberation, upon the rediscovery by the saint of his own radical liberty, in salvation, in society, or in both.[13] There is no need to abandon that emphasis; it retains validity; but we have been obliged to set beside it the perception that seventeenth-century men were still premodern creatures for whom authority and magistracy were part of a natural and cosmic order, and that the starting point of much of their most radical thinking was the unimaginable fact that, between 1642 and 1649, authority in England had simply collapsed.[14] In this reading, the central polemic of the English Revolution is not the Putney Debates, but the Engagement Controversy; and to say this is not to be describing an ideological reaction by conservative scholars to the events of 1968 or 1970. The line of research in question is some years older, and it presents English thinkers as responding with the greatest radicalism to the proposition that since authority had disintegrated, and God had withheld his word as to where it was now lodged, the individual must rediscover in the depths of his own being the means of reconstituting and obeying it. The pessimism of Anthony Ascham was a protest against the individual's being placed in this dilemma;[15] the patriarchalism of Sir Robert Filmer now became a demonstration that he did not possess the natural freedom which would otherwise place him in it;[16] but we can tabulate a list of singularly tough-minded responses to the challenge. Antinomianism itself was one: if the law had been withdrawn from men, it was that the spirit might take its place, and we can think of antinomianism as egg as well as chicken, as effect as well as cause of the English dilemma. But it is only one such response, and both Hobbes and Harrington can be depicted as answering the question what it was in men that ultimately made authority possible. To say that the individual sought to preserve himself, drew the sword to do so, but gave up his sword to Nimrod or Leviathan when he discovered the futility of the method, was one way of defining the roots of political capacity;[17] to say that the individual whose sword was rooted in property was free from fortune to pursue the goods of the mind, and could now join with others to form a political body whose soul was collective intelligence, was another and a very different way;[18] but both were answers to the question how men left with nothing but the sword could restore the rule of reason and authority. It is important to add that for both Hobbes and Harrington—and forming the closest link between their respective systems—a principal motive in reconstituting a natural politics was to deny separate authority to the clergy;[19] but nearly all the threads in the inconceivably complex texture of English thought in the first critical period can be attached to and deduced from the radical need to reconstruct authority, and though this is not the only valid mode of approach, it was quite certainly the one uppermost in the minds of most people then living and engaged in systematic thought. There can be no question of diminishing the radical libertarianism of the period when one points out the significance of the conservative impulse; the two were inherent in one another.

I want next to apply aspects of this analysis to the question of authority and property, which furnishes the first part of this paper's title. Debaters during the Puritan revolution had much to say about property, and began, as we know, to distinguish between the various historical modes in which it operated in society; and it is one of the most difficult, and valuable, questions before us to determine how far these discussions were based upon actual, if mediated, perceptions of the changing forms of property in contemporary reality. To begin with, it does us no harm to recall that the word is spelt in seventeenth-century printings both as *property* and as *propriety*; there is no consistent change in meaning between the two spellings, and had there been a tape recorder as well as a shorthand writer in the church at Putney, we might have learned something by hearing how Ireton and Rainborough pronounced the word. The point is that *property* was a juridical term before it was an economic one; it meant that which was properly one's own, that to which one properly had a claim, and words such as *proprium* and *proprietas* were applied as much to the right as to the thing, and to many things as well as the means of sustenance or production. Clearly, the word was often used in its crudely obvious sense; when a speaker in Richard Cromwell's Parliament says, "All government is founded in property, else the poor must rule it,"[20] there is not much point in being sophisticated about him; and it is often valuable to search behind the word in its juridical uses for perceptions of what we mean when we employ it in its economic-productive sense. This is what some important seventeenth-century analysts were doing. It is now naive to become excited whenever we espy the word "property" in seventeenth-century debate, and suppose that masks are being cast aside and we now see what the debate was really about. Sometimes they are not being cast aside, and sometimes we cannot be sure that they were masks at all. We have to know a good deal about the strategies of contemporary debate and the structures of contemporary language before we start peeling these down to assumptions about or perceptions of productive relations; and if this is going to be possible on some occasions, there are going to be other occasions on which analysis can only take us in other directions. This will have to be kept in mind even when we are dealing with seventeenth-century people

who specifically talked about changes in social relations consequent upon changes in the modes of holding or exploiting land or
movable goods.

Thus, when Ireton at Putney says that all he is arguing for "is
because I would have an eye to property,"[21] and proceeds to affirm
that the property that confers the franchise must be an inherit-
able freehold, he is not so much defending a particular form of
property as seizing the high ground in debate. The Levellers are
visibly uncertain whether they are trying to extend the franchise
to people who hold property in other legally determined ways, or
querying the necessity of the association between property and
franchise altogether, and Ireton is exploiting their uncertainty.
Had the Levellers seen themselves as playing the former role, the
debate at Putney could have resolved itself—as it never did—into
specific discussion and negotiation about the legally or economically defined categories of proprietor to whom the franchise
might be extended, and there might, when all is said and done,
have been an agreed compromise about that. Ireton had no commitment to freehold or to historic right as such; we know this
from other proposals which he was prepared to entertain. But
once the Levellers got upon the ground of manhood suffrage, or
anything near enough to it to suggest that the right to suffrage
might be established on grounds to which property was only
marginally related, they were raising the question of what the
political personality and its freedom really were and on what
grounds they could be established and talked about. This was the
question quite consciously before the minds of the variously
sophisticated debaters at Putney; it returns us to a known
seventeenth-century mental universe, one for which people at
that time had a wide range of words and ideas; and it reopens for
us the question of the authority by which people claim and exercise their liberty. Again and again in the Putney transcript, we
encounter moments at which the debaters get off the unfamiliar
ground of trying to clarify their feelings about property and
pursue instead what really concerns them and they really know
how to argue about: the problem of establishing the title by
which they are acting as they are; the real center of debate in the
first critical period—the basis in right of the *de facto*.

Right and principle, it can be no surprise to anyone to hear,
were more real in the minds of these debaters than social structure and change. Different assumptions concerning the basis for
action in right would have different consequences in action undertaken, and of course they knew that; but Ireton was not simply
aligning himself with those whose property was freehold and
defending their monopoly of the franchise—there is nothing to
suggest he would have objected to going some way outside that

group—so much as anchoring in social and historical reality his authority for being and acting as he was, and insisting that rights must be confined to those whose authority could be similarly anchored. And he did not see in the Levellers the spokesmen of a different group of proprietors with alternative claims to the franchise—a description they would not have recognized themselves—so much as people with no understanding of how to anchor authority in society at all, and no theory of property to be pitted against his. The fear that the poor will use an authority not rooted in property to redistribute property is, of course, present at Putney; but it is rather a stick to beat the Levellers with than a fear of anything specific. It is crude and unelaborated by those who express it, and rather ignored than answered by those who defend themselves against it; whereas the problem of authority at large can be and is discussed at great length by debaters on both sides, and by all contributors to the mid-century polemic, in language whose complexity defies reduction to the single issue of property.

On the assumption, then, that people think about what they have the means of verbalizing, and that relations between the center and the margins of a linguistically structured world must be problematical, we must often say that property in the mid-seventeenth-century crisis was discussed as part of the problem of authority, and rather less often that this order was reversed. This does not mean that minds of the period were unaware that the ways in which men held and exploited property, and behaved as social and political beings in consequence, were changing; on the contrary, a few contemporary theorists grounded their explanations of the whole crisis on precisely this perception, and it is of enormous importance in the history of social thought that this should have happened. But it is clearly not a sufficient explanation of its happening to say (1) that changes in property relationships were happening; (2) that a few people noticed; and (3) that everybody who did not notice nevertheless reflected the changes without noticing them. The patterns of human thinking at any period are more complex than that; and, especially when this order of change has never been noticed before, there must have been reasons inherent in the patterns of thought which led some people to notice—reasons which may or may not have been immediately connected with the changes that were noticed. On the assumption that ideas about authority and ideas about property were independent variables, I would like next to look into the seventeenth-century perception that property itself was changing.

C. B. Macpherson, as we all know, put forward some years ago, in *The Political Theory of Possessive Individualism*, the hypothesis that seventeenth-century political thought was importantly affected by the growth of a perception of property as marketable.[22] He constructed a model—an excellent one—of the social and political consequences of a set of market assumptions, and then tested for the presence of his model, or elements of it, in various seventeenth-century thinkers. As a result he was led to award middling high points to the Levellers and Harrington, much higher points to Hobbes and Locke, in proportion as he was able to find elements of the model in their thinking; and he concluded that the median score, so to speak, was high enough to justify the hypothesis that market assumptions were a constant determinant of thought in this period. Some of us were never altogether happy with this, because it never seemed quite dialectical enough; it all sounds rather as if something is known to have been going on, and various more or less sensitive instruments have recorded it with greater or less precision; and our notion of the behavior of consciousness in history has always been rather less barometric than that. We also thought that Macpherson's model tested for the presence of one thing at a time, and that if one started from the assumption that there were several kinds of possessive individual, and so of possessive individualism, and that there was argument going on as between several modes of property and individuality, a more dialectical and less barometric picture might result. In particular, there was doubt concerning his interpretation of Harrington, because Harrington had two models of property relationships, one defined by the presence of dependent military tenures and the other by their absence, and there was little need to involve the market in stating the difference between them. Everything relating to that debate is now in print elsewhere;[23] but it is possible to push the issue a little further, in a direction which takes us to the second part of my title: the question of liberal origins.

There is now a paradigm of liberalism, though one set up more by those who would attack than by those who would practice it. It is interesting to observe how the notion of liberalism is defined in much the same way, and attacked for much the same reasons, among political theorists and ideologues: on the one hand by socialist humanists—followers of Macpherson or Wolin or McWilliams or Lowi—and on the other hand by the classical conservative followers of Strauss or Arendt or Oakeshott.[24] Liberalism, as they all define it, is a view of politics founded on the conception of the individual as a private being, pursuing goals and safeguarding freedoms which are his own and looking to government mainly to preserve and protect his individual activity; and it is suggested that because this individual withholds from government so much of his personality—which he says is not the government's business but his own—government tends to become highly impersonal, and therefore paradoxically authoritarian in those areas from which it does not altogether abstain. The paradox of liberty and authority, on which I am basing my interpretations of seventeenth-century thought, was stated in these terms by Hume, and it is highly arguable that his formulation was prophesied by Hobbes; but through the nineteenth and twentieth centuries there has grown up a long tradition of attacking it. The attack is always, at least in form, humanist, and entails the charge that the liberal concept of individuality omits too much in the interactions of personality with politics and society which is essential to personality, and so tends to dehumanize both government and the governed. On the left the charge is one of failure in social humanism: the liberal individual is said to be engrossed in acquisitive activity, and so to detach himself from a politics which he pays to repress those whom acquisitiveness excludes. On the right the charge is one of failure in civic humanism: both the acquisitive individual and the wage-earning individual who looks to the state for protection against him are charged with abandonment of politics—by which is meant the heroic moralism of political and philosophical decision, practice, and contemplation. It is perhaps because the socialist concept of individuality has been heroic since its beginnings that the socialist and nonsocialist versions of antiliberalism so often look like mirror-images of one another. One has to have been attacked, from right and left simultaneously, for depoliticizing thought and dehumanizing history,[25] to realize just how far this brand of humanist heresy-hunt has been allowed to go.

Both versions of antiliberalism are intelligible and to that extent convincing, and there is a wide range of historical phenomena to which both are in various ways applicable. But the accusations which they level are becoming routinized—which is what one means by a heresy-hunt—and this gives one reason to believe that the range of phenomena to which they apply may have been exaggerated. The antiliberals of both camps tend to write as if the liberalism which they define had held the field—or had expanded its control of the field without effective opposition—from the days of Hobbes and Locke even to the days of Marx; and it is this supposition which recent historical research has tended to modify. If one expresses scepticism of the historic reality of such concepts as "liberal," or for that matter "bourgeois," the heresy-hunter will of course interpret that as meaning that one is a "liberal" or "bourgeois" in disguise; but among reasonable beings, there is a useful purpose to be served by going back to some doubts concerning Macpherson's "possessive individualism." We shall be engaged in the exercise of trying to get a paradigm into perspective, though readers of Kuhn will know that a covert attack on the paradigm may be entailed.

There is one English thinker of the first critical period who fits the Macpherson model very well indeed—so much so that his possessive individualism does not need to be brought to light by a complicated exegesis, but is expressly rendered in his own words. He depicted men in society as creatures who drove hard bargains with one another, the stronger party always dictating the terms of the bargain to the weaker; he said that this was peculiarly the characteristic of a society where property consisted in movable goods and wealth; he proposed that what was needed in so individualist a society was a sovereign and indeed absolute central authority to regulate the bargaining process; and he pointed out that in a commercial society such a sovereign could govern with the aid of salaried professional soldiers. So here we have one full-blooded possessive individualist in the middle of the seventeenth century, and where there was one there were doubtless more; we must not play the trick of isolating this man by seeming to emphasize him. But his name was Matthew Wren; his father was a Laudian bishop currently a prisoner in the Tower; and the circumstance that his grandfather had been a mercer will not really make a business spokesman out of him. Furthermore, he expressed these views in the form of a critique of James Harrington's *Oceana*, of which he was the leading contemporary opponent;[26] and he was attacking Harrington's doctrine that the form of property determining politics was land, whose stability—as opposed to the mobility of goods and money—set men free to be the rational political creatures which they were by nature. Harrington was, to some degree, an agrarian utopian, and he had affirmed that two girls left to share a cake would construct the choice rationally, by having one girl cut the cake and the other choose her piece. It was Wren who replied that the stronger girl would offer the other a small piece of cake to fetch her some water to drink with her larger share; as succinct a statement of the possessive individualist position as could be found.[27]

In the parable of the cake Harrington saw the image of the aristocracy proposing a range of choices and the democracy exercising the actual decision between them, which was not only his basic conception of the political process, but—he insisted—the essential means of infusing into the body politic a rational and political soul. This was the true target of Wren's attack: he was specific in denying that the body politic could possess a soul, and went so far as to remark that before we could even discuss such an idea we should have to know what the soul was and what the philosophy pertaining to it[28]—a rather startling remark from the son of a bishop and one who was much admired by other bishops. Harrington's ideas about the soul-body relationship in politics are rooted in ancient and medieval physics and medicine—"the contemplation of form," he once wrote, "is astonishing to man, and hath a kind of trouble or impulse accompanying it, that exalts his soul to God"[29]—and his agrarianism links him (though not directly) with the tradition of radical hylozoism, which I mentioned earlier: he is not immeasurably remote from Gerrard Winstanley, who conflated the relations of reason with matter, soul with body, Christ with mankind, and men with the earth in a system of social justice. It was Wren who was the modern, and only in the next century was Harrington seen as a pioneer of experimental science.[30] If we relate him in any degree to radical Puritanism, we commit ourselves to emphasizing the extent to which Puritan thought was rooted in antiquity.

The alliance with which Harrington felt himself confronted was that of mathematicians with clerics. From the time he read Wren's *Observations*, he began denouncing "mathematicians" as people who would reduce political society to a calculus of interested forces in order to deprive it of its rational soul. We might expect, given everything we have read or been given to understand concerning Hobbes, that Harrington would rank him among enemies of this stripe, and it is of course possible to argue that he should have. But the significant fact is that Wren attacked Hobbes as well as Harrington, and that Harrington defended Hobbes against both Wren and the Laudian doctor Henry Hammond,[31] the reason being that Harrington and Hobbes both desired to assert that Israel, from Moses to Samuel, had been a pure theocracy, and that consequently no order of clergy could claim a divine right to political authority.[32] We might suppose that this adventitiously deflected Harrington's attention from the fact that Hobbes also was among the mathematicians, were it not that Wren belonged to a largely clerical circle who repudiated Hobbes's mathematics as energetically as they repudiated everything else about him. Wren was a layman, but he was a protégé of John Wilkins, warden of Wadham College and founding father of the Royal Society, who serenely made the transition from being Cromwell's brother-in-law under the Protectorate to being bishop of Chester under the Restoration. It was Wilkins who had urged him to undertake the criticism of Harrington;[33] and the Oxford professors of mathematics, whom Hobbes had attacked in 1656, were all of the same kidney as Wilkins.[34] Harrington could see as little difference between protectoralists and royalists as he could between Presbyterians and Anglicans, and he was justified by his own perspective. Wren's commercially based theory of politics is the foundation of an antihylozoism which enables him both to undermine Harrington's republicanism and to restore the position of the clergy against the attacks of Harrington and Hobbes. It would be delightful to conclude by finding an ideological aspect to the differences between Hobbes's mathematics and those of the Oxford circle, but I do not know if this can be done.

At all events, here is the ideological context for the most specific piece of possessive individualism known so far. It was the bishops who promoted the "bourgeois ideology," the Latitudinarians who were the liberals. We have fallen in with that tradition which sees Restoration Arminianism, rather than Puritanism, as the ideological reinforcement of the scientific revolution and particularly with the important work of M. C. Jacob, who has argued that Newtonian science was promoted by a latitudinarian clergy, many of whom had made some sort of transition from the Laudian ranks, as an antidote to a lingering and potentially radical hylozoism, which had survived from the Puritan revolution and forms a kind of underground or dark underbelly to Restoration philosophy.[35] One can see how both a physics based on laws of motion, and a politics based on interest and acquisition, would serve their purpose, and there is much to be done with the notion of a hylozoistic and in some respects occultist underground, running through the Restoration and the clandestine aspects of the early Enlightenment, to surface again in the late eighteenth century. The immediate point I should like to make, however, is that the thesis that individualism points toward authoritarianism seems to be holding up well, but that we are obliged to leave a good deal of room for the possibility that the authoritarians promoted individualism for their own ends. I have been suggesting in this paper the usefulness of remembering that the notion of property might subserve that of authority, rather than the other way about; and we seem to have been looking at cases where a possessive-individualist view of society was promoted by members of a recovering ruling class, rather than by members of any new class which was replacing it. That the ruling classes of England became significantly more commercial in their membership and behavior during the first critical period seems much harder to maintain than that, during the same period, some of them discovered the utility from their point of view of a commercially based ideology. The clergy and other administrative elites may have invented a bourgeois ideology without belonging to, or recognizing the predominance of, any bourgeoisie that practised the ethic they described. This does not tell us, of course, how it became possible to invent such an ideology; but there has to be a non-Marxist reading of English history in which the ruling elites use the commercial classes without surrendering to them. This suggests an answer to the only problem that arises from Jacob's excellent study: if—as she insists—Hobbes was the apologist of market society, and the Latitudinarians and Newtonians were the apologists of market society, why was Hobbes the principal enemy whom the latter desired to overthrow?

But the Restoration of 1660 was the restoration of the established landholders as well as of the clerical and bureaucratic elites;[36] and therefore a view of political power based on the acquisition of movable goods is only one of the ideologies of property and authority possible in the era of history that then began, though it would be fair to say that the individual as magistrate was very rapidly replaced by the individual as proprietor. The second critical period, which we date from about 1675 to 1720, marks the beginnings of the *verità effettuale* of that tension between real and movable property which Harrington and Wren had prefigured, and our use and understanding of the liberal paradigm has to be re-examined in this light. Our histories of political thought in this second period have traditionally been dominated by the figure of Locke, and it has been established practice to interpret all contemporary and subsequent thought about politics with reference to his theories of consent, trust, and dissolution, and all thought about property with reference to his theories of labor and acquisition. But for about twenty years the received image of Locke has been subjected to some powerful solvents, as a result of which his role has been not so much diminished as rendered problematical. Peter Laslett demonstrated that the *Two Treatises* were written well before the Revolution of 1688, as a by-product of the Filmerian controversy of 1679–81; work carried out by myself on the ideological climate of the years beginning about 1675 seemed to uncover whole universes of discourse—the debate over parliamentary history, the neo-Harringtonian revival—which were of great importance to Locke's closest associates, but which Locke himself ignored while doing nothing to terminate; Philip Abrams and John Dunn brought to light readings of the theory of consent, and of Locke's politics in general, a good deal more angled toward the problem of authority than we used to think, and of such a character that it was doubtful how usefully the concept of liberalism could be employed in speaking of him.[37] There is now going forward a revision of the ideology of 1688, both in the months of revolution itself and in the ensuing twenty-five years, which indicates that Locke's position—his insistence that a dissolution of government was not a dissolution of society—while seemingly moderate, was in fact too radical to represent the emerging political reality. Some Whigs in the Convention not only insisted that there had been a dissolution of government, but were prepared to fill the vacuum with structures that recall the 1650s as much as anything in the *Two Treatises*;[38] but those Tories who had reluctantly accepted the revolution—and whose ideas dominate the thinking of the next quarter-century[39]—not only successfully maintained (and obliged the Whigs to agree) that there had not been a dissolution of government, but forced a general revival, reconsideration, and even reprinting[40] of the debate of 1649–51 concerning obedience to a *de facto* regime, which was to be of great importance to Edmund Burke a full hundred years later.[41] This was why the Whigs had to settle for a constitutionalist rather than a contractualist legitimation of the Revolution.

The effect of all this has been to create problems in the historical if not the philosophical understanding of Locke's political thought; our perception of the context in which he operated has been so greatly enlarged and complicated that we now have great difficulty in seeing how he should be connected with it, and this is rendered no easier by Locke's own secrecy, evasiveness, and denials of concern in aspects of debate which almost certainly did concern him.[42] It is not possible any longer to regard him as, in isolation, the philosopher of the Revolution, and it will be some time before this reconstruction of the context restores us to having the means of assessing his real importance in the history of ideas and ideology. That importance was probably great, but we have at present no very satisfactory way of evaluating it.

It is clear—to begin moving from an emphasis upon government toward an emphasis upon property—that Locke played no predominant role in the formation of what Caroline Robbins has called "the Whig canon" in the tradition of "the eighteenth-century commonwealthmen."[43] That group of middle and late seventeenth-century writers, and the Tories as well as Whigs of the second critical period who singled them out for canonization, are defined by their relation to the classical republican tradition, with which Locke had little if anything to do. They took a "country" as opposed to a "court" view of the ideal of the balanced constitution, which, following Corinne C. Weston,[44] we now date back to the *King's Answer to the Nineteen Propositions of Parliament*, published in 1642; and they saw this balance as threatened by the renewal of the crown's command of parliamentary patronage, which had first surfaced about 1675. For a century and a half, from the Bill of Exclusion through the American Revolution to the First Reform Act, the secret of English government, and the matter of English political debate, was to be the role of patronage, or, as its enemies termed it, "corruption"; and what still requires emphasis is that this was to be discussed in terms of the relation of property to personality. What troubled the "country party" or "commonwealth" thinkers—among whom, we now know, nearly all articulate Americans of the Revolutionary generations are to be included[45]—was less the encroachment of the executive's constitutional powers on those of the legislature, than the growth of the executive's capacity to bring the members of the legislature, and of society in general, into personal, political, and economic dependence upon it. This destroyed the balance of the constitution by destroying that personal independence which could only belong to men whose property was their own and did not consist in expectations from the men in government; and the moral quality which only propertied independence could confer, and which became almost indistinguishable from property itself, was known as "virtue." What we used to think of as the Age of Reason may just as well be called the Age of Virtue; or rather, what used to appear an age of Augustan serenity now appears an age of bitter and confused debate over the relations between reason, virtue, and passion.[46] I am looking ahead from a "second critical period" ending about 1720 to an eighteenth century which ended about a hundred years later because it is important to emphasize that the polemic against Alexander Hamilton which Jefferson and Madison conducted in the 1790s was to a remarkable degree a replay of an English polemic which had begun in the 1670s[47]—but which could not have been conducted in the fifties because the relation of patronage to property was not then in question.

What revisions may all this suggest in our thinking about possessive individualism, about the paradigm of liberalism and that antiliberal interpretation of modern political history whose different versions we looked at earlier? In the first place, it must be observed that our emphasis has moved forward in time. We no longer see the essential shifts in either the structure or the ideology of English property as taking place in the middle seventeenth century, still less in the so-called Tawney's century preceding it,[48] but in the quarter-century following the Revolution of 1688. It was then that what had been a highly theoretical debate between Harrington and Wren exploded and became a public issue, and a commonplace of debate came to be that major changes had occurred in the character of property itself, and consequently in the structure, the morality, and even the psychology of politics. All these things began, with spectacular abruptness, to be discussed in the middle 1690s; and compared with this great breakthrough in the secular consciousness of political society, the attempt to discover market connotations in Hobbes, or even Locke, sometimes looks rather like shadow play. There are some reasons for thinking that the great debate over property and virtue was conducted on premises not apparent to Hobbes or even Wren; as for Locke, the point to be made is that the debate seems to have been conducted with very little reference to anything he had said. An analysis of his writings will certainly define for him a position in relation to it, and we will some day find out when this analysis and definition were first conducted; but if one desires to study the first great ideologist of the Whig system of propertied control, one will not study Locke, but Defoe.[49] The articulation of political thought in the second critical period was moving from the control of philosophers into that of men of letters and semiprofessional journalists. Again, let me say that Locke will return to us, but he is at present moving along a remote orbit.

In the second place, the great debate over property was conducted in terms to which the Macpherson market model does not seem altogether crucial. Harrington—who remained a significant figure in the next century—had operated with a simple distinction between feudal and freehold tenure; Wren and others had pointed to the possible importance of commercial wealth; but there had really been, and was to be, very little attention paid to the thought that freehold land was liable to become a marketable commodity. What Harrington and Wren both desired to say, from opposite value positions, was that land, or real property, tended to make men independent citizens, who actualized their natural political capacity, whereas mobile property tended to make them artificial beings, whose appetites and powers could and must be regulated by a sovereign. If we are to move Hobbes into the latter camp—as is certainly possible—it was not apparent to the debaters in the 1650s that he belonged there, or that he was an advocate of a mobile-property society in the way that Wren was. But Harrington and Wren lived on the eve of a great reassertion of control by the landed elites in society, fully as important as the expansion of commerce and finance which was to accompany it; and the debate they had begun was to be continued in the context of a dialogue between real and mobile property within the post-1660 and post-1688 political order.

If we look at the history of events in the growth of political consciousness, we find that there was a confrontation between real property and government patronage before there was a confrontation between real and mobile property, and that when the latter occurred it was because mobile property presented itself in the guise not of a marketable commodity, but of a new and enlarged mode of dependence upon government patronage. The ideal of property as the basis of independence and virtue was first stated—and as always it was stated on behalf of the country gentlemen—as against the revival of patronage by the court politicians in the 1670s. No conflict with mobile property was entailed or implied, and the critique of patronage was as acceptable in London as in the shires. What escalated the great debate was not the political revolution of 1688, but its largely unanticipated consequence, the so-called financial revolution of the 1690s;[50] and this confronted the ideology of real property with a threat from the operations not of a trading market, but of a system of public credit. At very high speed there was created a new class of investors great and small—Locke was one of them—who had lent government capital that vastly stabilized and enlarged it, and henceforth lived off their expectations of a return (sometimes a marketable one) on their investments. The landed classes, and still more their ideologues to the right and left, saw in this process a revolutionary expansion not of a trading and manufacturing market, but of a system of parliamentary patronage. The mode of property which they now began to attack, and to denounce as a new force in history, transforming and corrupting society, was not property in exchangeable commodities—they called this "trade" and greeted it as a means to independence and virtue—but property in government office, government stock, and government expectations to which the National Debt had mortgaged futurity: there is a real sense in which the sense of a secular future is the child of capitalist investment.[51] They called this "public credit," a mode of property which rendered government dependent on its creditors and creditors dependent on government, in a relation incompatible with classical or agrarian virtue. It was a property not in the means of production, but in the relationships between government and the otherwise property-owning individual; these relationships could themselves be owned, and could be means of owning people. The perception of credit in many ways preceded and controlled the perception of the market; it can be traced in the literature how the Tory and Old Whig ideologues came to perceive "commerce" as a new and ambivalent force in history mainly in proportion as they came to perceive it as the precondition of "credit." It was the latter concept that was and remained crucial.

Once we are prepared to admit that the first widespread ideological perception of a capitalist form of political relations came into being, rapidly and abruptly, in the last years of the seventeenth century and the two decades following, a number of consequences follow. I have tried to show elsewhere that since capitalism in this form was perceived in terms of speculation rather than calculation, its epistemological foundation appeared as fantasy rather than rationality—with some interesting sexist implications—and that goods had to be reified, and the laws of the market discovered or invented, in order to restore reality and rationality to an otherwise purely speculative universe.[52] The interests succeeded the passions—as is beginning to emerge from the researches of several scholars[53]—as a means of disciplining and rendering them manageable and intelligible. But it was the individual as classical political being whose capacities for self-knowledge and self-command—expressed in the ideal of virtue—were rendered uncertain and dissolved into fantasy, other-directedness, and anomie by the corruptions of the new commercial politics. The social thought of the eighteenth century has begun to look like a single gigantic *querelle* between the individual as Roman patriot, self-defined in his sphere of civic action, and the individual in the society of private investors and professional rulers, progressive in the march of history, yet hesitant between action, philosophy, and passion. It seems perfectly possible that both classical economic man and classical socialist man were attempts to rescue the individual from this Faustian dissociation of sensibility.

This suggests that we might keep intact that important element of the antiliberal paradigm which presents classical political man as somehow destroyed by the advent of eighteenth-century capitalism; and we should indeed keep this generalization in view and try to state it correctly. But the juxtaposition of polity and economy—to borrow the language of Joseph Cropsey[54]—ought not to be stated as a simple antithesis; I want to argue that it was an unending and unfinished debate. The main historical weakness in the antiliberal position is that all its practitioners, right and left, are so anxious to find, that they antedate and exaggerate, some moment at which economy became emancipated from polity and market man, productive man, or distributive man declared that he no longer needed the *paideia* of politics to make him a self-satisfactory being. I cannot find such a moment (not even a Mandevillean moment)[55] in the eighteenth century, because the dialogue between polity and economy remained a dialogue, and because both political man and commercial man were equipped with theories of property as the foundation of political personality which could not be separated from each other. Once political virtue was declared to have an agrarian base, it was located in the past; and the movement of history toward credit, commerce, and the market was defined as a movement toward culture but away from virtue. Subject to these definitions, the formulation of a "bourgeois ideology," in the naive sense of a declaration that market behavior was all that was needed to make a human being a human being, was an extraordinarily difficult task, and we should doubt if it was ever naively accomplished. If we find someone who seems to us to have formulated such an ideology, we have to remember that he emerged from a context in which it was openly problematic whether such a thing could be done, and we should not be surprised to find in his ideology unresolved contradictions of which he was well aware. It might even be that the ideology of market society was perfected only by those who desired to destroy it.

I return in conclusion to the suggestion that Macpherson's market model explained only one group of phenomena and did not account for their opposites. I think that both socialist and classical antiliberals have been so intent on the location of economic man that they have taken account only of those phenomena which indicate his presence, and have suggested that one set of chromosomes always drove out another, with the result that somewhere in the eighteenth century or the nineteenth must be found the moment when political man died and economic man reigned in his stead. It is now in doubt if such a moment ever occurred at all. It seems that the classical ideal quite simply did not die; that it was reborn with the great recovery of aristocracy which marks the later seventeenth and early eighteenth centuries, with the result that property was always discussed in the political context of authority and liberty.[56] Property was the foundation of personality; but the acid test of personality was whether it required most to be affirmed in liberty or governed by authority. When modes of property arose that did not favor political virtue, they suggested private freedom and political sovereignty, and to that extent the antiliberal paradigm holds good; but—the strength of the classical ideal remaining—the apparition of an individual rendered nonpolitical and nonvirtuous by his property occasioned terrible conceptual problems. By the middle of the eighteenth century, the historically problematic individual, who could neither return to ancient virtue nor find means of completely replacing it, had made his appearance; and he was present, uneasily but effectively occupying the stage of history, before classical economic man, American democratic man—a close relative—or German dialectical and in due course socialist man, had arisen to suggest ways of escaping or resolving his problems. In this scenario, we can, of course, find highly systematic liberal philosophies occurring from time to time; but they always appeared in response to problems which they did not persuade everybody they had succeeded in solving, and they can be made to look as much like incidents as like turning points in the history of social consciousness. I am not calling in question the historical reality of "liberalism" or "possessive individualism," so much as those "liberal," or rather antiliberal, interpretations of history, in which everything leads up to and away from a monolithic domination of "liberal" ideas somewhere in the nineteenth century. I see the formulation of these ideas as always problematic and precarious, and I am even prepared to entertain the notion that "liberal" or "bourgeois" ideology was perfected less by its proponents than by its opponents, who did so with the intention of destroying it. What went on in the eighteenth century was not a unidirectional transformation of thought in favor of the acceptance of "liberal" or "market" man, but a bitter, conscious, and ambivalent dialogue. In contemporary scholarship, it is the Marxists who are the Whigs, their critics who command a dialectic.

## Notes

This essay originated as a paper presented to the 1976 convention of the American Political Science Association (Chicago, 2–5 September). I am indebted to Nannerl O. Keohane for organizing the panel and to C. B. Macpherson for taking the chair.

1. J. H. Plumb, *The Growth of Political Stability in England, 1675–1725* (London, 1967).

2. The study of the growth of the Whig order as leading to its partial disruption by the American Revolution became the theme of a conference held at the Folger Library, on 21–22 May 1976, and now published under the title *Three British Revolutions: 1641, 1688, 1776* (Princeton, 1980). See also John Carswell, *From Revolution to Revolution: England, 1688–1776* (London, 1973).

3. Cf. James H. Meisel, *Counter-revolutions: How Revolutions Die* (New York, 1966).

4. Norman Cohn, *The Pursuit of the Millennium*, rev. ed. (New York, 1967); William M. Lamont, *Marginal Prynne, 1660–1669* (London, 1963) and *Godly Rule: Politics and Religion, 1603–1660* (London, 1969); Sacvan Bercovitch, *Typology and Early American Literature* (Amherst, 1972). For Hill, see n. 6 below.

5. M. C. Jacob, *The Newtonians and the English Revolution, 1689–1720* (Ithaca, 1976); Charles Webster, *The Great Instauration* (New York, 1976).

6. Christopher Hill, *Puritanism and Revolution: Studies in Interpretation of the English Revolution of the Seventeenth Century* (London, 1958; New York, 1964); *Intellectual Origins of the English Revolution* (Oxford, 1965); *Society and Puritanism in Pre-Revolutionary England*, 2d ed. (New York, 1967); *God's Englishman: Oliver Cromwell and the English Revolution* (New York, 1970); *Antichrist in Seventeenth-Century England* (London and New York, 1971); *The World Turned Upside Down: Radical Ideas During the English Revolution* (New York, 1972).

7. Eric Hobsbawm, *Primitive Rebels* (New York, 1965).

8. Peter Laslett, *The World We Have Lost: English Society Before and After the Coming of Industry* (London, 1965).

9. George Rudé, *The Crowd in History: A Study of Popular Disturbances in France and England, 1730–1848* (New York, 1964); *The Crowd in the French Revolution* (Oxford, 1959); *Wilkes and Liberty: A Social Study of 1763 to 1774* (Oxford, 1962); E. P. Thompson, *The Making of the English Working Class* (New

York, 1964]; *Whigs and Hunters: The Origin of the Black Act* (London, 1975]; "The Moral Economy of the English Crowd in the Eighteenth Century," *Past and Present*, 50 (February 1971): 76–136.

10. J. H. Hexter, "A New Framework for Social History," in *Reappraisals in History* (Evanston, 1961), was the first to propose this restorationist perspective.

11. Keith Thomas, "Women in the Civil War Sects," in *Crisis in Europe, 1560–1660*, ed. Trevor Aston (New York, 1965).

12. The distinction between the "magisterial" and "radical" Reformations may be studied in S. H. Williams, *The Radical Reformation* (Philadelphia, 1962). On Winstanley, see G. E. Aylmer, ed., "*England's Spirit Unfoulded,*" *Past and Present* 40 (July 1968): 3–15; J. C. Davis, "Gerrard Winstanley and the Restoration of True Magistracy," *Past and Present* 70 (February 1976): 76–93. On William Sedgwick, see article in *Dictionary of National Biography*; works in Donald Wing ed., *Short Title Catalogue . . .* , (3:224–25); and in particular *Animadversions upon a Letter and Paper, first sent to His Highness by certain gentlemen and others in Wales* (London, 1656).

13. William Haller, *Liberty and Reformation in the Puritan Revolution* (New York, 1955, 1963).

14. J. G. A. Pocock, *Order and Authority in Two English Revolutions* (Wellington, 1973).

15. Perez Zagorin, *A History of Political Thought in the English Revolution* (London, 1954); Irene Coltman, *Private Men and Public Causes* (London, 1962); and above all, John M. Wallace, *Destiny His Choice: the Loyalism of Andrew Marvell* (Cambridge, 1968).

16. For Filmer's role in the Engagement Controversy see Wallace, *Destiny His Choice*, and for a full and serious study of his thought, Gordon J. Schochet, *Patriarchalism in Political Thought* (Oxford, 1975). Also James W. Daly, *Sir Robert Filmer and English Political Thought* (Toronto, 1978).

17. Wallace, *Destiny His Choice*; and Quentin Skinner, "Hobbes's *Leviathan*," *Historical Journal* 7 (1964): 321–33; "History and Ideology in the English Revolution," *Historical Journal* 8 (1965): 151–78; "The Ideological Context of Hobbes's Political Thought," *Historical Journal* 9 (1966): 286–317; "The Context of Hobbes's Theory of Political Obligation," in *Hobbes and Rousseau: a Collection of Critical Essays*, ed. Maurice Cranston and Richard S. Peters (New York, 1972); "Conquest and Consent: Thomas Hobbes and the Engagement Controversy," in *The Interregnum: The Quest for a Settlement*, ed. G. E. Aylmer (Hamden, Conn., 1972).

18. James Harrington, *Oceana and Other Works*, ed. John Toland (London: 1700, 1737, 1747, 1771), particularly *The Prerogative of Popular Government*, book I, passim. See now J. G. A. Pocock, ed., *The Political Works of James Harrington* (Cambridge, 1977).

19. J. G. A. Pocock, *The Machiavellian Moment: Florentine Political Thought and the Atlantic Republican Tradition* (Princeton, 1975), pp. 396–400; "Time, History and Eschatology in the Thought of Thomas Hobbes," in *Politics, Language and Time: Essays in Political Thought and History* (New York, 1971); introduction to *The Political Works of James Harrington*.

20. Adam Baynes; see J. T. Rutt, ed., *The Diary of Thomas Burton . . .* , 4 vols. (London, 1828), 3:147–48.

21. A. S. P. Woodhouse, ed., *Puritanism and Liberty* (London, 1949), p. 57.

22. C. B. Macpherson, *The Political Theory of Possessive Individualism: Hobbes to Locke* (Oxford, 1962). Cf. Joyce O. Appleby, *Economic Thought and Ideology in Seventeenth-Century England* (Princeton, 1978).

23. J. G. A. Pocock, *The Ancient Constitution and the Feudal Law* (Cambridge, 1957; and New York, 1967), chap. 6; Macpherson, *Possessive Individualism*, chap. 4; Pocock, *Politics, Language and Time*, chap. 4; *The Machiavellian Moment*, chap. 11; Macpherson, chap. 5, and Pocock, chap. 3, of *Feudalism, Capitalism and Beyond*, ed. Eugene Kamenka and R. S. Neale (Canberra, 1975). See also the debate between Macpherson and John F. H. New, reprinted in *The Intellectual Revolution of the Seventeenth Century*, ed. Charles Webster (London, 1974), I–V.

24. Macpherson, *Possessive Individualism;* Sheldon Wolin, *Politics and Vision* (Boston, 1960); Wilson Carey McWilliams, *The Idea of Fraternity in America* (Berkeley, 1973); Theodore Lowi, *The End of Liberalism* (New York, 1969). For Oakeshott, see *Of Human Conduct* (Oxford, 1975).

25. Richard Ashcraft, *Political Theory* 3 (1975): 13, 15, 22–23; Dante Germino, *Virginia Quarterly Review* 51 (1975): 628–32; Neal Wood, *Political Theory* 4 (1976): 104. Compare Hexter's review of *The Machiavellian Moment* in *On Historians.*

26. [Matthew Wren], *Considerations upon Mr. Harrington's Commonwealth of Oceana, restricted to the First Part of the Preliminaries* (London, 1657); Matthew Wren, *Monarchy Asserted, or the State of Monarchicall and Popular Government, in Vindication of the Considerations upon Mr. Harrington's Oceana* (Oxford, 1659). Harrington's replies are *The Prerogative of Popular Government,* book 1 (London, 1658); *The Art of Law-Giving,* book 3, and *Politicaster* (both London, 1659); all in Toland, *Oceana and Other Works.*

27. Wren, *Considerations,* p. 36.

28. Ibid., p. 20.

29. Harrington, *A System of Politics,* in Toland, *Oceana and Other Works,* 1771 edition.

30. Duncan Forbes, *Hume's Philosophical Politics* (Cambridge, 1975), chap. 1, contains interesting evidence on this.

31. Harrington, *The Prerogative of Popular Government,* book 2.

32. *The Machiavellian Moment,* pp. 397–98.

33. Wren, *Considerations,* unpaginated introduction; Barbara Shapiro, *John Wilkins, 1614–1672: An Intellectual Biography* (Berkeley and Los Angeles, 1969), pp. 116–17.

34. Hobbes, *Six Lessons to the Savilian Professors of the Mathematics* (1656), in *The English Works of Thomas Hobbes,* ed. William Molesworth, 11 vols. (London, 1845), vol. 7.

35. Webster, *Intellectual Revolution,* pp. xiv–xxv, is a useful anthology of writings on this question; Jacob, *The Newtonians and the English Revolution.*

36. For the last mentioned, see G. E. Aylmer, *The State's Servants* (London, 1973).

37. Peter Laslett, ed., *John Locke's Two Treatises of Government* (Cambridge, 1960, 1963); Pocock, *The Ancient Constitution and the Feudal Law,* chaps. 8–9; *Politics, Language and Time,* chaps. 3–4; *The Machiavellian Moment,* pp. 423–24, 435–36; Philip Abrams, ed., *John Locke: Two Tracts on Government* (Cambridge, 1967); John Dunn, *The Political Thought of John Locke: An Historical Account of the Argument of the Two Treatises of Government* (Cambridge, 1969). On Locke and liberalism, cf. M. Seliger, *The Liberal Politics of John Locke* (London, 1969), for whom the elements of authoritarianism in Locke are inherent in the liberal tradition. Dunn argues that they are anterior to it.

38. Julian H. Franklin, *John Locke and the Problem of Sovereignty* (Cambridge, 1978); Mark Goldie, "The Origins of True Whiggism," *Journal of the History of Political Thought* 1 (1980).

39. See J. P. Kenyon, *Revolution Principles: The Politics of Party, 1689–1720* (Cambridge, 1977); Martyn P. Thompson, "The Reception of Locke's *Two Treatises of Government,*" *Political Studies* 24 (1976).

40. See Skinner, "History and Ideology in the English Revolution."

41. See Burke's *Reflections on the Revolution in France* (1790) and *An Appeal from the New to the Old Whigs* (1794). H. T. Dickinson, *Liberty and Property: Political Ideology in Eighteenth-Century Britain* (London, 1978).

42. Thus, it is not possible to discover Locke's connection with the neo-Harringtonian writings sponsored by Shaftesbury in 1675–77, though he must have been very close by; K. H. D. Haley, *The First Earl of Shaftesbury* (Oxford, 1968), pp. 391–93. Locke and his friend Tyrrell are said to have composed replies to Filmer while sharing the same house, but without telling each other; Laslett, *John Locke's Two Treatises* (1960 ed.), pp. 59–61. For other instances see Laslett, passim, and Maurice Cranston, *John Locke: A Biography* (London, 1957).

43. Caroline Robbins, *The Eighteenth-Century Commonwealthman:*

*Studies in the Transmission, Development and Circumstances of English Liberal Thought from the Restoration of Charles II until the War with the Thirteen Colonies* (Cambridge, Mass., 1959).

44. Corinne C. Weston, *English Constitutional Theory and the House of Lords* (New York, 1965).

45. There is now an extensive literature on this subject; see Robert E. Shalhope, "Toward a Republican Synthesis: The Emergence of an Understanding of Republicanism in American Historiography," *William and Mary Quarterly*, 3d ser., 29 (1972): 49–80.

46. See chaps. 13–15 of *The Machiavellian Moment*. Such a synthesis, still necessary in histories of political thought, would be redundant to a historian of literature or philosophy.

47. See Lance Banning, *The Jeffersonian Persuasion* (Ithaca, 1977).

48. For a study of the historiography of the period from 1540–1640, see Lawrence Stone, *Social Change and Revolution in England, 1540–1640* (London, 1965), pp. xi–xxvi.

49. *The Machiavellian Moment*, chap. 13. The history of political thought—as distinct from that of the social awareness of literature—seems to be without a full-length study of him.

50. P. G. M. Dickson, *The Financial Revolution in England: A Study in the Development of Public Credit* (London, 1967).

51. See Pocock, "Modes of Political and Historical Time in Early Eighteenth-Century England," in *Studies in Eighteenth-Century Culture, volume 5*, ed. Ronald C. Rosbotton (Madison, 1976).

52. Kamenka and Neale, *Feudalism, Capitalism and Beyond; The Machiavellian Moment*, chaps. 13 and 14; "Mobility of Property and the Rise of Eighteenth-Century Sociology," in *Theories of Property, Aristotle to the Present*, ed. Anthony Parel and Thomas Flanagan (Waterloo, Ontario, 1979).

53. Albert Hirschman, *The Passions and the Interests* (Princeton, 1976).

54. Joseph Cropsey, *Polity and Economy: An Interpretation of the Principles of Adam Smith* (Chicago, 1957).

55. Thomas Horne, *The Social and Political Thought of Bernard Mandeville* (New York, 1977).

56. For a study of Adam Smith contrary to the liberal paradigm, see Donald Winch, *Adam Smith's Politics: An Essay in Historiographical Revision* (New York, 1978).

# The Published Works of J. H. Hexter: A Bibliography

## Books

*The Reign of King Pym.* Harvard Historical Series, volume 48. Cambridge, Mass.: Harvard University Press, 1941.

*More's Utopia: The Biography of an Idea.* Princeton: Princeton University Press, 1952. Reprinted, with an epilogue, Torchbook editions, New York: Harper and Row, 1965. Italian translation, *L'Utopia di Moro, biografia di un'idea,* Naples: Guida Editori, 1975.

*Reappraisals in History.* London: Longmans, 1961; and Evanston, Ill.: Northwestern University Press, 1961. Augmented edition, Chicago: University of Chicago Press, 1978.

*The Judaeo-Christian Tradition.* New York: Harper and Row, 1966.

*Doing History.* Bloomington: Indiana University Press, 1971.

*The History Primer.* New York: Basic Books, 1971.

*The Vision of Politics on the Eve of the Reformation: More, Machiavelli, Seyssel.* New York: Basic Books, 1973.

*On Historians.* Cambridge, Mass.: Harvard University Press, 1978.

## Books Edited

*Utopia*, edited with Edward Surtz, volume 4 of the *Complete Works* of Sir Thomas More. New Haven: Yale University Press, 1965. Introduction, pp. xv–cxxiv, and Appendix, pp. 573–76, reprinted in *The Vision of Politics* (1973), pp. 19–107 and 117–46.

General editor. *The Traditions of the Western World.* Chicago: Rand McNally and Co., 1967.

*Western Civilization*, edited by W. L. Langer. Volume 1: *Paleolithic Man to the Emergence of European Powers*, chapters 24–29. Volume 2: *The Struggle for Empire to Europe in the Modern World*, chapters 1–9. New York: Harper and Row, 1968. Revised edition, 1975.

## Articles

"The Protestant Revival and the Catholic Question in England, 1778–1829." *Journal of Modern History* 8 (1936): 297–319.

"The Problem of the Presbyterian Independents." *American Historical Review* 44 (1938): 29–49. Reprinted with an additional footnote in *Reappraisals* (1961), pp. 163–84.

"The Education of the Aristocracy in the Renaissance." *Journal of Modern History* 22 (1950): 1–20. Reprinted in *Reappraisals* (1961), pp. 45–70.

"The Myth of the Middle Class in Tudor England." *Explorations in Entrepreneurial History* 2 (1950): 128–40. Revised and reprinted (with footnotes added) in *Reappraisals* (1961), pp. 71–116.

"The Historian and His Day." *Political Science Quarterly* 69 (1954): 219–33. Reprinted in *Reappraisals* (1961), pp. 1–13.

"A New Framework for Social History." *Journal of Economic History* (1955): 415–26. Reprinted in *Reappraisals* (1961), pp. 14–25.

"Seyssel, Machiavelli and Polybius, VI: The Mystery of the Missing Translation." *Studies in the Renaissance* 3 (1956): 75–96.

"*Il principe* and *lo stato.*" *Studies in the Renaissance* 4 (1957): 113–38. Reprinted in *The Vision of Politics* (1973), pp. 150–78.

"Storm Over the Gentry." *Encounter*, May 1958, pp. 22–34. Revised and reprinted (with footnotes and appendices added) in *Reappraisals* (1961), pp. 117–62. Correspondence on "Storm over the Gentry" appears in the following issues of *Encounter*: July 1958, pp. 73–77; August 1958, pp. 75–76; September 1958, pp. 73–74; October 1958, pp. 68–70; November 1958, p. 81.

"Thomas More: On the Margins of Modernity." *Journal of British Studies* 1 (1961): 20–37.

"The Loom of Language and the Fabric of Imperatives: The Case of *Il principe* and *Utopia.*" *American Historical Review* 69 (1964): 945–68. Reprinted in *The Vision of Politics* (1973), pp. 179–203.

"Garret Mattingly, Historian." In *From the Renaissance to the Counter-Reformation: Essays in Honor of Garret Mattingly,* edited by C. H. Carter, pp. 13–28. New York: Random House, 1965. Reprinted in *Doing History* (1971), pp. 157–72.

"Claude Seyssel and Normal Politics in the Age of Machiavelli." In *Art, Science and History in the Renaissance,* edited by C. S. Singleton, pp. 389–415. Baltimore: Johns Hopkins Press, 1967. Reprinted in *The Vision of Politics* (1973), pp. 204–30.

"The Rhetoric of History." *History and Theory* 6 (1967): 3–13.

"Some American Observations." *Journal of Contemporary History* 2 (1967): 5–23. Reprinted as "Doing History" in *Doing History* (1971), pp. 135–56.

"Historiography: The Rhetoric of History." *International Encyclopedia of the Social Sciences,* 17 vols. (New York: Macmillan, 1968), 6:368–94. Reprinted as "The Rhetoric of History" in *Doing History* (1971), pp. 15–76.

"Publish or Perish—A Defense." *The Public Interest* 17 (1969): 60–77.

"Utopia and Geneva." In *Action and Conviction in Early Modern Europe: Essays in Memory of E. H. Harbison,* edited by T. K. Rabb and J. E. Siegel, pp. 77–89. Princeton: Princeton University Press, 1969. Reprinted in *The Vision of Politics* (1973), pp. 107–17.

"History, the Social Sciences, and Quantification." In *The Acts of the Thirteenth International Congress of Historical Sciences.* 5 vols. Moscow: 1970. Volume 1: 113–43. Reprinted as "History and the Social Sciences" in *Doing History* (1971), pp. 107–34.

"Doing History." *Commentary,* June 1971, pp. 53–62. Reprinted as "The Historian and His Society: A Sociological Analysis—Perhaps" in *Doing History* (1971), pp. 77–106, and in *The Professor and the Public: The Role of the Scholar in the Modern World,* pp. 73–121. The Leo M. Franklin Memorial Lectures, volume 20. Detroit: Wayne State University Press, 1972.

"Parliament Under the Lens: Reflections on G. R. Elton's 'Studying the History of Parliament'." *British Studies Monitor* 3 (1972): 4–15.

"The University and the Rites of Passage." *Washington University Magazine,* Summer 1973, pp. 27–31.

"Intention, Words, and Meaning: The Case of More's *Utopia.*" *New Literary History* 6 (1974–75): 529–41.

"Property, Monopoly, and Shakespeare's *Richard II.*" In *Culture and Politics from Puritanism to the Enlightenment,* edited by Perez Zagorin. Berkeley: University of California Press, 1980.

## Review Articles and Reviews

*Marlborough: His Life and Times,* volume 6: (1708–1722), by Winston S. Churchill. *Boston Evening Transcript,* 25 November 1938, p. 15.

*The Lord General: A Life of Sir Thomas Fairfax*, by M. A. Gibb. *American Historical Review* 44 (1939): 884–85.

*John Pym, 1583–1643*, by S. Reed Brett, and *Lucius Cary, Second Viscount Falkland*, by Kurt Weber. *American Historical Review* 46 (1940–41): 894–96.

*Essays in Modern English History in Honor of Wilbur Cortez Abbott.* *American Historical Review* 47 (1941–42): 329–30.

*The Dignity of Kingship Asserted*, by G. S., with an introduction by W. R. Parker. *American Historical Review* 48 (1942–43): 177.

*The Journal of Sir Simonds D'Ewes*, edited by W. H. Coates. *Yale Law Journal* 51 (1942): 1418–21.

*The Great Transformation*, by Karl Polanyi. *American Historical Review* 50 (1944–45): 501–4.

*Woman as Force in History*, by Mary Beard. *New York Times*, 17 March 1946, p. 5.

*The Liberal Tradition: A Study of the Social and Spiritual Conditions of Freedom*, by W. A. Orton. *American Historical Review* 51 (1945–46): 486–88.

*Written in Darkness*, by A. S. Somerhausen. *New York Times*, 28 April 1946, p. 7.

*Roots of American Loyalty*, by M. Curti. *New York Times*, 23 June 1946, p. 16.

*Concord and Liberty*, by José Ortega y Gasset. *New York Times*, 1 September 1946, p. 8.

*Ideas Have Consequences*, by R. Weaver. *Political Science Quarterly* 64 (1949): 300–302.

*The Merchant Class of Medieval London (1300–1500)*, by S. Thrupp, and *Social Structure in Caroline England*, by D. Mathew. *Journal of Economic History* 9 (1949): 223–25.

*Les institutions de la France au XVIe siècle*, volumes 1 and 2, by R. Doucet, and *Les institutions de la France au XVIe siècle*, by Gaston Zeller. *Journal of Modern History* 22 (1950): 162–64.

*The Elizabethan House of Commons*, by J. E. Neale. *Political Science Quarterly* 65 (1950): 469–70.

*Social Thought in America: The Revolt Against Formalism*, by M. G. White. *American Historical Review* 56 (1950–51): 152–54.

*From Puritanism to the Age of Reason: A Study of Changes in Religious Thought within the Church of England 1660–1700*, by G. R. Cragg. *American Historical Review* 56 (1950–51): 386–87.

"The Renaissance Again and Again." Review of *The Renaissance in Historical Thought: Five Centuries of Interpretation*, by W. K. Ferguson, and *The Counter-Renaissance*, by Hiram Hayden. *Journal of Modern History* 22 (1951): 257–61. Reprinted in *On Historians* (1978), pp. 45–59.

*The Great Frontier,* by W. P. Webb. *American Historical Review* 58 (1952–53): 963.

*Essays in Honor of Conyers Read,* edited by Norton Downs. *Journal of Economic History* 14 (1954): 72–73.

*The Gentleman of Renaissance France,* by W. L. Wiley. *Renaissance News* 7 (1954): 40–43.

*The World of Humanism, 1453–1517,* by M. P. Gilmore. *Journal of Modern History* 26 (1954): 372–73.

*Hugh Latimer: Apostle to the English,* by A. G. Chester. *American Historical Review* 60 (1954–55): 411–12.

*Members of the Long Parliament,* by D. Brunton and D. H. Pennington, and *The Long Parliament, 1640–1641: A Biographical Study of its Members,* by M. F. Keeler. *Political Science Quarterly* 70 (1955): 464–67.

*England and the Italian Renaissance: The Growth of Interest in Its History and Art,* by J. R. Hale. *American Historical Review* 61 (1955–56): 950.

"Puritanism—Root and Branches." Review of *The Strenuous Puritan: Hugh Peter, 1598–1660,* by R. P. Stearns, and *Liberty and Reformation in the Puritan Revolution,* by W. Haller. *William and Mary Quarterly,* 3d series, 13 (1956): 401–8. Reprinted in *Reappraisals* (1978 edition), pp. 241–48.

*An Elizabethan: Sir Horatio Palavicino,* by L. Stone. *American Historical Review* 62 (1956–57): 962–63.

*The Greatness of Oliver Cromwell,* by M. Ashley; *Lord Brook,* by R. Greville; *Naked to Mine Enemies: The Life of Cardinal Wolsey,* by C. W. Ferguson. *Nation* 186 (1958): 567–68.

*The Puritan Dilemma: The Story of John Winthrop,* by Edmund Morgan. *New England Quarterly* 31 (1958): 526–30.

*The Independents in the English Civil War,* by George Yule. *American Historical Review* 64 (1958–59): 362–63.

*Business and Politics Under James I: Lionel Cranfield as Merchant and Minister,* by R. H. Tawney. *American Historical Review* 64 (1958–59): 633–34.

*The Ancient Constitution and the Feudal Law,* by J. G. A. Pocock. *Renaissance News* 12 (1959): 33–35.

*The New Cambridge Modern History,* volume 2: *The Reformation 1520–1559,* edited by G. R. Elton. *English Historical Review* 74 (1959): 693–96.

*The Estates of the Percy Family 1416–1537,* by J. M. W. Bean. *Journal of Economic History* 20 (1960): 95–97.

*The Wealth of the Gentry, 1540–1660: East Anglian Studies,* by Alan Simpson. *American Historical Review* 68 (1962–63): 106–8.

*Order, Empiricism and Politics: Two Traditions of English Political Thought 1500–1700*, by W. H. Greenleaf. *American Historical Review* 72 (1966–67): 175–76.

*Analytical Philosophy of History*, by A. Danto, and *The Foundations of Historical Knowledge*, by M. White. *New York Review of Books*, 9 February 1967, p. 24.

"The English Aristocracy, Its Crises, and the English Revolution, 1558–1660." Review of the *Crisis of the Aristocracy*, by L. Stone. *Journal of British Studies* 8 (1968): 22–78. Reprinted in *On Historians* (1978), pp. 149–226.

"Fernand Braudel and the Monde Braudellien . . ." Review of *The Mediterranean and the Mediterranean World in the Age of Philip II*, by Fernand Braudel. *Journal of Modern History* 44 (1972): 480–539; reprinted in *On Historians* (1978), pp. 61–145.

*Seventeenth-Century Economic Documents*, edited by J. Thirsk and J. P. Cooper. *Journal of European Economic History* 3 (1974): 814–17.

"The Burden of Proof." Review of *Change and Continuity in Seventeenth-Century England*, by Christopher Hill. *Times Literary Supplement*, 24 October 1975, pp. 1250–52. Reprinted in *On Historians* (1978), pp. 227–51.

*Radical Reform and Political Persuasion in the Life and Writings of Thomas More*, by Martin Fleisher. *American Historical Review* 81 (1976): 128.

*The Machiavellian Moment: Florentine Political Thought and Atlantic Republic Tradition*, by J. G. A. Pocock. *History and Theory* 16 (1977): 306–37. Reprinted in *On Historians* (1978), pp. 255–303.

"Power Struggle, Parliament, and Liberty in Early Stuart England." *Journal of Modern History* 50 (1978): 1–50. Reprinted in *Reappraisals* (1978 ed.), pp. 163–218.

## Correspondence and Miscellaneous

Comment and discussion on "The General Crisis of the Seventeenth Century," by H. R. Trevor-Roper. *Past and Present*, 18 (November 1960): 14–18.

"Postscript to an Awfully Long Review." (On L. Stone's comment on "The English Aristocracy, Its Crises, and the English Revolution, 1558–1660.") *Journal of British Studies* 9 (1969): 45–48.

Correspondence in *Quantification in History*, by W. Aydelotte, pp. 162–63, 166–70. Reading, Mass.: Addison-Wesley Publishing Co., 1971.

"Collaborating with Father Surtz." *Moreana* 8 (1971): 15–18.

# Contributors

*William J. Bouwsma*, Sather Professor of History at the University of California at Berkeley, is the author of *Concordia Mundi: The Career and Thought of Guillaume Postel (1510–1581), Venice and the Defense of Republican Liberty*, and various studies of Renaissance humanism. He is currently working on a general interpretation of Renaissance culture.

*G. R. Elton*, Litt.D., F.B.A., is professor of English constitutional history at the University of Cambridge and past president of the Royal Historical Society. Author of The *Tudor Revolution in Government, England under the Tudors, Policy and Police, Reform and Renewal: Thomas Cromwell and the Common Weal*, and other works, he is now studying bills and acts in the Parliaments of Elizabeth I.

*Elizabeth Read Foster* is professor of history at Bryn Mawr College, where she formerly served as dean of the Graduate School of Arts and Sciences. She has long been associated with the Yale Center for Parliamentary History. Her publications include *Proceedings in Parliament 1610* and *The Painful Labour of Mr. Elsyng*. She is engaged in research on the House of Lords in the early seventeenth century.

*Robert R. Harding*, author of *Anatomy of a Power Elite: The Provincial Governors of Early Modern France*, is associate professor of history at Yale University.

*Brian P. Levack* is associate professor of history at the University of Texas at Austin. His publications include *The Civil Lawyers in England, 1603–1641: A Political Study.*

*Barbara C. Malament,* the editor of this volume, is a Fellow of the Society for the Humanities, Cornell University, for 1977–78. She has written "Baldwin Re-Restored?" *Journal of Modern History* (1972), "W. E. Gladstone: An Other Victorian?" *British Studies Monitor* (1978), and "British Labour and Roosevelt's New Deal," *Journal of British Studies* (1978), in addition to articles on seventeenth-century England. She is completing a study of *British Politics and the Crisis of 1931.*

*H. C. Erik Midelfort* is the author of *Witch Hunting in Southwestern Germany, 1562–1684: The Social and Intellectual Foundations.* He is associate professor of history at the University of Virginia.

*Louis O. Mink,* Kenan Professor of Philosophy and Senior Tutor in the College of Social Studies, Wesleyan University, is associate editor of *History and Theory* and the author of *Mind, History, and Dialectic: The Philosophy of R. G. Collingwood, A Finnegans Wake Gazetteer,* and numerous essays on the philosophy of history and other subjects.

*Howard Nenner* has written *By Colour of Law: Legal Culture and Constitutional Politics in England, 1660–1689.* He is currently engaged in an examination of property and the succession in seventeenth-century England, and a larger study on the image of the Stuart monarchy. He is associate professor of history at Smith College.

*Laura Stevenson O'Connell* has published "Anti-Entrepreneurial Attitudes in Elizabethan Sermons and Popular Literature" in the *Journal of British Studies* (1976) and is working on a monograph concerning social perceptions in Elizabethan popular literature. She lives in Santa Barbara, California.

*Linda Levy Peck* teaches English history at Purdue University. Her articles include "Problems in Jacobean Administration: Was Henry Howard, Earl of Northampton, a Reformer?" *The Historical Journal* (1976) and "The British Case: Corruption and Political Development in the Early Modern State," in *Before Watergate: Corruption in American Society,* edited by Hoogenboom and Trefousse (1979). She is completing a study of the career of Henry Howard, earl of Northampton.

*J. G. A. Pocock,* professor of history at the Johns Hopkins University, is the author of *The Ancient Constitution and the Feudal Law, Politics, Language and Time,* and *The Machiavellian Moment.* He has edited *The Political Works of James Harrington* and *Three British Revolutions: 1641, 1688, 1776* (for the Folger Institute). He plans further work on British political and historical thought.

*Quentin Skinner* is the professor of political science at the University of Cambridge. From 1976 to 1979, he was a member of the School of Social Science at the Institute for Advanced Study at Princeton. He is the author of numerous articles, and of a two-volume study of *The Foundations of Modern Political Thought.*

*Lawrence Stone,* Dodge Professor of History and Director of the Shelby Cullom Davis Center for Historical Studies at Princeton University, is the author of *The Crisis of the Aristocracy, The Causes of the English Revolution, The Family, Sex and Marriage in England, 1500–1800,* and other works. He is a member of the American Philosophical Society and Fellow of the American Academy of Arts and Sciences.

*David Underdown* is professor of history at Brown University. He is author of *Royalist Conspiracy in England, 1649–1660, Pride's Purge,* and *Somerset in the Civil War and Interregnum.* He is engaged in a study of popular allegiance in the English Civil War.